The Facts of English

K. Seb
Apr. 1978

To Margaret
Xmas '83
K.

Pan Reference Books

The Facts of English

RONALD RIDOUT · CLIFFORD WITTING

(Revised by Ronald Ridout and Anthony Hern)

Pan Books London and Sydney

First published 1964 by Ginn and Co Ltd
This revised edition published 1973 by
Pan Books Ltd, Cavaye Place, London SW10 9PG
2nd printing 1976
© R. R. Productions Ltd and C. Witting 1964
New material © R. R. Productions Ltd
and Anthony Hern 1973
ISBN 0 330 23534 6
Printed in Great Britain by
Richard Clay (The Chaucer Press) Ltd, Bungay, Suffolk

PREFACE

OUR purpose has been to provide a reference book giving in alphabetical order the literary and linguistic facts of the English language, with such examples and explanations as will make them intelligible to the non-specialist.

There are just over 1,000 entries, some only a few words in length, others running to several pages. They include: grammatical terms; literary terms; general language terms; the derivation of words; confused words; overworked words; new words; acceptable and unacceptable usage of words; pronunciation; punctuation; prosody; logic; and such other matters as American English, foreign words and phrases, and terms used in printing, advertising, music and drama. Because they are not readily available elsewhere, we have also made a point of including in this new edition a number of recent coinages and VOGUE WORDS which will be found under such headings as ADVERTISING, DRUGS, PORNOGRAPHY, and so on.

More erudite books of this kind take it for granted that the student has already reached a high standard of education. *The Facts of English* makes no such assumption, and although the entries range widely in difficulty, all elementary matters – what a noun is, how a comma is used, the agreement of subject and verb in a sentence, and so on – are fully dealt with. The new terms of modern linguistics, or such of them as have gained common acceptance, are also included. The book should therefore be helpful to the many students who have previously found this type of reference book unsuited to their needs.

The entries are fully cross-referenced. For example, under the main heading **prosody** are listed nearly a hundred entries relevant to poetry in general. A word (or words) printed in SMALL CAPITALS in the body of an entry indicates that more information can be found under that heading. Thus, on page 156, **hyperbole** is described as a FIGURE OF SPEECH, on referring to which the student finds listed all the other figures of speech discussed in the book. In this way cross-references will act not only as a guide to interrelated entries but also, it is hoped, as an incentive to further exploration of these pages.

Derivation is shown wherever it helps to clarify the meaning of a word, since many a long word of forbidding appearance loses its fearsomeness when broken down into the English equivalents of its component parts in Latin or Greek. As an instance of this, that six-syllabled monster **onomatopoeia** means simply 'word-making'.

Pronunciation is shown by means of phonetic symbols, which are listed in the Guide to Pronunciation immediately following; and at the end of the book (page 342) are to be found biographical particulars concerning writers and others mentioned in the text, together with the titles of reference books cited.

R. R.
C. W.
A. H.

GUIDE TO PRONUNCIATION

I⊤ has not been considered necessary to give the pronunciation of all the words discussed in this book. Any doubt can soon be dispelled by reference to a good dictionary. Where pronunciation *is* indicated in these pages it is done by means of the system by which the forty-four sounds that make up the English language have been given international phonetic symbols. The advantages of this system are considered under PRONUNCIATION.

Below is a complete list of the twenty vowel sounds and the twenty-four consonant sounds that make up the English language. The international phonetic symbol for the sound is given and then examples of the words containing the sound. These words are repeated in phonetic symbols. Stressed syllables are marked by a vertical stroke (ˈ) immediately following.

Vowel Sounds

1. ʌ as in *up* (ʌp), *clump* (klʌmp), *mongrel* (mʌnˈgrəl)
2. aː as in *art* (aːt), *charm* (tʃaːm), *guard* (gaːd)
3. i as in *it* (it), *biscuit* (bisˈkit), *forfeit* (foːˈfit)
4. iː as in *tea* (tiː), *brief* (briːf), *league* (liːg)
5. u as in *put* (put), *cook* (cuk), woman (wumˈən)
6. uː as in *boot* (buːt), *glue* (gluː), *crew* (kruː)
7. e as in *egg* (eg), *metal* (metˈəl), *leopard* (lepˈəd)
8. æ as in *at* (æt), *snag* (snæg), *plait* (plæt)
9. o as in *on* (on), *doll* (dol), yacht (jot)
10. oː as in *all* (oːl), *cork* (coːk), *swarm* (swoːm)
11. ə as in unstressed *the* (ðə), *today* (tədai), *alone* (əloun)
12. əː as in *fur* (fəː), journey (dʒəːˈni), *connoisseur* (konəsəːˈ)
13. ei as in *pay* (pei), *eight* (eit), *reign* (rein)
14. ou as in *so* (sou), *goat* (gout), *throw* (θrou)
15. ai as in *my* (mai), *cider* (saiˈdə), *awry* (ərai)
16. au as in *house* (haus), *howler* (haulə), *bough* (bau)
17. oi as in *toy* (toi), *boil* (boil), *buoy* (boi)
18. iə as in *gear* (giə), *sphere* (sfiə), *pier* (piə)
19. eə as in *stair* (steə), *scarce* (skeəs), *their* (ðeə)
20. uə as in *cure* (kjuə), *sure* (ʃuə), *doer* (duə)

Notes on Vowel Sounds

No. 11 is called the neutral vowel sound. It never occurs in stressed syllables, and in rapid speech it becomes the *ure* in *nature*, the *our* in *labour*, the *ough* in *thorough*, the *u* in *suppose*, the *a* in *thousand*, the *er* in *pattern*, the *a* in *collar*, the *o* in *actor*, the *o* in *gallop*, the *e* in *silent*, etc. Notice also that Nos. 13–20 are made up of more than one sound. When two sounds glide together to make a single unit we call them DIPHTHONGS. Nos. 13–20 are diphthongs.

Consonant Sounds

21. p as in *park* (paːk), *popped* (pɒpt), *happy* (hæˈpi)
22. b as in *bark* (baːk), *burst* (bəːst), *bought* (bɔːt)
23. t as in *tip* (tip), *bust* (bʌst), *Turk* (təːk)
24. d as in *dip* (dip), *dare* (deə), *loved* (lʌvd)
25. k as in *kill* (kil), *cap* (kæp), *chord* (kɔːd)
26. g as in *got* (gɒt), *gun* (gʌn), *great* (greit)
27. m as in *mat* (mæt), *mother* (mʌðə), *sum* (sʌm)
28. n as in *nag* (næg), *nail* (neil), *nun* (nʌn)
29. ŋ as in *sing* (siŋ), *long* (lɒŋ), *among* (əmʌŋˈ)
30. f as in *file* (fail), *life* (laif), *rafter* (raːfˈtə)
31. v as in *vile* (vail), *live* (liv), *never* (nevˈə)
32. θ as in *thin* (θin), *both* (bouθ), *method* (meθˈəd)
33. ð as in *then* (ðen), *they* (ðei), *heather* (heðˈə)
34. r as in *ran* (ræn), *rare* (reə), *around* (əraundˈ)
35. h as in *hate* (heit), *heart* (haːt), *unheard* (ʌnhəːd)
36. s as in *sat* (sæt), *place* (pleis), *cats* (kæts)
37. z as in *was* (wɒz), *these* (ðiːz), *dogs* (dɒgz)
38. ʃ as in *shut* (ʃʌt), *ash* (æʃ), *mission* (miʃən)
39. ʒ as in *measure* (meʒˈə), *massage* (mæsˈaːʒ), *vision* (viʒˈən)
40. tʃ as in *chance* (tʃaːns), *match* (mætʃ), *church* (tʃəːtʃ)
41. dʒ as in *jug* (dʒʌg), *agile* (æˈdʒail), *manage* (mænˈidʒ)
42. l as in *lack* (læk), *bale* (beil), *bulls* (bulz)
43. w as in *way* (wei), *won* (wʌn), *women* (wimˈən)
44. j as in *yes* (jes), *year* (jiə), *pure* (pjuə)

Notes on Consonant Sounds

Nos. 21–6 are made by air that escapes with a small explosion and are called *plosives*. Nos. 25 and 26 are also called GUTTURALS because they are produced by using the back of the tongue. Nos. 27–9 are made by the air passing through the nose, and are called NASALS.

Nos. 30–9 are made by friction of the air, and are called FRICATIVES. Nos. 40 and 41 are made by a combination of explosion and friction, and are called AFFRICATES. Because they are sounded with a hiss, Nos. 36–41 are also called SIBILANTS. In No. 42 the air passes round the sides of the tongue, and so *l* is called a LATERAL. Nos. 43 and 44 are called *semi-vowels* because the obstruction of the passage of air is so slight. Notice that No. 44 is sounded in a great many words where it is not represented by any letter, e.g. *curious* (kjuəˈriəs), *Muriel* (mjuəˈriəl), *pupil* (pjuˈpəl), *cube* (kjuːb), *few* (fjuː), *ewe* (juː).

A

a, an These are technically known as indefinite articles. The first is used before all words beginning with a consonant except the silent *h*, e.g. *a* cat, *a* mouse, *a* horse. The second is used for most words beginning with a vowel or the silent *h*, e.g. *an* egg, *an* orange, *an* honest man, in *an* hour's time, *an* heir to the throne. Exceptions to this are words beginning with the sound of *y* or *w*, e.g. *a* ewer of water, *a* unique opportunity, *a* one-man band. Once it was fashionable to drop the *h* sound at the beginning of certain words (such as *hotel*) in imitation of French pronunciation. Now that the *h* in such words is always sounded (aspirated), it is unnecessary to speak of *an* hotel, *an* historian.

When, of two nouns in a sentence, one calls for *a* and the other *an*, do not let one indefinite article do duty for both. 'He was often mistaken for a Canadian or American (or *an* American).' 'Write your name and address on an envelope or postcard (or *a* postcard).'

See also THE

abbreviation (L. 'to shorten') The following notes may help:

1. *Months* May, June and July should not be abbreviated. The others should be abbreviated as follows:

Jan. Feb. Mar. Apr. Aug. Sept. Oct. Nov. Dec.

2. *Counties* Leaving out the full stop after abbreviations is common, e.g.:

> Bedfordshire = Beds. or Beds
> Lancashire = Lancs. or Lancs
> Staffordshire = Staffs. or Staffs

The full stop should not be used after Hants (Hampshire), Northants (Northamptonshire) or Salop (Shropshire).

3. *Organisations and Societies* When abbreviating, the modern style favours doing without full stops, e.g. GLC (Greater London

Council), RSPCA (Royal Society for the Prevention of Cruelty to Animals), BBC (British Broadcasting Corporation). This tendency to do without full stops has been reinforced by the extensive use of ACRONYMS (see below).

4. *Acronyms or Protograms* Take the initial letters of a series of words to form a pronounceable word, e.g. *Ernie* (Electronic Random Number Indicator Equipment), *Radar* (radio detection and ranging). The armed forces are especially quick to form acronyms: *Anzac* (Australian and New Zealand Army Corps) dates from World War I. Every British serviceman became familiar in World War II with *Naffy*, so pronounced from the initials (NAAFI) of Navy, Army and Air Force Institutes. *Pluto* stood for Pipe Line under the Ocean (supplying oil). Initials used to convey messages may also become acronyms, e.g. *Swalk* (Sealed with a Loving Kiss).

5. *Titles and forms of address* When curtailed these should be followed by full stops, e.g.:

Capt. (Captain) Esq. (Esquire) Lieut. (Lieutenant)
M. (Monsieur) Prof. (Professor) Rev. (Reverend)

But when contracted in such a way that the final letter is retained, they should not be followed by full stops, e.g.:

Bart or Bt (Baronet) Dr (Doctor) Kt (Knight)
Ld (Lord) Messrs (Messieurs) Mlle (Mademoiselle)
Mme (Madame) Mr (Mister) Mrs (Mistress)

Some would include the abbreviation of Saint (St) in this second list, but St. with a full stop is well established. The French *Saint* is abbreviated *S.* and the feminine *Sainte* is abbreviated *Ste* without a full stop.

6. *Plurals* In (a) below, the *s* is retained; in (b) it is omitted:

(a) caps. (capitals), gals. (gallons), hrs. (hours), Nos. (numbers), pts. (pints), qts. (quarts), yds. (yards)
(b) cm. (centimetres), cwt. (hundredweights), p. (pence), deg. (degrees), gm. (grammes), in. (inches), lb. (pounds), min. (minutes), mm. (millimetres), oz. (ounces), sec. (seconds)

A few plurals are formed by repeating the letter, e.g. cc. (chapters or cubic centimetres), pp. (pages), vv. (verses).

The apostrophe should not be used for such plural abbreviations as M.P.s (not M.P.'s), Q.C.s (not Q.C.'s), N.C.O.s (not N.C.O.'s). See also APOSTROPHE (1).

7. *Symbols*   The following should not be followed by full stops: 1st (first), 2nd (second), 3rd (third), 4th (fourth), etc.; 4to (quarto), 8vo (octavo).

8. *Points of the compass*   These should be followed by full stops when used singly, but in combinations the only full stop comes at the end, e.g.:

N.   S.   E.   W.   NE.   NW.   SE.   SW.   NNE.   SSW.

9. *London postal districts*   With the introduction of postal codes, these should never be given full stops.

10. When an abbreviation followed by a full stop comes at the end of a sentence, do not add another full stop.

Wrong: The shop sold newspapers, magazines, etc..

Right: The shop sold newspapers, magazines, etc.

Wrong: Write to your M.P.. He is your representative in the House of Commons.

Right: Write to your M.P. He is your representative in the House of Commons.

11. *Christian names or forenames*   These fall under two headings:

(a) formal abbreviations, e.g. *Wm., Fredk., Thos., Robt., Edw., Jas., Geo.*

(b) informal abbreviations, e.g. *Will, Fred, Tom, Bob, Ted, Jim.*

In writing, we should not follow an informal abbreviation with a full stop, unless, of course, it ends a sentence.

Wrong: On the way to the football match Fred. and I met Ben. and Pete. and also a boy called Stan., who is Ben.'s cousin.

Right: On the way to the football match Fred and I met Ben and Pete and also a boy called Stan, who is Ben's cousin.

The full stop is required only if the abbreviation is intended to be read as if the name had been written in full. Thus *Sam Weller* is to be read *Sam Weller*, but *Sam. Pepys* is to be read *Samuel Pepys*. Such distinction does not arise when abbreviations are clearly not intended to be read as spelt, e.g. *Wm., Fredk., Thos.* With these the addition or omission of a full stop is a matter of personal taste. We may write 'Wm. Shakespeare' or 'Wm Shakespeare', 'Fredk. Stevens' or 'Fredk Stevens'. But we must not write 'Will. Shakespeare' or 'Fred. Stevens' if we wish them to be read as 'Will' and 'Fred'.

12. *Shortened words*   Many abbreviations have become shortened words in their own right; others are in colloquial use; others are still

SLANG. (See also CONTRACTION.) Whether in formal writing or in dialogue, they are better shorn of all full stops, apostrophes or inverted commas, unless not yet fully accepted, or liable to be misunderstood. Here are a few: *bus* (omnibus), *cab* (cabriolet), *taxi* (taximeter cabriolet), *cycle* (bicycle), *pram* (perambulator), *maths* (mathematics), *exam* (examination), *prep* (preparation), *rhino* (rhinoceros), *zoo* (zoological gardens), *perm* (permanent wave in hair-dressing), *phone* (telephone), *vet* (veterinary surgeon), *cello* (violoncello).

Whatever our personal feelings about the word *telly* as a shortened form of *television*, it has obviously come to stay and should therefore not be written in inverted commas, particularly in dialogue. This looks bad: 'May we have the "telly" on, Dad?' asked Jack.

The list that follows is by no means complete. It is intended primarily for the guidance of the student of English.

Entries marked with an ASTERISK are treated more fully under their own headings in the body of the book. A dagger indicates fuller treatment under LATIN WORDS AND PHRASES.

A1, a first-class ship in Lloyd's register. Also used colloquially, e.g. 'My new tennis racket is absolutely A1.'

acc., accusative*

*A.D., *Anno Domini*, the Year of Our Lord

A.D.C., *aide-de-camp*, an army officer acting as assistant to a general

adj., adjective*

*ad lib., *ad libitum*, at pleasure

adv., adverb*

A.G.M., Annual General Meeting

a.m., *ante meridiem*,† before midday

Anon, anonymous; used when the writer's name is not known or when he does not wish it to be known

A.S., AS., A-S., Anglo-Saxon

A.V., Authorized Version (of the Bible)

BBC, British Broadcasting Corporation

*B.C., Before Christ; British Columbia

BR, British Rail

Bros., Brothers (in names of companies)

B.S.T., British summer time

*c., *circa*, about

Cantab., *Cantabrigiensis*, a member of Cambridge University; also in degrees, e.g. M.A. (Cantab.)

caps, capitals, i.e. capital letters
cf., *conferatur*, compare
cm., centimetres
Co., Company; County, e.g. Co. Durham
C.O.D., Concise Oxford Dictionary; cash on delivery
co-ed., co-educational
c/o, care of (addressing of letters)
C. of E., Church of England
comp., comparative*
compd., compound*
compl., complement*
con, *contra*,† against
conj., conjunction*
cont., contd., continued
cwt., hundredweight(s); 112 lb. = 1 cwt.; 20 cwt. = 1 ton
dat., dative*
decd., deceased (legal or pompous word for *dead*)
deg., degree(s)
dept., department
do., ditto, the same
doz., dozen(s)
Dr, Doctor
D.V., *Deo volente*,† God willing
E., East
E. & O.E., errors and omissions excepted
EEC, European Economic Community
EFL, English as a foreign language
EFTA, European Free Trade Association
*e.g., *exempli gratia*, for example
Esq., Esquire
*etc., *et cetera*, and the rest
et seq., *et sequitur*,† and the following
etym. dub., etymology dubious, used in dictionaries to indicate
    that the origin of a word is uncertain
exor., executor
fcp., foolscap,* a size of paper
fem., feminine (of gender)*
fig., figure; figuratively
foll., following
Fr., French; Father (R.C.)
ft., foot (feet) = 12 in.

Ger., German

G.B., Great Britain, i.e. England, Wales and Scotland. See also U.K. below

G.B.S., George Bernard Shaw

gen., genitive*

ger., gerund*

Gk., Greek

Glos., Gloucestershire

GMT, Greenwich Mean Time

Govt., Government

GPO, General Post Office

gym., gymnasium, gymnastics

h. & c., hot and cold water

Hants (no full stop), Hampshire

H.M.S., His (Her) Majesty's Ship

Hon., Honorary; Honourable

Hon. Sec., Honorary Secretary

Hon. Treas., Honorary Treasurer

h.p., hire purchase; horse-power

H.Q., headquarters

H.R.H., His (Her) Royal Highness

ib., *ibid.*, *ibidem*,* in the same place

IBA, Independent Broadcasting Authority

*i.e., that is

in., inch(es)

incog., incognito*

ind., indicative*; indirect

inf., infinitive*

infra dig., *infra dignitatem*, beneath one's dignity

inst., *instante mense*, in the present month, used in business correspondence, e.g. '14th inst.', the fourteenth day of the present month

int. alia, *inter alia*,† among other things

interj., interjection*

intr., intransitive*

IOU (no full stops), 'I owe you', a written acknowledgment of debt

I.Q., Intelligence Quotient (psychology)

i.t.a., initial teaching alphabet*

ital., italics

ITV (no full stops), Independent Television

jnr., jr. (American), junr., junior, e.g. *John Smith Jnr.* Note no comma after *Smith*

J.P. (plural J.P.s), Justice of the Peace, in England and Wales, a local magistrate

K.C., King's Counsel, a senior barrister. See Q.C. below

£, pound(s) sterling

£A., pound(s) Australian

lab., laboratory. The abbreviation (plural *labs.*) is often used colloquially, e.g. 'He's been working in the lab all night.'

l.b.w., leg before wicket (cricket)

l.c., lower case,* a term used in printing

LP (no full stops), a long-playing gramophone record

LSD, a hallucinatory drug (lysergic acid diethylamide)

£. s. d., pounds, shillings and pence; British currency before decimalisation in 1971

Ltd. or Ltd, Limited (Liability Company). Strictly speaking, it is incorrect to refer to a 'limited company', since it is not the company but the liability that is limited

M., *Monsieur*, a French form of address, e.g. 'M. Georges Simenon'

M.A., *Magister Artium*, Master of Arts

mack (or mac), a colloquial abbreviation of mackintosh*

mag., magazine

masc., masculine (of gender)*

M.C., Master of Ceremonies, e.g. 'The dance was held in the Town Hall, with Mr Fred Nuttall acting as M.C. in his usual genial and efficient manner.'

MCC, Marylebone Cricket Club

M.E., Middle East

M.E. or ME, Middle English

mem., memo, memorandum

Messrs (no full stop), from the French *Messieurs*, plural of *Monsieur*. It is used when addressing correspondence, etc. to more than one person, e.g. 'Messrs Lawson & Co.', and is pronounced 'Messers' in English

Mlle (no full stop), *Mademoiselle*, a French form of address equivalent to the English 'Miss'

MM., *Messieurs*. This is the abbreviation used in French

mm., millimetre(s)

Mme (no full stop), *Madame*, a French form of address equivalent to the English 'Mrs'

M.P., Member of Parliament

m.p.g., miles per gallon

m.p.h., miles per hour

Mr (no full stop), Mister

Mrs (no full stop), Mistress, the form of address for a married
   woman and pronounced mis¹iz

ms. (plural *mss.*), manuscript(s)

mun., municipal

Mx., Middlesex

N., North

n., noun

N.B., *nota bene*,† note well

N.E.B., New English Bible

nem. con., *nemini contradicente*,† no one speaking against

No. (plural Nos.), number(s), from the Latin *numero*

nom., nominative*

non seq., *non sequitur*,* it does not follow

nr., near, used in postal addresses to identify a small place with a
   larger one, e.g. 'Little Meldon, nr. Lulverton'

N.T., New Testament

ob., *obiit*,† he died

obj., object*

obs., obsolete

O.E. or OE, Old English

O.E.D., *Oxford English Dictionary*

O.F. or OF, Old (Norman) French

O.H.M.S., On His (Her) Majesty's Service

O.K., all correct, everything is fine, agreed

op. (plural *opp.*), opus*

op. cit., *opere citato*, in the work quoted

O.T., Old Testament

O.U.P., Oxford University Press

Oxon., Oxfordshire; of Oxford University, e.g. M.A. (Oxon.)

oz., ounce(s). 16 oz. = 1 lb.

p. (plural *pp.*), page(s)

p.a., *per annum*,* by the year

par., para. (plural *pars.*, *paras.*), paragraph(s)*

P.A.Y.E., pay as you earn, a British system by which an employer
   deducts income tax from staff salaries before making payment

P.C., Privy Councillor

P.c., Police constable

p.c., postcard; per cent*

pd., paid

per pro. or *p.p.*, *per procurationem*, by proxy, used when a person signs
a document on behalf of another or others

Ph.D., Doctor of Philosophy

pl., plural*

plup., pluperfect*

P.M., Prime Minister

p.m., *post meridiem*,† after midday

P.M.G., Postmaster-General

pp., pages

p.p., past participle*; *per pro.* (see above)

pred., predicate*

pref., prefix*

prep., preposition*

pres., present (tense)*

pres. part., present participle

pro, professional. The abbreviation is used colloquially in such
contexts as: 'After playing as an amateur for seven years, he
has now turned pro'

Prof., Professor

pron., pronoun*

pro tem., *pro tempore*,† for the time being

prox., *proximo mense*, in the next month, formerly used in business
correspondence, e.g. 'Please expect delivery on 4th prox.'

PS (plural PPS); postscript*

P.T., physical training

pt., past (tense)*

P.T.O., 'Please turn over', written at the foot of a page to show
that the letter continues overleaf

Pty, proprietary, a collective noun for a body of proprietors. In
Australia it is equivalent to the English 'Co.', e.g. 'A. K. Watson
Pty Ltd'

pub, public house. The abbreviation is in widespread use, e.g.
'Old George spends too much time drinking in the pub, if you
ask me.'

Q.C., Queen's Counsel, a senior barrister. See K.C. above.

Q.E.D., *quod erat demonstrandum*,† that which was to be proved

qto (or 4to), quarto*

q.v., *quod vide*, which see

R.C., Roman Catholic

Rd., Road, used in addresses, e.g. '16 Park Rd.'. The abbreviation (or the capital letter) is not used in such contexts as: 'The London road', i.e. the road to London

R.D.C., Rural District Council

recd., received

ref., refer; reference

refl., reflexive*

rel., relative (grammar)

Rep., Repertory company*

rep., representative. The abbreviation is used in such contexts as: 'I rang up the wholesalers and asked for their rep to call in and see us.'

Rev., Reverend

R.I.P., *Requiescat in pace*, 'May he rest in peace', a wish or prayer for the repose of the dead. The plural is *Requiescant*

rly., railway

rom., roman type as distinct from italics

R.S.V.P., 'Répondez, s'il vous plaît'. See under FRENCH WORDS AND PHRASES

Rt. Hon., Right Honourable. See HONORARY, HONOURABLE

R.V., Revised Version (of the Bible)

S., South; *Saint* (French)

s., singular*; shilling

$, dollar sign

s.a.e., stamped addressed envelope

Salop (no full stop), Shropshire

Sc., Science; Scene (of a play), e.g. 'Act 1, Sc. 2'

s.c., small capitals (type)

S.E., South-East

Sec., Secretary

sec., second(s) (time)

Sig., Signor (Ital.)

sing., singular*

snr., sr. (American), senior, e.g. *John Smith Snr.*, used when father and son have the same first name. Note no comma after *Smith*

Soc., Socialist; Society

S.O.S., 'Save our souls', a distress signal, in Morse Code: (s) · · · (o) — — — (s) · · ·

St., Saint; Street, e.g. 'High St.'

Ste (no full stop), *Sainte* (French feminine)

subj., subject*; subjunctive*

suf., suffix*

sup., superlative*

Supt., Superintendent, a senior title, e.g. in the Police Force

syn., synonym*; synonymous*

t., transitive*

taut., tautology*

Thos., Thomas

Tote, Totalisator, a machine for registering bets on racecourses

trad., traditional, applied, for example, to folk music

ts., typescript

T.T., teetotaller, a total abstainer from strong drink

TV (no full stops), television

U.D.C., Urban District Council

U.K., United Kingdom of Great Britain and Northern Ireland. See also G.B. above

ult., *ultimo mense*, in the previous month, formerly used in business correspondence, e.g. 'Yours of 30th ult. to hand.' This kind of writing is to be avoided

v. or vb., verb*

v. (plural *vv.*), verse(s)*

v., versus,† against

van, advantage (in tennis scoring)

Ven., Venerable, a form of address

verb. sap., *verbum sapienti*,† 'a word to the wise (is enough)'

vet, veterinary surgeon. The abbreviation is used colloquially in such contexts as: 'I thought our dog had mange, so I took him to the vet, who said there was no need to worry.'

V.G., very good

V.H.F., very high frequency (radio)

V.I.P., very important personage

*viz., namely

V.P., Vice-President

W., West

w.c., water closet

w.e.f., with effect from. The abbreviation is used in the Services in such contexts as: 'Increased family allowances for other ranks will be paid w.e.f. 1st Jan. next.'

w.p.b., waste-paper basket

Xmas, Christmas, an abbreviation to be avoided, difficult though it may be

yd. (plural *yds.*), yard(s) = 3 ft.

Z., zero

zoo, a zoological garden where live animals are kept, particularly the Zoological Gardens in London

See also SIGNS AND SYMBOLS.

absolute (L. 'to set free')   in grammar a construction that is set free from the rest of the sentence in grammatical agreement.

The *nominative* absolute is a construction in which a participle is preceded by a noun or its equivalent that looks as if it is going to be the subject of a verb to follow, but is not; it stands on its own, grammatically free from the rest of the sentence. It is called a nominative absolute because the noun, though not the subject, is felt to be the subject and is therefore in the nominative, e.g. '*The season being over*, I put away my cricket gear.' Here the absolute construction is set free from agreement with any of the remainder of the sentence, since it is in fact not the subject or object of any verb, nor is it governed by a preposition. The nominative case is evident when a pronoun is used in the absolute construction, e.g. '*He being rich and I being poor*, everyone took his side against me.'

A common error is the insertion of an unnecessary and misleading comma between the noun and the participle in an absolute construction, e.g. 'My father, being at home at the time, I asked his advice.' This should read: 'My father being at home at the time, I asked his advice.' The mistake arises from the general practice of inserting a comma between the noun and the participle in sentences in which the noun standing first is the subject of the main verb, e.g. 'My *father*, being at home at the time, *gave* me his advice.' In the former sentence, the subject of the main verb ('asked') is not the noun 'father' but the noun equivalent 'I'. See also COMMA.

abstract nouns   Deriving from the Latin, *abstract* means 'drawn away from everything else; not concrete'. We often talk about the *thinness* of a person or an object as if it were something that existed on its own. But really there is no such thing as thinness apart from the person or thing possessing it. Thinness is the quality possessed by a thin person or a thin object. In the same way *pity* cannot exist apart from the person who feels it, and an *arrival* cannot exist apart from the person or thing that arrives. In other words, things like thinness, pity and arrival are qualities, feelings and actions that have been taken away from or abstracted from persons or things. Nouns that name such qualities, feelings and actions are called abstract nouns.

Other abstract nouns are *love, hate, scorn, health, mercy, speed, flight, action, truth, height, depth, heat, cold.* Many more are formed by adding suffixes to common nouns, adjectives or verbs. Below are a few of them.

1. Formation from nouns is made by adding the following suffixes:
   - *-dom*   boredom, martyrdom, serfdom
   - *-hood* brotherhood, childhood, manhood, motherhood
   - *-ism*   chauvinism, communism, hitlerism, mannerism
   - *-ship* fellowship, salesmanship, scholarship
   - *-cy*   bureaucracy, democracy, infancy
2. Formation from adjectives:
   - *-dom*   freedom, wisdom
   - *-ism*   classicism, neuroticism, romanticism, socialism
   - *-ity*   familiarity, liberality, maturity, morality, solidity
   - *-ness* dullness, eagerness, rudeness, sweetness, ugliness
3. Formation from verbs:
   - *-ance* deliverance, endurance, ignorance, perseverance
   - *-ation* damnation, fixation, temptation
   - *-ence* concurrence, convergence, precedence, transference
   - *-ion*   abstraction, constitution, speculation, toleration
   - *-ment* agreement, derangement, resentment

   See also SUFFIXES, NOUNS.

abstractions   ideas expressed in general or abstract terms. The opposite of using abstractions is to use concrete terms. Thus instead of saying 'inclement weather conditions', we could say concretely, and therefore more precisely, 'a blizzard', 'a wet day' or whatever it exactly was. By their very nature, abstractions are vague and lead to imprecise writing unless accompanied by concrete examples.

acatalectic (ækætəlek'tik) (Gk. 'not stopping short')   In PROSODY an acatalectic line is one that has a complete foot at the end of it. It is the opposite of a CATALECTIC line and is referred to more fully under that heading. See also METRE.

accent   This can be defined as the stronger tone of voice given to a particular syllable of a word. In, for example, *elephant* and *tiger* the accent is on the first syllable; in *abundance* and *discovery* the accent is on the second syllable; in *guarantee* and *engineer* the accent is on the last syllable. In dictionaries the accented syllable is usually indicated by means of a stroke or a dot, e.g. *el'ephant* or *e·lephant*; *abun'dance* or *abun·dance.* A change of accent often denotes the difference between the noun and the verb, e.g. *an ab'stract* and *to abstract'*, and the verb and the adjective, e.g. 'He *frequent'ed* the tennis club.' 'He made *fre'quent* visits to the tennis club.'

In PROSODY accent (or stress) is indicated by the *macron* (–), which indicates a stressed sound, and the *breve* (∪), which indicates an unstressed sound. This is dealt with under METRE and SCANNING.

See also under PRONUNCIATION.

accidence (L. 'that which happens') the branch of grammar that has to do with INFLEXION, under which heading it is treated in this work.

accusative (objective) case the case of the direct object of a verb or preposition; the person or thing upon which an action takes effect, e.g. (a) 'The dog scattered the *sand.*' (b) 'The dog buried the *bone* in the sand.' (c) 'The bully hit *him.*' (d) 'She gave the bread to *us* and not to *them.*'

The following points arise in connexion with the use of the accusative case:

(a) When two pronouns are the object of a verb, they must both be in the accusative case, e.g.:

Wrong: Let you and I do it together.

Right: Let you and me do it together.

In the same way, when two pronouns are the object of a preposition, they must both be in the accusative, e.g.:

Wrong: John comes after you and I.

Right: John comes after you and me.

See also BETWEEN YOU AND ME.

(b) The word *than* is, grammatically speaking, a conjunction and should not be used as a preposition, e.g.:

Wrong: Michael is taller than me.

Right: Michael is taller than I am.

The first sentence is elliptical. Its full form is given in the second sentence. On this argument, *me* is wrong because it is an ELLIPSIS of *I am* and should therefore be *I*, with *than* functioning correctly as a conjunction. Yet most educated people now accept *me* in this construction, and it can in fact be justified, since if *than* is considered to be a preposition (even the conservative Concise Oxford Dictionary now allows that it may be used as a quasi-preposition) the accusative form *me* is required. The accusative form can, however, be ambiguous, e.g. 'She likes me better than you.' To avoid ambiguity, the sentence should be written in full: 'She likes me better than she likes you' or 'She likes me better than you do.'

(c) When an interrogative pronoun is governed by a preposition, it should be in the accusative case, e.g.:

Wrong: Who were you talking to just now?

Right: To whom were you talking just now?

The accusative form of *who* is not, however, very popular. Very few educated people, at any rate in speech, would use our corrected sentence, or even 'Whom were you talking to just now?' Usage now runs against *whom*, so that in this instance many modern grammarians would accept our first sentence as correct. We should nevertheless understand the point. If we wish to be correct in the traditional manner, we should write 'To whom were you talking just now?'

(d) A RELATIVE PRONOUN agrees with its ANTECEDENT in number and person, but its case is determined by its function in its own CLAUSE, e.g.:

Wrong: The boy who you rescued from drowning has recovered.

Right: The boy whom you rescued from drowning has recovered.

Here the pronoun is the object of the verb *rescued* and should therefore be accusative. Nevertheless, as in (c) above, there is no question of ambiguity, and the accusative form of *who* is likely to die out.

(e) Sometimes a writer uses *whom* when even grammatically it is incorrect, e.g.:

Wrong: They chose the candidate whom they thought would have most initiative.

Right: They chose the candidate who they thought would have most initiative.

The relative pronoun is the subject of the verb *would have* and should therefore be in the nominative case. The confusion arises from wrongly thinking that the relative pronoun is the object of the verb *thought*. In fact the clause *they thought* is parenthetical ('who, they thought, would have') and does not influence the case of the pronoun.

See also CASE.

acknowledge   This is sometimes misused.

(a) *Wrong*: I have to acknowledge your letter.

      Right: I have to acknowledge the receipt of your letter.

In this context *acknowledge* means 'inform you of'.

(b) *Wrong*: The prisoner's wild denials acknowledged his guilt.
  Right: The prisoner's wild denials proved his guilt.

A person can acknowledge, can admit to be true, but a thing cannot.

acronym (ak'rounim)   see ABBREVIATIONS (4)

acrostic   an arrangement of words in such a way that their initial letters form words or phrases. In a double acrostic the last letters also form a word. This is a double acrostic:

```
M  U  S  I  C
O  D  D  L  Y
T  O  N  I  C
O  R  I  E  L
R  O  U  S  E
```

active voice   see VOICE.

A.D.   abbreviation of *Anno Domini*, which means 'in the Year of Our Lord'. In the writing of dates it precedes the figures, e.g. A.D. 1066. See also B.C.; CENTURIES.

addendum (plural **addenda**)   an appendix; something to be added, as, for example, a list of new words at the end of a dictionary.

ad hoc (L. 'for this')   as arranged for a particular or special purpose, e.g. 'When the question of new premises was raised at the annual general meeting, an *ad hoc* committee was formed to look into this matter and report back to the main committee.'

adjacent, contiguous (*g* hard)   The first means 'lying close to', whilst the second means 'lying so close as to be touching'. Jersey and Guernsey are *adjacent*; Surrey and Sussex are *contiguous*; Jersey is adjacent to Guernsey; Surrey is contiguous to (not *with*) Sussex.

adjective   the part of speech that qualifies (or describes) what is named by a noun or pronoun, e.g. 'a *black* cat'; 'a *tall* man'; '*Lucky* you!' Care must be taken to place an adjective as near as possible to the noun it qualifies. Should another noun be placed between them, the adjective is liable to be read as qualifying this other noun. 'Short children's stories are always in demand.' (Short children?) 'Striped men's pyjamas are now reduced in price.' (Striped men?) 'The beautiful engineer's wife.' (Beautiful engineer?) See also TRANSFERRED EPITHET.

An adjective may be either *attributive*, where it stands with its noun (usually before), e.g. 'The *wild* creature sprang upon us', or *predicative*, where it stands in the predicate as the complement of the verb, e.g. 'These animals become very *wild* in a storm.' (See also ATTRIBUTIVE; PREDICATE.)

Adjectives may also be classified as: *descriptive*, 'The *next* boy looked *ill*'; *demonstrative*, 'I like *those* cakes best'; *interrogative*, '*Which* cakes do you like best?'; *possessive*, '*My* book is red, but *your* books are both green'; *numerical*, 'In the *fourth* picture you can see *eight* trees'; *distributive*, '*Each* kind should be given to *every* child'.

Demonstrative adjectives must agree in number with the nouns they qualify, e.g.:

(a) *This apple* is sweeter than *those plums*.
(b) *That girl* is taller than *those boys*.

'These kind', 'those sort', etc. have become so common that they are allowable in conversation, but in formal writing it is best to avoid them, e.g.:
Wrong: These kind of mistakes often occur.
Right: This kind of mistake often occurs.
A possessive adjective should always agree with any personal pronoun to which it relates, e.g.:
Wrong: One should always do their best.
Wrong: One should always do his best.
Right: One should always do one's best.
  or: People should always do their best.
Possessive adjectives are treated more fully under POSSESSIVE ADJECTIVES AND PRONOUNS.

See also PROPER ADJECTIVES, and also under ADVERB.

adjectival clause (or **adjective clause**) a subordinate clause functioning as an adjective and therefore qualifying a noun or pronoun in another clause; sometimes called a relative clause. It may be introduced by a relative pronoun, e.g. 'The man *whom he visited* is a cousin of mine'; by a relative pronoun governed by a preposition, e.g. 'The man *in whom I have the greatest faith* is no longer here'; by a relative adverb, e.g. 'Do you remember the time *when we won the cup*?' or by any of the foregoing understood but not expressed, e.g. 'What was the name of the man (*whom*) *we met yesterday*?'

See also NON-DEFINING CLAUSES; CONTACT CLAUSES.

adjectival phrase (or **adjective phrase**)   a phrase functioning as an adjective and therefore qualifying a noun or pronoun. There are three main types of adjectival phrases: prepositional, e.g. 'The name *at the top* was mine'; participial, e.g. '*Weakened by fever*, he soon began to totter'; infinitive, e.g. 'The task *to be accomplished* was not easy.'

ad libitum (L. 'at pleasure')   abbreviated *ad lib.* and used in music to mark a passage that may be varied according to the player's taste. Colloquially it occurs in such contexts as: 'Refreshments were *ad lib*, so we all had enough to eat.' In the theatrical world to *adlib* is to extemporise, to fill in awkward gaps by using one's own words instead of the playwright's, e.g. 'Mary missed her cue and I had to *adlib* until she made her entrance.'

admission, admittance   These are sometimes confused. Generally they are interchangeable, but usage insists on 'No admittance' for warning notices and 'the price of admission' for entrance money. Usage now also insists that when we admit something we make an *admission*, e.g. 'His frank admission that he had made a mistake led me to forgive him for what he had done.'

admit, admit of   Do not use the preposition except when the meaning is 'to leave room for', e.g.:

Wrong: He admitted of having been near the house on the night of the crime.

Right: He admitted having been near the house on the night of the crime.

Right: That he had been near the house on the night of the crime admitted of several conclusions.

adventitious, adventurous   The first means 'accidental; casual; incidental'. The second means 'venturesome; enterprising; ready to take risks'.

'The adventurous undergraduate was prevented from reaching the top of the steeple by the adventitious arrival of the proctor.'

adverb   the part of speech that usually modifies a verb, but may also modify an adjective or another adverb. We therefore have adverbs of manner, e.g. 'He behaved *sensibly*'; of time, e.g. 'Finish it *now*'; of place, e.g. 'Bring it *here*'; of degree, e.g. 'It is *quite* clear that he worked *too* hard'; of reason, e.g. 'He was *therefore* disqualified'; of assertion, e.g. '*No*, you cannot go'; of interpolation (see SENTENCE ADVERBS), e.g. 'We refused to pay the price, *however*, and went elsewhere.'

Though many adverbs have been formed by the addition of *-ly* to adjectives, by no means all fall under this heading, e.g. *everywhere, how, more, much, otherwise, perhaps, seldom, today, very, yonder.* Some adverbs are the same as the adjectives, e.g. *fast, hard* (try hard, work hard, etc.), *leisurely, less, more, much, only, overmuch, sideways, straight.*

When both adjective and adverb end in *-ly*, the adverbial use can look awkward. 'He behaved cowardly.' 'The matron treated me beastly.' 'I drove leisurely through the woods.' We feel they should be *cowardlily, beastlily* and *leisurelily*. To avoid this awkwardness, we can rearrange the sentence without altering the meaning, e.g. 'He behaved in a cowardly way.' 'The matron was beastly to me.' 'I took a leisurely drive through the woods.' Other adjective-adverb words are *deadly, doubly, niggardly, slovenly, untimely.* A few words do have the second adverb, e.g. *friendly, friendlily; kindly, kindlily,* but they are too awkward to be popular.

It is sometimes difficult to decide whether to use the adjective or the adverb, e.g. (a) 'The children arrived home safe'; or (b) 'The children arrived home safely.' The important thing here is that the children were safe when they arrived, so (a) is better than (b). 'After coming safely through the woods the children arrived home.' Here the adverb is correct because it describes how they came through the woods.

Adverbs of emphasis, such as *only, even, merely,* must be placed near the words they modify, for the sense of the sentence changes according to their position in it. ONLY is treated under that heading. Here are some examples of the other two:

(a) Even Mary burst into tears when I told them this. Mary even burst into tears when I told them this. Mary burst into tears when I told them even this.

(b) In the uproar and angry exchange of blows that followed, the women were merely spectators. In the uproar and angry exchange of blows that followed, merely the women were spectators.

The same thing applies to adverbs in general: they must be placed, with the adjectives they modify, as near as possible to the noun qualified by the adjective, e.g. 'The newly painted ladies' cloakroom' should be 'The newly painted cloakroom for ladies' or 'The ladies' newly painted cloakroom.'

See also TRANSFERRED EPITHET.

adverbial clause (or **adverb clause**)   a subordinate clause functioning as an adverb. Adverbial clauses may therefore be: of time, e.g. 'They sang *as they walked along*'; of place, e.g. 'I planted it *where you suggested*'; of cause or reason, e.g. '*Because I was late*, I missed my turn'; of purpose, e.g. 'I removed them *so that I should not be reminded of my failure*'; of result, e.g. 'He walked so slowly *that he missed the bus*'; of condition, e.g. '*If we do not hurry* we shall keep them waiting'; of concession, e.g. 'She failed *though she did her best*'; of manner, e.g. 'They completed the task *as they were instructed*'; of degree or comparison, e.g. 'John is taller *than his brother was at that age.*'

adverbial particle   a common adverb that can also be used as a preposition, which is added to a main verb to form a PHRASAL VERB that functions as a unit and usually has a new meaning that is not just the sum of its parts, e.g. to sum *up*, to go *off*, to hold *over*, to carry *out*, to keep *on*.

adverbial phrase (or **adverb phrase**)   a phrase functioning as an adverb. Adverbial phrases may be: prepositional, e.g. '*Along the road* they walked *in full view*'; infinitive, e.g. 'I come *to bury Caesar*, not *to praise him*'; participial, e.g. '*Standing on the chair*, I just managed to reach it'; the nominative absolute, e.g. 'The child, *there being no one in sight*, decided to escape.'

adverse   This means 'contrary; hurtful; hostile'. It should not be confused with *averse*, which means 'disinclined'.

(a) The explorers were prevented by adverse weather from reaching their objective.

(b) With the weather rapidly worsening, the leader of the expedition was averse to going on.

For the use of *to* or *from* after *averse*, see AVERSE.

advertising proclaiming of wares primarily by way of paid announcements in the Press, on film, or on commercial broadcasting (TV and radio) channels. The practice has developed into a major industry in the field of communications, and has produced its own contribution to the language both by adding new words and by modifying the meaning of established ones, e.g. *trailer* (advertisement preceding [!] an event); *puff* (to inflate a claim; also as a noun); *impact* (effect); *slogan* (orig. a war-cry); *market research* (a semi-scientific method of finding out what potential customers need); *test surveys* (part of *market research*); *consumer* (often merely he who used to be a *customer* or a *client*); *copy* (words embodying the advertiser's *message*); *medium* (means of communicating the message – printed word, recorded word, televised or cinematograph film); a *mass medium*, e.g. the national *Press* (see also MEDIA and MCLUHAN); *public relations* (a method often using personal *contacts* of establishing an advertiser's *image*); *hard sell* (direct, sometimes blatant, advertising – the converse is *soft sell*, an insidiously casual approach: both methods may sometimes be seen or heard consecutively in *TV commercials*); *packaging* (dressing up a product, especially a retail item, to catch a consumer's eye at *point of sale*); *angle* (slant given to *copy* to make a special appeal: in advertising *jargon*, a *campaign* may be specially *angled* to *catch* the *women's market*); *visual* (an artist's *rough* impression of what e.g. a magazine advertisement should look like: the accompanying words are supplied by a *copywriter* employed by an *advertising agency*); *appropriation* (the amount of money set aside by an advertiser for the *promotion* of his product over a given period); *space buyer* (an *agency executive* who buys advertising space for his client in selected publications: his colleague may be a *time* buyer, dealing with broadcasting); *spot* (the seconds of commercial TV time secured to advertise a product).

advice, advise The first is the noun, the second is the verb. To *advise* is to give *advice* and should not be used when we simply mean to give information, since the verb *to inform* is already available for that. 'His doctor advised him to take a month's holiday.' 'We have the pleasure to advise you that the television set will be delivered tomorrow.' The first sentence is correct; in the second sentence *advise* should read *inform*.

Æ, Œ (æ, œ) see VOWEL LIGATURES.

aeroplane, aircraft The first was the original word for a flying-machine, but it has been superseded by the second, which is also the plural form, e.g. *aeroplanes = aircraft*. In everyday use *plane* (*planes*) is general, the apostrophe (*'plane*) being omitted, as in *bus* (*omnibus*) and *phone* (*telephone*). The use of *plane* is likely to grow, as it is also American, whereas the American for *aeroplane* is *airplane*.

aesthetic (esθet'ik) (Gk. 'perceptible by the senses') adjective and noun meaning 'having to do with the beautiful'. An aesthetic temperament is one that attaches more importance to beauty than to anything else. Keats wrote in his *Ode on a Grecian Urn*:

> 'Beauty is truth, truth beauty,' – that is all
> Ye know on Earth, and all ye need to know.

In a derogatory sense an aesthete is one who pays too much attention to beauty, or, worse still, pretends to despise the ordinary or the matter-of-fact.

affect, effect The first is always a verb and means 'to influence'. Though *effect* is usually a noun meaning 'result' ('The effect of the drought was a serious shortage of water'), it is sometimes a verb meaning 'to bring about', e.g. 'The coach effected a remarkable improvement in our play.'

affinity attraction; liking; mutual regard. Thus there is an affinity *between* two persons, and each of them has an affinity *with* the other. *Affinity to* and *affinity for* are therefore to be avoided.

affirmative see NEGATIVE.

affixes prefixes or suffixes added to a root word to build a new one. Many hundreds of words have been formed in this way from Greek and Latin roots. See also PREFIX; SUFFIX; WORD-FORMATION.

affricates in PHONETICS the sounds made by a combination of explosion and friction. See GUIDE TO PRONUNCIATION on page 9.

aged We pronounce this in two ways. When we speak of an aged man, we pronounce it ei'dʒid with two syllables; when we speak of a man aged sixty-five, we pronounce it eidʒd with one syllable.

aggravate   to make worse. 'His loneliness was aggravated by the loss of his parents.' The present participle, however, is now commonly used in the sense of *provoking* ('Don't be so aggravating, Tommy!'). This is a pity, since there are plenty of adjectives such as *annoying, vexing, exasperating, irritating* that already have this meaning and it would have been better to reserve *aggravating* for its original meaning. See also CORRECT ENGLISH.

ago, since   Do not use these adverbs together; use one or the other, to avoid redundancy, e.g.:
    Wrong: It is over a year ago since we met.
     Right: It is over a year since we met.
       or: It was over a year ago that we met.

agreement (or **concord**)   a grammatical term meaning that certain words must agree in GENDER, NUMBER, CASE or PERSON. Three examples are quoted below.

  (a) The subject and the verb must agree in number, e.g. 'The *cat was* in the house. The *dogs were* in the garden.'
  (b) The subject and the verb must agree in person, e.g. '*He swims* well, but *I swim* badly.'
  (c) The demonstrative adjective must agree in number with the noun it qualifies, e.g. '*This apple* is sweeter than *these plums*.' '*That girl* is taller than *those boys*.'

Agreement is treated in this work under the following headings: ABSOLUTE; ACCUSATIVE (OBJECTIVE) CASE; ADJECTIVE; ATTRACTION; BETWEEN YOU AND ME; BOTH, EACH; COLLECTIVE NOUNS (under NOUN); CONJUNCTION; EITHER . . . OR; GOVERN; NOMINATIVE CASE; NOT ONLY . . . BUT ALSO; NUMBER; PRONOUN; SEQUENCE OF TENSES (under TENSE).

al-, all   *almighty, already, altogether* and *always* are all right, but *alright* is all wrong; *all right* is the correct spelling. There is a distinction between *all ready* and *already, all together* and *altogether*, and *all ways* and *always*. Here are examples of each:

  (a) By seven o'clock the travellers were all ready to depart.
     By seven o'clock the travellers had already departed.
  (b) The fifty guests were all together in the room. The room was altogether inadequate for the fifty guests.

(c) He looked all ways before he crossed the road. He always looked before he crossed the road.

Alexandrine in PROSODY a form of verse probably deriving from a French rhyming romance about Alexander the Great written in twelve-syllable lines rhyming aabb. In English poetry an *Alexandrine* is an iambic HEXAMETER, i.e. it consists of six feet (twelve syllables) with the stress falling on the second syllable of each FOOT. It is sometimes used to vary the monotony of iambic pentameters (see PENTAMETER). For example, Spenser's *The Faerie Queene* is written in iambic pentameters with the exception of the last line of each stanza, which is an Alexandrine. Here is the fourth stanza of Canto IV:

A stately Pallace built of squared bricke,
Which cunningly was without morter laid,
Whose wals were high, but nothing strong nor thick
And golden foile all over them displaid,
That purest skye with brightnesse they dismaid:
High lifted up were many loftie towres,
And goodly galleries far over laid,
Full of faire windowes and delightful bowres:
And on the top a Diall told the timely howres.

Pope, that master of the iambic pentameter, was very scornful of this use of the iambic hexameter, declaring in his *Essay on Criticism*:

Then, at the last and only couplet fraught
With some unmeaning thing they called a thought,
A needless Alexandrine ends the song,
That, like a wounded snake, drags its slow length along.

alienation a technical term used by the German dramatist Bertolt Brecht to describe his distinctive approach to the theatre. Instead of actors seeking to involve the audience in the drama, producing *empathy* and making them *feel*, the cast of a Brecht play would be instructed to alienate the audience, making them aware all the time that they were watching actors act. In this way, the audience would cease to *feel* and would start to *think* about what the actors were conveying. Brecht was a Communist and his view of the role of the drama was conditioned by the need to make the stage another medium for influencing society (propaganda is a DEROGATORY term for it).

allege   to assert without proof. It is a useful word when one wishes to be careful what one says, e.g. 'She is alleged to have run off with an actor.' In legal circles a man must not be called a criminal until he has been found so in a court of law. Until then he is referred to as 'the alleged housebreaker' or 'the alleged spy', and the crime he is thought to have committed as 'the alleged crime' or 'the alleged offence'. As an example of this legal caution there can be mentioned the solicitor who chased a man down the street shouting, 'Stop alleged thief! Stop alleged thief!'

allegory   a FIGURE OF SPEECH; a narrative description of a subject under the guise of another suggestively similar. It is therefore like a SIMILE extended into a complete story. An example is *The Pilgrim's Progress* by John Bunyan, in which a man named Christian goes on a long and difficult journey. It is thus apparently a story of the pilgrim's adventures on the way, but its underlying and more important meaning is the nature of a Christian's life.

A PARABLE is an allegory in short form.

allergic   (ælə:ˈdʒik) (Gk. 'other work', i.e. 'reacting in a different way')   As a medical term the noun *allergy* (ælˈə:dʒi:) means 'an abnormal reaction to a food or substance innocuous to other people'; and to be *allergic* is to be highly susceptible to certain things, either eaten, touched or breathed in. For example, sufferers from hay-fever are allergic to the pollen of various grasses and plants. Note that it is the sufferer who is allergic.

Wrong: Some foods are allergic to people who have asthma.

Right: People who have asthma are allergic to some foods.

Allergy does not denote dislike; we may be allergic to tomatoes and still be very fond of them. In recent years, however, *allergic* has joined the ranks of VOGUE WORDS, being used in the sense of 'having an aversion to'. When we say that we are allergic to sugar in tea, we do not mean that it gives us a stiff neck or brings us out in spots, but merely that we much prefer our tea unsweetened. Or we may say: 'John is very fond of classical music, but he's allergic to this modern stuff'; or, 'I'm allergic to men who use purses.'

alliteration   the repetition of a sound, usually a consonant and usually at the beginning of words, in order to help the sense, e.g. '*A*fter life's *f*itful *f*ever he sleeps well.' '*S*ister *S*usie's *s*ewing *s*ocks for *s*oldiers.' It was the poet Charles Churchill who referred to 'apt alliteration's artful aid', but in good writing it should be used sparingly and with discretion.

allude   to refer to, but not in a straightforward way. 'The president then alluded to the great generosity of Mr Smith.' This is incorrect. Had he alluded to it, he would not have mentioned it outright but by implication. 'The president then referred to the great generosity of one of the members. He did not mention his name, but it was clear that he alluded to Mr Smith.'

allusion, elusion, illusion, delusion   These are sometimes confused. The first is the noun of the verb *to allude*. 'In proposing the toast to the school, Mr Robinson quoted Goldsmith's famous lines, "And still they gazed, and still the wonder grew, That one small head could carry all he knew." This allusion to Mr Whackham caused much amusement among the boys present.'

An *elusion* is an avoidance by clever means; an escape by clever means; bafflement. The verb (*elude*) and the adjective (*elusive*) are more often met with than the noun. 'He eluded the police for nearly a year.' 'The elusive law-breaker was finally traced to a boarding-house in Brighton.' 'Although I tried hard to remember it, the name of my benefactor eluded me.'

An *illusion* is a false impression or belief; a deception (an *illusionist* is another name for a conjuror). 'Everyone thought him a rich man, but that was an illusion.' 'A boy loses many of his illusions as he grows into manhood.'

A *delusion* is not quite the same as an illusion. To quote from *Modern English Usage*: 'The existing thing that deludes is a delusion; the thing falsely supposed to exist, or the sum of the qualities with which an existing thing is falsely invested, is an illusion. Optimism (if unjustified) is a delusion; Heaven is (if non-existent) an illusion. If a bachelor dreams that he is married, his marriage is an illusion; if he marries in the belief that marriage must bring him happiness, he may find that marriage is a delusion . . . What a conjuror actually does – his real action – is a delusion; what he seems to do is an illusion.'

alphabet (Gk. *alpha*, *beta*)   a series of symbols in which a language is written. In a number of languages – Spanish, for example – there is close correspondence between the written word and the spoken word, but, as is mentioned under PRONUNCIATION, spoken English has changed so much since spellings were fixed in the eighteenth century, that English cannot now be described as a phonetic language. Numerous attempts at a reformed alphabet have been made, one of which, intended for the assistance of beginners, is treated under INITIAL TEACHING ALPHABET.

alphabetical order   the order of words when arranged according to the alphabet. Lists, indexes, dictionaries, directories, encyclopaedias and similar reference books are arranged alphabetically. If the words begin with different letters, you clearly arrange them according to the first letter. Thus *Belgium* comes before *Denmark* because B comes before D in the alphabet. If they begin with the same letter, they are arranged according to the second letter; *banks* comes before *boats* because A comes before O. If they begin with the same two letters, they are arranged according to the third letter; and so on. Thus *banks* comes before *baskets* because N comes before S, and *basins* comes before *baskets* because I comes before K. There is only one difficulty: if two words have the same letters but one goes on farther than the other, you put the shorter word first. Thus *pen* comes before *penal*, and *penal* comes before *penalty*.

This can be seen more clearly in practice from the following list of words, which is repeated in alphabetical order on the right:

rich	neuter
rice	number
rhyme	questions
riches	rhyme
number	rice
questions	rich
neuter	riches

In listing personal names alphabetically, it is normal to order those with the same surname according to the initials of their first names. Thus *Smith, Brian* comes before *Smith, Donald*; *Jones, S. J.* comes before *Jones, T. A.*; *Baker, P.* comes before *Baker, P. B.*; and *Taylor, Jack* comes before *Taylor, J. C.* It is also common practice to consider *St.* as *Saint* for alphabetical purposes. The prefixes *M'* and *Mc* are both treated as if they were *Mac*, and the next letter in the name determines its position in the list.

alright   See AL-, ALL.

also   This is an adverb, not a conjunction. It cannot join words, phrases or clauses unless preceded by a conjunction, e.g. *and* or *but*.

 Wrong: Many of the children, also some of the parents, were ill after the party.

 Right: Many of the children, and also some of the parents, were ill after the party.

Care must be taken to place *also* in its right position in the sentence. As with ONLY its position governs the meaning of the sentence, e.g.:

 (a) I also have given five pounds to this good cause. (Others have given five pounds and so have I.)

 (b) I have also given five pounds to this good cause. (Besides helping in other ways, I have given five pounds to this good cause.)

 (c) I have given five pounds to this good cause also. (Besides giving five pounds to other good causes, I have given five pounds to this one.)

alternate, alternative   These two adjectives are sometimes confused. *Alternate* means coming by turns, one after the other. 'The walls were covered in alternate stripes of red and blue.' *Alternative*, on the other hand, means offering a choice between two. 'If red is not desired, an alternative colour is blue.' Strictly speaking, *alternative* should be used only where there is a choice between two. Thus, instead of saying, 'we were faced with three alternatives', it would be better to say, 'we were faced with three choices'.

although   see THOUGH.

ambiguity (æmbigju'iti) (L. 'to move on both sides')   something that can be taken in two ways. The main reasons for ambiguity are:

 1. The misplacement of word, phrase or clause, e.g. (a) 'In Paris there are over three million inhabitants alone.' ('In Paris alone there are over three million inhabitants.') (b) 'David's father told him to be quiet in a loud voice.' ('David's father told him in a loud voice to be quiet.') See also ONLY.

 2. The doubtful reference of personal pronouns, e.g. 'She likes me better than you.' ('She likes me better than she likes you'; or 'she likes me better than you do'.)

 3. The omission of necessary words, e.g. 'The teacher's next experiment was not the least interesting.' ('The teacher's next

experiment was not the least interesting of those he carried out that afternoon.')

4. Defective punctuation, of which some examples are given under COMMA and HYPHEN.

5. The use of words with more than one meaning, e.g. 'Australia at that time possessed no capital.' ('Australia at that time possessed no capital city.')

6. Phrases or constructions that in their context can have more than one interpretation, e.g. 'The crew of the ship intended nothing less than mutiny.' This means either that the crew fully intended to mutiny, or that they had not the slightest intention of mutinying.

As pronouns are so frequently used to avoid repetition of nouns, No. 2 above is a major cause of ambiguity. Where the pronouns are of different gender there is no ambiguity, e.g. 'Mrs Baker tried to ring the butcher but found her telephone was out of order.' But if her husband made the call 'her telephone' becomes 'his telephone', which may be Mr Baker's or the butcher's. This ambiguity can be avoided by altering the sentence round to fit the facts, thus: 'Mr Baker found his telephone was out of order when he tried to ring the butcher'; or 'Mr Baker found the butcher's telephone was out of order when he tried to ring him.'

Here are a few more examples of ambiguity: 'Harry made a point of seeing Jack before he went to America.' Before who went to America – Harry or Jack? 'When the bully attacked him he punched him on the nose.' Whose nose was punched? 'Her mistress was not satisfied until she had dusted all the ornaments.' Who did the dusting? 'He removed the basket from the car and jumped into it.' Jumped into the basket? 'Tired of being a spectator, I asked my friend to lend me a gun so that I could shoot myself.' 'The old gentleman went into the garden and watched the goldfish smoking his pipe.' Then there was the notice in the chemists' window: 'We dispense with accuracy.'

Not all ambiguities are so obscure that we cannot get at their meaning, but such woolliness is to be avoided in clear writing. See also ELLIPSIS; HARD, HARDLY.

Deliberate ambiguity is a form of FALLACY. See also EQUIVOCATION.

American English   It has been said with more than a little truth that Great Britain and the United States are two countries divided by the same language. The differences are not merely in pronunciation and spelling: *labour – labor, programme – program, theatre – theater*, *catalogue – catalog, through – thru, anaemia – anemia, cheque – check*. Nor does it perplex us when an American asks 'Do you have a match?' instead of 'Have you a match?' or when he invites us to have a seat instead of to take one. We know too that a *pavement* in London is a *sidewalk* in New York, yet we might be somewhat alarmed to learn that a car was approaching us at great speed along the pavement, unless we were aware that pavement is the American for *roadway*. Again, if we have just started a conversation on the telephone and the operator breaks in with 'Are you through?', we must remember to say 'Not yet,' for if we say 'Yes, thank you' the operator will think we have finished and will clear the line.

A book like *Modern American Usage* by H. W. Horwill (O.U.P.) takes 350 pages to list all the differences, so it is obvious that we can refer here to only a few of them. As is discussed under DERIVATION, many American words and phrases have been absorbed into our language, but there are still many that have not. Some of these are given below, and we are very grateful to Mr Michael Avallone, the American writer, for his generous assistance in checking our draft list (and writing 'Never!' against some of the entries).

A few words of explanation are called for. First, it should be understood that a word in one column is not necessarily synonymous with a word in the other column in all its senses. For example, although Americans use *raise* instead of *rise* to mean an increase in pay, in other contexts they use it in the same way as we do, and when they say *cunning* they do not always mean *dainty* or *cute*; a cunning baby is a most attractive infant in the U.S.A.; a cunning man is a crafty fellow on both sides of the Atlantic. Secondly, although one American may describe a pocketbook for paper money as a *billfold*, another may call it a *wallet*, just as we do. Our purpose is to show what is meant by *billfold* – or *flatware* or *custom built* or *notions* or a *round-trip ticket*, which doesn't entitle the holder to make a circular tour.

American	British
aisle	long narrow passage; corridor of a train
aluminum	aluminium
apartment	a flat
approbate	approve
bellhop	pageboy
bill	note (paper money)

American	British
billboard	hoarding
billfold	wallet
billion	a thousand millions
bourbon	whisky distilled from corn and rye
brakeman	guard of a goods train
bureau	chest of drawers
business suit	lounge suit
calling card	visiting card
candy	sweets
car (of train)	carriage
carry	have in stock
casket	coffin
check	cheque
checkers (game)	draughts
checking account	banking account
checkroom	cloakroom
city	large town
city hall	town hall
city ordinance	by-law
clerk (klə:k)	shop assistant
clothes-pin	clothes-peg
collar-button	collar-stud
come by	to call on a person; to look in
comfort station	public convenience
composition book	exercise book
conductor	guard of a passenger train
conservatory	school of music
cookie (cooky)	small sweet cake
corn	maize
cracker	biscuit
crematory	crematorium
crystal	watch-glass
cunning	dainty; cute
custom built	made-to-order
cycler	cyclist
declination	refusal; non-acceptance
derby (də:ˈbi)	bowler hat
district attorney	public prosecutor

American	British
draft	draught
dresser	dressing-table
druggist	chemist (pharmacist)
drugstore	chemist's shop, also selling stationery, magazines and sometimes soft drinks
drummer	commercial traveller
dry goods store	draper's shop
dumb	stupid
elevator	lift
fall	autumn
faucet	water tap
first floor	ground floor
fix	(see page 45)
flat (noun)	puncture (of a car tyre)
flatware	table cutlery
floorwalker	shopwalker
frame	to fabricate evidence against a person
freight train	goods train
freshman	first-year student at university or college
gas(oline)	petrol
get across	make clear; explain
gotten	got
grain	corn
gridiron	football field
grip	suitcase
handle	deal in
highball	whisky and soda, etc. served with ice in a tall glass
hog	pig
hog-pen	pig-sty
homely	plain-featured
hood (of a car)	bonnet
huckster	costermonger
janitor	caretaker
kerosene	paraffin
lawn party	garden party
lawyer	solicitor or barrister
line busy (telephone)	number engaged
locomotive engineer	engine driver

lumber	timber
mad	angry
mail (n. and v.)	post
mailman	postman
melt up	melt down
mistreat	maltreat
molasses	treacle
mortician	undertaker (funeral director)
news-stand	bookstall
normalcy	normality
notions	haberdashery, small articles such as ribbons, cotton, needles, pins, buttons, sold in one department – or at the 'notion counter' – of a store
Oxford (or oxford) shoe	laced shoe
paddle	spank
panhandler	street beggar
pants	trousers
parkway	wide thoroughfare, closed to heavy traffic, its verges planted with trees, grass, etc.
parlor	not only a sitting-room but also a term for certain businesses where customers are gathered together under social circumstances, e.g. *ice-cream parlor*, *beauty parlor*
pasteboard	cardboard
patrolman	police constable
pavement	roadway
penitentiary	prison
pen-point	nib
period (punctuation)	full stop
pitcher	jug
porch	veranda
private school	public school
public school	school maintained by public funds, i.e. state school
purse (woman's)	handbag
railroad	railway
raise (increase in pay)	rise

American	British
roast	joint of meat
round-trip ticket	return ticket
run	to stand for office
saloon	public house
scratch-pad	scribbling-block
shine up to	try to please
shingle	wooden roof-tile
shoe-string	bootlace or shoelace; also very small amount of money used to start or carry on a business
shy of	short of; lacking in
sick	ill
sidewalk	pavement
silent partner	sleeping partner
slick up	tidy up
soapboxer	tub-thumper; ranting orator
solicitor	not a member of the legal profession but any person who solicits, even a street beggar
sophomore	second-year student at university or college
spool of thread	reel of cotton
station agent	station master
stay over	stay the night
store	shop
subway	underground railway
sundown	sunset
sunup	sunrise
suspenders	braces for trousers
switch (railway)	points
terminal	terminus
thread (for sewing)	cotton
thrifty	thriving; prosperous; of plants, growing vigorously
thumbtack	drawing-pin
trailer	caravan
truck	lorry; van
trunk (of car)	boot
trunk line (railway)	main line
tuxedo	dinner jacket

American	British
vanity	dressing-table
vest	waistcoat
visit	a friendly chat, wherever it takes place
washcloth	face flannel
yen	yearning

The word *fix* has a variety of uses in America; it is nearly as over-worked as *got* is in English. Here are a few examples:

(a) I'll fix the highballs while you fix the fire. (I'll see to the drinks while you light the fire.)

(b) Do you have a comb for me to fix my hair? (Have you a comb for me to tidy my hair?)

(c) He's fixing to get over to Europe in the fall. (He's trying to get over to Europe in the autumn.)

(d) I figured the fresh air would fix my head. (I thought the fresh air would clear my head.)

(e) It surprised him to find a woman fixing flowers in the apartment. (It surprised him to find a woman arranging flowers in the flat.)

(f) The bookmaker fixed the trainer to give the horse a fix. (The bookmaker bribed the trainer to dope the horse.)

(g) Because the stores were closed we had to eat the roast with no fixings. (Because the shops were closed we had to eat the joint without trimmings.)

(h) The addict had a 'fix'. (He had an injection of heroin.)

among   see BETWEEN, AMONG.

amongst   The best thing we can do with this preposition is to regard it as obsolete. All the necessary work can be done by *among*.

amount, number   The first should be used of uncountable things; the second of countable things. 'The boy did a large amount of work, but unfortunately made a large number of mistakes.'

ampersand   the sign (&), which stands for *and*. In formal writing it is reserved for the names of companies, but it is much used in note taking and other hurried writing. At one time the ampersand was used with *c* to form *&c* as an abbreviation of *et cetera*.

amphibrach (æmˈfibræk)   in PROSODY a trisyllabic FOOT with the stress on the second syllable, e.g. rĕvōltĕd. See METRE.

an   see A, AN.

-ana   a Latin neuter plural ending used as a suffix (sometimes with an 'i' interposed for the sake of euphony) to denote a collection of sayings by or about famous people. Thus *Shakespeariana* are collected items relating to Shakespeare, and *Keatsiana*, *Churchilliana* and *Americana* are collected items relating to John Keats, Sir Winston Churchill and the United States of America.

anachronism (ənækˈrənizm)   a reference that is out of time. It would be an anachronism for the author of a mediaeval romance to describe how a monk in the fifteenth century switched on the electric light when he entered his cell. This is a mistake not likely to be made; others are less obvious, but are still anachronisms, which are not only references too early in time but also references too late in time. 'On the outbreak of war in 1914 he went to the United States in the White Star liner *Titanic*.' He could not have done this because the *Titanic* sank during her maiden voyage in 1912.

anagram   the formation of a new word by rearranging the letters of another word, or the formation of a new sentence by rearranging the letters of another sentence. Thus 'meat' becomes 'team', 'angle' becomes 'glean', and 'Tower of London' becomes, most appropriately, 'now one old fort'. Anagrams are much favoured by the compilers of CROSSWORDS. Here is a clue from puzzle No. 2,023 in the *Sunday Times*: 'Make our wench get it into the opposite scale! (7-6).' The figures at the end indicate that we need two words, one of seven letters and the other of six, joined by a hyphen, thirteen letters in all. We study the clue and notice the words 'Make' and 'into', which suggests that the words between – 'our wench get it' – form an anagram of something that has to do with 'the opposite scale'. By rearranging the letters of 'our wench get it' we arrive sooner or later at 'counter-weight', which solves the clue.

analogy (ænælˈədzi)   a certain likeness in two things that are different in other ways, a similarity in function but not in origin. Thus there is an analogy between the wings of a butterfly and those of a bird, an analogy between the branches of a family and those of a tree. If we say that a sock is to the foot as a hat is to the head, we are pointing to the similarity of attributes in the sock and the hat: they both cover something. We are drawing an analogy between the sock and the hat. All metaphors and similes are based on analogy. In language many changes take place by analogy. For example, *all right* by analogy with *already* is nowadays often spelt *alright*.

The adjective *analogous* is pronounced æˈnæləgəs, with a hard *g*.

See also FALSE ANALOGY.

anapaest (ænˈəpist)   in PROSODY a trisyllabic foot with the stress on the third syllable, e.g. rĕfĕrēe. See METRE.

and/or   This means 'one or both', e.g. 'The contractor shall be responsible for any tools and/or materials left on the premises over-night.' An attempt in recent years to introduce the compound word *andor* did not meet with any success.

Anglo-Saxon English (Old English)   see DERIVATION.

anomalous finites   those special verbs that have the attributes of finites but are irregular: *am, is, are, was, were, have, has, had, do, does, did, shall, should, will, would, can, could, may, might, must, ought, need, dare, used.* Most of them can also be used as AUXILIARY VERBS. In their finite forms they are the only verbs that can be negated by adding *not* after the verb, e.g. 'I am not sure,' 'he dare not.'

See also FINITE VERBS.

Antarctic   see ARCTIC.

ante-, anti-   As a prefix *ante-* means 'before', whilst *anti-* means 'against'. Thus *antediluvian,* 'before the Flood', the inundation men-tioned in Genesis; *antemeridian,* 'before midday'; *antichristian,* 'against Christianity'; *antiseptic,* 'against putrefaction'. Colloquially the second is used in such contexts as: 'That chap seems to be anti everything.'

antecedent   a word grammatically related to a word that follows it in the sentence, but especially the noun or pronoun to which a relative pronoun is related. Thus 'story' is the antecedent of 'that' in this sentence: 'The story of coincidence that he told us was pure fiction.'

See also PRONOUN, section 3.

anthology (Gk. 'a gathering of flowers')   a collection of poems or prose extracts by various authors. Perhaps the most famous of English anthologies is *The Golden Treasury of Songs and Lyrics* by Francis T. Palgrave, first published in 1861.

anticipate   to be before in doing or speaking; to use in advance; to enjoy beforehand; to forestall. 'He anticipated the arrival of the police by committing suicide.' 'Harry anticipated his birthday by holding the party on the previous Saturday.' To anticipate does *not* mean 'to expect or suppose'. These are wrong: 'We anticipate a very large attendance at this meeting.' 'The anticipated income from this source is £500 per annum.' Use *expect* or *expected*.

anticipatory subject   referring to the pronoun *it* when it stands before the verb in place of the real subject, which then comes after the verb, e.g. 'It is no use crying over spilt milk' instead of 'Crying over spilt milk is no use.' The *it* here clearly stands for and anticipates the real subject, *crying over spilt milk*.
  See also IDIOM; PRONOUN.

anticlimax   a building up to a climax that is accidentally or deliberately made to look ridiculous by a sudden descent to something quite trifling, e.g. 'The bomb completely destroyed the cathedral, the new cinema, several dozen houses and my dustbin.' See also BATHOS; CLIMAX.

anti-hero   In the struggle between right and wrong that forms the basis of many works of fiction, the hero is on the side of right, the villain on the side of wrong. In modern fiction a new character has appeared: the anti-hero, who, although the principal person in the book, is anything but a hero in the classical sense. Lucky Jim, in Kingsley Amis's novel with that title, is an early specimen.

antipodes (æntip'ədi:z)   The literal meaning of this is 'opposite feet' and it refers to places, and those living in them, on the other side of the globe. Thus for those living in Great Britain the antipodes are Australia and New Zealand.

antistrophe (æntis'trəfi)   in PROSODY the second stanza of a Pindaric ode. See ODE.

antithesis (æntiθˈəsəs)   contrast between words, ideas, etc., e.g. 'To err is human, to forgive, divine.' In literature when it is used deliberately by placing contrasting terms or ideas close together to emphasise their difference and give the effect of balance, it becomes a FIGURE OF SPEECH, e.g. 'For many are called, but few are chosen.' See also SENTENCE.

antonyms (ænˈtənimz)   words of opposite meaning. Thus *blunt* is an antonym of *sharp*, and *pleasant* is an antonym of *disagreeable*. Words of the same meaning are called SYNONYMS.

anxious   An anxious man is one not easy in his mind, or one earnestly wishing for something. 'He was anxious about the children left in the empty house.' 'Our host was anxious to avoid any un-pleasantness.' 'The would-be dictator was anxious for power.' But let us not use *anxious* in lesser matters. 'Anxious to buy a stamp, he strolled into the post office.' His lack of haste suggests that the stamp was not urgently required, so there was no element of anxiety, as there would be in: 'Anxious to buy a stamp, he dashed into the post office just as it was about to close.'

aphorism (æfˈərizm)   a short, pithy sentence stating a general truth or maxim, e.g. 'Blood is thicker than water.' 'Live and let live.' The term includes the PROVERB, the EPIGRAM, the PARADOX and any other concise, pithy statement or observation.

Apocrypha (əpokˈrəfə)   books of the original Old Testament not now included in the Bible, but which 'the Church doth read for example of life and instruction of manners'. The adjective *apo-cryphal* now refers to anything of doubtful authenticity or author-ship; anything sham, counterfeit or false. It is frequently encountered in such contexts as: 'The story is probably apocryphal, but it is said that . . .'

apologia (æpəlouˈdʒiə)   a defence, not an apology. Cardinal New-man, a convert from the Established Church to the Catholic faith in Victorian England, correctly entitled his autobiography *Apologia pro sua Vita*. 'He entered with a long apologia to explain why he was late' is wrong as well as being long winded.

a posteriori   see A PRIORI.

apostrophe (1) a punctuation mark represented by a raised comma and used to denote:

1. Contractions, e.g. *don't, isn't, I'd, he's, e'er, 'tis, tho', o'clock, John o' Groat's* (not *Groats*), *the 'thirties* (1930–9).

2. The possessive form of nouns and certain indefinite pronouns, where it originally represented the Old English *e* of the genitive ending in *es*, e.g. *my only brother's wife, my three brothers' wives*. The possessive form of *'s* or *s'* is restricted to (a) the names of living things, e.g. *Susan's hat, the cat's paws, the boys' bicycles*; (b) the names of personified things, e.g. *winter's bite, time's flight, life's disappointments*; (c) certain expressions of time, e.g. *a week's wages, a day's work, three months' imprisonment*; (d) *for heaven's sake, for goodness' sake*. In all other instances we must use *of* to denote possession, e.g.:

Wrong: The house's front was shaded by trees.

Right: The front of the house was shaded by trees.

When a word already ends in *s* and, in making it possessive, we give it another syllable, it is now customary to add an *s* as well as the apostrophe, e.g.:

Wrong: Jones' idea is a good one.

Right: Jones's idea is a good one.

As mentioned under PLURAL, names ending in *s* or *es* add *es* for the plural. To make these possessive we add the apostrophe at the end, e.g. 'The Joneses' idea is a good one.' If in making it possessive we do not give the word another syllable, we do not add *'s* but the apostrophe only, e.g. *for goodness' sake, Euripides' tragedies*.

3. The plural form of certain letters and figures. There is not complete agreement on the use of the apostrophe to denote a plural form, but the following are generally accepted: *minding your p's and q's* (being careful how you behave); *dotting the i's and crossing the t's* (putting the finishing touches); but, *the 1930s* (now more usual than *the 1930's*). Note that in *the '30s* and *the 'thirties*, the initial apostrophes denote the omission of *19* and *nineteen*. The apostrophe should not be used when there is no contraction, e.g. *he was in his thirties*; *the temperature was well up in the eighties*.

Note also that the apostrophe is omitted in the plural forms of abbreviations, e.g. *M.P.s, Q.C.s*. The apostrophe is used to denote possession, e.g. *the M.P.'s* (belonging to the Member of Parliament), *the M.P.s'* (belonging to the Members of Parliament).

See also ABBREVIATION; CONTRACTION; ELISION; GENITIVE (POS-
SESSIVE) CASE; INVERTED COMMAS.

apostrophe (2)   a FIGURE OF SPEECH in which a direct address or
appeal is made to an absent person as if he were present, e.g. 'Milton!
thou should'st be living at this hour' (Wordsworth). It is often found
in PERSONIFICATION, e.g. 'Glide gently, thus for ever glide, O
Thames.'

apposition (L. 'putting to')   the placing of a noun or noun-
equivalent beside another for the purpose of fuller explanation or
description. Thus the things in apposition are one and the same,
though differently expressed, e.g. 'The news *that he had won* surprised
Tom, *a raw lad of eight*.' The clause is in apposition to the noun *news*,
and the phrase is in apposition to the noun *Tom*.

a priori, a posteriori   Both derive from the Latin, the first meaning 'from what comes before'; the second meaning 'from what
comes after'. Philosophers through the ages, from Aristotle to
Herbert Spencer, have interpreted the terms in a variety of ways.
Roughly, an *a priori* argument is one that works forward from cause
to effect, or from a general rule to a particular case, whilst an *a
posteriori* argument works backward from effect to cause, or from a
particular case to a general rule. *A priori* is therefore argument by
DEDUCTION and *a posteriori* is argument by INDUCTION.

apropos (æprəpou¹)   from the French *à propos*, which means 'to
the purpose'. We use it to introduce a remark on some matter that
arises from the main subject under discussion but, although relevant
to it, is not part of it. For example, let us assume that we are talking
about the migration of birds and one of us happens to mention that
Mr Foster, who lives along the road, saw some swallows fly over his
house last week. Another of us then says: 'Really? It's very early in
the season, even for swallows.' A third then says: 'Apropos of Mr
Foster, is it true he's just bought a new car?'

Apropos may be followed also by *to*, in the sense of 'in relation to'
or 'regarding', e.g. 'Apropos to the suggestion made in your
letter . . .' In conversation the preposition is often omitted, e.g.
'Apropos the cricket match next Saturday . . .'

See also *malapropos* under MALAPROPISM.

apt, likely, liable   Each of these adjectives has several different meanings, but we are concerned here with *apt* in the sense of 'having a tendency to'; *likely* in the sense of 'to be expected'; and *liable* in the sense of 'open to' or 'exposed to'. Let us first consider the difference between *apt* and *likely*. The first implies a regular occurrence, something that has happened before and may well happen again, whilst *likely* implies the possibility that a certain thing will happen, e.g.:

(a) Temporary regulations are apt to become permanent.
(b) These temporary regulations are likely to remain in force for some months.
(c) He is apt to call in here on Wednesday afternoon. (He has done it before on a number of occasions and can be expected to do it again, if not next Wednesday, then the one after.)
(d) He is likely to call in here on Wednesday afternoon. (We can expect him to call in next Wednesday afternoon.)

The third of these, *liable*, promises more unpleasant consequences than do the other two, e.g.:

(e) He is liable to call in here at awkward moments.
(f) He is liable to lose his temper when he calls in here.
(g) If you do not wear your thick overcoat you are liable to catch cold.
(h) Milk is liable to go sour in hot weather.

Arabic numerals   see NUMERALS.

arch-   the prefix denoting pre-eminence. It is used in a good sense, e.g. *archangel, archbishop, archdeacon, archduke,* and in a derogatory sense, e.g. *arch-enemy, arch-fiend, arch-knave, arch-liar, arch-villain.* In the case of *archangel*, the prefix is pronounced a:k; in all the others, a:tʃ.

archaism   (a:kᶦeiizm)   a word, spelling, phrase or construction that has become out of date, e.g. *albeit* (though), *anent* (concerning), *quoth he* (he said), *peradventure* (perhaps), *burthen* (burden), *eke* (also), *alarum* (alarm), *nathless* (nevertheless), *prithee* (pray thee = please). Some archaisms persist in particular contexts, often in tautological terms. For example, in 'without let or hindrance', the word *let* has its archaic meaning of 'hindrance', the very opposite of its meaning

today. Again, the archaic word *an*, meaning *if*, survives in the
nursery rhyme:

> If 'ifs' and 'ans'
> Were pots and pans,
> There'd be no need for tinkers!

See also OBSOLETE.

aren't I? see GRAMMAR.

Argentina, Argentine The country was formerly known as the
Argentine Republic and is still often referred to as the Argentine
although the official name is now Argentina. An inhabitant of the
country is an Argentine, and the adjective is also Argentine. The
ending of Argentina is pronounced ti:nə; the ending of Argentine
is pronounced tain.

arguing in a circle This is known by logicians as *petitio principii*,
which means 'assumption of the beginning'. It is using a premise (an
assumption made for the purpose of the argument) to prove a conclusion, and then using the conclusion to prove the premise, e.g.:

Lord Nuffield was a very generous and public-spirited man.
Therefore he gave away vast sums of money.
Lord Nuffield gave away vast sums of money. Therefore he was a
very generous and public-spirited man.

Arguing in a circle is a logical FALLACY. Of a somewhat similar
nature is BEGGING THE QUESTION.

argument (L. 'to prove') Here we are not concerned with argument in a colloquial sense ('I had a bit of an argument with the
ticket-collector'), but with argument in the sense of 'reasons and
facts given for or against a matter under discussion'. In its literal
sense the argument is not the discussion; it is the statement of one
point of view in the discussion, and the purpose of it is to convince
the other side (or in a debate, the audience) that it is the right point
of view. Although partisanship is justified, and EMOTIVE LANGUAGE
permissible, care must be taken that the enthusiasm is soundly based
on fact and logic; an argument is not proved merely by shouting.
A misleading argument is known as a FALLACY.

argumentum ad hominem   For this and *argumentum ad populum*
and *argumentum ad baculum* see IRRELEVANCY.

articles   The definite article (*the*) indicates one particular person
or thing. The indefinite article (*a, an*) indicates a single but not a
particular person or thing. See also A, AN; THE; ELLIPSIS.

artist, artiste   Though now becoming blurred, there is a useful
distinction between them. An artist is a person who is skilled in one
of the fine arts; an artiste (pronounced a:ti:st) is any professional
performer on the stage or in show business in general. In recent years
the term *artiste* has, however, been largely taken over by the more
trivial end of show business. As a consequence it has been so cheap-
ened that a serious professional singer or ballet dancer might now
feel slightly insulted by being so described.

as, like   The incorrect use of the second (a preposition) for the
first (a conjunction) is treated under PREPOSITION.

as, than   'Mr Brown's house is as big if not bigger than Mr
Robinson's.' The word *big* should be followed by *as*. Even then, such
sentences are clumsy. 'Mary is as attractive as, if not more so than,
Elizabeth.' It is better to rephrase the sentence, e.g. 'Mary is perhaps
even more attractive than Elizabeth.'

as follows   an accepted introduction to one or more items,
matters, etc. The O.E.D. defines it as 'a prefatory formula, impersonal in construction, and therefore to be always used in the
singular', e.g.:
  Wrong: The main points raised at the meeting were as follow:
  Right: The main points raised at the meeting were as follows:

aspirate   The noun is pronounced æsˈpərət, the verb is pronounced æsˈpəreit. They come from the Latin *aspirare*, which means
'to breathe upon or in the direction of'. The noun is usually taken to
refer to the letter *h*. It is in fact a letter or combination of letters pronounced with a breathing sound. The *th* in *thistle* is aspirated, but the
th in *the* is not; the *f* in *front* is aspirated, but the *f* in *of* is not; the *ch*
in *loch* is aspirated, but the *ch* in *chord* is not. For the use of *a* or *an*
before words beginning with *h*, see A, AN.

assimilation   the changing of a sound by the influence of an adjacent one. Thus the *p* in *cupboard* takes on the sound of the adjacent *b*. More usually, however, the spelling changes as well. Thus the *n* of *in+mortal* becomes *m* (*immortal*) and the *d* of *ad+saltare* becomes *s* (*assault*). By wrong division *a nadder* became *an adder* and *a napron* became *an apron*. The Old English word *nædre* meant a serpent. In *napron* we can see the connexion with *napery* and *napkin*.

assonance   in PROSODY the agreement of vowel sounds in two syllables without the agreement of consonant sounds which would make a rhyme, e.g. *roam – bone, leap – neat*. An example is to be found under BALLAD, e.g.: 'We banged the tins, and bawled the hymns.'

Wilfred Owen, a poet of World War I (he was killed a week before Armistice Day, 1918) developed a form of rhyme that was not assonance in the strict sense, but 'near rhyme'. One might say of it that it would be blank verse if there were not a vague similarity of sound between the last word in one line and the last word in the next. Here are the opening lines of his unfinished poem, *Strange Meeting*:

It seemed that out of battle I escaped
Down some profound dull tunnel, long since scooped
Through granites which titanic wars had groined.
Yet also there encumbered sleepers groaned,
Too fast in thought or death to be bestirred.
Then, as I probed them, one sprang up, and stared
With piteous recognition in fixed eyes,
Lifting distressful hands as if to bless.
And by his smile, I knew that sullen hall,
By his dead smile I knew we stood in Hell.

See also RHYME and EYE RHYME.

asterisk   the sign (*). It is derived from the Greek *asteriskos*, meaning 'a small star', and is treated under FOOTNOTE.

astrologer, astronomer   An *astrologer* is one who claims to be able to foretell the future by reading the stars and to divine personal characteristics by considering the individual's birthdate. An *astronomer* is one who studies the sun, moon, planets and stars. *Astrology*, some would say, is a false science, *astronomy* is not.

attraction   the tendency of plural nouns or pronouns to draw into the plural verbs that should agree with a singular subject, e.g.:

(a) 'The clerk in the office, as well as the manual worker, the technician and the research chemist, are affected by these new regulations.' Here 'are' should be 'is'.

(b) 'It is he, not they, who demand an answer.' Here 'demand' should be 'demands'.

(c) 'A wide range of washing-machines and refrigerators are displayed in our showrooms.' Here again 'are' should be 'is', since the subject is the singular 'wide range'.

See also AGREEMENT; NUMBER.

attributive   An adjective is said to be attributive when it stands with the noun it qualifies, e.g. 'He saw a red rose.' It is said to be predicative when a verb stands between the adjective and the noun it qualifies, e.g. 'The rose was red.'

aught   see NAUGHT.

autobiography   a person's life written by himself. If it is written by somebody else it is called a BIOGRAPHY. See also MEMOIR.

auxiliary verbs   the verbs *be, have, do, shall, will, may,* which assist others to form their tense, voice or mood, e.g. *he has eaten; he will eat; he should eat; he has been eating; does he eat?; had it been eaten?; it may have been eaten.* These little verbs are not auxiliaries, of course, when used on their own, e.g. 'He does these things perfectly.'

See also INFINITIVE; ANOMALOUS FINITES.

averse from, to   Some pedants insist that *from* is correct because the Latin derivation is *avertere*, 'to turn away'. Modern usage favours *to*, e.g. 'I am averse to travelling by air.' For the noun *aversion* the choice of the preposition is a matter of personal taste. If we dislike a thing we can have an aversion *to, from* or *for* it. A *pet aversion* is a particular object of dislike, e.g. 'My pet aversion is tapioca pudding.'

See also ADVERSE.

avoirdupois   the system of weight in which there are sixteen ounces in the pound. The word derives from the French *avoir du pois,* 'to have weight'. The English pronunciation, ævə:djupo:zı, or an approximation of the French pronunciation are both commonly acceptable.

awful, awfully   Some observations on this jaded pair are to be found under OVERWORKED WORDS.

awhile, a while   The first is an adverb meaning 'for a short time'; the second is a noun meaning 'a period of time', which may be short or long. So although it is correct to write 'let us rest awhile' it is not correct to write 'Let us rest for awhile'. This should be 'let us rest for a while'.

ay, aye   The first, pronounced ai, means 'yes'. It is an affirmative answer and is often used in the plural, e.g.:

'Those in favour?' asked the chairman.
Twenty-five voters raised their hands.
'Those against?'
Fourteen voters raised their hands.
'The ayes have it,' announced the chairman, and the secretary noted in the minutes of the meeting that the proposal had been adopted.

The second, pronounced ei, means 'ever', 'always'. It is OBSOLETE except in the tautological term, 'for ever and aye' (see TAUTOLOGY).

B

back-formation   The word *editor* long existed on its own without a verb. Because it ended in *-or* people thought it must have been formed from the verb *to edit*. There was no such verb: it was formed back from the noun *editor*. Another back-formation is *to nestle* from the noun *nestling*. Others are *to burgle* from *burglar*, *to conscript* from *conscription*, *to enthuse* from *enthusiasm*, *to resurrect* from *resurrection*, *greed* from *greedy*, *televise* from *television* and, jocularly, *to butch* from *butcher*

and *to buttle* from *butler*. A very recent addition to the list is *to emote*,
which is to give expression to emotion.

backward, backwards   Modern usage seems to prefer the first as
the adverb, but the second is by no means obsolete; in fact there is a
natural tendency to use it in such contexts as: (a) 'He fell over backwards.' (b) 'The brakes failed and the car ran backwards down the
hill.' See also FORWARD, FORWARDS.

ballad   from the Portuguese *balada*, 'a dancing-song'. At one time
it was a song intended to accompany a dance. It is now a simple song
of any kind, with a *fa la* burden or chorus. *Widecombe Fair* is a ballad
of eight stanzas, the second line of each being 'All along, down along,
out along lee', and the last line of each being 'Old Uncle Tom
Cobley and all'.

The term applies also to a narrative poem, one that tells a story,
usually tragic. The form used in the old narrative ballads was a four-
line stanza of alternate four-feet and three-feet lines, with only the
second and fourth lines rhyming. Here are two stanzas from *Chevy
Chase*, a ballad that goes back to the fifteenth century:

> The gallant greyhounds swiftly ran,
>   To chase the fallow deer;
> On Monday they began to hunt,
>   Ere daylight did appear;
>
> And long before high noon they had
>   An hundred fat buck slain;
> Then having dined, the drovers went
>   To rouse the deer again.

Later ballads varied in metrical form. Here are two stanzas from
The Ballad of Reading Gaol, written by Oscar Wilde while he was
serving a sentence there in 1896:

> We tore the tarry rope to shreds
>   With blunt and bleeding nails;
> We rubbed the doors, and scrubbed
>   the floors,
>   And cleaned the shining rails;
> And, rank by rank, we soaped the plank,
>   And clattered with the pails.

We sewed the sacks, we broke the stones,
  We turned the dusty drill:
We banged the tins, and bawled the
    hymns,
And sweated on the mill:
But in the heart of every man
  Terror was lying still.

The modern revival of interest in folk-song and 'Country-and-Western' music has widened the acceptable use of ballad to include the words to such songs. In the 1960s the mournful nasal notes of such ARTISTES as Bob Dylan singing 'ballads' won immense appreciation among the young.

ballade (bæla:dⁱ)   This has the same derivation as *ballad* above, but is verse of a different metrical form. It consists usually of three stanzas of eight lines, with the same three or four rhymes throughout. It ends with an ENVOY of four lines, and the last line of the first stanza is repeated as a refrain in the last lines of the second and third stanzas and of the envoy. In this repetition it is similar to the RONDEAU.

Basic English   an international language devised by C. K. Ogden and I. A. Richards in 1929. It has a vocabulary of 850 words, some 70 per cent of them nouns, 18 per cent adjectives and adverbs, 2 per cent verbs, and the remaining 10 per cent miscellaneous structural words. Basic has been criticised on the score that the scarcity of words leads to circumlocution in order to express often quite simple meanings, and that many of the essential idioms of the language remain a complete mystery to those who have learnt only Basic. The word *Basic* is a PROTOGRAM; it is made up of the initial letters of the words *British, American, Scientific, International* and *Commercial*.

bathos (beiθⁱos) (Gk. 'depth')   the same as ANTICLIMAX. Napoleon is reputed to have said after the retreat from Moscow in 1812: 'Du sublime au ridicule il n'y a qu'un pas.' ('From the sublime to the ridiculous is but a step.') That is bathos, a fall from a splendid height to an absurd depth. PATHOS carried too far can descend into bathos.

B.C.   abbreviation of 'Before Christ'. In the writing of dates it comes after the figures, e.g. 55 B.C. See also A.D.; CENTURIES.

beatnik   In the mid-1950s a reasonably small but highly visible group of young Americans in their twenties and early thirties be-came known as the *Beat Generation*. When the Russians produced their first earth satellite they gave it the name of *sputnik*. The suffix was added to *beat*, giving *beatnik*, which describes one who renounces material ambition and conventional society, preferring to live in squalor, untidy and unwashed.

begging the question (petitio principii)   assuming the truth of the very thing being argued about or to be proved. If I contend that bull-fighting is not cruel because the bulls enjoy it, I am begging the question; I am assuming that the bulls enjoy it in order to prove that it is not cruel. If I say that laws are necessary because a country cannot be run without them, my argument is that laws are necessary because they are necessary. Again I am begging the question.

In ARGUMENT begging the question is a FALLACY.

begin, commence   Never use the second if you can use the first, which is a much stronger word. The first verse in the Bible is: 'In the beginning God created the heaven and the earth.' Compare this with: 'At the commencement God created the heaven and the earth.' Avoid also such deplorable variation as 'Jack began to read his book as Mary commenced to write her letter.' It is much better to repeat 'began'.

behave   to conduct oneself, whether it be well or badly, e.g. (a) 'The children behaved excellently.' (b) 'The treasurer behaved in a dishonourable way by absconding with the funds of the cricket club.' Colloquially, however, it has come to have the meaning of behaving well, without any modifying adverb or adverbial phrase, e.g. 'Our father told us that if we did not behave ourselves he would not take us to the pantomime.'

belles-lettres (bel'let'rə)   writings of a purely literary kind, e.g. essays, poems, parodies. It is a term used almost solely for classifica-tion purposes.

beloved   has either two or three syllables according to the con-text, e.g.:

   (a) 'He was beloved by the whole community.' Here there are
      two syllables: bəlʌvd'.

(b) 'He spoke in tender terms of his beloved wife.' Here there are three syllables: bəlʌvˡed.

beside, besides The first means 'alongside' or 'next to', e.g. 'John sat down beside Mary.' The second means 'in addition to', e.g. 'A number of guests besides Mary were in the room when John entered.'

between, among We say that something is shared *between* two persons, but when there are more than two we say it is shared *among* them. When there is no question of apportionment we use *between*, even when referring to more than two persons or things. 'We had to choose between Tom, Dick and Harry.' 'The field was shown on the map as a green-coloured area between the three points of a triangle.' 'Open warfare broke out between the four rival factions.'

between each 'There was an interval of ten minutes between each race.' This is impossible, since only a single race is mentioned. The sentence should read: 'There was an interval of ten minutes between one race and the next.'

between you and me This is correct, and so are such others as 'between him and me' and 'between him and her', since the ACCUSATIVE form of the pronoun is required after a PREPOSITION.

bevy If you are referring to a company of ladies, larks, maidens, quails or roes (small deer), by all means call them a bevy, but no bevies of motor-buses, or bevies of spectators at a football match, please.

bi- a prefix with a number of meanings, such as 'twice', 'doubly', 'having two', 'once in every two', e.g. *bicentenary* (two-hundredth anniversary), *bicoloured* (of two colours), *biconcave* (concave on both sides), *biconvex* (convex on both sides), *bicycle* (having two wheels), *bigamy* (having two wives), *bilateral* (having two sides), *bilingual* (using two languages), *biped* (a two-footed animal), *biplane* (an aircraft with two planes, one above the other), *bisect* (to cut into two). It is in combinations denoting periods of time that this prefix can give rise to ambiguity. For example, *bi-monthly* can mean twice a month or once every two months, whilst *bi-weekly* can mean twice a week or once a fortnight. It is better to say 'twice a month' and 'every two months'; 'twice a week (or semi-weekly)' and 'every two weeks (or fortnightly)'. *Biannual* is treated below.

biannual, biennial The first means 'half-yearly'; the second 'every two years'. To avoid confusion or misunderstanding it is better to say 'half-yearly' and 'every two years'. As a noun, *biennial* is a plant that lives two years.

bibliography Many books are the result of research, and it is customary to include in these a list of the works that have been consulted, or in which fuller information is given, so that the student may refer to them should he wish. This list is called the bibliography.

billion When an Englishman talks of a billion he means a million million, but to an American a billion is a thousand million.

biography a person's life written by someone else. If he writes it himself it is called an autobiography. Edmund Clerihew Bentley, the inventor of the CLERIHEW, once wrote:

Geography is about maps,
But Biography is about chaps.

blank verse in PROSODY verse that scans but does not rhyme. Although the term is applied to unrhymed verse in general, true blank verse is written in iambic pentameters (see PENTAMETER), the lines being each divided into five metrical feet, each foot consisting of two syllables, with the stress on the second syllable, e.g.:

So spake/the ser/ aph Ab/diel, faith/ful found
Among/ the faith/less, faith/ful on/ly he.

Note here also the use of ALLITERATION.

Some of the greatest poems in our language are written in blank verse. The above quotation is from Milton's *Paradise Lost*. Much of Shakespeare's plays is written in blank verse. Here, for example, are the opening lines of *Henry V*:

O for a Muse of fire, that would ascend
The brightest heaven of invention,
A kingdom for a stage, princes to act
And monarchs to behold the swelling scene!

See also ENJAMBMENT; METRE.

blessed has either one or two syllables according to the context, e.g.:

(a) 'He was blessed with good health and good looks.' (Here the word is single-syllabled: blest.)

(b) 'Blessed are the meek: for they shall inherit the earth.' (Here the word is disyllabic: bles'ed.)

The first (or *blest*) is used colloquially in such expressions as: 'Well, I'm blessed! Fancy meeting you!' The second is similarly used in such euphemistic expressions as: 'Where's my blessed hat?'

blurb According to Gelett Burgess, the American who coined it in 1907, the verb *to blurb* is 'to make a sound like a publisher'. A blurb is an inspired testimonial printed on the dust jacket of a book, telling briefly what it is about and praising it highly.

bombast In Elizabethan times men of fashion padded their clothing with cotton, tow and other materials. This padding was called *bombast* (from the Old French *bombace*) and the word came to be used figuratively to describe shallowness of thought dressed up in extravagant and high-sounding language. Webster defines it as 'language above the dignity of the occasion'. Public speakers often resort to bombast.

'How long,' thundered Mr Tompkins from the platform, 'are we to submit to this disgraceful and deplorable state of affairs? Are we – the long-suffering, abused and afflicted general public – people of all ages and conditions – the elderly, the lame, the sick – mothers with tiny mites in their arms – schoolchildren with their satchels over their shoulders and a posy of sweet-smelling flowers for the teacher clutched in their little hands – are we all to continue to be deprived of that sanctuary – that vital and all-important – nay, essential and indispensable amenity in a town otherwise famed for its progressive, enlightened policy, a town whose history goes back to those far-off days when Norman William stormed our shores – are we, I say with all the sincerity and eloquence at my command, to be helpless against the forces of Nature, when a brazen sun throws down its pitiless heat and glare, or when the very vault of heaven opens and drenches us with rain, bruises us with hail, and blinds us with snow, or when the wind from the frigid north stabs like the murderous knife of the assassin?' He paused to draw breath, then went on, thumping the table with his fist: 'How long – and our patience is wearing thin – how long will it be before the administrative wheels begin to turn, slowly at first and then, we must hope, with increasing momentum, until at last there stands a bus-shelter in the High Street?'

both, each   These are not interchangeable. *Both* means 'taken together', e.g. 'Both these books cost a pound.' The total cost of the two books is one pound. *Each* means 'taken separately', e.g. 'Each of these books costs a pound.' The total cost of the two books is two pounds.

Note also that *both* requires a plural verb, whilst *each* requires a singular verb. Below are examples of both (below is an example of each):

(a) Both John and Mary were invited to the party.
(b) Each of the fifty guests was given a present.

See also AGREEMENT.

bowdlerise (baud'ləraiz)   to expurgate; to remove from a book, play, etc. anything thought to be objectionable. The word derives from the surname of Thomas Bowdler, who published in 1818 *The Family Shakespeare*, from which were omitted 'those words and expressions which cannot with propriety be read aloud in a family'. (He clearly had a very dirty mind.)

brackets   punctuation marks used to enclose a PARENTHESIS and show that it is grammatically separated from the rest of the sentence, e.g. 'My next walking tour (I was young and fit in those days!) took me halfway across Europe.' They may also be used to add examples, e.g. 'The precious metals (gold, platinum, silver, etc.) resist corrosion.' Square brackets have a particular function, which is to indicate that the words within them were not written by the original author but were added afterwards by someone else for the purpose of explanation or clarification, e.g. 'As rumours were afloat of a projected attack on the Isle of France [Mauritius], it occurred to me that such information as I possessed might be useful to the Government.'

Brackets can be very useful in such sentences as this: 'The appointment is open to any boy (or girl) in his sixteenth year who has passed his examinations and has been given a good character by the headmaster of his school.' By placing 'or girl' in brackets we separate it grammatically from the rest of the sentence and avoid such awkward constructions as 'in his or her sixteenth year', 'his or her examinations', and 'headmaster or headmistress of his or her school'.

breve (L. 'short')   the mark (˘) placed over a vowel to show that it is short, e.g. *făt*. The mark showing that the sound is long (–) is known as a MACRON, e.g. *fāte*. For the use of the breve in PROSODY see MACRON. See also ACCENT; METRE; PRONUNCIATION; SCANNING.

bull   Often called an *Irish bull*, this is an amusing mistake in language. It is said to derive from the story of the Irishman who said, 'If you saw four cows lying down in a field and one of them was standing up, that would be the bull.' Here is another example:
The motorist who had lost his way pulled up and asked an old man leaning on a gate: 'How do I get to Dublin, please?'
The old man considered the matter for some time, saying at length: 'If Oi were you, Oi wouldn't start from here at all.'

bureaucracy   One of the meanings of the French word *bureau* is 'government department'. The Greek suffix *-cracy* means 'rule of' or 'rule by', so that bureaucracy means 'rule by government departments'. The derogatory term *bureaucrat* refers to an official with exaggerated ideas of his own importance – one who is (to quote Shakespeare) 'drest in a little brief authority'. We now also have the *Eurocrats* who administer the Common Market. See also DEMOCRACY.

burlesque (bəːleskˡ) (It. 'absurd')   a comic imitation, especially of literary and dramatic work, not intended satirically, but to cause laughter. *Don Quixote* is a burlesque because it makes fun of chivalry. On the stage Gay's *The Beggar's Opera* mocked Italian opera.

burnt, burned   Modern usage tends towards the first for the past tense and past participle of *burn*.

bus   a contraction of *omnibus*, a vehicle for carrying fare-paying passengers. No apostrophe is needed, e.g. 'He caught the next bus to the station.' The plural is *buses*. A *busman's holiday* is a holiday spent doing the work one does every day, e.g. 'During the weekend Mr Robinson, who was a carpenter by trade, enjoyed a busman's holiday by building a shed in his garden.'

business, busyness The first (pronounced biz'nəs) can be defined as one's trade or profession, the occupation by which one earns a living. 'Mr Harrison carried on the business of bookseller.' The second (pronounced bizi'nes) is the state of being busy. 'The busyness of all members of the staff showed that the firm's affairs were prospering.'

business letters See CORRESPONDENCE.

but When used as a coordinate conjunction *but* indicates that the clause or phrase following it is in opposition to what has gone before it, e.g. (a) 'We thought it was going to rain, but it didn't.' (b) 'Mrs Thorpe kept her temper, but her husband was very angry.' When there is not this element of opposition – no suggestion of *not this, but that* – the use of *but* is incorrect, e.g.:

Wrong: Tom remained silent, but it was Harry who answered.

Right: Tom remained silent, and it was Harry who answered.

Wrong: He knew that his pursuers must eventually capture him, but they did not slacken their pace for a moment.

Right: He knew that his pursuers must eventually capture him, for they did not slacken their pace for a moment.

Wrong: She was not frightened by the lightning, but what alarmed her was the thunder.

Right: She was not frightened by the lightning; what alarmed her was the thunder.

Wrong: He agreed to our proposals in general terms, but then specified those to which he objected.

Right: He agreed to our proposals in general terms, then specified those to which he objected.

The insertion of a comma before *but* depends largely on the length of pause required by the context. In the first example below, a comma is unnecessary; in the second it is optional; and in the third it is essential.

(a) He was poor but honest.

(b) He was poor, but always ready to help others.

(c) When I arrived it was still broad daylight, but all was in darkness when I came away.

There are some who would deny us the right to begin a sentence or a paragraph with *but*. This rule is as out-moded as that against ending a sentence with a preposition or that against splitting an infinitive.

but that, but what   These are SOLECISMS, e.g.:
  Wrong: I don't deny but that he is clever.
  Wrong: I don't deny but what he is clever.
  Right: I don't deny that he is clever.

by, bye   The first is a preposition meaning 'near; at; beside; in the neighbourhood of'. The second is a noun meaning 'a subordinate or incidental thing', e.g. a run made from a missed ball at cricket, or the advancing to the next round of a tournament without playing. In compounds the following are recommended: *by and by* (but *by the bye*), *by-blow, bye-bye* (nursery word for sleep and also variant of *good-bye*), *by-election, bygone, by-lane, by-law, bypass, bypath, by-play, by-product, bystander, by-street, by-walk, by-way, byword*. The prefix *bi-*, meaning 'twice' or 'doubly', is not to be confused with *by* or *bye*.

C

c.   abbreviation of the Latin *circa*, meaning 'about'. Its use is largely confined to dates, indicating that they are only approximately correct, as in this encyclopaedia reference: *Chaucer, Geoffrey* (*c. 1340–1400*). Sometimes a QUESTION MARK is used instead.

-c   Words ending in -c add *k* before *-ed, -ing, -y, -er*, e.g. *bivouac – bivouacked – bivouacking*; *traffic – trafficked – trafficking*; *picnic – picnicker – picknicked – picknicking*; *panic – panicky – panicked – panicking*.

caesura (sezjurˈə) (L. 'a cutting off')   in PROSODY a rhythmic break occurring near the middle of a line; the point at which a line naturally falls into two parts, e.g.:

  Stiff in opinions, / always in the wrong,
  Was everything by starts / and nothing long.

See METRE; INTERNAL RHYME; LEONINE VERSE; and, for fuller reference to the above quotation, EPITOME.

can, may The careful speaker used to make a distinction between these. Strictly, the former means 'to be able to', and the latter means 'to have permission to'. Thus if a child wanted permission to go to the cinema he would say, 'May I go?' If he wanted to know if someone was able to swim he would say, 'Can you swim?' But nowadays 'can' has almost taken over both functions, and he is far more likely to say, 'Can I go to the cinema?'

cannon, canon The first is a gun, a piece of ordnance. The second has several meanings: (a) a rule or standard by which something is judged, e.g. *the canons of literary taste, the canons of gentlemanly behaviour*; (b) the list of Bible books accepted by the Church (the books excluded from the canon are known as the APOCRYPHA); (c) the name given in the Church of England to a member of the cathedral chapter. *Canon law* governs the ecclesiastical affairs of the Church. To *canonise* is to declare a person to be a saint, e.g. St. Thomas Aquinas, St. Catherine, St. Peter the Martyr.

cannot This is the accepted spelling. The Americans write *can not*, probably because when they speak it they tend to stress the second syllable, not the first as we do. The abbreviation *can't* is now acceptable in even formal spoken English, and is becoming increasingly common in written English.

cant see SLANG.

canto a division of a long poem. Dante's *Divine Comedy* contains one hundred cantos.

canvas, canvass Both these come from the Latin meaning 'hempen cloth'. An early meaning of the verb *to canvass* was to shake up by tossing in a sheet of cloth, and so to agitate and, figuratively, to arouse interest. Today it means to solicit business, or votes in an election, by going from house to house. To canvass public opinion is to take a sample poll.

capital letters   These are used:

1. At the beginning of every sentence, e.g. 'He is a very good cricketer.'

2. At the beginning of a passage of direct speech, even if it is not the beginning of the sentence, e.g. 'A moment later he said, "My purse is not here." '

3. Traditionally to begin each line of verse, e.g.:

Little drops of water, little grains of sand,
Make the mighty ocean and the pleasant land.

In much modern verse this convention is disregarded.

4. To begin proper nouns, e.g. 'Mr Charles Brown, who has been living in Onslow Square, South Kensington, has now emigrated to Toronto, Canada.'

5. To begin the first word and other main words in the titles of books, poems, music, films, articles, etc., e.g. *It is Never too Late to Mend, Ode to a Nightingale, Land of Hope and Glory, Gone with the Wind.*

6. For titles, e.g. Her Majesty, the Queen of England, the Prince of Wales, the Archbishop of Canterbury, the President of the United States.

7. For the pronoun *I* and the vocative *O*, e.g. 'The first boy I saw was Johnny.' (No other pronoun is spelt with a capital letter unless it begins a sentence or forms part of a title, etc.) 'O death, where is thy sting?' Note also that although *Oh* is spelt with a capital when it begins a sentence, it is not when it comes in the body of it, e.g. 'We had little money in those days, but oh, how happy we were!'

In German all nouns begin with a capital letter, but generally speaking in English only proper nouns begin with a capital. Here are a few examples:

(a) *Church* may be regarded as a proper noun when used in such phrases as 'Church and State'. It should then be given a capital, e.g. 'The Church stood out against this new legislation.' But when the reference is to a building for public Christian worship, the capital should not be used, e.g. 'The church stood on top of a hill.' If the church is named it should have a capital, e.g. 'The Church of the Good Shepherd stood on top of a hill.'

(b) *Father* and *Mother* should have capitals when used as terms of address, e.g. 'Please will you buy me a bicycle, Father?' 'I've brought you some apples, Mother.' They should not have capitals in such sentences as 'I asked my father if he would buy me a bicycle';

and 'I told my mother that I had brought her some apples.' *Aunt* and *Uncle* are dealt with in the same way. When used with names they should have capitals, e.g. 'My Aunt Mary came to stay with us.' 'My Uncle Henry was very kind to me.' But 'My uncle, Henry Smith, was very kind to me.' *Cousin* does not require a capital, e.g. 'My cousin George is a sailor'; but a capital may be used when the sentence takes this form: 'I wrote to Cousin George, who is a sailor.'

(c) Although we speak of the 'First World War' and the 'Second World War' (or 'World War I' and 'World War II'), we do not use a capital letter in such sentences as: 'When the war broke out in 1939 he immediately enlisted.'

(d) The *Army* and the *Navy* should have capitals when they refer to the country's whole armed force on land or sea, but a body of troops or a fleet of vessels is called an *army* or a *navy*, e.g. 'Under a fierce bombardment by the enemy navy, the army defending the port stood firm.'

(e) Words derived from proper names should not be printed with capitals, e.g. *brussels sprouts*, *diesel engine*, *french polish*, *herculean*, *morocco leather*, *pasteurise*, *quixotic*, *volt*, *watt*.

(f) For geographical locations use a capital for the compass point when it forms part of the place-name, e.g. *North America*, *South Australia*, *Western Australia*, *East Anglia*, *the West Riding of Yorkshire*, *North Finchley*, *West Norwood*. When indicating position or direction do not use capitals, e.g. 'Tulcan is a town in north (or northern) Ecuador.' 'We were fifty miles south of the Equator.' 'To the east lay the Pacific Ocean.' 'He lived in a small house in west Surrey.' 'A north-easterly gale was blowing.'

cardinal (L. 'a hinge') fundamental; of first importance; main; chief. The *cardinal virtues* are justice, prudence, temperance and fortitude, on which hinge all other virtues. The *cardinal points* of the compass are north, south, east and west. The *cardinal numbers* are the basic numbers, 1, 2, 3, 4, etc. (see NUMERALS), whilst the ORDINAL NUMBERS are 1st, 2nd, 3rd, 4th, etc. A *Cardinal* is an official of the Roman Catholic Church, next below the Pope. The colour, *cardinal red*, is called after the deep scarlet of a cardinal's robes.

caret (L. 'it is lacking') the sign (∧) used in writing and proof-reading to show where an addition is to be brought into the text. The addition is usually written above, e.g.:

An Englishman and∧Frenchman met by accident in Rome.

case   grammatically, the form of the noun, pronoun or adjective which, in inflected languages, expresses its relation to other words in the sentence. As English has largely become an uninflected language, case is shown only in the genitive of some nouns (John's, girls') and in the accusative (me, him), genitive (mine, hers) and dative (to us, to her) of certain pronouns. Cases are treated under NOMINATIVE; ACCUSATIVE (OBJECTIVE); GENITIVE (POSSESSIVE); DATIVE; VOCATIVE. See also APOSTROPHE (1).

cast, caste   The first has many meanings, including the names of those taking part in a play; the second has but one. It derives from the Portuguese *casta*, meaning 'breed', 'race', 'lineage', which in turn derives from the Latin *castus*, meaning 'pure'. It refers in particular to the hereditary system by which no son can rise above his father's caste (or social level). In general it means an exclusive class of persons. To *lose caste* is to descend in the social scale.

catalectic (kætəlek|tik)   a rather imposing word used to describe something very often met with in PROSODY. It derives from the Greek meaning 'stopping short' and refers to a line that has an incomplete foot at the end of it. A line with a complete foot at the end of it is called ACATALECTIC. In the following stanza from Longfellow's *A Psalm of Life* lines 1 and 3 are acatalectic, and lines 2 and 4 are catalectic:

> Lives of/ great men/ all re/mind us
>   We can/ make our/ lives sub/lime,
> And, de/parting,/ leave be/hind us
>   Footprints/ on the/ sands of/ time.

See also METRE.

catastrophe (kətæs|trəfi)   a disaster or great calamity. In the classical theatre the catastrophe is the DÉNOUEMENT of a tragedy, bringing about the death or ruin of the principal character. The catastrophe of *Othello* is reached when he stabs himself at the end of the play.

catchword   Makers of dictionaries print catchwords (or GUIDE WORDS) at the top of each page. The one on the left tells us the first word dealt with on that page, and the one on the right tells us the last one dealt with. In an index the catchword is the first word of each entry. When the subject of the entry is more than one word, the main one is made the catchword, e.g. *Trafalgar, Battle of.*

A catchword is also a word or phrase used as a slogan and repeated parrot-fashion, e.g. 'Down with this!' 'Down with that!' 'Hands off the other!' 'We want freedom!' 'Yanks, go home!' Comedians try to increase their prestige by inventing catchwords, which are taken up by the public, repeated *ad nauseam* for a time, and then discarded in favour of others. Here are a few that come to mind: 'Very tasty, very sweet.' 'I'm proper poorly.' 'Don't be like that.' 'Not a word to Bessie about this.' 'Can I do you now, sir?' 'You must be joking!'

catharsis (Gk. 'purging') the effect on an audience of a great tragedy or on the reader of a great novel. The mind is thought to be emotionally cleansed of dross by contact with the certainties of life and death presented by the act of genius.

cedilla (sədil'ə) the mark (,) used in French to indicate that the letter *c* is to be given the sound of *s*, e.g. *garçon* (boy). Although distinctly useful, it is not used in English.

centre, middle The centre of anything is a definite point; the middle of anything is somewhere near the centre. We speak of *the centre of attraction*, but *the middle of the night*. It is more correct to say *the middle of the road* than to say *the centre of the road*, because a road has length and width but no centre.

(a) He found himself the centre of an angry demonstration.
(b) He found himself in the middle of an angry demonstration.

In (a) the demonstration was directed against him personally. In (b) he happened to be present at the time of the demonstration, in which he was not personally involved.

centuries periods of one hundred years, specifically the hundred-year divisions of the Christian era or of the preceding period. Thus the first century B.C. was from 101 B.C. to the birth of Christ; the first century A.D. was from A.D. 1 to A.D. 100 inclusive; and the second century A.D. was from A.D. 101 to A.D. 200. We are now in the twentieth century, A.D. 1901–2000. The year 1900 was the last year of the nineteenth century, not, as is often supposed, the first year of the twentieth.

It is better to spell out than to use ORDINAL NUMBERS, e.g. 'the twentieth century', not 'the 20th century'.

See also A.D.; B.C.; DATES; NUMERALS.

childish, childlike   We must differentiate between these when we use them to describe a grown-up person. 'His childish attempt to write a play met with the derision of both public and critics'. 'The old hermit's demeanour was childlike in its simplicity and charm.'

chorus   In Greek drama the chorus was a band of dancers and singers commenting on the action of the play. In Elizabethan drama the chorus was reduced to a single actor speaking the PROLOGUE and again commenting on the action at a few set times, as in *Henry V*. In modern times, the chorus has been revived by Brecht and T. S. Eliot. The term chorus is also used to denote a group of singers and sometimes dancers in OPERAS and MUSICALS.

Christian names   are first names as opposed to surnames. Originally taken from the Bible, hence their name, many English first names nowadays have nothing to do with Christianity. Consequently there is a growing tendency, especially in America, to call them forenames or first names rather than Christian names.

Christmas, Xmas   It is bad enough to write 'Xmas'; it is even worse to use it in conversation.

chronic (kro'nik)   This adjective means 'having gone on for a long time; inveterate'. It is therefore correct to speak of chronic rheumatism if it has lasted several months, even if it has not been very severe; but it is a misuse of the word to speak of a sudden chronic pain, however severe it may be. Used as a synonym for *unpleasant*, *objectionable*, etc. – e.g. 'The weather was chronic' – it is SLANG.

See also OVERWORKED WORDS; VOGUE WORDS.

circulus in probando   see ARGUING IN A CIRCLE.

circumlocution (L. 'talking around')   any roundabout method of expression sometimes to lend dignity, sometimes (as in the following) for humorous effect: 'After an earnest colloquy with the custodian of the vehicle it was agreed that our transportation should be accomplished for the sum of fifty pence.' Another name for it is *periphrasis*, a Greek derivative.

circumstances   Should we say 'in the circumstances' or 'under the circumstances'? The word *circumstance* derives from the Latin meaning 'to stand around', so it would seem that 'in the circumstances' is correct; in that they are, as it were, surroundings, whatever is affected by them must be inside them and not under them. In his *Modern English Usage* Fowler described this objection to *under* as 'puerile'. The *Oxford English Dictionary* has this to say: 'Mere situation is expressed by "*in* the circumstances", action takes place "*under* the circumstances".' On this definition we can base these examples:

(a) 'In these circumstances we have no alternative but to agree to your proposals.'
(b) 'Under the circumstances arising out of loss of orders from overseas, the factory has been closed down.'

Perhaps this distinction can be made, yet we are not without the thought that we are more likely to be chided for using *under* than for using *in*.

classic   from the Latin meaning 'of the first class', referring to the highest rank in the Roman social system. We use the word to refer to the Greek and Latin authors, or to anything of Greek or Roman antiquity. A *classic style* is one that is simple, harmonious, regular and restrained. Hence conformity to the rules and models of Greece and Rome is called *classicism*, the opposite of *romanticism*.

The *classics* are the literature of ancient Greece and Rome. In modern times a *classic* is a writer, artist or work of the first rank. Shakespeare is a classic; his plays are classics. Milton's *Paradise Lost* is a classic, *Robinson Crusoe* is a classic, and so are Dante's *Divine Comedy*, and *Don Quixote* by Cervantes, not forgetting *Alice in Wonderland* by Lewis Carroll.

A *classical scholar* is one well-versed in the classics, and when we speak of a *classical education* we mean one based on the study of the classics, rather than on subjects such as physics, zoology, economics and engineering.

In horse-racing the *classics* are the five chief races of the year – the 2,000 Guineas, the 1,000 Guineas, the Derby, the Oaks and the St. Leger.

clause It is advisable to read this section in conjunction with points treated under SENTENCE, particularly as to classification according to clause structure.

In grammar a clause is part of a sentence, but, unlike a PHRASE, is a complete sentence in itself, having a subject and predicate. As soon as it stands on its own it ceases to be a clause and becomes a simple sentence. Every clause has a definite function within the sentence. It may be a main clause, a co-ordinate clause or a subordinate clause.

A *main* clause is one that does not depend on any other clause. *Co-ordinate* clauses are two or more main clauses joined by co-ordinate conjunctions. A main clause is main to the extent that it can usually stand on its own, regardless of a *subordinate* clause, which, as its name implies, is any clause dependent upon another.

Consider this complex sentence, i.e. a sentence consisting of a main clause and one or more subordinate clauses: 'We will go to the theatre tonight if we can get tickets.' The main clause, which could stand by itself, is 'We will go to the theatre tonight'; the subordinate clause, which could not stand by itself, is 'if we can get tickets'.

Now consider this compound sentence, i.e. a sentence consisting of two or more co-ordinate clauses: 'We will go to the theatre tonight and see the new play.' Here are two clauses of equal importance joined by a conjunction; tonight we will do two things: we will go to the theatre and we will see the new play.

Now consider this compound-complex sentence, i.e. a sentence consisting of two or more co-ordinate clauses and one or more subordinate clause: 'We will go to the theatre tonight and see the new play if we can get tickets.'

From this it will be seen that subordinate clauses are found only in complex or compound-complex sentences. The three types are treated under ADJECTIVAL CLAUSE; ADVERBIAL CLAUSE; NOUN CLAUSE.

clerihew (kleri'hju) a form of humorous verse named after its inventor, Edmund Clerihew Bentley, who also wrote a famous if over-praised detective story, *Trent's Last Case*. A clerihew is in rhymed couplets, but the lines do not have to scan. Here is one (not by Mr Bentley):

Cortés is famous for standing with his men
Silent upon a peak in Darien.
There were also one or two rumours
About a daughter of Montezuma's.

(C. W.)

See also BIOGRAPHY.

cliché (kli:ʃ'ei)   This comes to us from the French and its literal
meaning is a stereotype plate, used for printing. Its figurative meaning is any phrase that has become hackneyed through constant
reproduction. We can hardly get along without some clichés such as
stock SIMILES (*as hard as nails*), stock idiomatic expressions (*to get down
to brass tacks*) or, for humorous purposes (*the long arm of the law, filthy
lucre, the inner man*), pompous phrases (*the founder of the feast, the winds
of change*) or JOURNALESE (*dramatic new move, last-ditch attempt, storm of
protest*). It is worth remembering that every cliché was once new
minted and most are useful in everyday communication. But an
overdose of clichés gives a second-hand effect, especially in writing.

client, customer   The first is thought to be the more polite word
and is used euphemistically when the second would be better. It is
an advantage to reserve *customer* for a person who buys things, and a
client for a person who pays for professional services.

climax (Gk. 'a ladder')   a FIGURE OF SPEECH in which a series of
expressions rises step by step, each exceeding the one before it in importance or force, e.g. 'For some men gambling leads to penury,
penury to petty theft, petty theft to robbery, robbery to armed
violence, and armed violence to murder.'
  See also ANTICLIMAX.

closed couplet   see HEROIC COUPLET.

c/o   abbreviation of 'care of', used in the addressing of letters, e.g.
'Miss Janet Green, c/o Mrs Masters, 3 High Street, Paulsfield,
Downshire.' It should not be used when the name of the addressee's
host or hostess is not mentioned. The word *at* should be used
instead, e.g. 'Miss Janet Green, at 3 High Street, Paulsfield, Downshire.'

collective noun   see under NOUN.

colloquialism   an expression used in common speech, but unsuitable for more dignified literary usage, e.g. *have a go*; *I'm broke*; *a nice chap*; *to take the rap*; *to stage a come-back*; *to cut no ice*; *to take it lying down*; *at a loose end*. There are many others. The difference between colloquial language and SLANG is that the first is the more respectable. We may say that *bored to tears* is colloquial, but *browned off* is slang. For all that, the slang of yesterday becomes the colloquialism of today. *To cut no ice* was a slang expression when first used in 1896. Colloquial speech is of course perfectly acceptable in everyday conversation. It is one of the REGISTERS. It would be unacceptable, because inappropriate, to use too formal language with one's friends. Every REGISTER has its place. See also JARGON.

colon   a punctuation mark (:) slightly less final than a full stop. The colon is used:

1. To separate two co-ordinate clauses, the second of which elaborates the first or is in antithesis to it, e.g. 'He was not feeling well: a numbing pain was creeping up his spine.'
2. To introduce a list, e.g. 'He was a first-class exponent of five games: badminton, hockey, cricket, tennis and golf.'
3. To introduce a conclusion or climax, e.g. 'Taking all the circumstances into account, we did the only thing possible: we fled.'
4. To introduce a passage of direct speech when the verb of saying rather suggests 'as follows', e.g. 'This is in fact what he said: "The bridge can be built only in the dry season."'
5. To introduce a quotation or an extract, e.g. 'As Shelley wrote in his *Ode to the West Wind*: "If Winter comes, can Spring be far behind?"' Longer quotations or extracts are usually given a separate paragraph, e.g.:
'The whole of his philosophy is summed up in this passage from his autobiography:'
(Here, beginning with a new paragraph, follows the extract.)
6. To introduce sub-sections in regulations, etc., e.g.:
'If any parcel is not called for or accepted by the consignee or the consignor the Company shall be entitled without giving notice:'
(Here, numbered i, ii, iii, etc., follow the steps the Company reserves the right to take.)
Frequently in such usage the colon is followed by a dash (:—).

collocation   a term used in modern linguistics to denote a group of words that tend to go together as a result of long usage, e.g. *in due course, by no means, cool and collected, bless my soul, a well-stocked larder*. The term is sometimes more loosely used to refer to any group of words that are to be considered as a unit, such as a nominal phrase or an adjective phrase.

colossal   see OVERWORKED WORDS.

comedy   a drama with a happy ending. A drama with an unhappy ending is called a TRAGEDY. Comedy need not be all comic. When the comic goes beyond the realms of probability it becomes FARCE. *Twelfth Night* is a comedy and so is *The Frogs* by Aristophanes. A *musical comedy* is a light-hearted stage or film production with a slender plot that is secondary to the music, songs, dancing and costumes. A famous musical comedy was *The Maid of the Mountains*, first produced in 1917, which ran for 1,352 performances. *My Fair Lady* is a musical comedy based on *Pygmalion*, the stage play by Bernard Shaw.

In *The Divine Comedy* by Dante and *The Human Comedy* by Balzac, the word *Comedy* does not mean that these are humorous works, but rather that, though serious, they show truth or life in such a way that the reader is not left with any painful or tragic impression. In modern literature *Black Comedy* has heavy satiric overtones. It is TRAGEDY viewed flippantly.

comic   In its literal sense this means 'of comedy'; it is the opposite of *tragic*, which means 'of tragedy'. The alternative adjectives are *comical* and *tragical*. In its secondary sense *comic* means 'funny; laughable; ludicrous', e.g. 'Mrs Perkins was wearing a comic hat, which looked like a bird's-nest.' Used as a noun, *comic* may refer to a music-hall or radio comedian, or to a magazine featuring strip-cartoons, an early example of which was called *Comic Cuts*.

Comic opera is comic in the literal sense; it is the opera of comedy. See OPERA.

comma   the punctuation mark (,) indicating the least separation or pause. Nevertheless, it is a punctuation mark of great importance. Oscar Wilde once confessed that he had spent the whole morning putting in a comma, and the whole afternoon taking it out again. It is used:

1. To separate (a) two or more adjectives defining one noun, e.g. 'He was a quiet, gentle, compassionate man.' (b) two or more adverbs modifying one verb, e.g. 'My offer of help was scornfully, contemptuously declined.' No comma is necessary after 'compassionate' in (a) or after 'contemptuously' in (b); nor is it necessary in such phrases as 'a famous American poet', 'a pretty little girl', 'a tall young man', 'a huge brown bear'. It is the opinion of some authorities that when 'and' is placed before the final adjective, the conjunction should be preceded by a comma, e.g. 'a quiet, gentle, and compassionate man', yet as the meaning is clear enough without the comma, there seems no need for it. (Printers describe 'copy' overloaded with commas as being 'thick'.)

2. To separate individual items in a list, e.g. 'I noticed books, pens, papers, some broken pencils, boxes of all sizes, a couple of packets of cigarettes, two chairs, a table and a dead body.'

Usually in such lists 'and' is not preceded by a comma, but there are occasions when it is necessary, e.g. 'Those present included Mrs Brown, Mrs King, Mrs Jackson and her daughters Mary and Jane, and Mrs Edwards.' The comma after 'Jane' avoids any suggestion that Mrs Edwards was also a daughter of Mrs Jackson. Here is another example: 'The books in the library were classified under such headings as Educational, Classics, Fiction, Art and Architecture, Botany, and Chemistry.' The comma after 'Botany' indicates that 'Botany' and 'Chemistry' are separate headings, unlike 'Art and Architecture', which are classed together.

3. To mark off words or phrases in APPOSITION, e.g. 'Fleetwood, this year's favourite for the Derby, was seen out exercising yesterday.'

4. To mark off words in PARENTHESIS, e.g. 'The lawns, always green and fresh, were a delight to the eye.'

5. To mark off words used in addressing a person, e.g. 'Believe me, my dear fellow, he is almost penniless.'

6. To mark off SENTENCE ADVERBS (adverbs of interpolation). This sentence, for instance, contains one.

7. To mark off participial phrases, e.g. 'My brother, seeing my plight, quickly came to my rescue.'

8. To separate VERBS OF SAYING from direct speech, e.g.:

'Have you a watch?' he asked.
'No,' I replied, 'I have not.'

Note that the question mark after 'watch' comes inside the quotation mark, as do also the comma after 'No' and the full stop after 'not'. See also INVERTED COMMAS; TURNED COMMA.

9. To separate two co-ordinate clauses when a conjunction is used and the second subject is expressed, e.g. 'I looked everywhere for my coat, but I could not find it.' In modern usage there is a tendency to omit the comma here altogether.

10. To separate an adverbial clause from a following main one, e.g. 'Although it rained in the night, the pitch is now quite dry.'

11. To separate two or more co-ordinate noun clauses, e.g. 'He told me that he was leaving, and that his post would be advertised.' But in modern usage there is a growing tendency to omit the comma altogether here.

12. To mark off a non-defining relative clause, which, instead of defining the antecedent, merely adds some information about it, as if in parenthesis, e.g. 'They presented me with a book, which I shall keep to the end of my life.'

13. To mark off a nominative absolute construction, e.g. 'The weather turning cold, he put on his thick overcoat.'

ADDITION AND OMISSION

All too often commas are misused, either by addition or by omission. Let us consider first the sin of addition.

(a) 'Motorists, who ignore traffic signs, are a menace.' This condemns all motorists as a menace because they all ignore traffic signs; but that is not the intention, which is to condemn only such motorists as ignore the signs, i.e. 'Motorists who ignore traffic signs are a menace.' By marking off the adjectival clause with commas, we add some information, but we do not restrict the meaning of the noun. Here is a descriptive clause correctly used: 'John, who is a vegetarian, refused the next dish.'

(b) 'At the picnic none of the children behaved themselves, as their parents had hoped.' Had the parents hoped that the children would not behave themselves?

(c) 'I was not afraid of the bully, because he was stronger than I.' This means that because the bully was the stronger of the two, I was not afraid of him, which is nonsense. Delete the comma after 'bully' and the meaning is clear: the fact that the bully was stronger than I did not make me afraid of him.

For further notes on misleading commas see under ABSOLUTE.

We have seen under section 2 how the omission of commas can cause misunderstanding or AMBIGUITY. Here are a few more examples:

(i) 'Mrs Mason, who is this year's president, was supported on the platform by Lady Langston, Mrs Davis-Jones and Miss Protheroe, all past presidents of the association and three of the twenty-four founder members.' It is reasonable to assume that the past presidents were the three ladies named, but were they also the three founder members? If they were not, there should be a comma after 'association', or, better still, a comma followed by 'and by'.

(ii) 'The boy having tripped over the cat fell down the stairs.' It may be asserted that only a half-wit would take this to mean that the cat fell down the stairs, but that if we *must* be pedantic, all we have to do is put a comma after 'cat'. But something is still wrong somewhere. We feel that 'The boy having tripped over the cat' should be followed by something arising out of the accident, for example: 'his mother rebuked him for his carelessness'. But that was not so, for the boy fell down the stairs; and because he did, 'boy' is the subject of the verb 'fell', and 'having tripped over the cat' is a participial phrase (see section 7 above), which should be marked off by commas, giving us: 'The boy, having tripped over the cat, fell down the stairs.'

(iii) 'He contracted a heavy cold followed by pneumonia after a night spent in the open.' What resulted from the night spent in the open – the heavy cold, pneumonia, or both? 'He contracted a heavy cold, followed by pneumonia, after a night spent in the open.' The commas now show that the night in the open caused first the cold and then the pneumonia. 'He contracted a heavy cold, followed by pneumonia after a night spent in the open.' The omission of the second comma now shows that he had a heavy cold, then contracted pneumonia after a night spent in the open. How the sentence is to be punctuated depends on the facts. Our main concern here is that the sentence as first set out in this paragraph is ambiguous.

(iv) 'The city is now without gas and electricity and public services are seriously affected.' There should be a comma after 'electricity' to prevent a false linking of 'public services' and 'electricity'.

(v) 'I went to the dance with Margaret and her sister Hilda came along later.' There should be a comma after 'Margaret'.

(vi) 'Helping at the Christmas party will be the vicar's wife, who

will cook the turkeys and about six women members of the church.'
A comma after 'turkeys' would avoid any suggestion of cannibalism.

Commas should not be used after street numbers in addresses (26
Lime Tree Grove) or in dates (14th November 1963 *or* 14 November
1963).
The insertion of a comma before BUT is discussed under that
heading.

command   the form taken by a sentence when it expresses an
order or a request, e.g. (a) 'Run away!' (b) 'Fetch me a glass of
water, please.' Commands are, grammatically speaking, expressed
by the IMPERATIVE. A command may therefore be referred to as an
imperative.

commence   see BEGIN.

common noun   see under NOUN.

common sense   Used as a noun this should not be written as one
word. The adjective, *common-sense*, is hyphenated.

commuter   This noun, with the verb *to commute*, came to us from
the United States. A commuter in America is one who travels daily
between a suburban home and an office in the city. We have
widened its meaning by applying it, first to a season-ticket holder
and then to any frequent traveller, thus gaining a useful synonym for
what was previously a circumlocution. The verb is similarly used,
e.g. 'Paul Horst was an American of German origin who made
money from hops. His son commutes between Paris, Switzerland and
Deauville.' – *Evening Standard*. And it is used to refer not only to the
traveller but also to the train, e.g. 'An eight-coach mail train commutes each night between East and West Berlin.' – *Observer Weekend
Review*.

comparative   the form of the adjective or adverb indicating the
second degree of comparison, e.g. prettier, better, more beautiful,
more sensibly, quicker. See COMPARISON, DEGREES OF.

comparison   the act of comparing one thing with another. Simile
and metaphor are both based on comparison; the SIMILE acknow-

ledges a comparison between things that are for the most part different, whilst the METAPHOR implies a comparison without explicitly stating it. Here we are concerned with literal comparison.

First, things compared must be of the same class.

Wrong: The price of sugar has risen less than any other food.

Right: The price of sugar has risen less than that of any other food.

It is impossible to compare price and food. By inserting *that of* we make a sensible comparison between the price of sugar and the price of other food.

Secondly, if we wish to compare one of a group with the whole group, we must exclude the single member from the group with which it is compared.

Wrong: Yorkshire is larger than any county in England.

Right: Yorkshire is larger than any other county in England.

In the first sentence the writer is suggesting either that Yorkshire is not in England, or that it is larger than itself. Clearly, Yorkshire must be excluded by inserting 'other'. In the same way we cannot say that we prefer pears to any fruit, since pears are fruit.

Just as the comparative degree requires the inclusion of 'other' in such sentences as the above, the superlative degree requires its exclusion, e.g.:

Wrong: Of all the other books in my library, this is the one I most treasure.

Right: Of all the books in my library, this is the one I most treasure.

comparison, degrees of   There are three of these – *positive, comparative* and *superlative* – and they are indicated by the form of the adjective or adverb, e.g.:

Positive: The *small* boy ran *fast*.

Comparative: The *smaller* boy ran *faster* than the *taller* one.

Superlative: The *smallest* boy ran (the) *fastest*.

The superlative should not be used when only two persons or things are referred to, e.g.:

Wrong: Of the two boys the *youngest* is the *tallest*.

Right: Of the two boys the *younger* is the *taller*.

The comparative should be used also when one person or thing stands compared with a number of others, e.g.:

Right: Our house is *larger* than the bungalows along the road.

When a word is already comparative it should not be preceded by *more*, e.g.:

Wrong: What more finer sight can there be than a ship under full sail?

Right: What finer sight can there be than a ship under full sail?

Similarly, when a word is already superlative it should not be preceded by 'most'. We know that Shakespeare made Marcus Antonius say in *Julius Caesar*: 'This was the most unkindest cut of all.' But this is no excuse to follow his example. The superlative 'unkindest' cannot be heightened by 'most'. If we use 'most' we must say 'most unkind'. There is, however, such a thing as POETIC LICENCE and, in any case, usage has changed since Shakespeare's time.

Inasmuch as the superlative is the highest degree of comparison, only one thing can be last or first. We can, of course, refer to 'the last two', but 'the two last' is an impossibility, e.g.:

Wrong: John and Robert were the two last to reach home.

Right: John and Robert were the last two to reach home.

A choice between the comparative and the superlative is sometimes difficult to make. Assume that of three brothers Tom is the first, Dick the second and Harry the third. If Tom refers to 'my youngest brother' when speaking of Harry, he is implying that he has more than two brothers. Should he refer to 'my younger brother', it is not clear whether he is referring to Dick or Harry. It is better, therefore, for him to refer to 'the elder of my two brothers' or 'the younger of my two brothers'.

Words that have no comparative or superlative are treated under UNIQUE. See also COMPARISON above.

complement, compliment   The first means 'a full quantity; that which is necessary to make complete'. The second is an expression of regard, a pleasing word or act.

In grammar, *complement* has a special meaning. Some intransitive verbs are known as *verbs of incomplete predication* because, unlike other intransitive verbs, they are not complete in themselves and require a complement to complete them. 'He has become' is meaningless till we add a complement such as 'a doctor'. Such verbs are *be, appear, seem, look, grow* and *become*. The noun, noun-equivalent or predicative adjective completing the verb is known as the *complement*. 'He is *a good player* and with practice will become *first-rate*.' In this sentence *a good player* and *first-rate* are the complements of the verbs *is* and *become*. See also NUMBER; PREDICATE; VERB.

complex sentence   see under SENTENCE.

compound   a word created by joining two or more words together. At first the compound is hyphenated, but when it becomes accepted it usually drops the hyphen. A compound has sometimes a more limited meaning than the words from which it has been formed. Thus, many birds are black, but a *blackbird* is in a class by itself, and the hen blackbird is not black. Again, many human beings are men of war, but *men-of-war* are warships.

Here are but a few of the hundreds of compounds in our language: *bedroom, downtrodden, farewell, footsore, goldfish, good-looking, half-dead, hereafter, house-proud, landmark, makeshift, mother-in-law, nevertheless, outdo, rainbow, two-thirds, walk-over, welfare.*

A compound word often saves a much longer phrase. For example, having uneven, broken or projecting teeth can be condensed into *snaggle-toothed*; a bed of loose wet sand that readily swallows up men, animals, ships, etc. can be condensed into *quicksand*; and a person who is good for nothing and will never make a success of anything can be briefly described as a *ne'er-do-well*.

See also WORD-FORMATION; and for the plural of compound nouns see PLURAL.

compound sentence, compound-complex sentence   see under SENTENCE.

compound verbs   a term formerly used to describe any verb made up of two or more words. In modern linguistics we are more likely to describe these as verb phrases.

concave, convex   A *concave* surface is one hollowed out like the interior of a circle or sphere. A *convex* surface is just the opposite, curving like the outside of a circle or sphere. A saucer is concave on one side, where we place the cup, and convex on the other.

concession   is mainly expressed by an ADVERBIAL CLAUSE, e.g.

' *Whatever you may say*, I still think he is innocent.'
'He won the race, *although he did no training*.'

' *Thin as he is*, he is very strong.'
It may also be expressed by a phrase, e.g.
' *In spite of his large size*, he was quite agile.'
' *Though outnumbered*, they refused to surrender.'

concord   the agreement in number, person or case of one word
with another in the sentence. A verb, for example, agrees with its
subject in number and person (he *flies*, but they *fly*), and a demonstrative adjective agrees with its noun in number (*this* book, but
these books).

Another name for concord is AGREEMENT, under which heading
the matter is more fully discussed.

concordance   an alphabetical index, differing from an ordinary
index in that it is largely verbal – that is to say, it is a list of the principal words used in a book or series of books. It shows the places
where each word is to be found in the book, with its context in each
place. The best known is Alexander Cruden's *Complete Concordance*,
which was published in 1737 and was described as 'forming a dictionary and alphabetical index to the Bible, with a concordance to
the proper names of the Old and New Testament, and the books
called Apocrypha'. There are concordances to the Koran and to the
works of Shakespeare and other authors.

concrete noun   see under NOUN.

concrete terms   see ABSTRACTIONS.

conjugation   (L. 'a yoking together')   In grammar this means
'derived from the same root' and refers to the inflexion of verbs in
VOICE, MOOD, TENSE, NUMBER and PERSON. The verb is *to conjugate*.

conjunction   the part of speech that joins words, phrases or
clauses. It is either (a) *co-ordinate* or (b) *subordinate*.

(a) Co-ordinate conjunctions include *and, but, yet, as well as, so, or,
nor, both, however, therefore*. They are used to join words, e.g. 'bread
and jam', and phrases, e.g. 'He tried hard, but without success', and
also co-ordinate clauses, i.e. clauses of the same kind or function,
e.g. 'He said that we should fail *and* that he would be glad, *but* his
words proved false.' Pairs of words acting as single co-ordinate con-

junctions are known as correlative conjunctions. They include *either ... or, neither ... nor, both ... and, not only ... but also*. They are called correlative because they are dependent on each other and are nearly always used together.

When using correlative conjunctions, take care to place the parts before the words they should join, e.g.:

Wrong: He not only played the piano but also the violin.
Right: He played not only the piano but also the violin.
Wrong: She neither was in the house nor the garden.
Right: She was in neither the house nor the garden.

For verb forms required by alternative subjects see EITHER ... OR. See also NOT ONLY ... BUT ALSO.

    (b) Subordinate conjunctions include *after, before, since, for, as, if, than, because, though, when, where, now that, whatever*. They are used to join main clauses and subordinate clauses, e.g. 'He was angry *because* he was late.'

connotation   A word's connotation is to be contrasted with its DENOTATION. A word denotes no more than what its bare definition states. The word *father*, for example, denotes one who has begotten. In contrast, a word may connote any of the attributes associated with it. Thus *father* may have the connotation of male sex, responsibility for upbringing, breadwinner, affection, experience, leadership, disciplinary authority, etc.

connection, connexion   see under -XION, -CTION.

consonants   in PHONETICS the sounds formed by stopping the breath or by obstructing it in some part of the mouth or throat so that it passes with audible vibration. The letters representing such sounds are also referred to as consonants. They are all the letters of the alphabet except *a, e, i, o* and *u*, which are VOWELS. Their name derives from the Latin *cum* (together) and *sono* (I sound), which means that they can be sounded only with a vowel or a semi-vowel (*w* or *y*). Consonant sounds and vowel sounds are treated under GUIDE TO PRONUNCIATION on page 7.

constructional, constructive   The first means 'having to do with construction'; the second is the opposite of *destructive*.

    (a) The architect explained to the builder the constructional details of the new block of offices.

(b) 'This meeting has been called,' said the chairman to the inter-
rupters at the back of the hall, 'not to listen to destructive
criticism, but to consider any constructive suggestions that
may be made.'

contact clauses ADJECTIVE CLAUSES in which the RELATIVE PRO-
NOUN is omitted as unnecessary, e.g.:

'The man (whom) you want is not here.'
'This is the best book (that) there is on the subject.'

contemptible, contemptuous These adjectives must be clearly
distinguished. The first means 'deserving of contempt'; the second
means 'showing contempt for someone else'. We are therefore contemptuous of contemptible people.

contents (stress on first syllable) that which is contained in a
book. A *table of contents*, printed at the beginning of a book, gives a
summary of its subject-matter. Usually the details are limited to (a)
the numbers of the chapters; (b) the headings of the chapters; and
(c) the page on which each chapter begins. When the chapters of the
book have no headings – that is, no indication of what they are about
– (b) is omitted from the table of contents (or the table of contents
may be omitted altogether). When the book is divided into parts –
Part I, Part II, etc. – these are shown on the table. In some books
where there is a SYNOPSIS at the head of each chapter, the synopsis
appears also in the table of contents, but this is not normal practice.

context (L. 'weaving together') the parts that precede or follow a
given word or passage. Normally all words have to be considered in
their context, as they have no precise meaning out of it. On the other
hand, the meaning of a word can often be ascertained by studying
its context. For example, let us assume that we do not know the
meaning of *unilateral* and we come across this sentence in a newspaper: 'As a result of this unilateral agreement, entered into all too
hastily by the previous Government, we now find ourselves bound to
accept the products of Ruritania, whilst that country is under no
obligation to accept ours.' From this we see that one country under-
took to follow a certain course and the other country did not. It was
therefore a one-sided agreement, and as it is referred to in the early
part of the sentence as a unilateral agreement, we can take it that
unilateral means 'one-sided'.

To quote the writings and sayings of others without reference to the context can be to commit a serious offence. 'Why,' asked Mr Thomson, 'should we lavish our sympathy on those rendered homeless by the flooding?' Certainly Mr Thomson said that, but he went on: 'All the sympathy in the world will achieve nothing. What is needed here is action – immediate help for these unfortunates.' To quote the first sentence by itself is to take it out of its context and to do Mr Thomson wrong.

See also SEMANTICS.

contiguous   see ADJACENT.

continual, continuous   These are often confused. It is worth remembering that a continuous performance can be continually interrupted by fresh arrivals. *Continual* means 'frequent', but *continuous* means 'going on without a break'.

contraction (L. 'a drawing together')   the shortening of words or groups of words by elision or combination, the missing letters being indicated by apostrophes. For example, *o'clock* is a contraction of *of the clock*, and *'twas* is a contraction of *it was*. Contractions such as *can't, don't, isn't, shan't, won't, I'm, he'd, she'll, we're, you've* are regularly used in conversation and are becoming acceptable in writing, but the full form retains advantages in the matter of emphasis or formality.

The shortening of words by dropping letters or syllables from the middle of them (e.g. *e'er* for *ever*) is known as SYNCOPE or ELISION.

See also APOSTROPHE (1).

conundrum   a more precise term than RIDDLE when applied to a question depending on some fanciful likeness between things quite different, the answer to which involves a pun, e.g.:

Question: Why are our feet like fairy-tales?
Answer: Because they are leg ends (legends).
Question: Why are a tailor's children like vegetables?
Answer: Because they're parsnips (their pa snips).

convex   see CONCAVE.

copy   see PRINTERS' PROOFS.

correct English The whole concept of correctness in language has undergone a radical change in the last few decades. Till the turn of the century, most educationists thought they knew precisely what was correct and what was incorrect by reference to a body of immutable rules drawn up by schoolmasters and going right back to Latin grammar. More recently, greater attention has been paid to the fact that language is and always has been in a constant state of change, and, as usage changes, so do the 'rules'. Thus 'It's me' after long usage has become fully acceptable and therefore 'correct', though only a short while ago the purist was still crossing it out and writing 'It's I' as demanded by the old rigid rules.

By 1962, Prof. Quirk could already count on the full support of modern thinking when he wrote: 'There is more convention than logic in matters of dress, and the same applies to language. And the conventions of language are nearly as changeable as those of dress.' He applies this as much to SEMANTICS as to grammar by adding: 'It is futile to try to stop words from being used in a sense different from that in which they were used at some earlier period. Such an "etymological fallacy" betrays, in any case, a lamentable ignorance of the nature of language.' As he rightly points out, if we were to disallow such changes in the meanings of words, we should have to rewrite a substantial part of the modern dictionary, since thousands of words have in fact changed their meanings in this way over the years.

If usage always wins, why resist change? The compilers of *The Facts of English* do not believe in unnecessary resistance, but feel they must step a little cautiously whenever a large body of educated opinion is still resisting change, for some changes are more readily acceptable than others, and it is just possible that a few changes that have gone a fair distance may still be seen to be wrong-headed.

There is also much to be said for retaining a STANDARD ENGLISH that, whilst fully susceptible to change, does not jump too unthinkingly into acceptance of all and any change. What is right for an informal language situation is not necessarily right for a situation where standard English is used. 'I haven't done no homework' may not be acceptable in the classroom where standard English is practised, but it is perfectly comprehensible and acceptable in the streets of Bethnal Green. The double negative was also acceptable in Shakespeare's day and, who knows, may one day again find acceptance among the educated. The modern approach to correctness is very much a matter of conforming to a convention, and there is a different convention for every language situation. This accounts for the growing concern with REGISTERS in the teaching of English, and the insistence that there are many kinds of appropriate language rather than just one 'correct' one.

correlative conjunctions   pairs of words acting as single co-ordinate conjunctions. See CONJUNCTION; EITHER . . . OR; NOT ONLY . . . BUT ALSO.

correspondence   The purpose of personal letters, those written to friends or relatives, is to keep in touch and cultivate the relationship. Departures from STANDARD ENGLISH, the use of COLLOQUIALISMS and SLANG, are therefore acceptable roughly in proportion to the degree of intimacy of the relationship. If the correspondent is at all well known, it is probable that you will greet him with his first name, e.g. *Dear Peter*. If he is a mere acquaintance with whom you are not on 'Christian-name terms', you will give him his title, e.g. *Dear Mr Jones, Dear Dr Brown*. The normal way of ending a personal letter is now universally *Yours sincerely*, but with greater intimacy this becomes *Yours ever, Yours as always*, or *Yours*. To a close relative it is still usual to end with *With love from*, but *Yours affectionately* is dying out fairly rapidly. To those you know well you will normally sign the letter with your first name only; to those you know less well it is usual to add your surname, e.g. *Norman Jackson*. Because it is a signature, you must not incorporate your title; if you wish to indicate your status, this must be done in brackets after the signature, e.g. *Brenda Smith (Miss), Richard Milton (Dr)*.

Being formal, business letters allow of no departure from standard English. On the other hand, the old flowery formality of 'we beg to thank you for your esteemed favour of the 10th ult.' has entirely disappeared, to be replaced by the absolutely straightforward 'thank you for your letter of 10th February'. As time is money, the essence of the good modern business letter is to be brief and absolutely to the point. As in a personal letter, we set out our own address and the date at the top right; under it against the margin on the left we make it quite clear to whom we are writing by giving the name of the official, his firm's name and address. The greeting is a formal *Dear Sir, Dear Madam* or, if to the firm rather than an individual, *Dear Sirs*. Though *Yours truly* is still occasionally used, the ending of a business letter has been practically standardised as *Yours faithfully*. Such endings as *Yours respectfully, Yours humbly, Yours obediently*, except in very peculiar circumstances, have been banished as alien to the modern social climate. The signature contains the full name, or the surname and initials. It is polite to decipher the signature by typing it out underneath or, if handwritten, by repeating it in capital letters. Where a business correspondent has already written with a reference number, it is customary to add this reference in brackets after thanking him for his letter or to put it at the top under the date. This brief example gives the standard format:

**37 New Street
Godalming
Surrey**

**The Secretary   10th February 1972
World-Wide Travel Agents
18 Hertford Street
London W1**

Dear Sir,

> **Thank you for sending me your brochure. I should be glad if you would now send me further details of the type of holiday referred to on page 20.**

Yours faithfully,

Margaret Taylor (Miss)

correspondent, co-respondent   The first is a person who writes letters, or one employed to send news, e.g. 'Our Motoring Correspondent'; 'Foreign Correspondent of the *Evening Clarion*'. The second is a joint respondent in a divorce suit. If a husband or wife sues for divorce, the co-respondent is the person accused of adultery with the erring wife or husband. If a suit is brought by a wife, the 'other woman' is not technically a co-respondent; she is 'named'.

corrigendum (*g* soft as in *general*; plural **corrigenda**)   an error needing correction, especially in a book. If the error is discovered before the book is published but too late for the text to be emended, a note or slip is included, e.g.:

CORRIGENDA

p. 125, line 5: for '1963' read '1863'
p. 238, line 2 from foot: for 'not' read 'now'
p. 300, line 8: for 'sturgeon' read 'surgeon'

Though strictly a list of errors, *errata* (singular *erratum*) is used almost synonymously with corrigenda.

See also ADDENDA.

council, counsel The first is a noun meaning 'an assembly; a meeting for the consideration or laying of plans; an administrative body of a town or county'. The second is (a) a noun meaning 'consultation; a taking and giving of advice'; (b) a verb meaning 'to give advice'. A *councillor* is a member of a council, e.g. *Privy Councillor*; *County Councillor*. A *counsellor* is one who gives advice. *Counsel* is a pleader in court, a barrister, hence Q.C., Queen's Counsel. The word stands by itself: not *a* Counsel or *the* Counsel, but Counsel, which is both singular and plural, e.g. 'Counsel for the prosecution and for the defence conferred together.'

countable nouns those naming things that can be considered separately and counted, e.g. boy – boys, glass – glasses, idea – ideas, as opposed to UNCOUNTABLE NOUNS, which name things that cannot be counted but must be treated as a whole and therefore have no separate plural form, e.g. milk, cement, wisdom. 'Glass' meaning a drinking vessel is thus a countable noun, while 'glass' meaning the material is an uncountable noun.

couplet in PROSODY a general term for two successive lines of verse, rhyming with each other and of equal length. Here is John Gay's *My Own Epitaph*:

Life is a jest; and all things show it.
I thought so once; but now I know it.

Couplets are described as being 'closed' or 'open'. A closed couplet is one in which the sense is complete. The above is a closed couplet, as is a HEROIC COUPLET. An *open couplet* is one in which the sense is not complete and flows over into the next line. *Endymion*, the long poem by Keats, is written in open couplets. Here are the opening lines:

> A thing of beauty is a joy for ever:
> Its loveliness increases; it will never
> Pass into nothingness; but still will keep
> A bower quiet for us, and a sleep
> Full of sweet dreams, and health, and quiet breathing.
> Therefore, on every morrow, are we wreathing
> A flowery band to bind us to the earth,
> Spite of despondence, of the inhuman dearth
> Of noble natures, of the gloomy days,
> Of all the unhealthy and o'er-darkened ways
> Made for our searching: yes, in spite of all,
> Some shape of beauty moves away the pall
> From our dark spirits . . .

This flowing on of one line into the next is known as ENJAMBMENT.

-cracy a Greek suffix meaning 'rule of' or 'rule by'. It is treated under BUREAUCRACY; DEMOCRACY.

credible, creditable The first means 'believable'; the second means 'worthy of putting trust in; bringing credit, praise or honour to'. It is as well to remember this distinction. The explorer or big-game hunter who has told you some of his hair-raising experiences may be flattered if you say, 'it's hardly credible'; but he is likely to take offence if you say, 'it's hardly creditable'.

criticism the act of careful judgement. The word *critic* derives from the Greek meaning 'fitted to judge'. This shows that it is the duty of a critic not merely to censure, not merely to 'criticise' in the general acceptance of the word, but to consider carefully and give an honest opinion. The literary critic, the dramatic critic, the music critic, the radio critic – all may find fault, but when they praise, that is also criticism, the decision of an impartial judge.

cross-question In a court of law a witness gives evidence for one side and is then questioned by the other side in order to test the truth of what he has said. This second process is known as the *cross-examination*, and the questions put are known as *cross-questions*. It follows, therefore, that to cross-question is not merely to ask questions, so that it is incorrect to say that when Johnny arrived home late he was cross-questioned by his father, who wanted to know where he had been.

cross-reference   reference from one part of a book, index, etc. to another. For example, those who refer to AFFIRMATIVE in this book will find the cross-reference 'see NEGATIVE', which means that affirmative and negative are treated together under the second heading. A cross-reference may also refer the reader to another entry for additional information. Thus in *The Facts of English* after ASSONANCE will be found the cross-reference 'See also RHYME'. By turning up RHYME, the reader will find additional information loosely relevant to assonance.

crosswords   word puzzles, a development of the ACROSTIC. Originating in the U.S.A. in the early 1920s, they were soon immensely popular and have continued so ever since. Today most if not all newspapers include crosswords, ranging from easy ones for children to abstruse problems for the very learned and clever. Here is an elementary example, with no complicated clues of the type referred to under ANAGRAM.

Across

1. An upstart (7)
5. In small measure (T)
6. Inspiring reverence (7)
7. A deadly poison (7)

Down

2. A vaulted entrance (7)
3. Deer's flesh used as food (7)
4· Wet earth from a famous river (4, 3)

-ction, -xion   see -XION, -CTION.

curb, kerb   Use the first to describe anything used as a check or for the purpose of holding back. Use the second to describe the edging stone of a pavement – a kerb-stone – and as another word for *fender*, which in older houses keeps burning coal from falling from the fireplace into the room.

customer see CLIENT.

D

dactyl (dækˈtil)   in PROSODY a trisyllabic foot with the stress on the first syllable, e.g. *mournfully*. See METRE.

dare say Never write this as one word. It has two meanings, as will be seen from these examples: (a) 'You dare say that again!' (b) 'I dare say we shall meet when I am next in London.'

dash the punctuation mark (–), longer than a hyphen, used:

1. To mark a parenthesis instead of commas or brackets, e.g. 'I at once rang up Jones – he's my solicitor – and asked his advice.'
2. To indicate an abrupt change of thought, e.g. 'The following year we fared better – but that is another story.'
3. To separate a repeated word, e.g. 'The offer was accompanied by conditions – conditions that we were not prepared to accept.'
4. To indicate the omission of a word or part of it when the use of the full word might be undesirable, e.g. (a) 'It was during one of these trips to Paris that I met Mr C—.' (b) 'A man at the back of the hall called out that the speaker on the platform was a —.' (c) 'D— it!' It is from the use of the dash to represent the once rude word *damn* that the milder form 'Dash it!' derives.

data (deiˈtə)   the plural of *datum* and used much more frequently than the singular form. *Data* are things known or granted; given facts from which other facts may be inferred. *Data* is the plural form and should never be used in a singular context. 'The data he collected was sufficient to establish that Mr Robinson had never been within a hundred miles of Manchester.' In this sentence 'was' should be 'were'.

dates The most logical order is day, month, year, e.g. 14th November 1972 or 14 November 1972, omitting *th*. There should be no comma after the month because it is unnecessary, whereas it might be considered necessary to separate the figures when the order is month, day, year, e.g. November 14, 1972.

The lack of standardization can cause ambiguity when only figures are used, e.g. 4.1.72. Does this refer to 4th January or 1st April? (Part of the confusion stems from the fact that American usage is month, day, year both when the month is written out and when figures are used. Thus 4.1.72 would always mean 1st April to an American.) Many educated people are avoiding this ambiguity by using roman figures for the month. It is argued that 1.IV.72 refers more clearly to 1st April.

When years are linked by hyphens, all unnecessary figures should be omitted. The following are examples of the correct forms: 1895–1900, 1901–9, 1910–17, 1917–24, 1924–6, 1927–42. It should be noted, however, that in 1910–17 the second date should not be abbreviated still further; 1910–7 is incorrect. Another point is that when dates are preceded by 'from' the hyphen should not be used, e.g.:

Wrong: He lived in Paris from 1950–1972.

Right: He lived in Paris from 1950 to 1972.

For correct abbreviation of the names of months see ABBREVIATION, section 1. See also CARDINAL NUMBERS; CENTURIES.

dative case   the case of the indirect object (see under OBJECT), which is the word naming the person or thing indirectly but not primarily affected by the action of the verb, e.g. 'Jack sent Tom an invitation.' The direct object of 'sent' is 'invitation'; the indirect object is 'Tom', which is therefore in the dative case. 'He poured his friend a drink.' The indirect object is 'friend', again in the dative case.

In English neither nouns nor pronouns have any special inflexion to show the dative case. Pronouns, however, have the same form in the dative as in the accusative. Thus *me, us, them, whom* may be datives. (a) 'He threw me out of the house.' (b) 'He threw me the book.' In (a) 'me' is in the accusative; in (b) 'me' is in the dative, being the indirect object of 'threw'. (c) 'I will send whom I wish an invitation to my party.' Here 'whom' is in the dative. But this is to use Latin terminology. In modern linguistics the term 'dative' is rarely if ever used, since it is applicable only to inflected languages like Latin. It is considered more helpful to talk about indirect objects than datives, or about nouns governed by prepositions.

See also under CASE.

decasyllabic (dekə'silæb'ik)   having ten syllables. The lines of a SONNET and of BLANK VERSE are decasyllabic – that is, ten syllables divided into five disyllabic feet. See METRE.

declension   This noun and the verb *to decline* both come from the Latin meaning 'to bend'. In grammar declension is the giving of the different endings to nouns, pronouns and adjectives according to their relation to other words in the sentence – that is, according to their case. Thus the declension of *he* is: nominative case, *he*; accusative case, *him*; genitive case, *his*; dative case, *him*. But this is Latin terminology, which does not sensibly apply to English as it is not an inflected language. We do not normally talk about the declension of English nouns or pronouns. See also CASE.

deduction   a form of reasoning in which we start with a general truth or PREMISE and draw conclusions from it, whereas in INDUCTION we start from particular cases and evolve a general rule about them. If, for example, we know that all birds have two legs, we can deduce from the general truth the particular truth that an owl has two legs. Deductive reasoning can usually be reduced to a SYLLOGISM, which would here take the form:

All birds have two legs.
An owl is a bird.
Therefore an owl has two legs.

See also A PRIORI.

defence, defensive   Note that in British English the first is spelt with a *c*, the second with an *s*. Americans use an *s* for both.

definite, definitive   There is a difference between these two adjectives. The first means 'clear; precise; not vague; with exact limits'. The second means 'decisive; final; conclusive'. A *definite answer* is a precise answer, which can be modified should that be found necessary; a *definitive answer* is one from which there is no withdrawal. In the world of books the term *definitive edition* means a final edition. Thus, after the death of Rudyard Kipling there was published a volume containing all the poems he had ever written. As he would never write any more, this was called *The Definitive Edition of Rudyard Kipling's Verse*.

degrees of comparison   see COMPARISON, DEGREES OF.

delusion   see ALLUSION.

democracy   from the Greek meaning 'rule by the people'. *Aristocracy* is 'rule by the best'. *Autocracy* is 'rule by one person'. *Plutocracy* is 'rule by the rich'. Hence *democrat, democratic*; *aristocrat, aristocratic*; *autocrat, autocratic*; *plutocrat, plutocratic*. There are also such humorous variations as *foolocracy, snobocracy* and *gawkocracy* (television viewers). See also BUREAUCRACY.

denotation   Its meaning is brought in contrast with CONNOTATION.

dénouement   (deinuːˈmon)   The literal meaning of this French word, often used without the accent in English, is 'unknotting'. The dénouement of a play or story is the eventual solution, when all the knots are unravelled. In a novel of detection the dénouement is traditionally the moment when the villain is unmasked. The dénouement of a classic stage tragedy, usually the death of the principal character, is also known as the CATASTROPHE.

dependant, dependent   The first is the noun, one who depends on another, e.g. 'Although not a rich man, he had a number of dependants to support, including his widowed mother and two nieces orphaned by the death of their parents.' The second is the adjective. Instead of 'dependants' in the foregoing sentence, one might write 'dependent *relatives*' (but not 'dependant relatives'). The adjective has also the meaning of 'contingent', e.g. 'This appointment was dependent upon his passing the entrance examination.'

deprecate, depreciate   The first means 'to express disapproval of', e.g. 'He deprecated the use of force in the settlement of disputes.' The second means 'to go down in value or quality', e.g. 'Perishable goods depreciate very quickly.'

derivation   Where have all our words come from? In a sense they have all been borrowed, and the borrowings have been most numerous whenever there was an invasion of one sort or another. A pure-bred English language has never existed; it is aggressively mongrel. To change the metaphor, it is an interweaving of all the borrowings and their derivatives down the ages.

We need go back no farther than the time when Britain was in-
habited by the Ancient Britons, who were really Kelts speaking
Keltic. The number of Keltic words still surviving in our language
is very limited, but probably includes: *bannock, clout, crock, dam,
drudge, glen, hassock* (tuft of coarse grass), *knob, mattock, mug, pool, taper*.
Avon and *Ex*, which appear in the names of rivers and both mean
'water', are two more words borrowed from the Kelts.

Before the Kelts were driven out of England they were invaded in
55 B.C. by the Romans, who ruled the country for several centuries.
Very few Latin words from this period remain in our language, and
those few were mostly left behind in the names of places. *Castra* (a
camp) appears in Lancaster, Winchester, Leicester; *strata* (a paved
way) in Stratford, Stratton, Streatham; *colonia* (a settlement) in
Colne, Lincoln; *fossa* (a trench) in Fosseway, Fossebridge; *portus* (a
harbour) in Portsmouth, Bridport. Three common nouns borrowed
from the occupying Romans are: *mile* (mille passus), *wine* (vinum),
wall (vallum).

By the fifth century A.D. the Roman Empire was in decay and the
occupying forces in Britain could not prevent the Jutes from settling
in Kent and the Isle of Wight in A.D. 449. A Saxon invasion in the
west followed shortly after, and then came the Angles to the east.
The new invaders sent for their wives and families and quickly established their own language, traditions, religion and customs. They
seem to have had little use for the Ancient Britons, who mostly fled
to Wales, Cornwall and Scotland, where the Keltic language survived. Indeed, the newcomers called them *Wealhas* (foreigners), from
which the modern word *Welsh* derives.

Because they were such dominating invaders, the Jutes, Angles
and Saxons established their own language, taking over very little of
Keltic or Latin. Thus if we are to speak of an original English language, this must be it. We call it **Old English**, but actually there
were several dialects, and it is a curious fact that the dialect from
which modern English is mainly descended was that spoken by the
Saxons, though we call it English as if it were rather the language of
the Angles. Even so, modern English is very different from any kind
of Old English, but different though it is, there is a solid core of Old
English in it. Most of our short everyday words are of Old English
derivation, e.g. *and, bright, come, find, good, hand, it, Tuesday, through,
trough, two, under, was, we, well, when, would*.

Although, unlike Keltic, Old English was never ousted but remained at the centre of the growing English language, it was con-

tinuously modified by a succession of further invasions. The first of these was the arrival of Christianity from Rome with the mission of St. Augustine in A.D. 597. As a result, Old English added a number of words of a religious character, for which no native words existed, such as *altar, bishop, candle, Christmas, disciple, mass, monk, priest.*

Towards the end of the eighth century the Danish Vikings started invading the east coast of England. Within a hundred years their settlements had grown numerous. The Vikings were absorbed into the life of the Anglo-Saxons and so was their language. In exchange the Danish or Norse languages gave English many new words and altered the pronunciation of many more.

We can see the influence of Danish especially in the names of places where the Vikings settled. The Danish word *by*, meaning 'a town', appears in Grimsby, Whitby, Selby; *toft*, meaning 'a holding', appears in Lowestoft; *thwaite*, meaning 'a clearing', appears in Crosthwaite, Linthwaite, Slaithwaite; *thorpe*, meaning 'a village', appears in the surname Thorpe (or Thorp), and in many place-names such as Scunthorpe, Goldthorpe, Mablethorpe. Some of the commonest words that we owe to the Danish invasion are: *are, by-law, call, clip, clumsy, fellow, firth, get, hit, husband, knife, low, outlaw, take, them, they, want.*

The next invasion was similar but more far-reaching as far as language was concerned. William of Normandy conquered England in 1066 and rewarded his officers by making them lords of many of the English manors. For nearly three hundred years Norman French was the language of the English Court, nobility, law courts, learned professions and schools. Indeed, grammar-school pupils were taught in Norman French right into the fourteenth century. But the common people and many of the remaining Anglo-Saxon nobles went on speaking their own native tongue. There were therefore two languages spoken from 1066 till early in the fourteenth century. The native language was considered crude and was rarely used in writing, whilst Norman French was considered polite and fit for literature. But gradually, as the Normans became cut off from France and intermarried with the Anglo-Saxons, the two languages mingled and became **Middle English**. Though much more Old English than French, the new language owed many hundreds of words to Norman French. It was held in sufficient esteem by 1386 for Chaucer to write his *Canterbury Tales* in it, and it is interesting to note that about 13 per cent of Chaucer's vocabulary was French in origin.

What sort of words did Middle English borrow from Norman

French? For the most part they had to do with the more polite and cultured life for which the Anglo-Saxons had few words. It is amusing to observe, as Scott did in his novel *Ivanhoe*, that while the peasant tended his oxen and called them by that Old English name, as soon as they entered polite society in the form of roast meat they became beef, from *bœuf*, the French word for ox. In the same way pig became pork (from *porc*), sheep became mutton (*mouton*) and calf became veal (*veau*). Other common words of French origin are: *abbess, abbot, assize, cardinal, charity, comedy, courtesy, draper, haberdasher, humour, justice, larceny, repentance, security, tragedy, trespass, verdict*. Many of these words look as if they come from Latin, and at one remove most of them do, because French is a language largely derived from Latin.

One of the results of borrowing so many French words is that we often have two words for the same thing, one being Anglo-Saxon and the other French. These are considered under SYNONYMS.

The English language was destined to become even more hybrid than Middle English, for the next 'invasion' brought with it a flood of Latin and Greek words, many of which soon became permanently absorbed into our language. The full tide of the revival of learning called the RENAISSANCE reached England about 1500. It was based on the recently rediscovered classics of Latin and Greek. The Latin language was held in such respect for a time that it became a sort of international language among educated people, and for more than a century was the only language recognised in English schools. Latin words began to invade our language by the thousand. Most of them had a literary flavour when first borrowed, but in course of time they acquired a wider application. The part played by the Renaissance in producing the English language of today can be seen from the following, all of which were borrowed at this time: *accommodate, capable, capacious, compute, distinguish, estimate, experiment, insinuate, investigate, manufacture, manuscript, master, pagan, persecute, radius, senior, tradition*.

Many of the words borrowed from the Norman French had been derived from the Latin, e.g. *royal*, from the Latin *regalis*, meaning 'of or belonging to a king (*rex*)'. So to the Old English *kingly* were added the two synonyms *royal* and *regal*. Many new pairs of words came to us in this way. For example, from the Latin *debitum* there came *debt* indirectly through the Norman French, and *debit* directly from the Latin. With the passage of time the words in some of these pairs have taken on different shades of meaning, so that *feat* (N.F.) and *fact*, both from the Latin *factum*, are no longer synonymous, nor are *money* (N.F.) and *mint*, both from the Latin *moneta*; *poor* (N.F.) and *pauper*, both from the Latin *pauper*; *sure* (N.F.) and *secure* from *securus*; *sever* (N.F.) and *separate* from *separare*.

During the Renaissance, Ancient Greek began to be drawn upon too, but never to the same extent as Latin. Its importance can be gauged from the following selection of words that came in at that time: *apology, apostrophe, climax, drama, emphasis, encyclopaedia, epidemic, episode, epithet, grammar, hypothesis, hysterical, paragraph, parallel, physical, synonym*.

This flood of words from Latin and Greek did not cease with the Renaissance. Whenever we have needed a new word to name a new thing or new idea we have tended to look to Latin or Greek, e.g. *aerodrome* (Gk.), *bicycle* (L. & Gk.), *cinema* (Gk.), *penicillin* (L.), *phenol* (Gk.), *radio* (L.), *radium* (L.), *telegraph* (Gk.), *telephone* (Gk.), *uranium* (Gk.). *Television* is a mixture of Greek (*tele*, from afar) and Latin (*visus*, vision).

By the time the English language had digested its Renaissance borrowings in the middle of the seventeenth century, it had more or less taken on its present form as far as grammar, spelling and pro-nunciation are concerned. There have of course been slight changes since, especially in PRONUNCIATION, which has meant that spelling no longer always agrees with sound. But in general the language from 1650 on is essentially **Modern English**, and its main development has been that of enlarging its vocabulary and modifying the meaning of existing words. Even if we regard the Renaissance as the last major linguistic invasion, we must not forget that there have been dozens of minor ones since, and they are still going on.

For example, the invasion of Italian culture, mainly in the eighteenth century, gave us many musical and painting terms, such as *andante, concerto, fresco, mezzotint, replica*. The (literal!) invasion of Dutch sea power brought us *bulwark, deck, dock, yacht*. The invasion of science, especially since 1850, has given us a host of new technical terms, such as *analysis, automatic, bacteria, electron, impedance, oxygen, refrigeration, supersonic, telescope*. Then there has been an invasion of American popular culture, especially films, bringing in its wake words like *big shot, boom* (in the commercial sense), *bootlegger, commuter, crook, elevator, fan* (supporter), *frame-up, gangster, go-getter, graft* (political bribery, etc.), *gunman, guy, hobo, once-over, outfit* (group of persons), *pep, phoney, public enemy No. 1, racket, rough-house, rubberneck, set-up, spotlight, stenographer, sucker, yes-man*.

Here are but a few of the terms that gained currency as a result of World War I: *big noise* (important person), *binge, breeze* (or *wind*) *up, bunce, camouflage, civvy, cushy, embus* (to put troops into buses for transport), *pill-box* (small fort), *quids in, scrounge, spot of bother, U-boat, umpteen, zero hour, zoom.* The end of World War II saw us with more additions to our vocabulary: *ack-ack, airstrip, back-room boys, black market, black-out, blitz, block-buster, boffin, bull, bulldozer, Chindits, dam-buster, D-day, fifth column, Gestapo, G.I., Home Guard, jeep, lease-lend, near miss, paratroops, quisling, sabotage, spiv, under the counter, V.I.P., Waaf, wishful thinking.* There were many others.

Our Servicemen and merchants engaged in world-wide trade have brought back words gathered abroad. Foreign merchants brought their native words with them and sometimes left them here. In this way there have been many invasions from the Indian languages, Malay, Turkish, Arabic, Persian, Russian, Chinese, Portuguese, Spanish, German, various African languages, and so on, all enriching what Ralph Waldo Emerson, the famous American philosopher, once described as 'the great metropolitan English speech, the sea which receives tributaries from every region under heaven'.

See also NOUN; OVERWORKED WORDS.

derogatory (dərogˡətri) Disparaging or slightly contemptuous words like *banal, puerile, stupid, greedy, ignorant, layabout* are derogatory by nature. Words like *agitator, propaganda, tycoon, faction, anarchistic, appeasement, fascist, Red, drop-out* have become derogatory by association. The use of derogatory terms in ARGUMENT is discussed under EMOTIVE LANGUAGE. See also ARCH-.

deteriorate, deterioration The verb means 'to get worse', and that is what often happens to the pronunciation of it, which becomes 'deteriate', whilst the noun becomes 'deteriation'. Give these words their full quota of syllables.

deus ex machina When the characters in classical drama were faced by superhuman problems, a god was brought on the stage by means of a mechanical contrivance to rescue them from their predicament. In modern times, a *deus ex machina* is someone who arrives unexpectedly at a critical moment and puts matters right.

device, devise The noun is spelt with a *c*, the verb with an *s*.

diaeresis (daiə:ˡəsis) (Gk. 'to divide') the mark (¨) placed over the second of two vowels to show that they are not one sound but two, e.g. *aërate*, *Noël*. It is sometimes used to indicate two sounds when the last letter of a prefix is the same as the first letter of the root word, e.g. *coöperate*, *preëminent*. More usually the hyphen is used for this purpose, e.g. *co-operate*, *pre-eminent*. The word *diaeresis* is used not only for the mark but also for the separation of vowel elements in a word; it is the opposite of SYNAERESIS.

dialect a variation of a language peculiar to a certain geographical area within the total area of the language. Thus Cockney is a dialect of English once peculiar to a part of London.

dialogue conversation in print or on the stage. It is direct speech written down in such a way that the reader knows the exact words spoken and who spoke them. Except in printed plays, INVERTED COMMAS are used to separate the direct speech from the explanatory matter. Here is an example of dialogue:

'How would you like it cut, sir?' asked the talkative hairdresser. 'If possible in silence,' replied the customer.

When we refer in this book to certain grammatical errors being permissible in dialogue, we mean that the characters in novels, short stories, plays, films, TV series, do not all speak perfect English, for many would be very unconvincing if they did. So although an author must respect the rules of grammar in his narrative, his characters have full freedom of speech, with all its errors and inconsistencies.

See also REPORTED SPEECH.

did, done Do not confuse these. It is wrong to say 'I done it' when you mean 'I did it'. Remember that 'done' is never used on its own; it always needs a helping AUXILIARY VERB, e.g. 'I *have done* it'; 'she *has done* well'; 'it *is done* like this'.

didactic (dədækˡtik) (Gk. 'to teach') referring to the teaching of some moral lesson. The children's story of *Black Beauty* is didactic to the extent that it teaches its readers to treat horses kindly. Pope's *Essay on Criticism* is a didactic poem because it teaches the canons of literary taste. The FABLE and the PARABLE are didactic stories, whilst satire is a form of didactic writing. The noun is *didacticism*.

differ with, from Be careful to use the correct preposition. If we do not agree with a person, we differ *with* him; but our opinions differ *from* his.

See also PREPOSITIONAL IDIOM.

different from, to, than There are purists who argue that if one thing differs *from* another and not *to* it, the same thing applies when the adjective *different* is used. Others argue that *different to* is no less correct than *different from*. In practice, *different to* has become so common that it is now accepted as correct. But *different than*, though increasingly heard, is wrong, for *than* is never used as a preposition; it is a conjunction that follows comparatives; and *different* is not a comparative adjective. We tend to be lured into using *than* when it becomes separated from *different* or when the difference is a result of the lapse of time. 'When I returned to my old home after many years, everything seemed different in the house and garden than it had been when I was a boy.' Here 'than' should be 'from what' or 'to what'.

diffuse expressing ideas fully, but without sufficiently bothering to control or organise them. When we speak of a diffuse style, the word is invariably DEROGATORY.

digest The verb is pronounced dədʒestˡ; the noun is pronounced daiˡdʒest. A digest is a summary, a condensed version of some longer work. 'When he had digested all the available literature on the subject, he prepared a digest for the information of his colleagues, who had not so much time to spare.'

digraph (daiˡgraːf) a combination of two letters representing one sound, e.g. the *ea* in *meat*, the *ee* in *peel*, the *ch* in *chin*, the *ui* in *cruise*, the *au* in *pause*. Digraphs are often incorrectly referred to as DIPH-THONGS.

When two vowel letters are joined together to form one sound (æ, œ), this is called a VOWEL LIGATURE.

dimeter (dimˡətə) (Gk. 'two measures') a line of verse consisting of two feet. These lines from the nursery rhyme are in *iambic dimeters* – that is, two disyllabic feet with the stress on the second syllable of each foot:

The Queen/ of Hearts

She made/ some tarts

See METRE.

diminish, minimise   The first means 'to make or become less'; the second means 'to reduce to or estimate at a minimum'. They are therefore not synonymous. For example, to minimise the dangers of motor racing is not to diminish them; it is to make light of them by arguing that the risk is negligible.

diminutives   forms of nouns to express smallness, e.g. *codling* (small cod-fish), *coronet* (small crown), *duckling* (young duck), *eaglet* (young eagle), *gosling* (young goose), *granule* (small grain), *hillock* (small hill), *kitchenette* (small kitchen), *lambkin* (small lamb), *manikin* (little man, dwarf), *novelette* (short novel), *pannikin* (small metal pan), *particle* (small part or portion), *princeling* (petty prince), *rootlet* (small root), *statuette* (small statue), *wavelet* (little wave, ripple). Diminutives are sometimes used in token of affection, e.g. *darling* (little dear), or contempt, e.g. *lordling, manikin*.

See also MINI.

diphthong (dif'θoŋ, not dip'θoŋ)   in PHONETICS the sound of two vowels when pronounced rapidly so that they glide together to form one sound, e.g. the *a*: sound of *hard* plus the *u*: sound of *do* = the *au* diphthong of *count, how*, etc. It must be understood that a diphthong is a vowel *sound*. In the past the term has been used to mean the vowel *letters* representing one sound, e.g. the *eo* in *people* and the *ou* in *thought*. There are many of these combinations in the English language and the term for them is DIGRAPH.

See also GUIDE TO PRONUNCIATION on page 7.

diplomat, diplomatist   originally the (French) holder of a diploma of higher education, later restricted to a member of a country's Foreign Service accredited to a foreign court or government. All such *diplomats* constitute the Corps Diplomatique or Diplomatic Corps. *Diplomatist*, favoured by *The Times* newspaper, is nearer to the original French word. *Diplomatic* has the widespread secondary meaning of 'tactful'.

direct object   see OBJECT.

direct speech   see REPORTED SPEECH; INVERTED COMMAS

disinterested, uninterested   A disinterested person is one without self-interest, and is therefore very different from an uninterested person, who is bored because lacking interest in or enthusiasm for something.

dissociate   Do not fall into the error of saying 'disassociate'.

disyllabic (dai'silæb'ik) or **dissyllabic** (dis'ilæb'ik)   having two syllables, e.g. *wo-man, de-light, foot-ball*. See METRE.

documentary   an adjective (or noun) used to describe any film or TV programme that presents the drama of real life. Unlike a FEATURE film, the facts are always true, although they may be woven into a story, and slanted to produce a particular effect on the viewer.

doggerel   poetry of very poor quality. This is doggerel:

> Our hero then travelled afar
> Until he got to Africa,
> Where he made a famous name
> Shooting all kinds of big game,
> Including lions, tigers and elephants,
> Which he killed on his hunts.

Dog-Latin   Here 'dog' is used in the sense of 'mongrel'. Dog-Latin is bad Latin. Here is a mock example: '*Fumi negro diesel ex trux omnibusque erupit sed non taxis motorisque privati.*' ('Black diesel fumes belch from lorries and omnibuses but not from taxi-cabs and private cars.')

dogma (Gk. 'an opinion')   has two meanings: (a) an established principle, especially one laid down by the Church; a doctrine based on faith, not on experience and reasoning; and (b) as an adjective to describe an arrogant expression of opinion delivered with an air of authority, e.g. 'Why must you be such a know-all? You're so dogmatic that you never listen to other people's views, always ramming your own down their throats.'

done   see DID.

double negative see NEGATIVE.

doubtless This is already an adverb. There is no such word as 'doubtlessly'. The adverb ending in -*ly* is *undoubtedly*.

drama a stage or TV play or a film. *The drama* is a name for the dramatic art and the theatre in general (see METONYMY; STAGE; THEATRE). A writer of plays is a *dramatist* or *playwright*. To write in the form of a drama is *to dramatise* ('This is a dramatised version of the book of the same name'). The adjective *dramatic* refers to the drama and also to anything that resembles it, e.g. 'Recent dramatic events in the Middle East are causing much speculation in Europe.' *Amateur dramatics* are plays presented by unpaid performers.

    See also CATASTROPHE; COMEDY; DÉNOUEMENT; FARCE; KITCHEN-SINK DRAMA; MELODRAMA; METHOD; REPERTORY COMPANY; THEATRE OF THE ABSURD; THREE UNITIES, THE.

dramatic irony see IRONY.

drank, drunk, drunken The first is the past tense of the verb *to drink*. The second and third are the past participle and are also used adjectivally, e.g.:

(a) She drank two cups of tea while I was drinking one.
(b) She had drunk her second cup of tea before I had finished my first.
(c) Drunken in his habits, he lost one job after another.
(d) He was reeling about like a drunken man.

The use of *drunk* as a noun instead of *drunkard* is SLANG.

drugs Suddenly, in the late 1960s and thereafter, the 'drug problem' became news and the subject of heated discussions. The young, increasingly long-haired, were, it was said, taking up hallucinogenic drugs in place of (or sometimes as well as) their fathers' social solace of alcohol. The most popular drug was made of *cannabis resin* (Indian hemp) which was inhaled by smoking in cigarettes known as *joints* or *reefers*; it was illegal in almost every country, and prosecutions of both users and *pushers* (sellers) were frequent, in spite of the existence of a number of TRENDY persons in the universities and the mixed MEDIA who campaigned for it to be legalised. Due to both the spread of the habit and the ensuing controversy, new words about drugs came into the language by the usual fast route via SLANG and COLLOQUIALISM, e.g. *pot* became the accepted word for *cannabis resin*, which was also known as *hashish* (*hash*) and *marijuana*. *Addict*, already in the language, took on a new, restricted meaning: the term *addictive* was often used in connection with *pot* and *LSD* (in full, lysergic acid diethylamide), though technically it should be reserved for the more potent hard drugs: *methedrine*, *cocaine* and *heroin*. An *addict* was said to be *hooked*. Because all the drugs were illegal, they were given disguised names by addicts: *speed* (methedrine), *coke* (cocaine), *horse* and *smack* (heroin) were several. (Compare the original purpose of RHYMING SLANG.) Books based on experience of drug-taking were written by such serious writers as William Burroughs Jnr; and UNDERGROUND NEWSPAPERS devoted much space to the drug scene.

due to, owing to These should not be confused; they are not interchangeable. The former always introduces an adjectival phrase, and the latter an adverbial phrase. 'I noticed a number of mistakes due to carelessness.' 'He failed the examination owing to lack of preparation.' In the first, 'due to carelessness' stands instead of an adjective describing 'mistakes'; in the second, 'owing to lack of preparation' does not stand instead of an adjective describing 'examination', but instead of an adverb saying why he failed. Perhaps the confusion of the two has already gone too far to stop. See CORRECT ENGLISH.

E

each SEE BETWEEN EACH; BOTH, EACH.

eclectic (Gk. 'to pick up') Adjectivally it means 'chosen from many sources'. An *eclectic* is a person who is ready to consider all doctrines and methods, picking out those he considers to be best or true.

economic, economical   The first means 'pertaining to economics, the practical science of the production and distribution of wealth'; the second is used in the sense of 'thrifty; careful'. It is as well to distinguish them, e.g.:

  (a) The Chancellor of the Exchequer explained the present economic position of the country.
  (b) My mother is very economical; she never wastes anything.

-ed   by analogy with *built, swept, crept,* and because the ending is pronounced as if it were a *t,* the *-ed* ending of *burned, dreamed, leaped, spelled* is rapidly giving way to *t: burnt, dreamt, leapt, spelt.*

editorial   American for LEADING ARTICLE. In British English, too, the leading article is often referred to as the 'editorial'.

effect   see AFFECT.

e.g., i.e.   These two are often confused. The first is an abbreviation of the Latin *exempli gratia,* meaning 'for example'; the second is an abbreviation of *idem est* (sometimes shortened to *id. est*), meaning 'that is' or 'that is to say'. When we wish to quote an example or examples, we use the first, thus:

'Of the large family of birds known as finches, a number of varieties (e.g. the chaffinch, the greenfinch, the house sparrow and the linnet) are common in Great Britain.'

When we wish to add something by way of explanation, we use the second, thus:

'The Fringillidae (i.e. finches) are common in Great Britain and are to be found in most parts of the temperate zone.'

In the first sentence we name a few of the many varieties of finches; in the second we explain that the Fringillidae are known in non-technical language as the finches.

When brackets are not used, each of these abbreviations should be preceded by a comma, but inasmuch as they form in themselves an introduction to what follows, they should not be followed by a comma or a colon, unless, as frequently happens in this book, the abbreviation *e.g.* introduces a new paragraph.

The abbreviations *e.g.* and *etc.* should not be used together – that is, one at the beginning and the other at the end.

'In some of Britain's largest cities, e.g. Liverpool, Manchester, Leeds, etc., the population is still less than a million.'

By the use of *e.g.* we make it clear that these are a few examples, so *etc.*, meaning 'and the rest', is redundant.

egregious (egriːˈdʒəs) The literal meaning of this is 'towering above the flock'. Although it can be used to mean distinguished, excellent, notable, etc., we do not often intend it to be complimentary. We speak of 'an egregious ass' or 'an egregious blunder', and when we refer to 'the egregious Mr Jones' we imply that he is outstanding in no distinguished or excellent way.

either, neither Do we pronounce these aiðə and naiðə or iːðə and niːðə? According to the dictionaries both are permissible, but aiðə and naiðə are recommended here, since they are now the more common in educated English speech.

either . . . or a pair of words acting as a single co-ordinate CON-JUNCTION. The following points should be noted:

1. If the alternative subjects are singular, the verb is singular also, e.g. 'Either the boy or the girl *is* to blame.'
2. If both subjects are plural, the verb is plural also, e.g. 'Either the boys or the girls *are* to blame.'
3. If one of the subjects is singular and the other plural, the verb is plural, e.g. 'Either Tommy or the boys who live next door *are* to blame.' 'Either the boys who live next door or Tommy *are* to blame.'
4. If both subjects are singular and each requires a different form of the verb, the verb agrees with the subject immediately preceding it, e.g. 'Either you or I *am* to blame.' 'Either you or he *is* to blame.' 'Either he or you *are* to blame.'

These remarks apply equally to NEITHER . . . NOR and NOT ONLY . . . BUT ALSO.

See also AGREEMENT; NUMBER.

ejaculation another name for EXCLAMATION. See also INTERJECTION.

eke out to supplement; to increase one's scanty resources by taking on other work, usually equally unremunerative. 'She eked out her tiny pension by taking in washing.' It is incorrect to say: 'He eked out an existence by playing the concertina outside public houses.'

elder, older   Modern usage is to restrict *elder* and *eldest* to family relationships and to use *older* and *oldest* as the general comparative and superlative, e.g.:

(a) My elder brother is now in Canada.
(b) Elizabeth was the eldest of the three sisters.
(c) Elizabeth was the oldest girl in her class.
(d) St. Andrew's is an older church than All Saints'.

elegy   This derives from the Greek meaning 'mournful song'. Shelley's *Adonais*, a lament for the death of Keats in his twenty-sixth year, is an elegy. It contains these haunting lines:

He has out-soared the shadow of our night;
Envy and calumny and hate and pain,
And that unrest which men miscall delight,
Can touch him not and torture not again;
From the contagion of the world's slow stain
He is secure, and now can never mourn
A heart grown cold, a head grown grey in vain.

Perhaps the best-known elegy in the English language is Thomas Gray's *Elegy written in a Country Churchyard*, which begins:

The curfew tolls the knell of parting day,
   The lowing herd winds slowly o'er the lea,
The ploughman homeward plods his weary way,
   And leaves the world to darkness and to me.

eligible, illegible   We have always imagined that the use of the second instead of the first is a deliberate mistake made to raise a laugh, yet we have been solemnly informed by an old soldier that he hoped to be soon illegible for entry into Chelsea Hospital. Let it, then, be reiterated that *eligible* means 'fit to be chosen', and *illegible* means 'unreadable'.

elision   the suppression of a vowel or syllable in pronouncing a word, for the sake of METRE or EUPHONY, e.g.:

Star that bringest home the bee,
And sett'st the weary labourer free!
If any star shed peace, 'tis Thou
   That send'st it from above . . .
       (*Song to the Evening Star*, Thomas Campbell)

Note that 'bringest' in the first line is not elided, retaining its two syllables. At one time poets indicated elision in all words ending in *-ed* unless the *-ed* was to be separately pronounced, e.g. (a) 'The sedge has wither'd from the lake,' – Keats; (b) 'Still long'd for, never seen!' – Wordsworth. That the termination should be pronounced was indicated thus: *-éd*. We have both conventions in this line by Keats: 'Cool'd a long age in the deep-delvéd earth.' In modern practice the *e* is not elided when the word is pronounced as one syllable. The poet of today would write 'cooled', but he would still write 'deep-delvéd' – if he had the nerve.

ellipsis   the shortening of a sentence by the omission of a word or words that may be readily understood from the context or from general knowledge, e.g. (a) 'The first boy was reading, the second (boy was) writing a letter, and the third (boy was) playing in the garden.' (b) 'This is the racket (that) I bought from Peter. I bought it and then (I) wished I hadn't (bought it).'
Here are some examples of faulty ellipsis:

(a). *Wrong*: Mary's arithmetic is as good if not better than Jane's.
    Right: Mary's arithmetic is as good as if not better than Jane's.

The conjunction 'than' cannot do service for the omitted 'as'.

(b) *Wrong*: No government has ever or will ever adopt such a plan.
    Right: No government has ever adopted or will ever adopt such a plan.

The understood part of the verb must be the same as the expressed part; 'adopt' will not do service for the omitted 'adopted'.

(c) *Wrong*: A farmer and sailor look at the matter differently.
    Right: A farmer and a sailor look at the matter differently.

When two separate persons or things are intended, the article should be repeated. Here it looks as if the 'farmer and sailor' are somehow one and the same person.

(d) *Wrong*: The red and white jerseys of the two teams were soon
covered with mud.

Right: The red and the white jerseys of the two teams were
soon covered with mud.

(e) *Wrong*: Every student in the drawing class was given a hard
and soft pencil.

Right: Every student in the drawing class was given a hard
and a soft pencil.

The omission of 'the' before 'white' in (d) and 'a' before 'soft' in
(e) suggests that each jersey was coloured red and white, and that
each pencil was both hard and soft.

(f) *Wrong*: His life was long and his friends many.
Right: His life was long and his friends were many.

A singular verb cannot be made to do service for an understood
verb that is plural.

(g) *Wrong*: Please tell me whether he has or will be going to
America.

Right: Please tell me whether he has gone or will be going to
America.

As in (b) the understood part of the verb must be the same as the
part expressed.

See also ACCUSATIVE (OBJECTIVE) CASE.

elusion   see ALLUSION.

emend, emendation   terms used instead of *amend* and *amendment*
for the correction of manuscript, typescript and printed matter.

emigrate, immigrate   To *emigrate* is to leave one country and
settle in another. To *immigrate* is to come into one country from
another country to settle. Note *m* in *emigrate* and *mm* in *immigrate*.

eminent, imminent   The first means 'outstanding; distinguished;
well-known'. It comes from the Latin *minere*, 'to jut'. The second
means 'ready to fall or happen; threatening'. It comes from the
Latin *imminens*, 'overhanging'. 'Knowing that an attempt on his life
was imminent, the eminent politician sought the protection of the
police.'

emotion any of the feelings that move the mind. They include love, hate, fear, humiliation, scorn; and it is such emotions that EMOTIVE LANGUAGE seeks to exploit.

See also SENTIMENT, SENTIMENTALITY.

emotive language language tending to incite emotion. It is common in PROSODY, where it usually has a legitimate function, e.g.:

> With fingers weary and worn,
>   With eyelids heavy and red,
> A woman sat, in unwomanly rags,
>   Plying her needle and thread –
>   Stitch! stitch! stitch!
> In poverty, hunger, and dirt,
> And still with a voice of dolorous pitch
> She sang the 'Song of the Shirt'!
>
> (Hood)

It may also have a legitimate function in straightforward speech or prose. It is abused only when it is used to replace sound ARGUMENT; to sway the hearer or reader by playing on his emotions in order to influence his judgement; to gain his agreement by flattering him or by condemning others, e.g. (a) 'All fair-minded men will concede that ...' (b) 'It is only those whose actions are governed by self-interest who will assert that ...' In (a) we are arguing that our hearer must agree with our argument because he is fair-minded; in (b) we are arguing that he must agree with us because those who do not are governed by self-interest. We are, in fact, BEGGING THE QUESTION by using phrases that assume what is to be proved. There are many assumptive phrases of this kind: 'It is only too clear that ...' 'No thoughtful person will dispute that ...' 'It is beyond doubt that ...' 'Professional agitators will tell you that ...' 'It is only to be expected that vested interest ...' We should always be on our guard against these expressions, since they seek to persuade by flattery or derogation and not by proof.

Single words have the same assumptive quality, e.g.: 'Those who are genuinely patriotic are supporters of the United Nations.' There is no proof offered, but the matter is prejudged by the use of 'genuinely'. This loose use of words like 'true', 'sound', 'honest', 'proper', 'good', 'bad' needs watching in any argument where moral or aesthetic judgements are concerned. They become emotive words and are a form of FALLACY.

empirical   the opposite of theoretical; based on practical experience, experiment or observation. In a derogatory sense an *empiricist* may be a quack, one who relies too much on practical experience instead of on scientific training and study.

empty words   another name for structural words, as opposed to FULL WORDS or LEXICAL WORDS. See STRUCTURE.

enclose herewith   The second word is redundant.
   Wrong: I enclose herewith my cheque for five pounds.
   Right: I enclose my cheque for five pounds.

encyclopaedia (Gk. 'all-round education')   a book giving information on many subjects, arranged in alphabetical order. The most famous is the *Encyclopædia Britannica*, which is published in twenty-four volumes.
   The *Britannica*, first published in 1768, retains the VOWEL LIGATURE (æ) in its title, but the modern tendency is to use the spelling *encyclopaedia* or *encyclopedia*. In some works of reference, e.g. *Pears Cyclopaedia*, the abbreviated form is used.

end-stopped line   in PROSODY a line of verse, either blank or rhyming, with a definite pause at the end of it. Rossiter Johnson, the American author, wrote this and called it *Ninety-nine in the Shade*:

   O for a lodge in a garden of cucumbers!
      O for an iceberg or two at control!
   O for a vale which at midday the dew cumbers!
      O for a pleasure trip up to the Pole!

Here all four lines are end-stopped. When there is no pause at the end of a line and the sense runs on into the next, this is called ENJAMBMENT. See also COUPLET and HEROIC COUPLET.

English   The verb *to English* has a long history. Originally it meant 'to put in plain English'; for example, to reword a legal document so that it could be understood by the common man. Later, early in the nineteenth century, it came to mean 'to translate into English'. It then fell into disuse and not until quite recently does it seem to have come back into favour. An *Englisher* is not necessarily English; he may be a Frenchman, a Pole or a Ghanaian; anyone who translates into English is an Englisher.

enhance to heighten; to make larger; to raise the value of. It cannot be applied to a person.

Wrong: This struggling young artist was enhanced by his lifelike portrait of the Duchess of Surrey.

Right: The reputation of this struggling young artist was enhanced by his lifelike portrait of the Duchess of Surrey.

enjambment (or **enjambement**) This derives from the French meaning 'a flowing on; an encroachment'; literally 'a treading in', from *jambe*, meaning 'leg'. The English spelling and pronunciation are recommended. In PROSODY enjambment is the flowing over of one line into the next. An *enjambed line* is the opposite of an END-STOPPED LINE. Enjambment is particularly noticeable when it occurs in a poem written in HEROIC COUPLETS, for the true heroic couplet consists of two lines complete in themselves. Here is a paraphrase of the famous quotation from *Hamlet* about the 'enginer' being 'hoist with his own petar':

> Great sport and sweet retaliation 'tis
> To have the scientist blown up by his
> Own bomb. It teaches others to deplore
> The trade of those who forge the tools of war.

There is an enjambment in the third line, the first two words of which complete the sense of line 2. The same idea might be conveyed in 'closed' couplet form thus:

> Sweet irony it is when those who make
> Atomic bombs get blown up by mistake;
> Perhaps this teaches others to deplore
> The trade of those who forge the tools of war.

Enjambment is frequently met with in blank verse. Here is one of the many examples in Shakespeare's plays. In *The Famous History of the Life of King Henry VIII* two gentlemen meet in a street in Westminster on the occasion of the coronation of Anne Boleyn. The first gentleman answers one or two questions put to him by the other, who then asks what has become of Queen Katharine. The first gentleman replies:

> That I can tell you too. The Archbishop
> Of Canterbury, accompanied with other
> Learned and reverend fathers of his order,

> Held a late court at Dunstable, six miles off
> From Ampthill, where the princess lay; to which
> She was often cited by them, but appear'd not:
> And, to be short, for not appearance and
> The king's late scruple, by the main assent
> Of all these learned men she was divorced,
> And the late marriage made of none effect:
> Since when she was removed to Kimbolton,
> Where she remains now sick.

The second gentleman then obligingly completes the scansion of the last line by adding:

> Alas, good lady!

enlargement of the subject   see SUBJECT.

ensure, insure   The first means 'to make certain'; the second means 'to protect'.

- (a) To ensure that he caught the train, he arrived at the station half an hour early.
- (b) He insured his house against fire only a week before it was burnt down, which aroused the suspicions of the insurance company.

There is a further verb *assure*, commonly meaning 'to tell someone confidently', e.g. 'I assured him it was time'. This is also used in the insurance world. Most insurance companies still make a distinction between insuring property and assuring life; hence such titles as 'Hambro Life Assurance Society'.

envoy   This derives from the French meaning 'to send on the way'. In PROSODY it (or the alternative *L'Envoi*) is used to describe an author's postscript to a collection of verses, a postscript addressed either to the reader or to a patron referred to as 'Prince' or 'Princess' without any particular factual significance. Sometimes it forms the closing stanza, usually shorter than the rest, of a poem. For the sake of example, let us assume that a versifier has written a narrative poem, in the third person, about 'her' and 'him' – she a beautiful, innocent village maiden, he a young musician of promise and now very much in love. The ballad tells of their dreams of the future, when he, a virtuoso of world renown, will give her, his beloved wife, everything she wishes – furs, diamonds, a home in London's May-fair, and the finest car that money can buy. The poet then ends with:

L'ENVOI
Princess, it was today through Berkeley Square
  In mink you glided in your Cadillac,
  Not noticing (I thought to turn my back)
The shabby man who played the cornet there.

epic   a heroic poem of lofty style, involving great issues and glorify-ing the hero and, through him, mankind. Milton's *Paradise Lost* is an epic, as are the *Odyssey* and the *Iliad* of Homer.

epigram   a saying that conveys much meaning in a few words. The American poet, George Birdseye, once wrote this QUATRAIN:

The diamond's virtues well might grace
  The epigram and both excel
In brilliancy and smallest space,
  And power to cut, as well.

If it passes into popular culture an epigram becomes a PROVERB. Epigrams are not so much figures of speech as a method of expressing oneself in a pithy, striking way, e.g. (a) 'Revenge is a kind of wild justice.' (b) 'The road to hell is paved with good intentions.'

epilogue   By comparison with a PROLOGUE an epilogue comes at the end of a play, poem, etc. After a play it is often delivered by an actor who has taken part in the performance, as with the epilogue spoken by Prospero at the end of Shakespeare's *The Tempest*. In poetry, perhaps the best known is Robert Browning's *Epilogue to Asolando*, which was published on the day of Browning's death. It includes the famous lines:

One who never turned his back but marched breast
    forward,
  Never doubted clouds would break,
Never dreamed, though right were worsted, wrong
    would triumph,
Held we fall to rise, are baffled to fight better,
      Sleep to wake.

epitaph (Gk. 'on a tomb')   a short description, in prose or verse, of a dead person and sometimes inscribed on his tomb. In Covent Garden church is this epitaph on Claude Duval, the French high-wayman, who came to England during the Restoration and, having made for himself a reputation as a highway robber and a womaniser, was executed at Tyburn in 1670:

> Here lies DuVall; reader, if male thou art,
> Look to thy purse; if female, to thy heart.

epithet   a noun or adjective expressing some quality or attribute, e.g. William *the Conqueror*, Warwick *the King-maker*, Ethelred *the Un-ready*, *doubting* Thomas, *envious* Casca. Some epithets are abusive, e.g. 'You *stupid* idiot!'

epitome (ipitⁱəmi) (Gk. 'to cut short')   an abridgement or sum-mary of some longer work. 'Epitomes,' wrote Francis Bacon, 'are the moths and corruptions of learning.' Figuratively, an epitome is something that is a miniature representation of something else, e.g.:

> A man so various that he seem'd to be
> Not one, but all mankind's epitome:
> Stiff in opinions, always in the wrong,
> Was everything by starts and nothing long;
> But in the course of one revolving moon,
> Was chymist [chemist], fiddler, statesman, and buffoon.

This was John Dryden's opinion of George Villiers, second Duke of Buckingham.

Today we write a summary or PRÉCIS rather than an epitome of a long passage. We restrict the word *epitome* to its figurative use.

epode   the third and final stanza of a Pindaric ode. See ODE.

equable, equitable   The first means 'without variation; regular; steady; calm'. The second means 'reasonable; fair; disinterested; impartial'. For example, Mr Smith owed Mr Jones two hundred pounds, which he could not repay all at once. Knowing Mr Jones's equable temperament he was confident that he could come to some equitable arrangement with him, whereby the debt could be repaid by monthly instalments of 50 pence. That these hopes were dashed when Mr Jones took Mr Smith to court does not invalidate the dis-tinction between these two adjectives.

equally This means 'in equal shares or proportion; without difference; alike'. It is correctly followed by 'with', but not by 'as', e.g.:

> *Wrong*: King William III was ruler of England equally as his wife, Queen Mary II.
>
> *Right*: King William III was the ruler of England equally with his wife, Queen Mary II.

To use 'equally as' instead of one or the other is to be guilty of TAUTOLOGY, e.g.:

> *Wrong*: He is certainly a fine singer, but I have heard others equally as good.
>
> *Right*: He is certainly a fine singer, but I have heard others equally good.
>
> *or*: He is certainly a fine singer, but I have heard others as good.

equivocation (L. 'of equal voice')   an expression having two or more meanings. 'Equivocation,' wrote William Penn, 'is halfway to lying, as lying the whole way to hell.' To equivocate is to speak in a way that is intentionally vague or ambiguous. Mr Smith was asked his opinion of imperialists. He replied, 'It takes all sorts to make a world.' His answer was equivocal, leaving the questioner in doubt as to Mr Smith's real feelings.

In ARGUMENT equivocation is a form of FALLACY.

errata See CORRIGENDUM.

esoteric (esoute^lrik)   private; confidential; understood only by the select few. 'The play, as I remember,' says Hamlet, 'pleased not the million; 'twas caviare to the general.' Anything esoteric is 'caviare to the general'.

especial see SPECIAL.

-ess a suffix denoting a female, e.g. manageress, actress, steward-ess, tigress, heiress. It has been fairly active till recently when WOMEN'S LIB has frowned upon the sex distinction and some -ess words.

essay a short composition in prose on any subject. Great essayists of the past were Montaigne, Francis Bacon, Richard Steele, Joseph

Addison, Samuel Johnson, Oliver Goldsmith and Charles Lamb. Later came Robert Louis Stevenson, Hilaire Belloc, G. K. Chesterton, the young J. B. Priestley and others. In the modern rush we have too little time for this leisurely pastime. Some might think this no bad thing, since essays were frequently the elaboration of trivialities and had the unfortunate result of making written English affected and pretentious.

et cetera (or etcetera)   This is borrowed straight from the Latin and means 'and the rest'. It is nearly always used in its abbreviated form *etc.*, which is added to a list to indicate that there are others besides those mentioned.

'The conifers – pines, firs, larches, yews, etc. – are so called because they are cone-bearing.'

When the list is preceded by *e.g.* or *for example*, it is unnecessary to add *etc.* at the end.

Although the practice is not so frowned upon as it once was, it is advisable to avoid adding *etc.* to a list of names, as here: Mr Smith, Mr Brown, Mr Jones, etc. It is better to refer to 'Mr Smith, Mr Brown, Mr Jones and others' (or 'and several others', or 'and a number of others'), and to reserve *etc.* for lists of things other than persons or abstractions.

In *Modern English Usage* we find this: 'To resort to etc. in sentences of a literary character (*His faults of temper, etc. are indeed easily accounted for*) is amateurish, slovenly and incongruous.' The important words here are 'of a literary character'. In lists of items, e.g. 'tools, nails, screws, etc.', its use is not objectionable, but in lists of, say, virtues, e.g. 'patience, charity, kindliness, etc.', it *is* objectionable.

Nor should *etc.* be used in such sentences as: 'By way of excuse he said that his alarm clock had not gone off, that he had overslept in consequence, that he had mislaid his office keys, that he had slipped on a piece of orange peel on the way to the station, that the train had been late, etc.' It is better to bring this dismal recital to a close with 'and so on' or 'and so forth'.

There is a tendency among the uneducated to say 'and cetera'. This SOLECISM should be avoided in conversation. And if *etc.* has to be used in written work, once is enough. The duplication *etc., etc.* is inexcusable, because unnecessary.

-ette   a suffix denoting a female, e.g. *usherette, suffragette*, or denoting a diminutive form, e.g. kitchenette, novelette. As a feminine ending it is no longer active, whereas -ESS is. As a diminutive it has been outpaced by MINI.

See also DIMINUTIVES.

etymology (Gk. 'true description') in the grammar of the classics, the science treating of the meanings, history and inflexion of words. Nowadays it means an account of the origin and history of a word – or, roughly, its DERIVATION. See also PRONUNCIATION.

euphemism (jufəˈmizm) a FIGURE OF SPEECH. When we seek to hide the real nature of something unpleasant, or use a mild and indirect term for a blunt and direct one, we are said to commit a euphemism. It is prudery or a false sense of refinement that causes us to use *paying guest* for *boarder* or *lodger*; *domestic* for *servant*; *passing* for *death*; *undertaker* for *funeral arranger*; *tipsy* for *drunk*; *serviette* for *table napkin*; *turf accountant* or *commission agent* for *bookmaker*; *expectorate* for *spit*; *perspiration* for *sweat*. Sometimes a euphemism can be justified. In certain circumstances it may be necessary in order to spare a person's feelings. But it can be overdone, and once it is started there is seemingly no end. Up to the end of the eighteenth century the Old English word *belly* was perfectly respectable. But 'refined' people began to think it vulgar and used *stomach* instead. Then *stomach* too became rather vulgar and the faint-hearted talked about *tummies* instead, or referred to their indisposition as *tummy trouble* when they were suffering from the old-fashioned *belly-ache*. Luckily, we are now almost back where we started and are using *belly* once more.

The ADVERTISING industry has been prolific with euphemisms as it sought to avoid offending potential customers, e.g. *the fuller figure* instead of *fat*, *compact* for *small*, *budget* for *cheap*, *used* for *second-hand*. Any women's magazine will provide many examples for those with an inquiring mind.

euphony (jufˈəni) (Gk. 'having a pleasing sound') In practice the word refers to the tendency to phonetic change for ease of pronunciation: it is not a pleasing sound we are after, but a way of saying a word more quickly and with a minimum of effort. For example, it is for the sake of euphony that the longer words ending in -*ate* drop the -*ate* before adding -*able*, e.g. *appreciate* – *appreciable*, *calculate* – *calculable*, *estimate* – *estimable*, *navigate* – *navigable*. And it is for the sake of euphony that we have added an *n* to *tobaccoist* and now call him a *tobacconist*.

See also ELISION.

even   This adjective can change the sense of a sentence according to its position in it. This is discussed under ADVERB.

every day, everyday   The first is an adverbial phrase of time; the second is an adjective, e.g.:

   (a) He lunched at the same restaurant every day.
   (b) It was his everyday habit to lunch at the same restaurant.

everyone, every one   The examples below will help to distinguish between these.

   (a) Everyone much enjoyed the new-laid eggs we had for breakfast.
   (b) The grocer said they were new-laid eggs, but every one was bad.

evince   This verb should be avoided when the meaning is merely 'to show'. It smacks of JOURNALESE to write: 'His Royal Highness evinced great interest in the new Boys' Club.' The word should be confined to the meaning 'to show quality', e.g. 'His writings evince wide knowledge of archaeology.'

exceedingly, excessively   The first means 'greatly; extremely'; the second means 'immoderately; outrageously'. The verb *to exceed* means 'to surpass'; the noun *excess* means 'too much'. For example:

   (a) He welcomed me in such an exceedingly cordial manner that I was glad I called upon him.
   (b) He welcomed me in such an excessively cordial manner that I suspected his sincerity.

except   The misuse of this preposition as a conjunction is treated under PREPOSITION.

exceptional, exceptionable   Be careful how you use these adjectives. *Exceptional* means 'unusual', e.g. 'It was exceptional weather for the time of the year.' *Exceptionable* means 'objectionable', descriptive of something to which exception can be taken, e.g. 'The chairman of the committee regarded Mr Smith's remarks as exceptionable and asked him to withdraw them.'

exclamation, ejaculation Grammatically these are known as INTERJECTIONS. They are not exactly synonymous. An exclamation or 'crying out' can be long or short, whilst an ejaculation (deriving from the Latin for 'javelin' or 'dart'), an utterance 'thrown out' suddenly, is short. 'Damn!' 'Heavens!' 'Hell!' 'Fire!' 'Help!' are ejaculations. Exclamations are usually expressions of surprise or anxiety, more leisurely expressed than ejaculations, e.g. 'Goodness gracious! Look at the time!' 'What a lovely dress you are wearing!' 'Don't say we've missed the train!' 'Hullo, Jack! Fancy meeting you!' Some interjections can be either exclamations or ejaculations, depending upon the state of mind of the speaker. For example, 'Oh dear!' may be an exclamation of mild distress, e.g. 'Oh dear! I've broken my pencil', or an ejaculation of great distress on hearing bad news. 'Good Lord' is an exclamation in 'Am I married? Good Lord, no!' It is an ejaculation when used by itself to express sudden surprise.

exclamation mark the punctuation mark (!) used after all individual exclamations (or ejaculations) and exclamatory sentences, e.g. 'Good-o!' 'The devil take the man!' 'Milton! thou shouldst be living at this hour.' 'What wonderful weather we are having!' The exclamation mark is also used to indicate a special intonation of scorn, disgust, amusement, e.g. 'And he was supposed to be an expert!'

Like pepper and salt, exclamation marks should be used with restraint, or they will spoil the flavour. Beyond a certain point they will not add to the excitement of a descriptive passage: they will detract from it by making it look ridiculous, thus: 'The bull rushed at me across the field! I turned to run – and stumbled! In a flash I was on my feet again! I must reach the gate! How far away it seemed! The bull bellowed! He was gaining on me! I ran like a hare! Then I stumbled again!' – and so on, until we hope the bull will toss you into the next field.

There are certain words that call for exclamation marks on some occasions but not others. The marks are better omitted when the word is said in such a way that the speaker is clearly not exclaiming anything, e.g.:

(a) 'Hullo,' muttered the boy in reply, embarrassed by my greeting.

(b) 'Splendid,' murmured the professor, his mind on other things.

(c) We were, alas, never to meet again.

Others of this kind are 'Good-bye', 'Good morning', 'Good afternoon', etc.; 'Oh'; 'Glad to see you'. Conventional greetings do not need exclamation marks, which should be reserved for those occasions when the greetings are not conventional.

Some writers, especially those who prepare crossword puzzles, use the exclamation mark to indicate they have made a little joke.

The use of exclamation marks in pairs ('Was my face red!!') is not recommended, except perhaps in letters to friends.

See also INVERTED COMMAS; O, OH; REPORTED SPEECH.

expertise   This is the French word for a survey carried out by specially appointed surveyors (*experts nommés exprès*). *Faire une expertise* means 'to make a survey'. As is our way, we have stolen this word and given it a new meaning (see VOGUE WORDS), making it synonymous with 'expertness', e.g. 'The reconditioning of the ancient building was carried out with great expertise.' 'Young Harry's expertise in playing truant won the admiration of his schoolfellows.' Many men of letters prefer the down-to-earth English 'know-how'.

The word is pronounced as in the French: ekspə:ti:zᶦ.

explicit, implicit   The first means 'plainly expressed; clearly stated'. The second means 'implied; not plainly expressed, but meant indirectly'. It also means 'accepted without question'.

(a) He gave his staff explicit instructions not to leave the premises until he returned.
(b) That they resented these instructions was implicit in the silence with which they received them.
(c) I have implicit faith in your ability.

exposition   a setting forth of some matter to make it clear; a type of composition that aims at explaining. In *The Merchant of Venice* Shylock says to Portia:

It doth appear you are a worthy judge;
You know the law, your exposition
Hath been most sound.

extension of the predicate   see PREDICATE.

extenuate This derives from the Latin meaning 'to make thin'. We use it in the sense of 'to palliate; to excuse in part; to make a fault or an offence seem less than it is'. It must, however, be understood that it is the fault or the offence that is extenuated, not the person who committed it, e.g.:

Wrong: The lawyer extenuated his client by pleading extreme provocation.

Right: The lawyer extenuated his client's misdeed by pleading extreme provocation.

Extenuating circumstances are those that partially excuse an offence, as when a doctor exceeds the speed limit on his way to see a patient.

eye rhyme in PROSODY two words that seem to the eye to rhyme because of similarity of spelling, but have not similar sounds when spoken, e.g. *man – swan, great – treat, comb – bomb*. Here is a limerick from *Punch* that touches on the matter:

A certified poet from Slough,
Whose methods of rhyming were rough,
    Retorted, 'I see
    That the letters agree
And if that's not sufficient I'm through.'
                (C. W.)

See also RHYME and ASSONANCE.

F

fable a FIGURE OF SPEECH; a short story in prose or verse written so that a certain moral lesson may be learnt from it. Frequently the characters of the story are animals behaving like human beings, rather than human beings themselves. Fables may be very short stories as in the case of Aesop's fables, or they may run to several pages as in the case of *The Nun's Priest's Tale* by Chaucer. A writer of fables is known as a *fabulist*. The adjective from *fable* gave us the recent VOGUE WORD *fabulous*.

fabulous   has such meanings as 'relating to fables', 'legendary', 'mythical', 'exaggerated', 'incredible', 'beyond belief'. Recently it has become one of those OVERWORKED WORDS, e.g. 'It was a fabulous evening. The tickets were fabulously expensive, but the dinner was fabulous, the band was fabulous, and we got back home fabulously late. I've a fabulous headache this morning.'

fallacy   This derives from the Latin meaning 'to deceive'. It is not necessarily a deliberate attempt to deceive; sometimes it is the result of ignorance or error. We can usefully divide it into three classes, as follows:

1. In the strict sense of LOGIC a fallacy is any violation of the rules of the science of reasoning. These logical fallacies are dealt with under SYLLOGISM.

2. In the wider sense of ARGUMENT a fallacy is either a misstatement of fact or the wrong use of words. These are known as:

(a) *Material Fallacies*, which are discussed under ARGUING IN A CIRCLE; BEGGING THE QUESTION; FALSE ANALOGY; IRRELEVANCY; NON SEQUITUR; PREJUDICE; RATIONALISING; RHETORICAL QUESTION.

(b) *Verbal Fallacies*, which are discussed under AMBIGUITY; EMOTIVE LANGUAGE; EQUIVOCATION; INNUENDO; SOPHISTRY; SPECIOSITY; SUGGESTIO FALSI.

3. In a more general sense a fallacy is an erroneous idea. For example, it is a fallacy to assume that a man is happy because he is rich, just as it is a fallacy to assume that a man in a black suit is an undertaker because all undertakers wear black suits. It is also a fallacy to suppose that one must not end a sentence with a preposition. A *popular fallacy* is a general belief for which there is no factual foundation. That lightning never strikes twice in the same place is a popular fallacy.

See also PATHETIC FALLACY.

false analogy   the use of ANALOGY to establish unjustified conclusions. For example, we are justified in drawing an analogy between the branches of a family and those of a tree; but we are not justified in arguing that, because the smaller branches of a tree have to be lopped from time to time, and the larger ones sawn off the trunk if they become dangerous or inconvenient, it is perfectly

logical to adopt the same procedure with the branches of a family.
In ARGUMENT false analogy is a FALLACY.

farce   a form of drama in which the probability of what happens is
sacrificed to the main aim of exciting laughter; very broad COMEDY.
Charley's Aunt is a farce; the Laurel and Hardy film comedies are
farces. French farce, exemplified by the work of Feydeau, was suc-
cessfully revived in London theatres and on TV in 1970; it is much
concerned with marital infidelity and surprising encounters in bed-
rooms.

farther, further   These have been so confused that usage now
makes no distinction between them. Some careful writers, however,
like to reserve *farther* for 'greater distance', and *further* for 'more' or
'additional', e.g. 'A further point in his favour is that he has
travelled farther than we have.'

feasible   This derives from the Latin meaning 'able to be done'.
It is not always synonymous with *possible* or *probable*, e.g.:
   Right: 'To reach the roof by climbing up the drainpipe is
         feasible, but I don't recommend it.'
   Wrong: 'It's just feasible that he will come, even at this late hour.'
         (Use 'possible'.)
   Wrong: 'It's quite feasible that this foul weather has delayed him.'
         (Use 'probable'.)
See also VOGUE WORDS.

feature   an adjective (or noun) used to describe a newspaper
article (as distinct from a news story) or the main film at a cinema.
See DOCUMENTARY.

feminine ending   continuing a line of blank verse beyond the
final stressed syllable, e.g. 'To be / or not / to be: / that is / the
ques/tion.'

feminine rhyme   when the stressed syllables containing the
rhyme are followed by unstressed syllables that are identical, e.g. –
flatter – *matter*, *dancing* – *prancing*. See RHYME.

ferment, foment   Both verbs derive from the Latin, the first from
fermentum, yeast (from *fervere*, to boil); the second from *fomentum* (from

fovere, to warm), anything used for the purpose of warming, hence a warm application to a diseased part of the body. Though commonly regarded as synonymous when the meaning is 'to stir up trouble', they should be distinguished in careful writing, *fomenting* being confined to the application of hot dressings.

fewer, less   It is a useful distinction to use *fewer* for countable quantities and *less* for uncountable quantities. 'There has been less rain today, so that fewer people are carrying umbrellas.'

fidus Achates   In Virgil's epic poem, the *Aeneid*, the faithful follower of the Trojan hero Aeneas was Achates. The term *fidus* (faithful) *Achates* is now used when referring to a devoted supporter or henchman. For example, the *fidus Achates* of Sherlock Holmes was Dr Watson.

figures   see NUMERALS.

figures of speech   Figurative language is any departure from plain statement or the literal use of words. Each of the different types of departure from literal language is called a figure of speech. They are treated under ALLEGORY; ANTITHESIS; APOSTROPHE (2); CLIMAX; EUPHEMISM; FABLE; HYPERBOLE; INNUENDO; INVERSION; IRONY; LITOTES; MEIOSIS; METONYMY; MIXED METAPHOR; OXYMORON; PARABLE; PARADOX; PERSONIFICATION; PROLEPSIS; PUN; RHETORICAL QUESTION; SIMILE, METAPHOR; SYNECDOCHE.
  See also LITERAL, LITERALLY.

finite verbs   main verbs which have person, number and tense, and which can be used as a PREDICATE. They are complete verbs that are distinguished from the non-finite verbs, i.e. participles, gerunds and infinitives, which are incomplete.
  See also ANOMALOUS FINITES, TENSE.

first, firstly   In enumeration, *first* is technically correct, e.g. 'The reasons why I do not watch television are: first, it tires the eyes; secondly, it wastes time; and thirdly, I can't afford to buy a set.' Some modern grammarians consider it pedantic to deny that there is such an adverb as *firstly*, whilst others still prefer *first, secondly, thirdly*.

flowed, flown Do not confuse these two. They come from different verbs, the first from *to flow*, the second from *to fly*. Birds *fly*, rivers *flow*.

Wrong: Much water has flown under the bridge since then.
Right: Much water has flowed under the bridge since then.

foment see FERMENT.

foolscap a sheet of paper for printing, writing or drawing, approximately $13\frac{1}{2}$ in. wide by 17 in. long. The size *foolscap octavo*, which is a foolscap sheet folded three times to give eight leaves $4\frac{1}{4}$ in. wide by $6\frac{3}{4}$ in. long, is that used for most paperbacks and pocket editions of books. Foolscap typing paper is usually 8 in. wide (the same as quarto) by 13 in. long. The word 'foolscap' derives from the cap and bells of a court jester used as a watermark by the paper-makers of old.

See also OCTAVO; QUARTO.

foot In PROSODY a line of verse is scanned not by breaking it down into syllables but by dividing it into metrical units known as *feet*. A foot is one accented syllable with one or more unaccented syllables attached to it. For example, here are two lines from Rudyard Kipling's *Recessional*, each line containing four feet, with the stress on the second syllable of each foot:

The tu/mult and / the shout/ing dies;
The Capt/ains and / the Kings / depart

See also METRE; SCANNING.

footnote When we come to a word or name that has an asterisk (*) printed beside it, we glance down to the bottom of the page, where we find a footnote giving us further information or comment. Should there be a second footnote, our attention is drawn to it by means of a dagger or OBELUS (†). Where there are several footnotes to a page, the references are usually numbered [1], [2], [3], etc. in small figures. Footnotes are very useful because the information or comment they contain is not always directly connected with the matter under discussion and their inclusion in the text might interfere with the continuity. Here is an example:

They were married in the village church* on 16th March 1861 and in the following week sailed from Southampton on a voyage that was to take them halfway round the world.

* Destroyed by a German bomb in World War II.

forbear   As a verb this means 'to refrain from; to hold oneself in check'. The past tense is *forbore* and the past participle is *forborne*. Unlike *forego – forgo* below, in which there is a distinction between the prefixes *fore* (meaning 'in front') and *for-* (meaning 'abstention'), the noun *forbear*, meaning an ancestor (a 'for-be-er') does not take the *e* in modern English usage, although Americans still spell it *forebear*.

for ever, forever   Use the first; although Americans use the second, there is no justification for it in English. 'Forever and ever' should be banned for ever.

forego, forgo   The first means 'to go before'; the second 'to go without', e.g. (a) 'The speaker added that his foregoing remarks about non-attendance at meetings did not apply to those now present in the hall.' (b) 'To save money for the wedding he decided to forgo his summer holidays.'

foreword   the introduction to a book, usually written by someone other than the author, whereas the PREFACE is usually written by the author.

forlorn hope   We use this phrase when referring to an enterprise that is almost certain to fail, so little hope is there of success. It has, however, nothing to do with 'forlorn' or 'hope', for it derives from the Dutch *verloren hoop*, which means a 'lost troop', a picked body of men sent ahead of the main force to begin an attack and therefore unlikely to survive.

format   a printing term for the shape and size of a book, pamphlet, etc., nowadays loosely applied to any lay-out on paper.

former, latter   The first of two things is referred to as the *former*; the second of them as the *latter*. Neither may be used when there are more than two things; we must then use *first* and *last*. In other words, *former* and *latter* are comparatives, whilst *first* and *last* are superlatives. Their use, however, produces a very stodgy, artificial effect, and Dr Johnson's warning should be heeded: 'As long as you have the use of your pen, never, Sir, be reduced to that shift.' See COMPARISON, DEGREES OF.

forward, forwards Modern usage seems to prefer the first as the adverb, but the second is by no means obsolete; in fact there is a natural tendency to use it in such contexts as: 'I'm not running backwards and forwards every five minutes just to please you.' See also BACKWARD, BACKWARDS.

fount a printing term for the complete assortment of all characters of one size and design of a type. Americans write it *font*, which is how British printers pronounce *fount*.

four-letter words These are the short words, often Old or Middle English in origin, used to describe parts of the body or some bodily functions which convention prefers to veil in decent obscurity. An extension of their use, often indicative of the emotional state of the user, is as participial adjectives of abuse or derogation. In the 1930s a play with the title *One Damn Thing after Another* was often billed as *One D— Thing after Another*. Such prudery seems positively Victorian as viewed from the 1970s, a decade which saw the open emergence into print and drama of all the taboo words.

Frankenstein Mary Wollstonecraft Shelley was the second wife of the poet. In 1818 she published a book called *Frankenstein, or The Modern Prometheus*, the story of a university student who creates a monster, gives it life and develops a loathing for it. Frankenstein was not the name of the monster but the name of the student, Victor Frankenstein.

free verse SEE VERS LIBRE.

French words and phrases For nearly three hundred years after William of Normandy conquered England in 1066, Norman French was the language of the English court, nobility, law courts, learned professions and school, so that modern English contains many hundreds of French words or their derivatives (see DERIVA-TION). For example, all the following are of French origin: *abbot*, *assize, beef, charity, comedy, courtesy, draper, haberdasher, humour, justice, mutton, pork, repentance, tragedy, trespass, veal, verdict.* The list below is not of the words that have been absorbed by our language so that we no longer recognise them as French derivatives; it is a list of some of the words and phrases used by us, knowing them to be French, just as we use, for example, *hoi polloi*, knowing it to be Greek for 'the rabble', and *auf Wiedersehen*, knowing it to be German for 'till we meet again'. Entries marked with an asterisk are treated more fully under their own headings in the body of the book.

adieu, farewell; good-bye

aide-de-camp (ADC), an army officer acting as assistant to a general

aide-mémoire, note made as an aid to memory

à la (mode de), after the fashion of. We use it colloquially in such contexts as: 'If you think you can dictate to me, *à la* Hitler, you're very much mistaken!'

à la carte, by the bill of fare, with a stated price for each dish. The customer pays for such dishes as he chooses. See *table d'hôte*

à la mode, in the fashion; fashionable

amour, love; *amours*, love affairs

amour-propre, self-esteem; conceit

ancien régime, the old order of things

*à propos, to the purpose

arrière-pensée, not an afterthought, but a mental reservation, a thought not put into words

attaché, a member of the staff of an ambassador. An attaché case is a small leather case

au fait, well acquainted with a matter

au revoir, until we meet again

avant garde, advance guard; cultural pioneers

à votre santé, to your health

beau monde, the people of fashion

* *belles-lettres*, polite literature

bête noire, 'black beast'; a bugbear; a pet aversion

bêtise, stupidity; a stupid thing; a silly act

billet-doux, a love-letter

blasé, bored; sick of pleasure

bonhomie, good nature

bon mot, a clever remark

bonne bouche, a tasty morsel; a titbit

bon ton, good taste; good style

bon vivant, one fond of luxury and good food (*bon viveur* is not a
French phrase).

bon voyage, a good voyage or journey, e.g. 'I went down to the
docks to wish him *bon voyage* when he left for the Far East.'

bric-à-brac, odds and ends

café, coffee; a small restaurant; *café au lait,* coffee with milk; *café
noir,* black coffee (i.e. without milk)

carte blanche, full power; a free hand, e.g. 'I gave the builder *carte
blanche* to do whatever repairs he thought necessary.'

chaperon, a married or elderly woman who accompanies a girl on
social occasions

chargé d'affaires, diplomat who acts in place of an ambassador

chauffeur, a fireman or stoker. In modern usage a driver of a car
who is paid for his services

chef-d'œuvre, a masterpiece

chic, literally, a knack (*Il a du chic,* 'He is skilful, a dab hand'), but
used today in the sense of 'stylish', e.g. 'She wore a chic dress.'

* *cliché,* hackneyed phrase

comme il faut, as it should be

confrère, a fellow member; a colleague

contretemps, an unfortunate happening

coup de grâce, the finishing stroke; merciful killing, e.g. 'The poor
creature had broken its back, so I gave it the *coup de grâce* with a
bullet from my rifle.' The phrase is used figuratively in such
contexts as: 'In the third game Mr Jones administered the *coup
de grâce* with the ace of trumps.'

coup d'état, a change of government by sudden and violent means,
e.g. 'By this swift *coup d'état,* the army gained control of the
whole country.'

crème de la crème, 'cream of the cream'; the very best

cuisine, literally 'kitchen', but also used in the sense of the style in
which food is cooked or prepared, e.g. 'This little restaurant is
famous for its cuisine.' *Haute cuisine,* the *crème de la crème* of cooking

cul-de-sac, 'bottom of the bag'; a blind alley, open at one end only

débris (usually without the accent in English), scattered fragments;
piles of rubbish

début, a first appearance, e.g. 'Sir John Gielgud made his *début* at
the Old Vic in 1921, when he played the part of the herald in
Henry V.' The accent is sometimes omitted in English

déjeuner, breakfast; sometimes also luncheon

* *dénouement*, 'unknotting', the final solution of a play, novel, etc., e.g. 'In the exciting *dénouement*, the most unlikely character turns out to be the murderer.' The accent is sometimes omitted in English

de rigueur, required by etiquette or custom

de trop, too much; not wanted; in the way, e.g. 'Feeling that I was *de trop* I quietly withdrew and left the young couple alone.'

Dieu et mon droit, 'God and my right', the motto of Richard I, meaning that he held his right from God alone. Since then it has been inscribed on the royal standard of English kings and queens

double entendre, a double meaning; words that can be taken two ways, one of them indelicate or vulgar

doyen, senior; oldest member, e.g. 'The 87-year-old Ambassador for Ruritania is the doyen of the Diplomatic Corps.'

éclair, a finger-shaped puff of pastry filled with cream

élite (or *elite*), the best people; the *crème de la crème*

embarras du choix, embarrassment of choice; too many from which to choose

embarras de richesse, embarrassment of wealth; having so much of something that one does not know what to do with it

en bloc, in a lump; in bulk; wholesale, e.g. 'The ship's cargo was bought *en bloc* by a trading company as soon as she reached port.'

encore, again, once more; a demand for the repetition of a song, dance, etc. Oddly enough, the French themselves do not cry 'Encore!' but 'Bis!', which means 'Twice!'

en famille, at home; with one's own family

enfant terrible, a terrible child, one who asks awkward questions at the wrong moment, or repeats remarks he has overheard, e.g.: 'What's a wolf in sheep's clothing, Mr Johnson?' 'Why do you ask, Tommy?' 'Because that's what Dad says you are.'

en masse, in a mass; all together, e.g. 'On the approach of the enemy, the inhabitants fled from the city *en masse*.'

ennui, tedium; boredom

en passant, in passing; by the way

en rapport, in sympathy with

en route, on the way; bound for

entente cordiale, a friendly understanding or agreement

entourage, a retinue; a group of advisers, attendants, friends, etc., e.g. 'The crown prince and his entourage went riding in the royal park.'

entrée, right of admittance; freedom of entry; also a dish served between the fish course and the main course at a formal dinner

entre nous, between ourselves, e.g. 'I don't think she will make him a good wife, but that's *entre nous*. Don't tell them I said so!'

esprit de corps, the spirit of loyalty and comradeship among the members of a group, regiment, etc.

etiquette, the rules of behaviour in polite society. Professional etiquette governs the conduct of doctors, lawyers, accountants, etc.

fait accompli, an accomplished fact; a thing done and no longer worth making a fuss about

faute de mieux, for want of anything better

faux pas, a false step; an indiscretion; an error of judgement

fiancé (feminine *fiancée*), one who is engaged to be married

force majeure, superior force; greater strength, e.g. 'It's no use reasoning with those people. The only argument they understand is *force majeure*.'

* *gourmand, gourmet*. The first eats greedily; the second with discrimination

habitué, a frequenter; a regular customer

Honi soit qui mal y pense. This is the Old French for 'Shame be to him who thinks evil'. It is the motto of the Order of the Garter

hors de combat. Once translated by an English schoolboy as 'war-horse', this means literally 'out of the fight'; disabled

hors-d'œuvre, a side dish served as a relish at the beginning of a meal

idée fixe, a fixed idea, one that no persuasion or argument can alter

impasse, a blind alley; a deadlock

laisser-faire, the principle of non-interference, especially by a government in commercial matters

mal à propos (Anglicized malapropos), out of place; inopportune. See under MALAPROPISM

matinée, an afternoon performance, either theatrical or musical

mauvais quart d'heure, 'a bad quarter of an hour'; a short but unpleasant experience or interview

mauvais sujet, a worthless fellow; a scoundrel; a black sheep

menu, a bill of fare in a restaurant

messieurs, gentlemen, the plural of *monsieur*. Used in English in the abbreviated form *Messrs* (no full stop) when addressing a letter to more than one person, e.g. 'Messrs Taylor & Lawson' *mise en scène*, the scenery and general setting of a play. Figuratively, the surroundings of an event

naïve (usually without the diaeresis in English), artless, natural, ingenuous

* *née*, born

négligé (sometimes spelt *negligee* in English), informal dress; a woman's loose gown

noblesse oblige, meaning that rank brings obligations

nom de guerre, literally a 'war-name', but used figuratively for an assumed name under which one follows a calling or profession, e.g. 'When George Edward Wade began his long career as a music-hall comedian he adopted George Robey as his *nom de guerre*.'

nom de plume, a pen name. See under PSEUDONYM

nonpareil, without equal; matchless

outré, exaggerated; extravagant

panache, literally a tuft or plume worn in a helmet; figuratively it means 'display; swagger; bounce'

papier mâché, 'chewed paper'; paper pulp moulded into shape and used for various purposes, such as egg boxes

par excellence, pre-eminently; above all

parole, a military word meaning a promise not to escape, given by a prisoner to gain a measure of freedom

parvenu, a newcomer; an upstart

pâté de foie gras, a paste or a patty made with the livers of geese fattened for that purpose

patois, dialect

pièce de résistance, the centrepiece, of a meal, for example. It is also used in such contexts as: 'The *pièce de résistance* of the evening was a magnificent fireworks display.'

pied-à-terre, 'foot on the ground', a temporary lodging; a *pied-à-terre* in London might be a room or flat used in the week by someone whose home is in the country.

poste restante, letters sent to a post office to be called for

pourboire, 'drink money'; a tip

* *précis*, an abstract or summary

protégé, a man, usually young, under the protection of another man (fem. *protégée*)

purée, a thick soup made by pressing peas, beans, etc. through a sieve

qui s'excuse s'accuse, he who excuses himself accuses himself *qui vive*, 'Who lives?', a sentry's challenge. To be on the *qui vive* is to keep a sharp look-out

Répondez, s'il vous plaît (abbreviated R.S.V.P.), 'Reply, if you please', printed on invitations to dinners, parties, etc.

résumé, a summary

Revenons à nos moutons, 'Let us return to our sheep.' Figuratively, 'Let us return to our subject,' said when the conversation has drifted away from the main topic. The quotation is from *Patelin*, by the French dramatist, Pierre Blanchet (*c.* 1459–1519)

riposte, a smart retort

roué, a rake; a profligate

sabotage, deliberate damage, originally by Frenchmen wearing *sabots* or clogs, to railways, factories, machinery, etc. by discontented employees. In World War II it was used extensively to impede the enemy in the occupied countries

sang-froid, 'cold blood'; coolness; composure

sauve-qui-peut, 'save who can'; 'every man for himself'; a general panic; a headlong flight

savoir-faire, tact; knowing the right thing to do; presence of mind

soupçon, suspicion; a taste; a small quantity, e.g. 'Pink gin requires only a *soupçon* of angostura bitters.'

souvenir, a keepsake

table d'hôte, 'the host's table'; a set meal served at a set time and at a fixed price, unlike *à la carte* (see above), where the customer chooses his meal from the menu and pays for each dish

tête-à-tête, 'head to head'; a private conversation or interview between two persons, e.g. 'I waited outside the office while my wife had a *tête-à-tête* with the manageress.'

tour de force, a feat of strength; a striking exhibition of power or skill

tout ensemble, 'all together'; in costume and the arts, the general effect of anything considered as a whole, without regard to details

trousseau, a bride's outfit of clothing, etc.

voilà tout, that is all

vol-au-vent, 'flight on the wind'; a pastry case of light puff paste with a filling of chicken, prawn, lobster, mushroom, etc.

volte-face, a turning round; a change of front in an argument or in politics

See also ITALICS

fricatives in PHONETICS the sounds made by friction of the air. See GUIDE TO PRONUNCIATION on page 7 and also ASPIRATE.

full stop the punctuation mark (.) of the greatest finality, called by Americans the *period* and by printers and journalists the *full point*. It is used to end every sentence that does not require a question mark or an exclamation mark.

When we are quoting a part but not the whole of an extract we mark the omitted section with a row of full stops, usually three — technically known as a LACUNA. To take an example, William Pitt said in the course of a speech made on 6th March 1741: 'The atrocious crime of being a young man, which the honourable gentleman has, with such spirit and decency, charged upon me, I shall neither attempt to palliate nor deny.' We can reduce this in length without any loss of point by the use of the omission sign, thus: 'The atrocious crime of being a young man . . . I shall neither attempt to palliate nor deny.'

For the use of the full stop in marking words that have been contracted, see ABBREVIATION.

full words another name for LEXICAL WORDS.

further See FARTHER.

G

galley see PRINTERS' PROOFS.

gaol, jail The first may be favoured in official circles, but the second is surely the more sensible spelling; *gaol* is so like *goal* that one is in danger of making prison one's objective — or *vice versa*.

gasoline the American word for *petrol*, also spelt *gasolene*. Both spellings pronounced gæsˡəliːn. But *gas* has almost completely replaced the longer words.

gazette, gazetteer The first official newspaper was issued in Venice in 1566. A Venetian coin of small denomination was the *gazzetta*, and it is said that the word *gazette* derived from it and was used as a name for the news-sheet that developed into the newspapers that we know today. A *gazetteer* is a geographical dictionary forming a reference section to an atlas. It gets its name because it was originally provided for the information of writers of gazettes.

gender the grammatical classification of words according to whether they are masculine, feminine or neuter. Since English is now very largely an uninflected language (see INFLEXION) there is no gender in the true sense, except in a few pronouns where inflexion survives, e.g. *he*, *she*, *it*. Unlike the French, we do not have to remember that *pencil* is masculine whilst *pen* is feminine (but the word for a female swan is a *pen*!). (In French, because *majesté* is a feminine noun calling for the feminine adjective *sa*, one *seems* to refer to 'Her Majesty the King'; and in Old English, which was a highly inflected language with a complicated grammar, the gender of the word for woman was masculine!) We do, however, make changes in a limited number of words according to the sex of the creature named. There are four types of change:

1. We modify the masculine name, e.g. *man – woman*, or the feminine name, e.g. *bride – bridegroom, widow – widower*.

2. We add a suffix, e.g. *actor – actress, god – goddess, mayor – mayoress, negro – negress, sultan – sultana*.

3. We alter part of a compound, e.g. *billy-goat – nanny-goat, landlord – landlady, manservant – maidservant*.

4. We use an entirely different word, e.g. *son – daughter*.

Here is a list for reference. The male names are placed first.

abbot	abbess	executor	executrix	monk	nun
bachelor	spinster	fox	vixen	nephew	niece
baron	baroness	gander	goose	peacock	peahen
beau	belle	hart	hind	ram	ewe
boar	sow	heir	heiress	sir	madam
brave	squaw	hero	heroine	sire	dam
buck	doe	host	hostess	stag	hind
colt	filly	husband	wife	stallion	mare
dog	bitch	lad	lass	steer	heifer
drake	duck	lord	lady	testator	testatrix
duke	duchess	marquis	marchioness	waiter	waitress
earl	countess	masseur	masseuse	wizard	witch
emperor	empress	master	mistress		

generalisation   using one general term to cover a number of particular items. Thus 'excessive heat, hunger, thirst, disease, unrelieved toil and anxiety' might be generalised by saying simply 'hardships'. Generalisation is an important part of PRÉCIS work.

genitive (possessive) case   the case of a noun or pronoun that denotes possession or appurtenance. It is represented by: (a) special inflected forms of pronouns (*mine, yours, hers, ours, theirs, whose*); (b) the inflexion '*s* or *s*' in nouns naming animate things (*this boy's bat, these boys' bats*); (c) the case-phrase *of*+noun (*the hands of the clock*) or *of*+relative pronoun (*a table the leg of which is broken*).

The use of '*s* and *s*' is treated under APOSTROPHE (1).

See also under CASE; GERUND; INFLEXION.

gerund (*g* soft)   a non-finite part of the verb, ending in -*ing* and having the same form as the present participle. It has a verbal force though possessing all the functions of a noun. It can therefore be used as a subject, an object, or a complement, or be governed by a preposition, e.g. '*Selling* is only part of our problem' (subject); '*Seeing* is *believing*' (complement); 'He began *writing* the article yesterday' (object); 'After *travelling* so far, we are tired' (object of preposition). Like nouns, gerunds may be given an adjectival function, e.g. a *walking* stick. Here it is not a stick that walks but a stick for walking. This kind of gerund is called a *gerundial adjective*.

The gerund is frequently used in the GENITIVE (POSSESSIVE) CASE, e.g. (a) '*His reading* was extensive.' (b) 'I do not object to *your coming*.' (c) 'My *brother's walking* to school was an unusual event.' The incorrect use of *you* for *your* in (b) arises from the confusion of the gerund with the present participle, on which matter see *fused participles* under PARTICIPLES.

gimmick   originally a swindling device used by American hucksters, it is now extended on both sides of the Atlantic to indicate a bright idea leading to success. A young woman's *gimmick* might be to wear a monocle to draw attention to herself. Modern ADVERTISING is full of gimmickry.

glossary   a list giving explanations of technical or other terms used in a book.

got   'I got the bus from the corner of the road. When we got to the station I got off. I got my ticket at the booking-office, then got a magazine before I got on the train. I got a corner seat just as the train got moving. The sun got very hot, so when we got to the next station I got out and got an ice-cream.' That is an example of how this not very pretty word can be overworked to avoid the trouble of finding something suitable. Sparing use of *got* in this sense is therefore advisable. *Got* is the past tense of *get*, which means 'to obtain'. The use of *has got*, *have got* for simple possession is resisted by the purist on the grounds of redundancy and of there being no question of getting possession. 'Have you got a match?' is frowned upon by such purists, but in fact the intrusion of 'got' is now so widespread that it is actually taught as part of the language by compilers of textbooks for teaching English as a foreign language.

See also OVERWORKED WORDS.

gourmand, gourmet The former is a disparaging term and the latter a flattering one. The *gourmand* eats greedily, whilst the *gourmet* eats with discrimination. The cynic will say, perhaps, that a man cannot be a gourmet unless he has first been a gourmand!

govern In grammar a word is said to govern another word because it requires it to be in a certain case or mood. For example:

(a) A preposition governs the word to which it is attached, e.g. 'I bought it from *him*.' The preposition 'from' requires the accusative case 'him'.
(b) A verb governs its object by requiring it to be in the accusative case, e.g. 'Everyone loves *her*.'
(c) The conjunction *if* requires *were*, the subjunctive mood of the verb *to be*, e.g. 'I would not go if I *were* you.'

Government, government a useful distinction is conveyed by the use or otherwise of the capital letter. *The Government* refers to a particular ruling party or coalition; government, as in the phrase *wise government*, is an ABSTRACT NOUN, e.g. 'The Government may provide an example of wise government, although its political opponents will find this unlikely.'

graffiti plural of Italian singular noun, *graffito*, an inscription, scurrilous, obscene, ribald or jocose, scrawled on a wall. Early examples were found in the ruins of Pompeii; later examples may be studied on lavatory walls everywhere or on posters on the Underground in London. At their best they can rise to a level of mordant wit, e.g. on one Soho lavatory wall an introspective *graffiti* specialist wrote *My mother made me a homosexual*, to which an unsympathetic wag added *If I bought her the wool, would she make me one too?* At their lowest they are simply obscene.

grammar   Sigismund, king of Hungary, was elected German monarch and Roman emperor in 1411. At the Council of Constance in 1414 a prelate called attention to a grammatical error in the emperor's opening speech. Sigismund replied: 'Ego sum rex Romanus, et supra grammaticam.' ('I am king of the Romans, and above grammar.') Not all of us are in this favourable position; we must pay respect to grammar and its rules. Let it be added, though, that inasmuch as language is constantly changing, the rules of grammar change also. Our forefathers said 'Ain't I?' and not an eyebrow was raised by the well educated. We of our generation say 'Aren't I?', which has only usage to commend it. Perhaps our descendants will say 'Amn't I?', as some Irishmen do.

The word *grammar* derives from the Greek, meaning 'the science of letters'. The grammar of the classics (and English grammar too at one time) was divided into four sections: (1) *Orthography* ('writing correctly'), the art of spelling words correctly; (2) *Etymology* ('true description'), the science treating of the meanings, history and inflexion of words; (3) *Syntax* ('to put in order'), the science treating of the correct arrangement of words in a sentence; and (4) *Prosody* ('to a song'), the science treating of the QUANTITY of syllables and the rules of verse.

Although grammarians are at variance and attempts are constantly made to break away from the traditional arbitrary rules, modern grammar may be usefully divided into four branches, i.e. (1) *Phonology* ('description of sounds'), the science of vocal sounds, a branch of which is PHONETICS; (2) *Accidence* ('that which happens'), which has to do with inflexions; (3) *Syntax* ('to put in order'), the arrangement of words in a sentence, and the rules governing this arrangement; and (4) *Word-formation*, which deals with the formation of words, either by DERIVATION, or by joining two or more words together, or by adding AFFIXES to a root or a stem.

These four branches are treated under their own headings. Various other matters relating to grammar can be found by reference to such further main headings as AGREEMENT; CASE; GENDER;

MOOD; NUMBER; PARTS OF SPEECH; PERSON; REPORTED SPEECH; SENTENCE; SOLECISMS; TENSE; VOICE.

grand-dad, grandad   Both are informal, so there seems nothing against the use of the second. *Grand-daughter* (or *granddaughter*, as it is often spelt) should not be similarly treated; *grandaughter* is incorrect.

grandiloquent (grændil'əkwənt)   literally 'grand-speaking'; using lofty or pompous words; having a BOMBASTIC style of talk.

Greek alphabet   Below is the alphabet of ancient Greece. The signs in the third column are the small letters, known as minuscules. The second minuscule for *sigma* was used when it ended a word.

Name	Capital	Minuscule	English
Alpha	A	α	A
Beta	B	β	B
Gamma	Γ	γ	G
Delta	Δ	δ	D
Epsilon	E	ε	E (short as in *get*)
Zeta	Z	ζ	Z
Eta	H	η	E (long as in *she*)
Theta	Θ	θ	TH
Iota	I	ι	I
Kappa	K	κ	K
Lambda	Λ	λ	L
Mu	M	μ	M
Nu	N	ν	N
Xi	Ξ	ξ	X
Omicron	O	ο	O (short as in *got*)
Pi	Π	π	P
Rho	P	ρ	R
Sigma	Σ	σ ς	S
Tau	T	τ	T
Upsilon	Υ	υ	U
Phi	Φ	φ	PH
Chi	X	χ	CH
Psi	Ψ	ψ	PS
Omega	Ω	ω	O (long as in *go*)

guide words   another name for CATCHWORDS; used to show the first and last words on the page of a dictionary.

gutturals (L. 'throat')   the sounds produced by using the back of the tongue, e.g. the *k* in *kind*, the *g* in *go*, the *ch* in *loch*. As with the hard *g* in *go* (cf. the soft *g* in *gentle*), the letter *c* is a guttural when it is hard and sounded like *k*, e.g. *cat, recant, actor, relic*.

See also SIBILANTS, and GUIDE TO PRONUNCIATION on page 7.

H

hackneyed   In days gone by, a *hackney* was an ordinary horse – not a war-horse, a racehorse or a hunter, but a commonplace nag for pulling a carriage or a cab(riolet). By the nature of its duties, it became an overworked drudge, and from it we get the adjective *hackneyed* to describe a phrase that, from too much use, has become worn out. Another name for a hackneyed phrase is a CLICHÉ.

haiku   type of Japanese verse that has been described as 'butter-fly poetry'. A *haiku* has only three lines and only seventeen syllables, five in the first and third lines, and seven in the second. Here are two examples translated into English:

(i)	(ii)
Alone, in the room	Stillness! Through
Where no soul exists,	The rainy midnight,
A tall white poppy.	The sound of a bell.

half   An old catch question used to be: 'What is wrong with this sentence? – "You have kept the biggest half of the apple for yourself." ' The unwary would answer: 'As the apple has only two halves, "biggest" should be "bigger".' The right answer is, of course, that if a thing is divided into halves, each half is equal to the other. To divide a thing into two is another matter. 'Tom cut the other apple into two and gave the smaller piece to his brother.'

hanged, hung   If the law is just, only criminals have ever been hanged. They were never hung. Pictures, however, are regularly hung.

harass   Note the spelling.

hard, hardly   Unless we mean *hardly* in the sense of *no sooner* (see below), we should use *hard* as the adverb, since *hardly* can cause AMBIGUITY, e.g.:

Wrong: The crops were hardly hit by the frost.
Right: The crops were hard hit by the frost.
Wrong: The income he received was hardly earned.
Right: The income he received was hard earned.

Some compound adjectives with *hard* are: *-baked, -bitten, -boiled, -featured, -fisted, -fought, -headed, -hearted, -pressed, -won, -working.*

hardly, scarcely   When we mean these in the sense of *no sooner*, we should follow them by *when* or *before*, not by *than* as in *no sooner . . . than.* The first two sentences below show the use of *no sooner*; the others show the incorrect and correct use of *hardly* and *scarcely*.

Right: He had no sooner opened his mouth than he was shouted down.
Right: Autumn is no sooner over than the shops are filled with Christmas gifts.
Wrong: He had hardly opened his mouth than he was shouted down.
Right: He had hardly opened his mouth when (or before) he was shouted down.
Wrong: Autumn is scarcely over than the shops are filled with Christmas gifts.
Right: Autumn is scarcely over before the shops are filled with Christmas gifts.

Both these adverbs are virtually negative in character, and to use them with *no* or *not* is to produce a double negative.

Wrong: There isn't hardly any work that is too difficult for him.
Right: There is hardly any work that is too difficult for him.
Wrong: He's clever enough, I suppose, but he doesn't scarcely qualify as a genius.
Right: He's clever enough, I suppose, but he scarcely qualifies as a genius.
Wrong: There's a spot of grease on my jacket, but it doesn't hardly show.
Right: There's a spot of grease on my jacket, but it hardly shows.

harlequinade   a mixture of music, mime, character transformations and disguise, a type of PANTOMIME in which the two young lovers Harlequin and Columbine escape from persecution with the aid of magic and stage machinery; popular in the 1920s.

hectic   Although deriving from the Greek meaning 'habitual' this has come to be associated with the high colour caused by illness. One suffering from a fever has a hectic flush. Only colloquially can it be used to mean 'exciting' or 'busy', e.g. (a) 'It was three o'clock in the morning before the party ended – much too hectic for me.' (b) 'We're having a pretty hectic time at the office these days.'
    See also OVERWORKED WORDS; VOGUE WORDS.

heinous   (heinˡəs)   odious; giving great offence. We speak of 'a heinous crime'.

hemisphere   half a sphere, particularly half the world, either the Eastern and Western Hemispheres or (divided by the Equator) the Northern and Southern Hemispheres.

hence   an archaic adverb meaning 'from here', e.g. 'Get thee hence!' (in the modern idiom, 'Push off!' – or some other terse instruction). It is still used today in the sense of 'from this time', e.g. 'ten years hence', and 'as a result of this' (or 'for this reason'), e.g. 'I mistrust the man. Hence my reluctance to have dealings with him.'
    For 'from this time forward', both *henceforth* and *henceforward* are in current use, as are *thenceforth* and *thenceforward* for 'from that time forward'.
    See also WHENCE.

heptameter   (heptæmˡətə) (Gk. 'seven measures')   in PROSODY a line of verse containing seven feet. It can be regarded as a combination in one line of a TETRAMETER and a TRIMETER. For example, if the following were printed in one line instead of two, the single line would be a heptameter:

> Behind / a frown / ing prov / idence
> He hides / a smil / ing face.

See METRE.

herewith   see ENCLOSE HEREWITH.

heroic couplet   in PROSODY two rhyming lines, each line being an *iambic pentameter* – that is, having five disyllabic feet with the stress on the second syllable of each foot. This form of couplet, much favoured by Pope and Dryden, is called *heroic* because it was the form of verse used by the Greeks and Romans in writing of the lives and exploits of their heroes. It is usually 'closed' – that is, it conveys a complete thought and, although forming only part of a poem, is still a self-contained unit. Here are some lines from Pope's *Essay on Criticism*:

> True ease in writing comes from art, not chance,
> As those move easiest who have learn'd to dance.
> 'Tis not enough no harshness gives offence,
> The sound must seem an echo to the sense:
> Soft is the strain when zephyr gently blows,
> And the smooth stream in smoother numbers flows;
> But when loud surges lash the sounding shore,
> The hoarse, rough verse should like a torrent roar.

All these are closed couplets. *Open couplets* and ENJAMBMENT are discussed under COUPLET.

hexameter (heksæm'ətə) (Gk. 'six measures')   the quantitative (long-short sounds) metre used in the great classical epics, Homer's *Iliad* and *Odyssey* (Greek) and Virgil's *Aeneid* (Latin). It does not translate well into English stressed-unstressed verse. In English PROSODY a hexameter is any line of verse containing six feet. Its most frequent use is in an ALEXANDRINE, but some complete poems have been written in hexameters, usually with five dactyls ($-\cup\cup$) and a final trochee ($-\cup$) or spondee ($--$), and occasionally with a spondee elsewhere in the line. Here is a scanned extract from *Andromeda*, the poem in blank verse by Charles Kingsley:

> Over the / mountain a / loft ran a / rush and a / roll and a / roaring;
> Downward the / breeze came in/dignant and / leapt with a / howl to the / water,
> Roaring in / cranny and / crag, till the / pillars and / clefts of the / basalt

‾ ˘ ˘ | ‾ ‾ | ˘ ‾ ‾ | ‾ ‾ | ‾ ‾ ˘
Rang like a / god-swept / lyre, and her / brain grew / mad with
    ˘   ˘ ‾
the / noises . . .

Lines 1–3: dactyl, dactyl, dactyl, dactyl, dactyl, trochee.
Line 4: dactyl, spondee, dactyl, spondee, dactyl, trochee.

hiatus (haieit'ǝs) (L. 'to gape') in general usage, a gap or break, e.g. 'There is a hiatus in the manuscript, suggesting that several pages have been removed or lost.' It is used humorously in such sentences as: 'There was a hiatus between her blouse and her skirt.' In PHONETICS a hiatus is the pause in utterance between a word ending with a vowel and a word beginning with a vowel, e.g. 'pure Irish'. Slovenly speakers tend to ignore the hiatus and pronounce this 'pure Rirish'.

hiccup This, not *hiccough*, is the correct spelling.

historic present the present indicative tense used to give vividness in the narration of a past event, e.g. 'Suddenly, with a loud cry, he hurls himself over the edge.' This tense should not be mixed with the past tense, e.g. 'His pursuers were twenty yards behind. Suddenly, with a loud cry, he hurls himself over the edge. Below, the waves were breaking against the cliff.' It is confusing to chop and change like this. Use either the historic present or the past for the whole incident.
    See also *agreement of tenses* under TENSE.

homo This has two distinct meanings. The word *homo* (pronounced houmou) is the Latin for 'man'; it comes to us through the Norman French (cf. *homme*, the French for 'man'). The term *homo sapiens* refers to the human species, the whole of mankind. The epithet means literally 'wise' or 'learned', but in *homo sapiens* it has the meaning of 'thinking man'. This Latin derivation is to be found in *homage*, the acknowledgment by one person of the superiority of another, and in such combinations as *homicide* (the killing of a human being) and *homunculus* (a little man, a dwarf). By comparison, the Greek prefix *homo-* (pronounced homou) does not mean 'man' but 'the same'. From this are derived *homogeneous* (of the same kind), HOMOSEXUAL (of the same sex), and also HOMONYMS and HOMOPHONES.

homonyms (homˈənimz) (Gk. 'the same name') words spelt alike but meaning different things. They may be words that derive from the same source, but whose meanings have diverged. An example of this type is *box* meaning 'a tree', *box* meaning 'a container' and *to box* meaning 'to fight'. Or they may come from different sources and yet happen to be spelt alike and even pronounced alike. An example of this type is *port* meaning 'a wine' and deriving from the place of its origin, Oporto, and *port* meaning 'a harbour' and deriving from the Latin *portus* (harbour). There are also three other homonyms: *port* meaning 'an opening in a ship', from the Latin *porta* (a door); *port* meaning 'bearing', from *portare* (to carry); and *port* meaning 'the left side of a ship', from an unknown source. (It was originally called the *larboard* side, but was altered to *port* because of the verbal confusion between *larboard* and *starboard*.)

Homonyms must be spelt alike, although they need not be pronounced alike. Thus *bow* meaning 'a weapon to shoot arrows', *bow* meaning 'to bend' and *bow* meaning 'the fore-end of a ship' are homonyms. But words pronounced alike and spelt differently are not, strictly speaking, homonyms; they are HOMOPHONES.

Here is a short list of homonyms, with meanings distinguished:

bank, sloping ground; place where money is kept
bark, covering of tree trunks; cry of a dog
bear, animal; to carry
charger, large flat dish; officer's horse
corn, grain; horny place on foot
fair, market; beautiful; blond or blonde; satisfactory; reasonable
heel, lean of a ship; rear part of foot
lead, metal; to guide
leaves, plural of leaf; departs
like, similar to; to think well of
pole, long piece of wood; extremity of an axis, e.g. South Pole
shelves, plural of shelf; slopes gently; lays aside
stole, vestment; past tense of *steal*
tick, sound made by clock; parasitic insect; mattress cover; credit (slang), e.g. to get groceries on tick
till, to cultivate the soil; up to the time of; drawer for money

homophones (homˈəfounz) (Gk. 'the same sound') words pronounced alike but having different spelling and meaning or usage.

Sometimes they derive from the same source, as do *practice* (noun) and *practise* (verb). More frequently they derive from different sources, as do *maize* (corn) and *maze* (labyrinth). But in either case the different spelling is explained by the fact that English is not wholly phonetic, often using different letters to represent the same sound.

Here is a short list of homophones:

air, atmosphere; *heir*, inheritor
all, entire; *awl*, tool
bail, security given; *bale*, bundle of goods
bald, hairless; *bawled*, shouted
bare, uncovered; *bear*, animal; to carry
boy, male child; *buoy*, anchored float
braid, to plait together; *brayed*, cried like an ass
cereal, grain used for human food; *serial*, story in instalments
choir, band of singers; *quire*, twenty-four sheets of paper
fair, market; *fare*, price paid for journey
frays, fights; *phrase*, part of a sentence
gilt, thin layer of gold; *guilt*, wickedness
him, objective case of *he*; *hymn*, song of praise
knead, to work flour into dough; *need*, want
meat, flesh used as food; *meet*, to encounter; *mete*, to allot or portion out
reek, smoke; *wreak*, revenge
right, correct; *rite*, solemn ceremony; *write*, to set down on paper
rye, kind of grain; *wry*, twisted
sew, to use needle and cotton; *so*, therefore; *sow*, to plant seeds
son, male offspring; *sun*, heavenly body
steal, to purloin; *steel*, metal
wait, to stay for something; *weight*, heaviness

homosexual   of the same sex. In describing sexual activities or in-clinations, homosexual is in practice restricted to males: the female equivalent is *lesbian* (no need, now, for a capital *L*).

One of the many advantages of the PERMISSIVE Society, so-called, is that homosexuality may now be openly written about and openly confessed. It has clearly been a powerful creative force in some in-stances: Mahler, Tchaikovsky, Wilde, Somerset Maugham, E. M. Forster, Norman Douglas, Lytton Strachey, J. M. Keynes, Henry

James and A. E. Housman were all either overt or covert homosexuals. Whether the social necessity to conceal their natures was
responsible for so much original work by the men named is a question which is beyond the scope of this work. Certainly, while the
climate of the times condemned it, writing on a homosexual theme
tended to be either PORNOGRAPHIC or maudlin; and even a 'secret'
homosexual novel by E. M. Forster entitled *Maurice*, published after
his death, turned out to be sickly stuff.

With the easing of social restrictions, the 'secret sin', as Wilde's
circle knew it, became neither secret nor sinful. A successful
American play, *The Boys in the Band*, about a group of homosexuals,
did well in London; and in 1970, on both sides of the Atlantic, a Gay
Liberation Front was formed to demand an end to alleged discrimination against homosexuals. An American novel, *Last Exit to
Brooklyn*, was the object of a failed prosecution in Britain for obscenity in 1969.

Homosexuality has created its own JARGON. *Gay* is, at the moment,
the homosexuals' preferred adjective for themselves. *Butch* describes
an aggressively female homosexual. *Queer* is used to describe homosexuals by themselves and by heterosexuals, to the extent that it is
not possible to use it as a synonym for *odd* without possibly embarrassing confusion. Extravagant homosexual behaviour (fluttering of
hands, fluting of voice) is known as *camping*; to *camp* is to behave so.
Nancy, *pansy*, *sissy* are old established nouns with derogatory overtones; newer nouns of similar import are *poove*, *puff*, *queen* (used for an
older homosexual). Because of their history, all these words are
SLANG on their way to becoming COLLOQUIALISMS. Before long, they
may be fully acceptable.

honorary, honourable Both derive from the Latin *honor*, but
they differ in usage. The first is an adjective meaning 'given or done
as an honour', without payment. An *honorary member* of a club or
association is one who is given the honour of membership without
being otherwise entitled to it. An *honorary secretary* (abbreviated
Hon. Sec.) is one who carries out the duties of secretary without
salary or remuneration.

The second is an adjective meaning 'worthy of honour; high-
minded; upright; honest'. It also means 'having a title; having a
position of honour'. Children of peers below the rank of marquis are
known as 'the Honourable. . . .' (abbreviated Hon.). Right Honourable (Rt. Hon.) is a title of respect before the names of members

of the Privy Council, which is the British sovereign's body of advisers. See also COUNCIL, COUNSEL.

howler a glaring mistake. A *schoolboy howler* is an unconsciously funny answer to a question set in an examination paper. Here are a few examples:

'Sodium Sulphate is the Shah of Persia.'
'Livid was a famous Latin poet.'
'Letters in sloping type are in hysterics.'
'Soviet is another name for a table napkin.'
'Having only one wife is called monotony.'
'A mosquito is the child of black and white parents.'
'Samuel Pepys worked in the Admiralty and was always going to bed.'
'Cosmetics make people sick.'

hue and cry a tautological term. Here 'hue' is used in its old sense, which derived from the Old French *huer*, meaning 'to hoot; to shout'.

human an adjective meaning 'pertaining to man or mankind', e.g. *the human race, human nature, human beings*. Only colloquially can it be used as a noun, e.g. 'We humans are funny creatures.' The correct term in formal writing is *human being(s)*.

humane The final *e* provides a useful distinction, giving the adjective the meaning of 'merciful', 'compassionate'. Thus *human behaviour* is the behaviour of man as a race, whilst *humane behaviour* is the behaviour of one who has a kind and sympathetic nature.

humanism a cultural product of the RENAISSANCE. Concerning itself with human interests rather than theological or philosophical teaching, it was an attempt to break away from the rigid discipline of the Church. As wrote Pope in his *Essay on Man*:

Know then thyself, presume not God to scan,
The proper study of mankind is man.

The effect of humanism on English literature was considerable.
Its meaning in modern English is, however, more that of agnosticism. It has been taken over by all those who, believing the

existence of God unproved, place their faith in humanity. The modern humanist believes that humanity can and must evolve its own future, regardless of God.

humour   the sympathetic appreciation of the comic; the faculty that enables us to sympathise while we laugh, and to sympathise the better for our laughter. There is no sting in such laughter, no conscious superiority, as there may be in wit.

In American English it is spelt *humor*. We use the *u* in *humour*, *humourless* and *humoursome*, but omit it in *humorist* and *humorous*. The anatomist who translated the Latin word *humerus* as *funny-bone* showed he had a sense of humour.

hyperbole (haipə:ˈbəli)   a FIGURE OF SPEECH using exaggeration, not to deceive but to emphasise a feeling or to produce a humorous effect, e.g. (a) 'Belinda smiled, and all the world was gay.' – Pope. (b) 'The next wave caught me unawares and I swallowed a gallon of sea-water.'

hypercritical, hypocritical   The first means 'being too critical', too severe on those guilty of small faults; the second means 'being a hypocrite', one who pretends to be more virtuous than he is.

hyphen   the punctuation mark (-) used:

1. To link two or more words to form a single compound word, e.g. *son-in-law*, *mock-turtle*, *men-at-arms*, *governor-general* (plural *governors-general*), *court-martial* (plural *courts-martial*); and to link the words in certain place-names, e.g. *Southend-on-Sea*, *Chapel-en-le-Frith*, *Ashby-de-la-Zouch*, *Aix-les-Bains*.

2. To indicate, when a word is broken at the end of a line, that the rest of the word will be found at the beginning of the next line. These breaks should not be made haphazardly but in such a way that the first part will give the reader a clue to the whole word, e.g. not *pai- nful* but *pain- ful*; not *hig- hest* but *high- est*. In words like *written*, *puzzling*, *beginner*, the break should come between the double letters, e.g. *writ- ten*, *puz- zling*, *begin- ner*. Good typists, like good printers, remember such points as these.

3. To connect a prefix with a root when the latter begins with the same vowel letter as the prefix ends with, e.g. *co-operate*. See also DIAERESIS.

4. To indicate two different meanings of the same word, e.g. (a) 'I

recovered my umbrella from the lost-property office.' (b) 'The man in the shop re-covered my torn umbrella.' (c) 'When the recreation room was painted pink, six members of the club resigned.' (d) 'When the re-creation of the club had been decided upon, six of the former members re-signed.'

See also RECOUNT; REDRESS; REFORM.

5. To form compound adjectives, e.g. 'He is a first-rate cricketer and a well-known collector of seventeenth-century furniture.' It should be noted that in the case of *well-known* and such other compounds as *well-loved*, *well-nourished* and *worth-while*, the hyphen is unnecessary when the noun comes first, e.g. (a) 'The old man was well known for his eccentric behaviour.' (b) 'The children are well nourished and live in comfortable surroundings.' It should be noted also that no hyphen is necessary after the adverb in such combinations as: 'a beautifully furnished room'; 'a neatly typed letter'; 'a carefully prepared speech'.

6. To avoid creating a wrong impression, e.g. (a) 'a Dutch-cheese importer' (the cheese, not the importer, is Dutch); (b) 'an outstanding-rent collector' (the rent, not the collector, is outstanding); (c) 'a pickled-onion merchant'; (d) 'a coarse-cloth manufacturer'; (e) 'a sweet-shop assistant'; (f) 'a cleaner-caretaker'.

7. To act as a link in such phrases as: 'the Franco-Prussian War'; 'the Tory-Socialist coalition'; 'the London-Portsmouth road'; 'the England-Wales match'. There is some awkwardness when double names are linked, e.g. 'the Sheffield United-Manchester City match'. This suggestion of a united Manchester is easily avoided by describing the match as being 'between Sheffield United and Manchester City'.

8. To link such prefixes as *anti-*, *ex-*, *pre-* and *pro-* to nouns, e.g. *anti-slavery*, *ex-champion*, *pre-war*, *pro-British*. Here again, double words can cause misunderstanding, e.g. (a) 'anti-British Council' (a council that is anti-British?); (b) 'ex-gentleman jockey' (still a jockey but no longer a gentleman?).

See also DATES.

hypothesis (haipoθ¦əsis)   something assumed to be true for the sake of argument, or as a starting-point for an inquiry, although its truth has not been proved.

'I'm glad to hear,' said the superintendent of police, 'that you've got your man for the Paulsfield murder. What steps did you take?'

'Well, sir,' replied the detective-inspector, 'the medical evidence suggested that the murder had been committed by a left-handed person of great strength. Basing my case on this hypothesis, I circulated a description and we tracked down an ex-seaman in a cheap lodging-house in Portsmouth. He was a giant of a fellow, and when I asked him to write his name on a sheet of paper he did it with his left hand. At first he denied all knowledge of the Paulsfield killing, but he finally confessed.'

'Nice work,' smiled the superintendent. 'Your hypothesis was the right one.'

I

iambus (aiæmˈbəs)   in PROSODY a disyllabic foot with the stress on the second syllable, e.g. *immĕnsē*. See METRE.

ibidem (L. 'in the same place', abbreviated *ibid.* or *ib.*)   used in books of reference to indicate that this quotation is to be found in the same work, chapter or act as the quotation or quotations preceding it, e.g.:

He led his regiment from behind –
  He found it less exciting.

The Gondoliers, Act 1

Of that there is no manner of doubt –
No probable, possible shadow of doubt –
  No possible doubt whatever.

Ibid.

idiom   a form of expression peculiar to a language. Idiomatic expressions may be classified in four ways:

1. Grammatical, e.g. the impersonal IT used as an ANTICIPATORY SUBJECT, e.g. 'It is a long way to the station.'
2. Ungrammatical, e.g. 'It's me' instead of 'It is I'. See also NOMINATIVE CASE.

3. Metaphorical, e.g. 'He gave me the cold shoulder' (i.e. he ignored my presence).

4. Prepositional, e.g. 'We have run *out* of bread, and *of* course the shops are now shut.' See also PREPOSITIONAL IDIOM.

idyll   sometimes spelt *idyl* and may be pronounced ai¹dil or i¹dil. Originally it was a short descriptive poem of shepherd life, with a picturesque rustic or pastoral background. Tennyson extended the meaning of the term in his *Idylls of the King*, a series of poems in blank verse about King Arthur and the Knights of the Round Table. The adjective *idyllic* means 'pleasing in its natural simplicity', e.g. 'He led an idyllic existence on a tropical island, far from the distractions and artificialities of so-called civilisation.'

i.e.   an abbreviation of the Latin *idem est* (sometimes shortened to *id. est*), meaning 'that is' or 'that is to say'. It is often confused with *e.g.*, which is an abbreviation of *exempli gratia*, meaning 'for example'. The distinction between them is treated under E.G., I.E.

if I were   For the use of the subjunctive *if I were, if he were*, etc. see under MOOD. See also NOMINATIVE CASE for *if I were he (him)*.

ignoratio elenchi   see IRRELEVANCY.

illegible   see ELIGIBLE.

illusion   see ALLUSION.

imagery   the creation of images or pictures to help the poet achieve his intended purpose. These pictures are not as important in themselves as in the effect they produce in the reader's mind. Consider this image in a poem by Robert Burns:

Or like the snow falls in the river,
A moment white – then melts for ever.

This is mainly a visual image – a picture of a white snowflake suddenly vanishing for ever. Burns used this image, not because he wanted us to be interested in snowflakes but because by its means he hoped to make us understand more vividly the fleetingness of all life. If he had made the prosaic statement that life was transient, our imaginations would not have been roused and Burns would not have achieved his intended purpose; but by means of imagery he was able to bring the whole idea vividly alive in our minds.

Not all imagery is mainly visual; sometimes it may be mainly a sound picture, as in these lines from *The Rime of the Ancient Mariner* by Coleridge:

> With heavy thump, a lifeless lump,
> They dropped down one by one.

We see, of course, but we mainly *hear* what is happening this time. We also *feel* the heaviness of the impact as the mariner's shipmates drop dead one by one. Coleridge, however, is not really concerned with sound and heaviness. He is mainly using this image of sound and heaviness to make us vividly aware of the deadness and lifelessness on board the ship.

We should therefore always look for the purpose behind imagery. This is why poetry when paraphrased sounds so tame. As soon as we get rid of the imagery by means of which the poet makes his thought exciting and important in our minds, the thought falls very flat indeed.

immigrate   see EMIGRATE.

imminent   see EMINENT.

imperative   the form of the verb used to express requests, orders, COMMANDS, e.g. 'Keep off the grass,' 'Don't do that,' 'Please come here,' 'Would you mind shutting the door?'
See MOOD.

imperial, imperious   Though both derive from the Latin *imperium*, meaning 'command' or 'dominion', the first means 'of an empire or an emperor; supreme in authority; majestic'; whilst the second means 'haughty; arrogant; overbearing; domineering'.

(a) The imperial palace was attacked by the mob.
(b) His imperious demands caused great resentment.

impersonal 'it'   see ANTICIPATORY SUBJECT.

implicit   see EXPLICIT.

imply, infer The first means 'to suggest something without openly saying it', e.g. 'By his reference to the need for strict economy, the chairman implied that the financial position of the company was causing some concern.' The second means 'to draw a conclusion', e.g. 'From the chairman's reference to the need for strict economy, the shareholders inferred that the financial position of the company was causing some concern.'

impressionism in art and literature the style that attempts to convey the desired effect by broad, simple suggestions rather than by an exact reproduction of detail. Of the impressionistic school of painting, G. K. Chesterton wrote in 1937: 'Its principle was that if all that could be seen of a cow was a white line and a purple shadow, we should only render the line and the shadow; in a sense we should only believe in the line and the shadow, rather than in the cow. In one sense the Impressionist sceptic contradicted the poet who had never seen a purple cow. He tended rather to say that he had only seen a purple cow; or rather that he had not seen the cow but only the purple.'

The poet who had never seen a purple cow was Gelett Burgess. The poem is to be found under JINGLE.

incognito (incog¦nitou) see PSEUDONYM.

incomplete predication see under COMPLEMENT; VERB.

inculcate This means 'to teach by frequent repetition', but we cannot inculcate a person; we can only inculcate *in* or *upon* him, e.g.:
  Wrong: In his boyhood his parents inculcated him with a deep religious faith.
  Right: In his boyhood his parents inculcated in him a deep religious faith.

indentation In printing *to indent* is to leave a blank space at the beginning of a line. We ourselves indent when, writing a letter, we start the first line of a new PARAGRAPH a little way in from the margin. The noun *indentation* (occasionally *indention*) means either the act of indenting, or the blank space left by it. The indentation of lines of verse is discussed under RHYME.

index an alphabetical list of the subjects referred to in a book and giving the numbers of the pages on which reference to each subject is made. The plural is *indexes*, the Latin plural *indices* being confined to science and mathematics. See also CATCHWORD; CROSS-REFERENCE.

indicative mood   see under MOOD.

indict   to accuse; to charge with a crime. It is pronounced indait[1], as is *indite* meaning 'to write, inscribe'.

indirect object   see OBJECT.

indirect question   see REPORTED SPEECH.

indirect speech   see REPORTED SPEECH.

individual   When used as a noun this is not synonymous with *man*, *person, chap, fellow*. It means the particular as opposed to the general, a single human being as opposed to society or a collection of human beings. This is wrong: 'He struck me as a very shifty individual.' This is right (it comes from Henry Fielding's *Joseph Andrews*): 'I describe not men, but manners; not an individual, but a species.' And so is this, by the American humorist, J. Mason Knox:

> 'It ain't the guns or armament, or the money they can pay,
> It's the close co-operation that makes them win the day;
> It ain't the individual, nor the army as a whole,
> But the everlastin' teamwork of every bloomin' soul.'

See also VOGUE WORDS.

induction   At some point in history someone must have come to realise that every dog he had seen possessed four legs. From the observation of many particular instances he drew the general conclusion that all dogs are quadrupeds. He arrived at this conclusion by *induction*, which we can define as a mental process that observes many particular instances and then makes a general rule incorporating the truth of all the facts observed. Every GENERALIZATION is therefore arrived at by induction. A general truth is induced from particular truths. By contrast, in DEDUCTION we start with a general truth and apply it to particular cases.

See also A PRIORI.

infer   see IMPLY.

infinitive   the simplest form of the verb, normally preceded by *to*, e.g. *to work*. It is a NON-FINITE part of the verb and therefore, unlike FINITE VERBS, does not predicate (assert) anything about the person or thing named by the subject of a sentence, e.g. 'He began to work.' Though retaining the force of a verb, the infinitive may function as a noun, an adverb or an adjective. It does not, however, express person, number or exact time. Examples are: (a) '*To know* him is *to like* him' (subject and complement). (b) 'Do not forget *to come* early' (object). (c) 'I come *to bury* Caesar, not *to praise* him' (adverb of purpose). (d) 'Do you know of a house *to let*?' (adjective). It should also be noted that it is the infinitive form of the verb that is used with the auxiliaries *shall, should, will, would, do, may, might, can, could* to form compound tenses, e.g. (a) 'I shall *go* tomorrow.' (b) 'He can *swim* as well as you can.'

When the infinitive is the object of such verbs as *intend, hope, like, want, fear, plan, expect,* the time of the action expressed by the infinitive is always ahead of the time of intending, hoping, etc.

Wrong: I intended to have met him at the airport.

Right: I intended to meet him at the airport.

Wrong: I had intended to have met him at the airport.

Right: I had intended to meet him at the airport.

Whether we say 'I intended', 'I had intended', 'I should intend' or 'I should have intended', the meeting is yet to take place. The infinitive that follows must therefore express the future, and the future is expressed by the present infinitive *to meet*. Whatever past tense of these verbs we use, it cannot be followed by the perfect infinitive *to have met*.

See also SPLIT INFINITIVE.

inflexion (L. 'making curved')   any variation in the form of words to indicate grammatical relation in the sentence, e.g. *pen, pens; high, higher, highest; eat, ate, eaten, eating; he, him; girl, girl's.*

Old English was a highly inflected language, with a complicated grammar. There were two classes of adjectives, each declined differently, and every noun had a GENDER. The number of changes in the endings of words according to their grammatical function was very large indeed.

Modern English is very different, for our grammar is simple and has very few inflexions. Yet it has almost entirely descended from Old English grammar. What has happened is that there has been a gradual levelling out, so that inflexions have disappeared, leaving only one common ending. One inflexion to show the PLURAL has, however, survived and is today -*s*. In Old English there were several (we have another surviving in *ox–oxen*), but the most common was -*as*, which appeared in both the nominative (subject) and accusative (object) plural of many nouns. In the course of time it became the ending in all cases of practically all nouns, and shortened to -*s*. The only other inflexion left today is one to show possession (genitive). This survives from the Old English genitive's singular inflexion of -*es*, and is now shown by '*s* or *s*'.

Many other characteristics of English words may be traced to Old English and the way it gradually changed. The fact that we say, for instance, *to ride* but *have ridden*, *to drive* but *have driven*, is explained by a shift of accent leading to certain vowel changes in Old English before it arrived in England; whilst another change in vowel sounds that took place in England between A.D. 400 and 700 explains why we say *tooth* but *teeth*, *mouse* but *mice*, *long* but *length*, *food* but *to feed*.

Various inflexional forms of nouns, pronouns and other parts of speech can be found by references to CASE; COMPARISON, DEGREES OF; GENDER; MOOD; NUMBER; PERSON; PLURAL; TENSE. See also DERIVATION.

infra dig. a contraction of the Latin *infra dignitatem*, meaning 'beneath one's dignity', and usually spelt without a full stop, e.g. 'I considered it *infra dig* to quarrel with him in the street, so I kept my mouth shut and walked on.'

ingenious, ingenuous An ingenious man is one able to contrive clever plans or inventions, whilst an ingenuous man is one with a frank and open nature. Not all ingenious men are ingenuous, which is a pity.

ingratiate to work oneself into grace or favour. It is a REFLEXIVE verb and cannot be used unless followed by *oneself, myself, himself*, etc., e.g.:
Wrong: He did all he could to ingratiate his hostess.
Right: He did all he could to ingratiate himself with his hostess.

inimitable 'The cleverest performer at the concert was Mr John Phillips, who gave some life-like impersonations of a number of famous comedians, including the inimitable Frankie Howerd.' He must have been indeed a clever performer, for the meaning of inimitable is 'that cannot be imitated'. The adjective is used too freely as a complimentary description in the sense of 'the one and only'. Avoid it unless there is an element of imitation or comparative quality, e.g. 'He did not mention the author of the poem, but when he recited it I recognised the inimitable style of Algernon Swinburne.'

initial teaching alphabet (i.t.a.) an ALPHABET for teaching reading in the early stages, promoted by Sir James Pitman and formerly known as the Ehrhardt augmented lower-case alphabet. It is claimed that by avoiding capital letters and introducing certain new characters to represent sounds that have traditionally been represented by two or more separate letters, the beginner learns to read much more quickly. The new characters are so designed as to facilitate the transition to the traditional alphabet as soon as the beginner's reading has become fluent. Below are the 43 characters of the initial teaching alphabet. The number is sometimes quoted as 45, a figure which includes variants for characters 4 and 17. The character 4 variant is used in the very early stages to provide additional discrimination from character 2, and the character 17 variant is used in combination with certain vowel-characters to represent a particular vowel sound. At the end of the entry are two paragraphs printed in the new alphabet.

1. æ   long *a* as in *fate* (fæt), *same* (sæm); *ay* as in *way* (wæ); *ey* as in *they* (ꝥhæ)

2. b   *b* as in *be* (bεε), *before* (befor), *but* (but)

3. c   *c* as in *can* (can), *discarded* (discarded); *ch* as in *school* (scꬰl); *ck* as in *stick* (stick); with *s* as *cc* in *success* (sucsess)

4. d   *d* as in *do* (dꬰ); *ed* as in *achieved* (aꞔheεvd), *proved* (prꬰvd)

5. εε   *e* as in *be* (bεε), *medium* (mεεdium); *ee* as in *meet* (mεεt); *ea* as in *meat* (mεεt), *reading* (rεεdiŋ); *ie* as in *achieved* (aꞔheεvd); *ei* as in *received* (resεεvd)

6. f   *f* as in *fact* (fact); *ph* as in *alphabet* (alfabet)

7. g   hard *g* as in *good* (gꬰd), *figure* (figuer)

8. h   *h* as in *hat* (hat), *hate* (hæt), *have* (hav)

9. ie   long *i* as in *bite* (biet), *like* (liek); *igh* as in *might* (miet); *y* as in *why* (whie)

10. j   *j* as in *just* (just); *g* as in *German* (jerman); *ge* as in *change* (ꞔhænj), *language* (laŋgwæj)

11. k   *k* as in *kind* (kiend), *look* (lꬹk); with *c* as in *stick* (stick); with *s* as *x* in *six* (siks); with *w* as *qu* in *question* (kwestion)

12. l   *l* as in *learn* (lern); *le* as in *single* (siŋgl), *principle* (prinsipl)

13. m   *m* as in *most* (mœst)

14. n   *n* as in *not* (not); *gn* as in *sign* (sien); *kn* as in *know* (nœ)

15. œ   long *o* as in *most* (mœst); *ow* as in *own* (œn)

16. p   *p* as in *place* (plæs), *option* (opʃhon)

17. r   *r* as in *rate* (ræt), *reference* (referens); *wr* as in *wrong* (roŋ), *written* (ritten)

18. s   *s* as in *so* (sœ); *c* as in *policy* (polisy); *ce* as in *essence* (essens), *choice* (ʧhois)

19. ţ   *t* as in *true* (trœ), *deterred* (ḍeterḍ), but not as in *the* (ſhe), *both* (bœţh)

20. ue   *u* as in *future* (fuetuer); *ew* as in *few* (fue)

21. v   *v* as in *very* (very); *f* as in *of* (ov); *ve* as in *have* (hav)

22. w   *w* as in *will* (will), *world* (wurld); also for the *w* sound in *one* (wun), *once* (wuns)

23. y   *y* as in *yet* (yet), *any* (eny), *easy* (ɛɛsy)

24. z   *z* as in *zest* (zest); *ze* as in *emphasize* (emfasiez)

25. ʂ   *s* as in *is* (iʂ), *was* (woʂ), *easily* (ɛɛʂily); with *g* as in *example* (egʂampl)

26. wh   *wh* as in *which* (whiʧh), *where* (whær), *why* (whie)

27. ʧh   *ch* as in *change* (ʧhænj), *which* (whiʧh), *each* (ɛɛʧh)

28. ţh   *th* as in *thin* (ţhin), *thing* (ţhiŋ)

29. ſh   *th* as in *the* (ſhe), *that* (ſhat), *there* (ſhær)

30. ʃh   *sh* as in *shoe* (ʃhœ), *English* (iŋgliʃh); also for the sound of *sh* in *special* (speʃhal), *repetition* (repetiʃhon)

31. ʒ   *j* as in the French *déjeuner*, which same sound occurs in *measure* (meʒuer), *confusion* (confueʒon), *visual* (viʒueal)

32. ŋ   *ng* as in *sing* (siŋ), *writing* (rietiŋ)

33. ɑ   *a* as in *answer* (ɑnser), *example* (egʂampl), *palm* (pɑm)

34. au   *au* as in *taught* (taut); *ou* as in *bought* (baut); *a* as in *also* (aulsœ), *already* (aulredy); *aw* as in *dawn* (ḍaun)

35. a   short *a* as in *fat* (fat), *has* (haʂ)

36. e   *e* as in *bed* (beḍ); *ea* as in *read* (reḍ); *ai* as in *said* (seḍ); *a* as in *any* (eny)

37. i   short *i* as in *bit* (bit)

38. o   *o* as in *of* (ov), *not* (not), *more* (mor)

39. u   *u* as in *unless* (unless), *difficulty* (difficulty); *oe* as in *does* (ḍuʂ); *o* as in *become* (becum), *other* (uſher)

40. ɷ   *oo* as in *foot* (fɷt); *o* as in *woman* (wɷman); *ou* as in *should* (ʃhɷd)

41. ꭢ   *oo* as in *food* (fꭢd); *ui* as in *fluid* (flꭢid); *wo* as in *two* (tꭢ)

42. ou   *ou* as in *foul* (foul); *ow* as in *fowl* (foul), *however* (houever)

43. oi   *oi* as in *boil* (boil); *oy* as in *boy* (boi), *envoy* (envoi)

ſhis iʂ printed in an augmenteḍ rœman alfabet, ſhe purpos ov whiʧh iʂ not, aʂ miet bɛɛ suppœsḍ, tꭢ reform our spelliŋ,

but too improov ʃhe lerniŋ ov reediŋ. it is intended ʃhat when
ʃhe beginner has aʧeevd ʃhe iniʃhal sucsess ov flooensy in
ʃhis speʃhally eesy form, his fuetuer prœgress ʃhood bee
confiend too reediŋ in ʃhe present alfabets and spelliŋs ov
ʃhem œnly.

if yoo hav red as far as ʃhis, ʃhe nue meedium will hav
proovd too yoo several points, ʃhe mœst important ov whiʧ
is ʃhat yoo, at eny ræt, hav eesily mæd ʃhe ʧænj from ʃhe
ordinary rœman alfabet wiʃh convenʃhonal spelliŋs too
augmented rœman wiʃh systematic spelliŋ.

innuendo insinuation; conveying a meaning slyly by hinting,
usually because it is unpleasant, e.g. (a) 'I do not know him very
well, so perhaps I had better not say too much about him.' (b) 'It is
curious that Mrs Brown is now wearing a necklace similar to the one
lost by Mrs Green.' Innuendo is a FIGURE OF SPEECH and a form of
verbal FALLACY.

insignia, regalia Both these are plural nouns meaning 'badges of
honour or office'. The difference between them is that any person
may wear insignia, but only royalty may wear regalia, the word
deriving from the Latin *rex*, meaning 'a king'.

instructional, instructive The first is synonymous with 'educational'; the second with 'informative', e.g.:

(a) An instructional booklet entitled *Carpentry for Beginners* has just
been published.
(b) We spent an instructive afternoon in the cathedral city of
Canterbury.

intensive a word that emphasises, such as *very*, *vast* (*vastly*) or *extreme* (*extremely*). The verb *to demand* is an intensive, being more
peremptory than *to ask for*. The noun *superabundance* is an intensive
because it means 'more than abundance'; it emphasises the abundance of, say, this year's harvest of apples. Many fashionable adjectives and adverbs are intensives. They are very poor substitutes for
genuine intensives and, as is noted under OVERWORKED WORDS, they
are never too busy to deputise for each other, to which can be here
added that they are never too busy to deputise for a genuine (and,
in formal writing, dignified) intensive. Are not all the adverbs in the
following sentence intended to mean exactly the same thing as
extremely?

The weather was $\left\{\begin{array}{l}\text{awfully}\\ \text{terrifically}\\ \text{shockingly}\\ \text{fantastically}\\ \text{frightfully}\\ \text{dreadfully}\\ \text{fearfully}\\ \text{horribly}\\ \text{terribly}\end{array}\right\}$ cold.

interjection   the part of speech expressing EXCLAMATION or EJACULATION. As the etymology of their name implies, interjections are 'thrown into' the sentence and therefore have no part in its grammatical construction, e.g. (a) 'My aunt, *bless her heart*, gave me ten pounds on my birthday.' (b) 'He has kept me waiting over half an hour, *confound him*!' (a) 'The rain, *alas*, continued all day.' For the use of exclamation marks with interjections see EXCLAMATION MARK.

internal rhyme   a rhyme between a word in the middle of a line and a word at the end of it, e.g. 'Let dogs delight to bark and bite.' Another example of it is to be found under BALLAD, in the stanzas from Oscar Wilde's *The Ballad of Reading Gaol*. The point where the line breaks rhythmically into two ('Let dogs delight ǀ to bark and bite') is known as the CAESURA. Verse with a system of internal rhyming is called LEONINE VERSE.

international phonetic symbols   These are listed on pages 7 and 8. See also PRONUNCIATION.

into, in to   The first expresses motion or direction to a point within a thing; *to go into* is *to enter*, e.g. 'We went into the dining-room.' In the second, *in* and *to* have separate senses, e.g. 'We went in to dinner.' We did not enter the dinner; we entered the dining-room. The phrase 'to dinner' has the same meaning as the infinitive 'to dine'. The use of *into* to form an infinitive is clearly wrong, e.g.: 'Mary ran into tell her mother the news.' Here 'into' should be 'in to'. When we consider also that 'to run into' is 'to collide', we can appreciate the ambiguity of 'Mary ran into her mother'. See also ONTO, ON TO.

intonation   a general term used to denote the variation in PITCH of the human voice. Statements and commands are normally spoken with a falling pitch, whereas questions have a rising pitch. Intonation can therefore affect meaning. A statement can often be turned into a question simply by speaking it with a rising pitch. It is intonation, emphasis and pause that give an utterance its main spoken characteristics.

intransitive verbs   see under VERB.

inveigh, inveigle   These verbs are sometimes confused. The first (pronounced invei¹) means 'to attack with angry words; to speak violently against'; the second (pronounced invi:¹gəl) means 'to entice; to lead astray', e.g. 'Mr Lewis was inveighing against two men he had met on the train, who had inveigled him into playing cards with them and had cheated him out of five pounds.'

inversion   (L. 'to turn upside down')   the FIGURE OF SPEECH by which, to give emphasis, the parts of a sentence are arranged out of their natural order, e.g. (a) 'Happy is the country that has no history.' (b) 'Like a poleaxed ox he fell.' (c) 'Out ran the boys.' (d) 'Came the dawn.' In the *New Yorker* there appeared the following comment on writing that, like *Time* magazine which was being parodied, relies too much on inversion: 'Backward ran sentences until reeled the mind.'

Because of the demands of scansion and rhyme there is much inversion in poetry, e.g. 'the ocean wide'; 'roses red and violets blue'; and, to quote from Longfellow, 'This is the forest primeval.'

inverted commas   the punctuation marks (or 'quotes') used to indicate direct speech or quotation. Formerly, double inverted commas (" . . . ") were the convention, but the modern tendency in books is to use single quotes (' . . . '), with one TURNED COMMA at the beginning and one APOSTROPHE at the end.

Here is an example of DIRECT SPEECH, followed by some notes upon it:

'I must go home now,' I told my host.

'It is very cold,' he said; 'there is ice on the puddles. Would you like to borrow my coat?'

'No,' I replied, 'I am quite used to the cold.'

'I am glad of that,' he smiled. 'We need more men who do not expect life to be "roses, roses, all the way" and are not afraid to rough it.'

(a) Only the words actually spoken are enclosed in inverted commas. Explanatory matter, e.g. *I told my host*, remains outside.

(b) Punctuation marks are placed inside the inverted commas at the end of the words spoken.

(c) Even though the words spoken form a sentence in themselves, they are followed by a comma, with the full stop coming right at the end. If the words spoken are in the form of a question or an exclamation, the appropriate mark takes the place of the comma, e.g. (a) '*Must I go now?*' *I asked my host*. (b) '*How cold it is!*' *exclaimed my host*. (See also EXCLAMATION MARK; QUESTION MARK.)

(d) When a sentence is broken by the interpolation of a VERB OF SAYING, the verb of saying is marked off by commas, e.g. '*No*,' *I replied*, '*I am quite used to the cold.*', unless the sentence itself requires a semi-colon, which is then placed after the verb of saying, e.g. '*It is very cold,*' *he said;* '*there is ice on the puddles.*'

(e) When the use of double inverted commas was general, quotations within quotations were enclosed in single inverted commas. Now that the procedure is reversed, the quotation within the quotation is enclosed in double inverted commas, e.g. "*roses, roses, all the way*", which is from Browning's *The Patriot*. When inverted commas are used for a quotation that is not direct speech, following punctuation should be outside the inverted comma. The alternative is such an untidy sentence as: *His name was really John Brown but everyone called him* '*Buster.*'

Experimental writers, such as James Joyce in *Ulysses*, dispensed with inverted commas altogether. His example has sometimes been followed by less talented authors.

It should be noted that titles of books, names of ships, etc. are sometimes printed in inverted commas, but there is a growing tendency to put them into ITALICS. In handwriting the inverted commas are retained; but if we are writing something that is going to be printed, we should underline any words that we wish to appear in italics.

Inverted commas should not be used for abbreviations and colloquialisms that have become part of the language. Some of these are mentioned in section 12 of ABBREVIATION. The placing of slang words and phrases in inverted commas is liable to give the impression of condescension or, which is nearly as bad, to denote that the writer knows he is using slang but, because he can think of no other way of expressing his thoughts, excuses himself by using inverted commas, e.g. *The man was a 'bad lot', but we knew that he had 'got it coming to him', so we were not surprised when a 'copper' caught him 'on the hop'.*

irony a FIGURE OF SPEECH; a method of expression in which the ordinary meaning of the word is more or less the opposite of what the speaker intends. The waywardness of such expression draws attention to what is really intended and so emphasises it, e.g. (a) 'You're a nice one!' (b) 'This is a pretty state of affairs!' (c) 'That's a fine thing to say!' (d) 'George and Bill are a couple of bright specimens.' (e) 'I'm going to the dentist tomorrow – a pleasant prospect!' (f) 'Very clever!' All these are ironical remarks, not to be taken literally and said as if implying the addition of the idiomatic phrase, 'I don't think!' Here is an example of irony of a rather different kind: 'By a sudden and adroit movement I brought my eye right up against his powerful left fist.'

Irony is not so bitter, not so harshly intended as SARCASM.

The *irony of fate* is 'a result opposite to and as if in mockery of the promised or appropriate result' (Webster). For example: 'It was the irony of fate that Mr Richards, who had swum the Channel four times, was drowned in his own lily-pond.' There is little or no element of irony in the fact that it rained on the day of the garden party, or that Mr Williams failed to keep an important appointment because he overslept, so it is better not to use the term in such contexts as these.

Dramatic irony – or *tragic irony*, as it is sometimes called – is the speaking by a character in a play of words that have an inner meaning for the audience, who say to themselves, 'Little does he know, poor man . . .'

Socratic irony (named after Socrates) is the feigning of ignorance in a discussion or a debate, in order to provoke one's opponent and so get the better of the argument.

irregular verbs   see VERB; WEAK VERBS.

irrelevancy in ARGUMENT a common form of FALLACY. It is the deliberate diversion of attention from the matter in dispute. We can consider it under the following sub-headings:

Argumentum ad hominem
Any attempt to solve an argument by directing it irrelevantly towards an individual, appealing to his particular interests, sym-

pathies or prejudices, or taking advantage of his character or position in life. Suppose that Mr Harrison is arguing with Mr Mitchell, who is a shopkeeper, about how to solve the country's traffic problem. 'Surely,' says Mr Harrison, 'you're not in favour of one-way streets? Just think how they might affect your business if they were introduced in this town!' Mr Harrison has ignored the real point and appealed to the self-interest of Mr Mitchell. Here are three other examples of *argumentum ad hominem*: (a) 'Of course *you* are in favour of a capital levy; you are poor and stand to gain by it'; (b) 'Naturally, being a woman, you wouldn't understand why men join clubs'; (c) 'You're just the sort of half-witted moron to say a thing like that!'

Argumentum ad populum
Any attempt to solve an argument by directing it irrelevantly towards a number of persons – an argument designed to play on the emotions of the crowd. A splendid example of this is in *Julius Caesar*, when Mark Antony, addressing the citizens of Rome after the murder of Caesar, uses words and phrases with an emotional appeal to arouse anger in the minds of his hearers, the real point being entirely ignored. *Argumentum ad populum* can also take the form of appealing to popular prejudices or passions, e.g. (a) 'It's not cricket'; (b) 'It's un-American'; (c) 'We must be guided not by the head, but by the heart – the great heart of humankind . . .'
      See EMOTIVE LANGUAGE.

Argumentum ad baculum
The argument of the 'big stick'. It is a crude way of evading the point by threats, e.g. 'If you don't agree to my proposals I'll force you out of business!'

Ignoratio elenchi
This can be defined as 'the fallacy of the irrelevant conclusion'; in other words, avoiding the necessity of admitting that one is wrong by proving something quite different from what is under discussion. For example, when Mr Rogers was asked to justify his statement that the fluoridation of water had an injurious effect on children's teeth, he said that the *really* important advance in dentistry was the introduction of an air-turbine drill with air bearings.
      Mr Rogers evaded the point. Two other forms of *ignoratio elenchi* are *extension* and *diversion*. By the first, the arguer extends his oppo-

nent's assertion beyond what he intended and then discredits him for something he did not say. If, for example, Mr Turner is arguing in favour of the abolition of nuclear bombs, it would be an extension to try to discredit him by pointing out that to abolish nuclear fission would prevent progress. Diversion is a similar trick. For example, Mr Andrews says that it has been proved that black men when properly educated are just as able as white men. 'Well, if you think so,' retorts Mr Clarke, 'why don't you go and live with them?' The contention is not refuted; there is a diversion to an entirely different issue.

-ise, -ize When do we use the former verbal ending and when the latter? Etymologically we ought to use -*ize* for all those verbs that derive from the Greek -*izo*, a suffix meaning 'to make; to become; to use; to act like', e.g. *legalize* (to make legal), *fossilize* (to become a fossil), *economize* (to use economy), *tyrannize* (to act like a tyrant). It can be safely assumed that there are over five hundred verbs etymologically entitled to the -*ize* suffix. As distinct from these there are about twenty verbs having the suffix -*ise*, which derives from the Latin and does not have the meaning of 'make; become', etc. – verbs such as *advertise, advise, compromise, despise, exercise, revise, supervise, surprise*.

Despite the fact that there are many more words ending in -*ize* than in -*ise*, there is an increasing tendency to use -*ise* for all of them, as we have done in this book. By comparison the Americans adhere strictly to -*ize*, even going to the point of spelling *analyse* 'analyze' and *paralyse* 'paralyze'.

The compilers of this present work wish to be impartial and therefore confine themselves to setting down the following contrasting views. The *O.E.D.* states: 'The suffix, whatever the element to which it is added, is in origin the Gr. -ιζειν, L. -*izare*; and as the pronunciation is also with *z*, there is no reason why in English the special French spelling in -*iser* should ever be followed.' Most other English dictionaries (we are subject to contradiction here, for we have not examined every one) follow the same line. In *Modern English Usage* Fowler speaks out loud and clear for -*ize*. In *Usage and Abusage* Eric Partridge commends it. In the other camp, that champion of -*ise*, the late G. H. Vallins, once went so far as to say: 'The artificial distinction based on an etymological subtlety that cannot be known to the ordinary man is an unnecessary archaism, and ought to be abolished forthwith.'

it   The use of the *impersonal 'it'*, in English is highly idiomatic. As an ANTICIPATORY SUBJECT, it stands before the verb in place of the real subject, which then comes after the verb, e.g. 'It was a dark and stormy night' instead of 'the night was dark and stormy'. The use is more obvious in 'it is no good your making excuses', where the real subject is 'your making excuses', which *it* anticipates and stands for. Without this use, the sentence would have to be written: 'your making excuses is no good', which, though correct, is felt to be un-idiomatic.

See also IDIOM; PRONOUN; NEUTER.

italics   The adjective *italic* derives from the Greek *Italikos*, meaning 'pertaining to Italy apart from Rome'. In the sixteenth century Aldo Manuzio, a Venetian printer, introduced a sloping type that became known as *italic*. In printed matter italics are used for:

(a) Titles of books, plays, films, etc., e.g. 'We went to see *Oklahoma* after we had read about it in the *Sunday News*.'

(b) Names of ships, e.g. 'From the *Defence*, signals were repeated to the *Colossus*, stationed between the *Defence* and *Mars*, whence Duff communicated with the *Victory*.' (From *Nelson* by Carola Oman.) The tendency of modern naval writers, however, is to keep the names of warships in roman, perhaps because there are now so few of them.

(c) Emphasis, e.g. 'I *must* go to London.'

(d) Foreign words or phrases, e.g. 'Realising that I had been guilty of a *faux pas*, I immediately changed the conversation.'

(e) Differentiation, e.g. 'One of the simplest of the rules of spelling states that when the sound is like *ee* in *meet*, we use *i* before *e* except after *c*. The only exceptions to this rule are *seize, weird, counterfeit*.'

See also INVERTED COMMAS.

its, it's   It is easy to distinguish the two if we remember that the possessive *its* has no apostrophe (cf. *yours, hers, ours, theirs*), e.g. 'A blackbird has built its nest in our laurels.' The second is short for *it is* or *it has*, e.g. 'It's time we went home.' 'It's been a delightful party.'

See also POSSESSIVE ADJECTIVES AND PRONOUNS.

J

jail   see GOAL – no, see GAOL (and also LITERAL MISTAKE!).

jargon   the sectional speech of a small group of people, such as
those belonging to a particular religion, science, art, trade, profession or political party. It is full of the technical terms of the activity
concerned. When a person uses these too often in general conversation with those not engaged in that activity, it becomes bad manners.
It should be noted that some technical terms overlap SLANG. For
example, 'go into a flat spin' and 'off the beam' were originally
R.A.F. jargon, then they became R.A.F. slang, then they passed into
general slang, and later became fully acceptable colloquially. See
also COLLOQUIALISM; JOURNALESE.

jingle   a catchy little piece of verse, simple in construction and
having a jingling sound. Here is a jingle by Gelett Burgess, the
American satirist:

> I never saw a purple cow,
>   I never wish to see one;
> But I can tell you anyhow,
>   I'd rather see than be one.

Mother Goose's Nursery Rhymes are jingles.

Johnsonese   writing that is pompous in style and abounding in
words derived from the classics. It is named after Dr Samuel Johnson, but is not really descriptive of much of his prose, which is often
magnificent and has been ridiculed without just cause.

journalese   This is a derogatory term that still appears in school
textbooks to refer to the lazy pretentiousness that journalists used to
employ when they were in too much of a hurry to write simply and
freshly. In a cheap attempt to impress they filled out their writing
with long words, circumlocutions, pompous turns of phrase, stale
elegances and CLICHÉS. An extreme example is: 'The veteran custodian of the wicket was made the recipient of a gratuitous gift by
the next wielder of the willow who, not being born under a propi-

tious star, snicked the fleeting little leather sphere into his ever-vigilant gloves.'

But newspaper writing has become a good deal crisper than it used to be, so that we no longer criticise journalism quite so much in terms of long words and other pomposities; indeed some newspaper styles tend to be over-simple nowadays. Perhaps inevitably, however, there are still plenty of clichés and circumlocutions whose woolliness is often a disguise for slipshod thinking or sheer ignorance. The modern schoolmaster, therefore, if he still employs the term 'journalese', will use it to show up the staleness or emptiness of clichés such as 'dramatic new move', 'last-ditch attempt', 'storm of protest'.

K

kerb see CURB.

Kingston upon Thames Not *on*, and no hyphens.

kitchen-sink drama a derogatory label pinned to much of modern drama which sought to break away from middle-class drawing-room plays. Notable dramatists of this school are John Osborne in *Look Back in Anger*, Arnold Wesker in *Roots*, Samuel Beckett in *Waiting for Godot*, and Harold Pinter. In Pinter's *The Caretaker* 'a prominent object throughout was a bucket suspended from the roof of the grimy and cluttered-up living-room in which three men enacted their grisly little drama. Into the bucket dripped the rain from the roof.' (*Britannica Book of the Year 1961*)

See also METHOD; THEATRE OF THE ABSURD; THREE UNITIES, THE.

L

lacuna (L. 'a gap') the missing piece of text. If it is more than one word, the gap is usually indicated by a row of three full stops; if it is a single word or part of a word, by a dash.

lampoon This derives from the French *lampons*, which means 'let us drink' or 'let us guzzle' and came into a French drinking song of the seventeenth century. From this it came to mean a piece of scurrilous and malicious verse or prose, intended to wound a particular person. It is said that the following lampoon, in the form of a QUATRAIN, was written on the door of Charles II's bed-chamber by the Earl of Rochester:

> Here lies our Sovereign Lord, the King,
>   Whose word no man relies on:
> He never says a foolish thing,
>   Nor ever does a wise one.

lateral in PHONETICS the sound made when the air passes round the sides of the tongue. See GUIDE TO PRONUNCIATION on page 7.

Latin words and phrases Hundreds of these are in common use – perhaps too common, for there is often a perfectly acceptable English substitute, acceptable, at least, to those who do not wish to show off. Below is a selected list. Those asterisked are treated more fully under their own headings in the body of the book.

* *ad hoc*, for this
ad infinitum, to infinity; endless
* *ad libitum*, at pleasure
ad nauseam, to a disgusting extent, e.g. 'He repeated *ad nauseam* all the details of his many ailments.'
ad valorem, according to value
a fortiori, all the more; for a still stronger reason
Alma Mater, 'the bounteous mother', a name used by ex-students for their school or university
Anno Domini, in the year of our Lord. Abbreviated A.D. (*q.v.*)

ante meridiem, before noon. Abbreviated *a.m.*, e.g. 10.30 a.m. = half past ten in the morning

ave atque vale, 'hail and farewell'

Ave Maria, 'Hail Mary'; opening words of a prayer

bona fides, good faith, sincerity, genuineness, e.g. 'Assured of his *bona fides*, I handed him the keys of the house.'

caveat emptor, let the buyer beware

circa, about. Abbreviated **c.*

compos mentis, sound mind, e.g. 'The lawyer pleaded that his client had not been *compos mentis* at the time of the accident.'

contra, against. It is found in words such as *contradict* (speak against), *contravene* (come against), also in compound words such as *contra-regulations* (against regulations), and from it derives *counter*, e.g. *counteract*, to act against

cum, with. It is found in place names, e.g. Chorlton-cum-Hardy, and in such combinations as gardener-cum-chauffeur, a man who performs the double duties of gardener and chauffeur, and *shop-cum-garage*, where one can buy a pound of butter or a gallon of petrol

cum grano salis, with a gain of salt, used figuratively in the sense of not entirely believing a thing, e.g. 'I take all he says *cum grano salis*.'

de facto, in fact; existing, whether legal or not; the opposite of *de jure*

Dei gratia, by God's grace

de jure, by right; according to law. For example, a *de jure* government is one that has legal standing, whilst a *de facto* government is one that is in control, whether legally or not

Deo volente, God willing. Abbreviated D.V. 'I shall see you again next year, D.V.'

* *deus ex machina*, a god from the machine

dramatis personae, a list of the characters in a play, often with the names of the actors taking the parts

Eheu fugaces . . . labuntur anni. This is a quotation from the Roman poet, Horace. It means 'Alas, the fleeting years glide past.' It is our custom to use only the first two words, implying the rest, as if with a shrug of our shoulders

errare est humanum, to err is human

* *et cetera*, and the rest

et sequitur, and the following. Abbreviated *et seq.*

ex cathedra, 'from the throne', used of a Papal judgement, hence of any weighty statement *exempli gratia*, for example. Abbreviated* *e.g.*

exit (plural *exeunt*), a stage direction meaning 'he goes off'. The word is also used as a noun, e.g. 'They have their exits and their entrances.' 'The exit doors must be kept open in the interval.'

ex libris, from the library (of); printed at the head of a slip pasted inside the cover of a book and giving the owner's name

ex officio, because of one's office. The chairman of a main committee is an ex-officio member of all sub-committees that may be formed

felo de se, 'felon of self', one who takes his own life, e.g. 'The jury returned a verdict of *felo de se*.'

festina lente, 'Hasten slowly', a paradox attributed to the Roman emperor Augustus

* *fidus Achates*, a faithful follower

finis, the end, once regularly, but now very rarely printed below the text on the last page of a book

flagrante delicto, in the very act. Its literal meaning is 'while the crime is blazing'. 'A policeman arrived suddenly and caught the thief in *flagrante delicto*.'

hic jacet, 'here lies', often found on tombstones

* *ibidem*, in the same place

idem est, that is. Abbreviated **i.e.*

in camera. In Latin *camera* means 'a vault'. The term *in camera* is a legal one, e.g. 'The evidence was heard *in camera*.' That is to say, it was heard in the private chamber of the judge, not in open court

infra dignitatem, beneath one's dignity. Abbreviated *infra dig

inter alia, among other things, e.g. 'This book contains, *inter alia*, a list of Latin words and phrases.'

lapsus linguae, a slip of the tongue

lapsus memoriae, a slip of memory

laudator temporis acti, one who praises past times – 'the good old days'

locum tenens, 'holding the place'; a deputy, especially for a clergyman or a doctor. It is often abbreviated, e.g. 'Dr Harrison is acting as locum for Dr Brown, who is on holiday.'

magnum opus, great work; the chief production of an artist or a writer. See OPUS

mater, mother

mea culpa, by my own fault

mens sana in corpore sano, a healthy mind in a healthy body *meum et tuum*, mine and thine (yours). We use the term euphemistically in 'He doesn't know the difference between *meum* and *tuum*', which is another way of saying that we think he is a thief

mirabile dictu, wonderful to relate, e.g. '*Mirabile dictu*, the weather was fine.'

modus operandi, a way of working, particularly doing the same thing in the same way every time, e.g. 'The house had been entered through a skylight, which the police recognised as the *modus operandi* of a thief known to be in the neighbourhood.'

multum in parvo, much in little

mutatis mutandis, with any necessary change of detail, e.g. 'The new agreement shall be on the same terms, *mutatis mutandis*, as the existing agreement.'

nemine contradicente. Usually abbreviated *nem. con.*, this means 'no one speaking against', e.g. 'Mr Jones's proposal that the club-house should be redecorated was carried *nem. con.*'

ne plus ultra, 'not more beyond'; the utmost limit, e.g. 'In dress and appearance he was the *ne plus ultra* of good taste.'

* *non sequitur*, 'it does not follow'

nota bene, 'note well.' Abbreviated N.B., this is used to draw particular attention to what follows, e.g. 'The annual general meeting will be held on 25th October next. N.B. Subscriptions are now due.'

obiit, 'he died'. Abbreviated *ob.*, this is used as follows: 'Gibert Harding (*ob.* 16th Nov. 1960) was the most controversial broadcaster of his day.'

* *opus*, work

pater, father; hence *paternoster* (our father), the Lord's Prayer in Latin

paterfamilias, head of a family. Generally used facetiously or at one time to end a letter published in a newspaper, e.g. 'Dear Sir, Referring to recent correspondence in your columns, my belief is that school terms should be longer and holidays shorter. Yours faithfully, Paterfamilias.'

peccavi, 'I have sinned'

* *per annum*, by the year

per ardua ad astra, 'by hard ways to the stars' (the motto of the R.A.F.)

per capita, per head, i.e. for each person

* *per centum*, per hundred. Abbreviated *per cent* or %

per diem, per day

per mensem, per month

per procuriationem, by proxy; by the agency of. Abbreviated *per pro* or *p.p.* See *per pro* under ABBREVIATION

post meridiem, after noon. Abbreviated *p.m.*, e.g. 4.15 p.m. = quarter past four in the afternoon

post mortem, after death. A post mortem examination of a body is made to find out the cause of death

post scriptum, written afterwards. See POSTSCRIPT

prima facie, first impression, e.g. 'The *prima facie* evidence suggested that he had met with a fatal accident, but further investigations proved that he had committed suicide.'

pro patria, for one's country. It is to be found in Horace's *Dulce et decorum est pro patria mori*, 'Sweet and glorious it is for one's country to die'

pro rata, in proportion; proportionately

pro tempore, for the time being. Abbreviated *pro tem*, it is used in such contexts as: 'We hope to move into our new house at the end of the month and are living in a caravan pro tem.'

quod erat demonstrandum, that which was to be proved. In its abbreviated form Q.E.D. it is used at the end of Euclid's theorems. Q.E.F. (*quod erat faciendum*, that which was to be done) is used at the end of his problems

quod vide (abbreviated *q.v.*), 'which see' – used to indicate CROSS REFERENCES

rara avis, rare bird. It is used figuratively in such contexts as: 'The visitor to this little secluded village is a *rara avis* indeed.'

* *sic*, thus

sine die, 'without a day'; put off until some unspecified date in the future, e.g. 'It was considered too early to make a final decision, so the matter was deferred *sine die*.'

sine qua non, 'without which not'; an indispensable condition or qualification; something essential, e.g. 'In the art of public speaking, clear diction is a *sine qua non*.'

sotto voce, in an undertone

status quo, the existing state of affairs; the way things are now. To maintain the *status quo* is to ensure that things remain unchanged. To restore the *status quo* is to re-establish a former state of affairs

* *stet*, let it stand, remain as it was first

sub judice, 'under judgement (in a legal court)' and therefore not open to discussion *sub rosa*, 'under the rose', privately

terra firma, 'firm earth'; dry land, e.g. 'After a rough crossing of the Straits of Dover, we were relieved to be back on *terra firma*.'

ubique, everywhere. From it derives the adjective *ubiquitous*, e.g. 'All over the world the ubiquitous Englishman is to be found.'

ultima Thule, the utmost limit. *Thule* was the name given by the Romans to the most northerly country known to them, which may have been Iceland, Norway or the Shetland islands. It has been unnecessarily used in such contexts as: 'During my convalescence, when walking quickly tired me, my *ultima Thule* was the tobacconist's at the end of the road.'

ultra vires, beyond one's power or authority, e.g. 'The magistrates decided that the local council had acted *ultra vires* by closing this footpath to the public.'

vade mecum, 'go with me'. We may use the term for anything we carry about with us because we may need it at any time, particularly a handbook for ready reference, e.g. a tourist's vade mecum, an angler's vade mecum, a typist's vade mecum.

Vae victis! 'Woe to the conquered!'

vale (plural *valete*), farewell. The plural form is often used in school magazines to head a list of those leaving at the end of the term

verbum sapienti. The full phrase is *verbum sat sapienti*, meaning 'a word to the wise is enough', but we usually omit *sat* (enough) and abbreviate the rest to *verb. sap.* in such contexts as: 'Verb. sap.,' he said when she tried to explain. 'I can guess the rest.'

versus, against. It is abbreviated *v.* in sporting fixtures, e.g. England *v.* Scotland, Manchester City *v.* Tottenham Hotspur, and in legal cases, e.g. Andrews *v.* Jones

via, 'way; road'. We use it in the sense of *by way of*, e.g. 'He flew from London to Australia *via* Singapore.'

via media, sometimes *media via*, a middle way or road. We use it figuratively with the meaning of 'a middle course', which is safer than venturing too far to one side or the other, e.g. 'My doctor recommended me to take a month's holiday. I could not afford to be away so long from my business, so chose the *via media* and spent a fortnight at the seaside.'

vice, in the place of. A vice-president takes over the duties of the president when the latter is unable to attend. Also vice-admiral, vice-chairman, vice-captain (in cricket, football, etc.) and others. A viceroy is one who rules territory as the deputy of the sovereign. Lord Curzon was Viceroy of India from 1898 to 1905

vice versa, conversely; the other way round, e.g. 'After the collision the motorist blamed the driver of the lorry, and vice versa.' That is, they blamed each other

videlicet, 'one may see'. It is abbreviated **viz.*

vita brevis, ars longa, 'life is short, art is long'. An alternative version is *ars longa, vita brevis*

viva voce, 'with the living voice'; oral or orally, e.g. 'In the French examination, I passed the written test, but failed in the *viva* (*voce*) because my accent wasn't good enough.'

latter   SEE FORMER.

lay, lie   The verb *to lay* is misused by confusion with *to lie*. There are three things to remember. First, *to lie* means 'to recline', whilst *to lay* means 'to place or put down' an object, including an egg. Secondly, *to lie* is intransitive, whilst *to lay* is transitive. Thus you can lie somewhere, but you always lay something somewhere. Thirdly, the principal parts of *to lie* are *lay, lying, lain*, whilst those of *to lay* are *laid, laying, laid*, e.g.:

Intransitive: The boy lay (was lying, had lain) on the bed.
Transitive: The hen laid (was laying, had laid) an egg in the nest.

A useful MNEMONIC is: 'Even an eiderduck cannot lay down.'

The matter is further complicated by the existence of *to lie* meaning to tell an untruth. The principal parts of this are *lied, lying, lied*. It will help to remember that you can lay down the law, but you cannot lay down on the job; if you are lazy you lie down on it instead.

Which brings us to *lay-about*, a loafer. The old compound, *lie-abed*, which was not only equally descriptive but also grammatically sound, has been superseded in recent years by *lay-about*, which has no merit whatever, but looks, alas, as if it has come to stay.

Then there is *lay-by*. At first glance this seems to be yet another solecism, but it is not. The original lay-by was part of a waterway widened so that vessels could pass each other or be laid up. The term now refers also to a roadside recess in which vehicles can stop without obstructing the traffic. In that the motorist does not himself lie by but lays his vehicle by, the verb is transitive and therefore *lay-by* is correct.

leading article   a declaratory unsigned article in a newspaper setting forth the editor's views. Formerly such articles were 'leaded',
i.e. had lead 'slugs' placed between the lines of type to space them
out and draw attention to the importance of the article. In America
the leading article is called the EDITORIAL, a term which is becoming
increasingly widespread in Britain as well.

leading question   Here *leading* does not mean 'main', 'chief' or
'most important'. A leading question is one that leads the person to
whom it is addressed to give the answer required by the questioner.
In the following conversation John is prompting Harry by asking
him leading questions:

'You stole those apples from my orchard,' the farmer said to John
and Harry, who were not anxious to admit it.
'We didn't, did we, Harry?' said John.
'No, of course not,' said Harry.
'We bought them in a shop, didn't we?'
'Yes, at the greengrocer's.'

Leading questions are usually banned in courts of law.

learn, teach   The misuse of *learn* for *teach* is much frowned on by
the educated, who have been taught to learn. To learn is to receive
knowledge or to study; to teach is to convey knowledge to someone
else, e.g.:
Wrong: It learnt me a lesson I shall never forget.
Right: It taught me a lesson I shall never forget.

leonine verse   in PROSODY verse with a system of INTERNAL RHYME.
The song from *The Princess* by Tennyson is written in leonine verse,
thus:

The splendour falls on castle walls
    And snowy summits old in story:
The long light shakes across the lakes
    And the wild cataract leaps in glory.
Blow, bugle, blow, set the wild echoes flying,
Blow, bugle; answer, echoes, dying, dying, dying.

O hark, O hear! how thin and clear,
   And thinner, clearer, farther going!
O sweet and far from cliff and scar
   The horns of Elfland faintly blowing!
Blow, let us hear the purple glens replying:
Blow, bugle; answer, echoes, dying, dying, dying.

O love, they die in yon rich sky,
   They faint on hill or field or river;
Our echoes roll from soul to soul,
   And grow for ever and for ever.
Blow, bugle, blow, set the wild echoes flying,
And, answer, echoes, answer, dying, dying, dying.

The derivation of *leonine* is obscure; perhaps this form of verse is named after Leoninus, a thirteenth-century poet. There is another example of it under BALLAD, in the stanzas from Oscar Wilde's *The Ballad of Reading Gaol*.

less   see FEWER.

letters   see CORRESPONDENCE.

lexical words   dictionary words or words that have primarily a meaning content. They are contrasted with STRUCTURAL WORDS that create a grammatical framework in which lexical words are connected in meaning.

lexicon (Gk. 'to speak')   a dictionary. We usually refer to a Latin dictionary but to a Greek lexicon. The maker of a dictionary is called a *lexicographer*, defined by Dr Johnson as 'a harmless drudge'.

lexis   in modern linguistics roughly synonymous with 'vocabulary', but vocabulary considered mainly from the point of view of meaning content. STRUCTURAL WORDS are usually treated separately from lexis.

liable   For confusion with *apt* and *likely* see APT.

libel   see SLANDER.

libretto (plural **libretti**) (It. 'book')   the 'book' (words) of an opera or other long musical work. For example, in the Gilbert and

Sullivan operas the music was composed by Sullivan and the libretti were written by Gilbert. The words of a song are called the LYRIC.

licence, license   The noun is spelt with a *c*, the verb with an *s*.

lie   see LAY.

lifelong, livelong   The first means 'lasting throughout life', e.g. 'John Watson, his lifelong friend, survived him, but died before the year was out.' The second has no etymological connection with *life* in the sense of human existence; *live* derives from the Old English *léof*, meaning '*love*', and is used with *long* to intensify it, just as we use 'precious' to intensify 'few' in the phrase 'precious few'. When we speak of 'the livelong day' we mean 'the long, long day', e.g. 'That confounded cuckoo keeps at it the livelong day.'

lighted, lit   The two are interchangeable in such contexts as 'I have lighted (lit) the fire', but it is more usual to say 'a lighted match' than 'a lit match', and 'I have lit' than 'I have lighted'.

lightening, lightning   The first means (a) a reduction in weight, and (b) an increase in illumination. The second is a flash of electricity in the sky.

light opera (operetta)   see OPERA.

like, as   The incorrect use of the first (a preposition) for the second (a conjunction) is treated under PREPOSITION.

likely   For confusion with *apt* and *liable* see APT.

limerick   a form of humorous verse consisting of five lines in anapaestic metre – that is, each foot is trisyllabic, with the stress falling on the third syllable. Lines 1, 2 and 5 have three feet each, and lines 3 and 4 have two feet each. The second and fifth lines rhyme with the first, and the fourth with the third. Here is an example:

There was once a young girl from Australia,
Who attended a dance as a dahlia;
  But the petals revealed
  What they should have concealed
And the dress – as a dress – was a failure.

Often the anapaestic metre is not strictly adhered to. For instance, the above might begin:

There was a young girl from Australia,
Who went to a dance as a dahlia;

Some limericks owe their humour to the fact that the pronunciation of the last word in the first line is different from the spelling, e.g.:

There was a young fellow from Beaulieu,
Who was never presumptuous undeaulieu,
    And though he wrote reams
    To the girl of his dreams,
He always concluded 'Yours treaulieu'.

These little verses (many of them, including some masterpieces of bawdy, unfortunately unsuitable for publication in a book of this kind!) are said to get their name from the chorus sung by the company at convivial parties after an extemporised nonsense verse sung by each member in turn. The chorus ran:

Oh, won't you come up, come all the way up,
    Come all the way up to Limerick?

Edward Lear did much to popularise limericks, but he was not their inventor. The first limerick was published in 1820, in an anonymous work entitled *The History of Sixteen Wonderful Old Women*.
See also SCANNING and EYE RHYME.

lingua franca   a language which serves as a medium of communication over a large multi-lingual area. Swahili, for example, is the lingua franca of East Africa.

linguistics   the science of languages. In recent years it has completely replaced the term PHILOLOGY. See DERIVATION; ETYMOLOGY; GRAMMAR; STRUCTURAL LINGUISTICS.

liquidate   At one time *to liquidate* was to settle the affairs of a limited liability company that could no longer pay its way. Then in the days of Prohibition in the U.S.A. it took on another meaning, which was 'to get rid of'; the gangsters of Chicago liquidated their opponents with sawn-off shotguns. Opponents of the Communist regimes in Russia and Eastern Europe have at times been similarly eliminated.

literal, literally   These come to us through Norman French from
the Latin meaning 'a letter'. When we speak of 'the letter of the
law' we mean the exact wording of the law, the law taken literally,
rather than 'the spirit of the law', which is the real meaning of the
law as opposed to the verbal expression of it. For example, should
we see a child being attacked by a dog in a public park we keep the
letter of the law if we obey the notice reading 'Keep off the Grass',
but if we disregard the order and hasten to the child's rescue we do
not offend against the spirit of the law. Again, when we speak of 'a
literal translation' we mean a word-for-word translation. Thus a
literal translation of *pomme de terre* is 'apple of the earth', but when a
French housewife asks the greengrocer for *pommes de terre* it is potatoes
that she requires. It follows that, as in law, it is the *spirit* of the
original text that must be brought out by a translator.

According to the sort of language in which they are used, words
may be classified as either *literal* or *figurative*. Ordinary literal words
are those of our everyday vocabulary that have no hidden meaning
but mean just what they say, letter by letter. When we call a spade
a spade we are using the word literally; but if we call it 'a gardener's
right hand' we are using words figuratively. The different types of
figurative language are to be found under FIGURES OF SPEECH.

We come now to that overworked word *literally*. As explained
above, this adverb means taking words in their literal or non-
figurative sense. It is, then, clearly a misuse of it to say, 'He was
literally bursting with excitement.' The exact opposite is intended:
he was bursting figuratively, not literally. It is this misuse of the
word as an INTENSIVE that is the cause of the trouble. 'I was literally
snowed under by the replies I received.' 'It was literally raining cats
and dogs.' 'We were literally thunderstruck by this news.' 'All her
friends were literally green with envy.' 'My head was literally going
round and round.' The only justifiable use of the adverb is when a
figure of speech becomes factual, e.g. 'Private Snooks, who works in
the cookhouse, is always in trouble, but it was not until this morning,
when he lost his footing on the slippery floor, that he found himself
literally in the soup.' Apart from rare occasions such as this, intel-
ligent people will resist the use of this overworked word, even in conversation.

See also VOGUE WORDS.

literal mistake   a misprint, usually referred to as 'a literal'. See
PRINTERS' PROOFS.

litotes (lait'outi:z)   a FIGURE OF SPEECH; the description of something by the negation of the opposite, to give emphasis, e.g. (a) 'It
was not a bad party at all.' (b) 'Our success is due in no small
measure to the hard work done by Mr and Mrs Thorne.' (c) 'The
young man was not lacking in courage.'

See also MEIOSIS.

livid   anything of the colour of lead, such as a bruise. Extreme
emotion may have that effect upon a person's countenance, so that
he becomes livid with anger or rage. But *livid* is not synonymous with
angry. In the first example below, the use of *livid* is bad; in the second
it is unpardonable.

   (a) The manager was livid when I got to the office ten minutes
       late.
   (b) The manager was livid with me when I got to the office ten
       minutes late.

See also OVERWORKED WORDS.

logic   the science of reasoning. It consists mainly of putting arguments to the test to find out whether they are valid – whether they
are logical. The logician has therefore to examine the reasons and
items of evidence in an argument, to decide whether they support the
conclusion they claim to. The two main methods of reasoning are
INDUCTION and DEDUCTION. An argument based on deductive reasoning is known as a SYLLOGISM. Faults of logic – flaws in reasoning – are
called FALLACIES. Logical fallacies are dealt with under SYLLOGISM;
fallacies in ARGUMENT are dealt with under FALLACY.

lower case (abbreviated l.c.)   a printing term for small letters.
Type used to be kept in cases divided into compartments. The
capital letters (A, B, C, D, etc.) were in an upper case, and the small
letters (a, b, c, d, etc.) in another case below it. Hand-setting of type
has almost ceased with composing machines, but the terms remain.
See PRINTERS' PROOFS; UPPER CASE.

lucidity   clarity, especially in the arrangement of ideas.

luxuriant, luxurious   The two adjectives both derive from *luxury*
but they do not mean the same thing. *Luxuriant* means 'prolific';
growing abundantly'. *Luxurious* means 'very comfortable indeed'.

lyric   Its literal meaning is 'of or pertaining to the lyre', which was a stringed instrument of olden days. Lyrical poetry is that which gives direct expression to the poet's own emotions; SUBJECTIVE poetry by contrast with NARRATIVE poetry, which tells a story. The original lyrics of the ancients were usually personal but light-hearted songs. Today the more serious sonnet too would be called a lyric. The sonnet, the ode, the elegy, the carol, the folk-song – all these are lyrical poetry.

The term *lyric* refers also to the words of a song. For example, Oscar Hammerstein II wrote the lyrics for the musical play, *The Desert Song*, by the composer Sigmund Romberg. The words of an opera or long musical work are known as the LIBRETTO.

M

McLuhanism   Marshall McLuhan, a Canadian professor, put a NEOLOGISM into the Anglo-American language in the late 1960s. McLuhanism was the theory that, because of the universality of television, the printed word, relying on *linear concepts* (left to right reading) was obsolescent. The visual image was all that mattered. Universal electronics would reduce the whole world to a *global village*, relying on pictorial communications. Even more the MEDIUM would in some way achieve its own momentum: it would not merely be that the televisual message transcended the written message, but that transcendentally *the medium is the message*, which is the title of McLuhan's best-known book. Book? Ah yes, when it came to his own message, Professor McLuhan, with whatever reluctance, resorted with no great skill to the linear concept. Meanwhile, he was adopted with enthusiasm by the ADVERTISING industry as a sort of intellectual mascot, justifying tawdriness with transatlantic verbiage. By the 1970s McLuhanism was ceasing to be TRENDY.

macron (Gk. 'long')   the mark (–) placed over a vowel to show that it is long, e.g. *fāte*. The mark showing that the sound is short (◡) is known as a BREVE, e.g. *făt*. In PROSODY these two marks are used to denote stress on syllables, not the length of vowels, e.g.

$$\breve{\cup}\ -\cup\ -\ \cup\ -\ -\cup\cup\ -\cup$$

'To be or not to be: that is the question.'

magazine from the Arabic meaning 'storehouse'. Its original meaning in English was a building in which arms, ammunition, etc. were stored in time of war. In 1731 the *Gentleman's Magazine* was first published, and it is from that time that the word has been used to refer to a periodical published at regular intervals and devoted to short stories and articles on general topics. The term now includes local publications such as parish magazines, school magazines and other journals intended to convey information and news, rather than to entertain.

magnum opus see OPUS.

majority This means 'the greater number, numerically more than half'. It does not mean 'the greater part', e.g.:
  Wrong: The majority of the English lesson was devoted to syntax.
  Right: Most of the English lesson was devoted to syntax.
  But: The majority of our English lessons are devoted to syntax.
  Wrong: The home team was on the defensive for the majority of the game.
  Right: The home team was on the defensive for most of the game.

malapropism a ludicrous misuse of a word, especially in mistake for one resembling it. It derives from the French *mal à propos*, which means 'ill-suited to the purpose', and is associated with Mrs Malaprop, a character in Sheridan's *The Rivals*, who gives us such gems as:

'Illiterate him, I say, quite from your memory.'
'If I reprehend anything in this world, it is the use of my oracular tongue, and a nice derangement of epitaphs.'
'As headstrong as an allegory on the banks of the Nile.'
'I own the soft impeachment.'

This device was used earlier by Shakespeare and Fielding. It was Dogberry in *Much Ado About Nothing* who announced that 'comparisons are odorous' (Mrs Malaprop calls them 'caparisons'). Fielding's Mrs Slipslop had the trick, but she never sank to such delightful depths as Mrs Malaprop.

Malapropos (mæl¹æpropou¹) means 'out of place; inopportune; unsuitable', e.g. 'Although he spoke the truth and many of those present agreed with him, it was felt that his frank remarks were malapropos at this stage in the proceedings.'

See also APROPOS.

mannerism (of speech) some particular TURN OF EXPRESSION used from force of habit rather than from usefulness. Some people's mannerism consists of using 'I mean to say' before far too many things they utter. Others pepper their conversation with 'sort of' or 'you know'. The response of others to any statement or question is all too frequently 'just the job' or 'fair enough', whilst others add 'that's by the way' to many of the remarks they pass. More expressions of this kind are 'how right you are!', 'in a manner of speaking' and 'see what I mean?'

See also REPORTED SPEECH.

many, much The first refers to number, e.g. *many men, many times*. The second refers to quantity, e.g. *much rain, much laughter*. In other words, *many* refers to countable things; *much* to uncountable things. There are, however, certain exceptions. For example, *much* (not *many*) is used when referring to sums of money, weights, etc., e.g. (a) 'I had not thought it would cost me as much as fifty pence.' (b) 'We never buy as much as three tons of coal at a time.'

Usually *many* and *much* are used in questions and negative sentences, and *a lot of* in positive sentences, e.g.:

(a) 'Were there many cars on the road?'
    'There were not many cars on the road.'
(b) 'Was there much rain in the night?'
    'There was not much rain in the night.'
(c) 'There were a lot of cars on the road.'
    'There was a lot of rain in the night.'

masculine rhyme see RHYME

mask or masque a dramatic entertainment performed by amateurs and originating in the court masquerade. Popular in the fifteenth and sixteenth centuries, the mask sought to give pleasure by its verse, music, dancing and costumes rather than by plot or portrayal of character. Milton's *Comus* was a mask and there is another in Act IV of Shakespeare's *The Tempest*.

media Latin plural of *medium*, used specifically to refer to the means of mass communication – newspapers, radio, television, films. *Mixed media* is a way of referring to all such. People who work in *mixed media* are often consciously TRENDY. The phrase is from the JARGON of ADVERTISING but is a development of an original use of the word as in 'the medium of education', meaning the language used in teaching. In some schools in India for example, the medium of education is English, though the students' own language may be Urdu, Tamil, etc.

meiosis (maiouⁱsis) · a FIGURE OF SPEECH akin to LITOTES. This is an understatement for the sake of emphasis, often for humorous effect, e.g. (a) 'The suggestion that all school holidays should be abolished was somewhat unpopular.' (b) 'When one of the passengers in the railway compartment stepped heavily on my foot, I mentioned the matter to him.'

melodrama a form of DRAMA in which naturalness of character and action is sacrificed to the main aim of sensationalism. Tragedy becomes melodramatic when characters do sensational things without convincing us that they would really do such things in the circumstances given. Melodrama is sometimes described as being *transpontine*. This is derived from the Latin meaning 'over the bridge'. The reference is to the melodramas performed in the old days in theatres on the Surrey side of the Thames, the more serious theatres being north of the river.

memoir a report or essay on some learned or scientific subject. The word is more often used in the plural. *Memoirs* can be defined as an autobiographical record; an account of events in which the narrator took part. An AUTOBIOGRAPHY is the story of a person's life told by himself. Memoirs need not be so comprehensive; they can be confined to a certain period of the author's life: for example, he can write his memoirs (that is, his recollections) of his wartime experiences with the Royal Navy, or of the ten years he spent with the Ona tribe of Tierra del Fuego.

merely an adverb that can change the sense of a sentence according to its position in it. This is discussed under ADVERB.
    See also SIMPLY.

metaphor This is treated together with SIMILE. See also MIXED METAPHOR.

metathesis (mətæθˈəsis) (Gk. 'to change places') grammatically, the transposition of sound or letters in a word. For example, in Middle English *third* was *thrid*; and *wæps* was the Old English name for a wasp. The SPOONERISM is a form of metathesis.

Method In the nineteenth century a group of writers inspired by the French novelist, Emile Zola, developed naturalism in literature. The principles and methods of those who practised it included every unpleasant detail, with no reticence whatever. Naturalism, in effect, was REALISM carried farther. The pioneer of naturalism on the stage was the Russian director, Constantin Stanislavsky. A development of part of his teaching was called the 'New Method', later abbreviated to 'Method'. It demands that the actor identify with his part. He cannot express, say, jealousy or guilt merely by using his imagination; he must search within his own experience of jealousy or guilt. The film actor Marlon Brando was a notable recruit to Method acting.

See also ALIENATION; KITCHEN-SINK DRAMA; THEATRE OF THE ABSURD; THREE UNITIES, THE.

metonymy (metonˈəmi) a FIGURE OF SPEECH in which the thing really meant is represented by something closely associated with it, e.g. 'The stage [acting profession] is up in arms against this critic. He is even alleged to be addicted to the bottle [strong drink].' (b) 'All citizens of this country owe allegiance to the crown [monarch].' (c) 'Our son John has joined the colours [Army, *colours* referring here to the flag of a regiment].' Other examples are: *the turf* (horse-racing), *the Press* (newspapers in general), *the pulpit* (preachers and preaching), *Wall Street* (the American stock market), *the table* (food). The last means also those sitting round a meal table, e.g. 'His witty remarks kept the table highly amused' – or, using a cliché, 'He kept the table in a roar.'

metre the rhythm of lines of verse. This rhythm depends upon the emphasis given to certain syllables when spoken aloud. The arrangement of these *accents* or *stresses* in the form of a regular pattern is called *metre*, one of the two main divisions of PROSODY.

THE FOOT

The unit of metre is the *foot*, which is either *disyllabic*, i.e. with one stressed syllable and one unstressed syllable, or *trisyllabic*, i.e. with one stressed syllable and two unstressed syllables. The degree of emphasis of the sounds – stressed or unstressed – is known as QUANTITY. The symbols denoting quantity are the MACRON (–) for the stressed syllable, and the BREVE (◡) for the unstressed syllable. Thus a disyllabic foot may be denoted by –◡ or ◡–, and a trisyllable foot may be denoted by –◡◡, ◡–◡ or ◡◡–. It should be understood that in prosody the macron and the breve are used to denote stress; they are not used to denote the length of vowel sounds, as they are in PRONUNCIATION.

Trochee (–◡)
When the stress falls on the first syllable of a disyllabic foot (e.g.
–◡
(*sunset*) the metre is called *trochaic*. This derives from the Greek meaning 'running' and is so called because it gives the verse a tripping rhythm. The trochaic foot is known as a *trochee*. Here is an example from Browning's *Home Thoughts, from the Sea*:

> Nobly, / nobly / Cape St. / Vincent / to the / North-west /
>   died a / way;
> Sunset / ran, one / glorious / blood-red / reeking / into /
>   Cadiz / Bay.

Iambus (◡–)
When the stress falls on the second syllable of a disyllabic foot (e.g.
◡ –
immense) the metre is called *iambic*. This derives from the Greek meaning 'a lampoon', from the verb 'to assail', and is so called because it was used by the Greeks who wrote on satirical themes. The iambic foot is known as an *iambus* (plural *iambi* or *iambuses*). Here is an example from Tennyson's *In Memoriam*:

> I do / but sing / because / I must,
> And pipe / but as / the linn / ets sing.

Spondee (−−)
When the stress falls equally on both syllables of a disyllabic foot
(e.g. *boat-hook*, *waylay*) the metre is called *spondaic*. This derives from
the Greek meaning 'of a libation' because it was used in the solemn
chorus accompanying a libation, which was drink poured on the
ground as an offering to a god. The spondaic foot is known as a
spondee. It occurs with the *dactyl* (see below) and the *trochee* in the
classical HEXAMETER, but one rarely finds in English poetry a succession of spondees. Here is an example from Milton's *Paradise Lost*:

> Rocks, caves, / lakes, fens, / bogs, dens, / and shades / of death.

Dactyl (−˘˘)
When the stress falls on the first syllable of a trisyllabic foot (e.g.
laughable) the metre is called *dactylic*. This derives from the Greek
meaning 'a finger', in that it has one long 'joint' and two short ones.
The dactylic foot is known as a *dactyl*. Here is an example from
Browning's *The Lost Leader*, written when Wordsworth accepted the
poet laureateship:

> We that had / loved him so, / followed him, / honoured
>   him,
> Lived in his / mild and mag / nificent / eye . . .

Amphibrach (˘−˘)
When the stress falls on the second syllable of a trisyllabic foot (e.g.
revolted) the metre is called *amphibrachic*. This derives from the Greek
meaning 'short on both sides'. The amphibrachic foot is known as
an *amphibrach*. Here is an example from Campbell's *The Soldier's
Dream*:

> Our bugles / sang truce – for / the night-cloud / had lowered

Anapaest (˘˘−)
When the stress falls on the third syllable of a trisyllabic foot (e.g.
referee) the metre is called *anapaestic*. This derives from the Greek
meaning 'to strike back'; an anapaestic foot is a dactylic foot 'struck

back', i.e. reversed. The anapaestic foot is known as an *anapaest*. Here is an example from Byron's *The Destruction of Sennacherib*:

$$\breve{}\ \breve{}\ -\quad \breve{}\ \breve{}\ -\quad \breve{}\ \breve{}\ -\quad \breve{}\ \breve{}\ -$$

And the sheen / of their spears / was like stars / on the sea,

$$\breve{}\ \breve{}\ -\quad \breve{}\ \breve{}\ -\quad \breve{}\ \breve{}\ -\quad \breve{}\ \breve{}\ -$$

When the blue / wave rolls night / ly on deep / Galilee.

The LIMERICK is written in anapaestic metre.

SCANNING

To mark a line off into feet is to *scan* it. In SCANNING we must examine not only the *kind* of feet in a line but also the *number* of them. In prosody lines are known according to their metrical length, i.e.:

Monometer	1	metrical foot
Dimeter	2	metrical feet
Trimeter	3	do.
Tetrameter	4	do.
Pentameter	5	do.
Hexameter	6	do.
Heptameter	7	do.
Octameter	8	do.

These are discussed under their own headings elsewhere in this work.

By combining the kind and number of feet of which it consists, we can give each line of verse its full technical description. For example, in the lines by Browning quoted above under *trochee* there are eight feet, so we can call each line a *trochaic octameter*. In the lines by Tennyson quoted under *iambus* there are four feet, so we can call each line an *iambic tetrameter*. In the line by Milton quoted under *spondee* there are five feet, so we can call it a *spondaic pentameter*. Similarly, we can scan the second quotation from Browning as being in *dactylic tetrameters*; the quotation from Campbell as being in *amphibrachic tetrameters*; and the quotation from Byron as being in *anapaestic tetrameters*.

It will be noted that not all the lines in these quotations end with a complete foot. For instance, under *trochee* the lines end with *way* and *Bay*, which are monosyllabic instead of disyllabic. Because of this the lines are called CATALECTIC ('stopping short').

There are, of course, many variations in metrical scan. See, for example, *iambic hexameter* under ALEXANDRINE; *iambic pentameter* under BLANK VERSE and HEROIC COUPLET; SONNET; *iambic dimeter* under DIMETER; *trochaic tetrameter* under TETRAMETER; *iambic trimeter* under TRIMETER.

For convenience of reference all headings under which matters relating to prosody, metre and rhyme are separately treated in this work are listed under PROSODY.

middle see CENTRE.

Middle English see DERIVATION.

mini abbreviation of *miniature* used as a convenient prefix to indicate smallness, e.g. *mini-car*, *mini-skirt*. An earlier generation sought to add the dreadful suffix *-ette* to serve the same purpose, as in *wagonette*, *launderette* (a small, self-service laundry), *kitchenette*. In context, *mini* also serves as a noun.

minimise see DIMINISH.

miracle plays dramatic representations in the Middle Ages based on the Bible or the lives of the Saints. They were performed in the market place from the late fourteenth to the sixteenth centuries by the town guilds, usually in cycles, one episode being allotted to each guild. Though strongly religious, they contained some racy comic scenes.

misogamist, misogynist (misogˈəmist, misodʒˈənist) A *misogamist* hates marriage; a *misogynist* hates women.

misquotation In conversation this is a venial offence; it is usually of little consequence. When, however, we quote in our writing the works of others we should be more careful; we should verify our references: and the extract should be exact in wording, spelling and punctuation. (See SIC.) Some misquotations are, of course, deliberate. For example, we describe a man as having 'dined not wisely but too well', whereas Othello refers to himself as ' one that loved not wisely but too well'. Sometimes we alter a quotation to suit our needs, with the result that the emended version becomes the quotation and the original is forgotten. For example, we might speak of 'a beggarly array of empty bottles', but Romeo does not mention having seen bottles when he visited the apothecary, nor was there an array but an 'account'.

And in his needy shop a tortoise hung,
An alligator stuff'd and other skins
Of ill-shaped fishes; and about his shelves
A beggarly account of empty boxes,
Green earthen pots, bladders and musty seeds,
Remnants of packthread and old cakes of roses,
Were thinly scatter'd, to make up a show.

Below are a few other misquotations with the correct versions following in brackets:

(a) 'Discretion is the better part of valour.' ('The better part of valour is discretion.' – Shakespeare's *Henry IV*, Part I)

(b) 'Fresh fields and pastures new.' ('Fresh woods, and pastures new.' – Milton's *Lycidas*)

(c) 'Money is the root of all evil.' ('The love of money is the root of all evil.' – I Timothy, vi, 10)

(d) 'To gild the lily.' ('To gild refined gold, to paint the lily.' – Shakespeare's *King John*) To do these things, and to 'throw a perfume on the violet', is 'wasteful and ridiculous excess'. In other words, it is endeavouring to improve upon perfection.

See also CONTEXT.

mixed metaphor   a FIGURE OF SPEECH that combines two or more inconsistent metaphors. Perhaps the most famous is attributed to Sir Boyle Roche, the Irish politician: 'Mr Speaker, I smell a rat; I see him forming in the air and darkening the sky; but I'll nip him in the bud.' There is a mixed metaphor in the fourth line of Hamlet's soliloquy: 'Or to take arms against a sea of troubles.' Here are a few more: 'The skeleton at the feast was a mare's nest.' 'We're not through the wood yet by a long chalk.' 'All these whited sepulchres are tarred with the same brush.' 'He left no stone unturned until the apple of his eye had reached the top of the tree.'

See also SIMILE, METAPHOR.

mnemonics (niːmoˈniks)   This and the adjective *mnemonic* derive from the Greek meaning 'mindful'. (Mnemosyne was the goddess of memory.) It refers to any system devised to improve the memory, usually by the association of ideas. Most of us have our own little private systems. For example, we may remember the number of our car because it is the date of the Battle of Waterloo followed by the initials of Uncle Henry.

mock heroic   When a trivial incident is treated with mock serious-
ness and written up with all the formal style of the EPIC, we have a
mock heroic poem. Such is Pope's *Rape of the Lock* in which he
solemnly deals with the cutting of a lock of a lady's hair, in four
cantos.

Modern English   one of the periods into which the English language is divided. It dates from Elizabethan times and is discussed
under DERIVATION.

modify   in grammar, to qualify or describe more fully. It is chiefly
used in the definition of an adverb, which modifies a verb, an adjective or another adverb, e.g. (a) 'He shouted *angrily*' (modifying the
verb *shouted*). (b) 'He was *extremely* angry' (modifying the adjective
angry). (c) 'He was *quite* easily angered' (modifying the adverb
easily). When describing the functions of an adjective, grammarians
usually use QUALIFY.

monograph   a piece of writing on a particular subject. Sherlock
Holmes remarks to Dr Watson in *The Boscombe Valley Mystery*: 'I
found the ash of a cigar which my special knowledge of tobacco
ashes enables me to pronounce as an Indian cigar. I have, as you
know, devoted some attention to this, and written a little monograph
on the ashes of one hundred and forty different varieties of pipe,
cigar, and cigarette tobacco.'

monometer (monomˈətə) (Gk. 'one measure')   in PROSODY a line
of verse consisting of a single foot. The following epigram by W. N.
Ewer is in *iambic monometers*, the stress being on the second syllable
of each foot:

How odd
Of God
To choose
The Jews.

See METRE.

monosyllabic   having one syllable, e.g. *cat*, *dog*, *man*. 'Yes' and
'No' are monosyllabic replies. It is said that the longest mono-
syllable in the English language is, appropriately enough, *stretched*.

mood   the 'mode' or manner in which a verb expresses itself. There are three main moods for English verbs: *indicative, imperative* and *subjunctive*.

Indicative mood   This states a fact, e.g. 'He has left school', or asks a question, e.g. 'Has he left school?'

Imperative mood   This expresses a command, e.g. 'Go to bed!' or a request, e.g. 'Close the door quietly, please.'

Subjunctive mood   This expresses a state, event or act as possible, conditional or wished for, rather than as actual. The *Concise Oxford Dictionary* describes this mood as obsolescent in English. The only surviving inflexions to indicate the subjunctive are the third person singular present, e.g. 'if he have', 'lest he die', and in the present and past singular of the verb *to be*, e.g. 'if I be', 'lest you be', 'if I were'. But apart from a few lingering expressions, e.g. 'far be it from me', 'if I were you' and some useful INVERSIONS, e.g. 'Were I in a position to . . .', the use of these forms is now considered pedantic, even in serious literature. If the indicative does not suffice to suggest the doubt inherent in the original use of the subjunctive, the use of *may* or *should* will make good the deficiency. Instead of 'he is afraid lest I be taken ill', we today feel it to be more idiomatic to say 'he is afraid that I may be taken ill'. In 1933 Otto Jespersen said in his *Essentials of English Grammar*: 'Since the seventeenth century we see an increasing tendency to say *I wish he was . . ., if he was . . ., as if he was . . .* instead of the earlier *were*, a tendency which has to some extent been counteracted by the teaching of grammarians that *were* was the correct form, at any rate in serious literature. As, however, no inconvenience has ever been felt by the fact that there was no corresponding difference in other verbs (*if I had, did,* etc.), it seems doubtful whether the theoretic opposition to *if he was,* etc., will be strong enough to prevail against the natural evolution of the language.' In 1941 Somerset Maugham wrote: 'The subjunctive is in its death throes, and the best thing to do is to put it out of its misery as soon as possible.'

See also NOMINATIVE CASE for *if I were he* (*him*).

moral, morale   Their different usage is shown in the following:

(a) The moral of the story is that one should not count one's chickens before they are hatched.

(b) The morale of the troops is excellent; they are well trained and full of confidence.

morality plays   medieval verse plays of an allegorical kind, teaching lessons of virtue. The characters were personifications or abstractions such as Death, Good Deeds, Everyman, Beauty, Fellowship, Knowledge.

much   see MANY.

musical   used as a noun to refer to a musical comedy. G. B. Shaw's *Pygmalion* was turned into a musical called *My Fair Lady*.

musical directions   instructions printed with music to show how certain passages are to be played. Here are some of them:

accelerando, gradually increase speed
adagio, slowly and gracefully
ad libitum, as the player pleases; for as long as he wishes
allegretto, fairly briskly
allegro, more briskly than *allegretto*
andante, in fairly slow time
a tempo, in strict time
con anima, with feeling
con brio, with liveliness
crescendo, increase in sound
diminuendo, gradually decrease in sound
dolce, sweetly, softly
forte, loudly
fortissimo, very loudly
furioso, furiously
largo, very slowly and solemnly
legato, smoothly
lento, slowly
moderato, with moderate speed
molto adagio, very slowly
molto allegro, very quickly
non troppo allegro, not too quickly
pianissimo, very softly
piano, softly
rallentando, gradually more slowly
scherzando, in a playful manner
sforzando, with sudden emphasis
sostenuto, in a sustained or prolonged manner

staccato, jerkily
tardo, slowly and leisurely
vivace, in a lively manner

musical terms   Here are some of the very large number of terms
used in instrumental and vocal music:

accompaniment, music by an instrument going along with the voice,
   e.g. 'Mr Peters sang three songs. He was accompanied on the
   piano by his sister.'
anthem, a sacred song sung alternately by the two parts of a choir;
   a piece performed by the choir at a certain point in the church
   service
aria, a song for one voice to an instrumental accompaniment
ballad, see under BALLAD
berceuse, a lullaby or cradle-song; also a piece of soothing music
cadenza, an instrumental or vocal flourish at the end of a movement
calypso, a form of ballad that originated in the West Indies; it
   usually satirises current events and is sung in African rhythm as
   if the singer is making the words up as he goes along
cantata, a poem or lyrical drama set to music, with solos and
   choruses, but without dramatic actions such as there are in
   opera
caprice (or *capriccio*), a playful piece of music. The words derive
   from the frisky behaviour of a goat, in Greek: *capro*
chamber music, music adapted to performance in smaller surroundings than concert halls, theatres, etc.
choir, a band of singers; hence *choral*. In opera, the term is CHORUS
chord, a combination of notes sounded together
concerto, music for a solo instrument accompanied by an orchestra,
   e.g. a *piano concerto*, *violin concerto*. A famous example is Tchaikovsky's piano concerto in B flat minor
duet, a composition for two instruments or voices
étude, a 'study', a short piece of music, often giving practice in a
   specific technical difficulty
fantasia, a composition in which musical form takes second place to
   fancy
fugue, a composition in which the theme is taken up by the different
   parts (voices) or instruments one after another. Johann Sebastian Bach wrote a large number of fugues

intermezzo, a short musical performance between the acts of an opera or drama; a short piece of music

lyric, see under LYRIC

movement, a principal division of a musical work

musical comedy, see under COMEDY

nocturne, a dreamy piece appropriate to the night or evening. Chopin composed a number of beautiful nocturnes

obbligato, music accompanying a solo, but having a separate importance of its own. Note the spelling

opera, see OPERA

opus, any musical composition. Abbreviated *op.* and followed by a number, it shows a musician's composition in its order of publication, e.g. 'Chopin's fantasia, *op.* 49, was among the greatest of his musical works.'

oratorio, a composition for instruments and voices, dramatic in form, but performed without actions, scenery or stage costumes. Handel's *Messiah* and Elgar's *Dream of Gerontius* are oratorios

orchestra, see ORCHESTRA

overture, composition played by the orchestra as an introduction to an opera, oratorio, etc. A *concert overture* is an independent work, to be played at the beginning of a concert, e.g. Mendelssohn's *Fingal's Cave*

pizzicato, played by plucking the strings of a violin, cello, etc. with the fingers

polonaise, a piece of music for the slow Polish dance of the same name

quartet, a composition for four instruments or voices

quintet, a composition for five instruments or voices

rhapsody, an instrumental composition irregular in form, e.g. Liszt's Hungarian Rhapsodies

rondo, a work or movement having a main theme that is returned to after each subordinate theme. See also RONDEAU

scherzo, a light, playful movement, usually following a slow movement, in a symphony or sonata

serenade, music played or sung out of doors at night, especially by a lover beneath his lady's window; a nocturne

sextet, a composition for six instruments or voices

solo, a composition for one instrument, or voice (with or without instrumental accompaniment)

sonata, a composition for one or two instruments, usually consisting of three or more movements. Beethoven's *op.* 27, no. 2, the sonata in C sharp minor, is popularly known as the 'Moonlight' Sonata

suite, a series of instrumental movements, originally in dance style

symphony, a composition akin to the sonata but for a full orchestra. It usually has three or four movements in related keys but different rhythms and speeds

tempo, the speed at which music should be played as indicated by the directions (see above)

trio, a composition for three instruments or voices

voluntary, an organ solo played before, during or after a church service

mutual Careful writers will not confuse this adjective with *common*. To use *mutual* correctly there must be a relationship in which X is or does to Y as Y is or does to X. Thus we can say our admiration is mutual if you admire me as much as I admire you. But if X has a friend Z, and Y also has the same friend Z, Z is not their mutual friend; he is merely their common friend. Perhaps it is because *common* also means 'low' and 'vulgar' (*q.v.*) that we prefer to speak of 'our mutual friend'.

See also PLEONASM.

mystery plays another name for MIRACLE PLAYS. The name comes from an old use of 'mystery' meaning 'a religious truth divinely revealed'.

mythology A myth is a folk legend, a fictitious story told as if the incidents actually happened. Mythology is the study of myths or a collection of tales about them. Greek and Roman mythology includes such famous names as Zeus, Aphrodite, Pan, Apollo, Neptune, Mercury, Cupid, Hercules, Tantalus, Prometheus, Achilles, Jason.

N

narrative telling of events. We speak of narrative poetry and narrative composition. The *ballad* and the *epic* are narrative poetry because they tell a story. Famous examples of narrative poetry are Chaucer's *The Canterbury Tales*, Scott's *Marmion*, Coleridge's *The Rime of the Ancient Mariner* and, in more recent times, Masefield's *Reynard the Fox* and Chesterton's *Ballad of the White Horse*. There are many others.

nasals   in PHONETICS the sounds made by the air passing through the nose. See GUIDE TO PRONUNCIATION on page 7.

naturalism   a development beginning with Zola that aimed at making literature mirror life with the utmost directness and even crudity.
See also METHOD.

naught, nought   There is no fixed rule, but modern usage prefers *nought* for the cipher 0, reserving *naught* as a substitute for *nothing*. Even then it is falling out of use, except rhetorically, e.g. 'Say not the struggle naught availeth' (Clough). More common is the positive form, *aught*, e.g. 'For aught I know, he is a grandfather by this time.'

née (nei)   the feminine past participle of *naître*, the French verb meaning 'to be born'. It is used to show a married woman's maiden name by placing it after her married name, e.g. 'Mrs Annie Besant, *née* Page, was elected president of the Indian National Congress in 1918.' The word is often to be found in the personal columns of newspapers, e.g. 'On 3rd September 1964, to Jane (*née* Wright), wife of Frank Martin, a son (Anthony Paul).'

negative   the opposite of an AFFIRMATIVE. An affirmative says that a thing is so, e.g. 'The cat is black', or agrees that a thing is so, e.g. 'Yes, the cat is black' (or 'Yes, it is'). A negative says that a thing is not so, e.g. 'The cat is not black', or agrees that a thing is not so, e.g. 'No, the cat is not black' (or 'No, it isn't').

To say that the answer is 'in the affirmative' is the same as saying that the answer is 'yes'. To say that the answer is 'in the negative' is the same as saying that the answer is 'no'.

The effect of a double negative is that the second cancels out the first, e.g. 'I shan't be surprised if it doesn't rain this afternoon.' The speaker does not mean that he will not be surprised if the rain keeps off this afternoon; he will, in fact, be surprised if it does keep off. As the sentence stands, the negative 'doesn't' cancels out the negative 'shan't' and the result is an affirmative: 'I shall be surprised if it rains this afternoon.' There is the same effect in this exchange of remarks:

'Do you think it won't rain this afternoon?'
'No.'

If the second speaker is of the opinion that it will not rain, the correct answer is 'Yes' – in other words, 'Yes, I think it will keep fine this afternoon.'

Negative words are those that are made to negate the meaning of the base word, mainly by the use of the PREFIXES un-, in-, im-, il-, ir-, e.g. unspoilt, unsure, indirect, impossible, illegal, irrelevant.

See also HARDLY, SCARCELY.

negative questions   questions that incorporate the negative *not*. There are three main points:

1. Aren't you going to tell me what he said?
   Can't he swim?
   Isn't it a lovely day?
2. You do see what I mean, don't you?
3. You don't see what I mean, do you?

Examples 2 and 3 are also known as QUESTION TAGS.

neighbourhood   The incorrect use of 'in the neighbourhood' in the sense of 'about' or 'approximately' is treated under REGION, NEIGHBOURHOOD.

neither . . . nor   a pair of words acting as a single co-ordinate CONJUNCTION. The use of the first requires the use of the second, e.g.:
Wrong: Neither Jack or Frank was to blame.
Right: Neither Jack nor Frank was to blame.

Whether a singular or plural verb is required is discussed under EITHER . . . OR.

When *not* takes the place of *neither*, it is followed by *or*, not *nor*, e.g. 'The book was not in the study or in the bedroom.' We do, however, use *nor* in such sentences as 'The book was not in the study, nor was it in the bedroom.'

See also NUMBER; and, for the pronunciation of *neither*, EITHER, NEITHER.

neologism (niːolˡədʒīzm)   the coining or using of a new word. A neologism may consist of an entirely new invention, such as the name *polythene* for a new type of plastic; or it may consist of an old word with a new meaning, such as *viewer*, which now refers in particular to a person who watches the television (we have had to adapt the French word *voyeur* to indicate someone who views other people's sometimes illicit activities); and *summit*, which is no longer a mere peak or pinnacle but 'the highest level of officials; *esp.*: the diplomatic level of chiefs of state or heads of government' (Webster, 1961). A *summit conference* is a meeting of chiefs of state or heads of government, and a *summiteer* is one who attends such a conference.

Other recent words, among them some of the many noted in recent issues of the *Britannica Book of the Year*, are:

astronaut, cosmonaut, a space traveller
*beatnik, one of the *beat* generation expressing social protest by unconventional behaviour
bingo, the modern development of lotto
discotheque, a place where you dance to music played on records; the equipment for producing such music
exportise (export – expertise), the 'know-how' in export advertising
group, an ensemble performing modern popular music
hi-fi, high-fidelity recordings
motel, motorists' hotel, usually a group of furnished cabins near a main road and offering accommodation to tourists
motorcade, a modern equivalent of a cavalcade, with cars instead of horse-drawn vehicles in procession
pot, the drug made from dried Indian hemp leaves
redbrick, descriptive of a university of modern foundation (see REDBRICK)

See also DERIVATION; PORTMANTEAU WORDS; VOGUE WORDS.

nepotism (pronounced nepˡətism or niːpˡətism, the first being recommended here)   This comes from the Italian *nepote*, meaning nephew. It applied originally to the patronage of a Pope's illegitimate sons, who were conveniently known as nephews, and its present meaning is the showing of too great favour to relatives by those in high office, or, in the popular modern phrase, 'jobs for the boys'.

neuter (L. 'neither')   neither masculine nor feminine GENDER. In the past, English grammarians classified as neuter nouns all those that named things as distinct from living creatures. But that classification had to do with sex or absence of it, rather than with grammatical gender. In an uninflected language like English the neuter gender no longer applies. It survives only in the pronoun *it*.

See also INFLEXION; PRONOUN; VERB

neutral words   those that, unlike EMOTIVE words, show no emotional commitment on the part of the user. The word *old* is usually neutral, whereas *antiquated* shows disapproval, and *of mature age* shows approval. Similarly, *thin*, *youthful*, *reserved* are neutral, and *scraggy*, *childish*, *sullen* are emotive.

never   not ever; at no time. It should not be used in reference to one particular occasion, e.g.:
   Wrong: You never went to school this morning.
   Right: You did not go to school this morning.
   Right: You never go to school if you can avoid it.
   Never is used colloquially to express surprise, e.g. 'Well, I never! Fancy that!'

nice   a word that has undergone a series of changes in meaning. In the sixteenth century it had the meaning of the Latin derivation, 'stupid'. By the beginning of the seventeenth century it meant 'wanton'. Then it became 'affectedly coy or reluctant'. From that it took on the meaning of 'over-refined'. This led to its being used in the sense of 'difficult to satisfy', and thence to 'finely discriminating'. We still use it in this sense when we refer to 'a nice distinction', meaning a 'fine' one. By 1800 its more usual modern meaning of 'agreeable' had arrived and today it is in the category of OVER-WORKED WORDS.

nominative absolute   see under ABSOLUTE.

nominative case   the case of the subject of any verb. It indicates the source of an action, e.g. '*Dogs* bark.' It is also the case of the complement of verbs of incomplete predication (see under VERB), e.g. (a) 'It was *he* who was fond of her, not she of him.' (b) 'Her younger son became *a sailor.*'

   Errors arise from the use of the nominative case instead of the accusative, e.g.:
   Wrong: All things come to he who waits.
   Right: All things come to him who waits.

Wrong: I handed the tickets to she whom I took to be the oldest of the girls.

Right: I handed the tickets to her whom I took to be the oldest of the girls.

After the verb *to be* we should, strictly speaking, use the nominative case, e.g.:

Wrong: If I were him, I should tread warily.

Right: If I were he, I should tread warily.

There is, however, a growing tendency among educated people to use the accusative – so much so that it would be considered very pedantic in conversation to say 'It is I' instead of the universal 'It's me'. Though usage is clearly changing, it is perhaps safer to use the nominative in formal writing, except in direct speech. When a relative clause follows the pronoun, the nominative should always be used, e.g. 'It is I who am in the wrong.'

See also CASE.

non-conclusive verbs   those verbs not normally used in the continuous tenses because they are felt to signify actions that have no beginning or ending, such as *love, hate, think, believe, mean, remember, see, hear, wish, refuse*. We say 'I think he lives there', not 'I am thinking he lives there', 'I love eating here', not 'I am loving eating here'.

non-defining clause   a RELATIVE CLAUSE that is not strictly an ADJECTIVE CLAUSE, because it adds information about the ANTECEDENT but does not define it. Unlike an adjective clause, it must be separated from the antecedent by commas. The difference between the two clauses can be seen from these examples:

(a) Tom's brother, who retired last year, was a solicitor.
(b) Tom's brother who retired last year was a solicitor.

In (a) 'brother' is not defined. It means that Tom's brother (presumably he only has one) – he retired last year, by the way – was a solicitor. In (b) 'brother' is defined; it is the brother who retired last year, not any of the other brothers.

none   For the use of this as a plural pronoun see NUMBER.

non-finite   referring to those parts of verbs (i.e. PARTICIPLES, GERUND and INFINITIVE) which are not bounded by number and person. See also FINITE VERBS.

nonsense verse   a self-explanatory term for a form of poetry made popular by Edward Lear. This is from *The Jumblies*:

> Far and few, far and few,
>   Are the lands where the Jumblies live:
> Their heads are green, and their hands are blue;
>   And they went to sea in a sieve.

Perhaps the best-known piece of nonsense verse is called *Jabberwocky*. It comes in *Through the Looking-Glass* by Lewis Carroll, and begins:

> 'Twas brillig, and the slithy toves
> Did gyre and gimble in the wabe;
> All mimsy were the borogoves,
> And the mome raths outgrabe.

In chapter VI of the book Humpty Dumpty claims to be able to make sense of this, beginning by explaining that 'brillig' means 'four o'clock in the afternoon'.

non sequitur (L. 'it does not follow')   an illogical inference, e.g. 'Over six feet in height, he travelled regularly between London and Birmingham.' The inference here is that he travelled regularly between London and Birmingham because he was over six feet in height. The writer has been guilty of a *non sequitur* in an attempt to convey two separate items of information in the same sentence.

In ARGUMENT the *non sequitur* is called 'the fallacy of false cause' because it draws a conclusion that does not follow from the premises, e.g.:

> Watching television gives Tommy a headache.
> This evening he has a headache.
> Therefore he has been watching television.

It is a fallacy to argue that because he has a headache Tommy has been watching television. He may have been lying in the sun, miles away from a TV set.

not only . . . but also   a pair of words acting as a single coordinate CONJUNCTION. Points 1–4 noted under EITHER . . . OR apply equally to NOT ONLY . . . BUT ALSO, e.g.:

> 1. Not only the boy but also the girl *is* to blame.

2. Not only the boys but also the girls *are* to blame.
3. Not only Tommy but also the boys next door *are* to blame.
   Not only the boys next door but also Tommy *are* to blame.
4. Not only you but also I *am* to blame.
   Not only you but also he *is* to blame.
   Not only he but also you *are* to blame.

It is not essential to adhere strictly to the above forms; the alternative subject may be placed before *also*, e.g. 1. 'the girl also'; 2. 'the girls also'; 3. 'the boys next door also' (but not 'the boys also next door'); 'Tommy also'; 4. 'I also'; 'he also'; 'you also'.

It is grammatically incorrect to omit *also*, but modern usage seems to favour the shorter version in such sentences as: 'He not only won the mile race but came second in the high jump.'

not ... or   SEE NEITHER ... NOR.

nought   SEE NAUGHT.

noun   the part of speech (sometimes called the *substantive*) that names a person, thing or quality. Nouns may be divided into four classes:

1. *Proper nouns*, which name a particular person or thing and begin with a capital letter, e.g. *Peter, London, Frenchman, Protestant, High Street, Odeon Cinema, Mount Everest, Associated Television Ltd.*

Many common nouns, verbs and adjectives are derived from proper nouns. Below are a few of them, each being treated more fully under its own heading elsewhere in this work.

Nouns: atlas, dunce, epicure, italics, mackintosh, mnemonics, spoonerism

Verbs: bowdlerise, tantalise

Adjectives: herculean, jovial, laconic, martial, mercurial, quixotic, stentorian. (See also PROPER ADJECTIVES.)

2. *Common nouns*, which name things and creatures, e.g. *table, boy, crocodile, street, mountain.* They name whole classes, not particular things or creatures: a *city*, not *London*; a *girl*, not *Mary.*

3. *Abstract nouns* (*q.v.*), which name abstract concepts and qualities, e.g. *truth, emptiness, attraction, speed.* Any noun that is not abstract but names a thing that has physical existence is sometimes referred to as a *concrete* noun, e.g. *tree, house, river, sugar.*

4. *Collective nouns*, which name a collection of persons or things

considered as a whole, e.g. an *army* of soldiers; the *audience* in a theatre; a *board* of directors; the *congregation* in a church; the *crew* of a ship or aircraft; a *fleet* of ships or taxis; a *horde* of savages; the *jury* in a court of justice; an *orchard* of fruit-trees; a cricket or football *team*; a *troupe* of dancers.

Some collective nouns are known also as *nouns of assemblage* or *nouns of company*, applying in particular to animals, birds, fish and insects. Here are but a few of them: an *army* of frogs; a *charm* of finches; a *chattering* of starlings; a *colony* of gulls; a *congregation* of plovers; a *covey* of partridges or grouse; a *drove* of oxen; an *exaltation* of larks; a *flight* of doves or pigeons; a *flock* of birds or sheep; a *herd* of cattle, goats or seals; a *nest* of mice; a *pack* of hounds or wolves; a *plague* of locusts; a *pride* of lions; a *school* of porpoises or whales; a *shoal* of herrings, mackerel or other fish; a *swarm* of bees or eels; a *troop* of kangaroos or monkeys; a *watch* of nightingales.

When a collective noun is the subject of a sentence, the verb is singular or plural according to whether our attention is directed to the group as a single unit or to the individuals composing the group, e.g.:

(a) The class was really too large for one teacher.
(b) The class were exchanging papers among themselves.

But we must be consistent; we cannot change from singular to plural in the same sentence, e.g.:

(c) The jury was unable to reach a verdict, because some of them remained convinced that the man in the dock was innocent.

We must write either: 'The jury were . . .' or '. . . because some members were . . .'

(d) The committee has decided that they will write to the County Council, expressing their strong disapproval of the proposed road-widening, despite the fact that the County Council has expressed their firm intention of carrying out this work, which it considers to be in the best interests of the community. The committee feel that the community has a right to decide such matters for themselves.

The correction of this one is left to the reader!

In sport, usage dictates that a team name takes the plural: 'Arsenal were beaten by Spurs'; 'Kent are at home to Surrey today.'

See also APPOSITION; CAPITAL LETTERS; CASE; GENDER; NEUTER; NUMBER; PLURAL.

noun clause   a group of words containing a finite verb and functioning as a noun. Its different functions may be seen from these examples:

1. '*Whatever we do* is bound to be wrong' (subject of 'is').
2. 'The truth of the matter is *that she did not know*' (complement of 'is').
3. 'I had forgotten *that he was deaf*' (object of 'had forgotten').
4. 'The suspicion *that he was ill* grew upon me' (in apposition to 'suspicion').
5. 'My admiration for *what he said* cannot be denied' (object of preposition 'for').
6. 'It is essential *that we should be present*' (in apposition to the anticipatory 'it').
7. 'Liking *what he saw*, he went inside' (object of participle 'liking').
8. 'To find out *why he did it*, we must turn to Mr Jones' (object of infinitive 'to find out').

noun-equivalents   single words or groups of words that can function in the same way as a noun. They may be classified as:

1. All types of PRONOUNS.
2. Any part of speech that is for the time being used as a noun, e.g. 'I do not recall the *ins* and *outs* of the argument, but the *long* and *short* of it was that no agreement was reached.'
3. The infinitive, e.g. 'Her aim was *to win*.'
4. The gerund, e.g. '*Seeing* is *believing*.'
5. Noun clauses, e.g. 'I told him *that he would be welcome*.'
6. Noun phrases, e.g. 'He made a habit of *criticising the committee*.'

noun phrase   a group of words containing no finite verb but making a unit that functions as a noun, e.g. (a) '*Going late to bed* makes it more difficult to get up in the morning.' (b) 'John Lockwood Kipling, *father of the author of 'Kim'*, was a professor in the School of Art, Bombay.' In the first example the noun phrase is subject of the verb 'makes', and in the second it is in apposition to 'John Lockwood Kipling'.

novel   As an adjective this means 'new' or 'strange'. As a noun it refers specially to a piece of fiction long enough to fill one or more volumes. The first great English novelist was Henry Fielding, whose *Tom Jones* was published in 1749. A *novelette* is a short novel and written on a lower plane, usually taking the form of a love story making no great claims on the reader's attention or intelligence. For more serious short works of fiction, the word *novella* has been borrowed from Italy. A novel or novelette divided into sections and published in a newspaper or magazine is known as a SERIAL.

number   word form indicating whether singular or plural. Only three parts of speech in English may be inflected to denote number: nouns, e.g. *girl – girls, lady – ladies, wolf – wolves, potato – potatoes, man – men, medium – media*; pronouns, e.g. *I – we, he – they, me – us, her – them, that – those*; verbs, e.g. *I am – we are, she is – they are, he sings – they sing.*

1. Two nouns or pronouns connected by co-ordinate conjunctions, e.g. *with, along with, together with, as well as, in addition to, besides,* take a singular verb, e.g.:

Wrong: A tall man, as well as two little girls, were standing outside the house.

Right: A tall man, as well as two little girls, was standing outside the house.

The effective subject is the singular 'man'; 'as well as two little girls' is virtually in parenthesis.

2. When the subject consists of two nouns joined together by *and*, the verb must be plural, e.g.:

Wrong: In the garage there was a saloon car and a bicycle.

Right: In the garage there were a saloon car and a bicycle.

There are, however, certain combinations that are singular in character, e.g. 'bread and butter', 'whisky and soda', 'gin and tonic', and therefore take a singular verb, e.g. 'The bread and butter was thickly spread with strawberry jam.'

3. When a pronoun stands for more than one thing it should be in the plural, e.g.:

Wrong: He was not lacking in courage and resolution when there was need for that.

Right: He was not lacking in courage and resolution when there was need for those.

4. The conjunctions *or* and *nor* take a singular verb when both the subjects are singular, e.g.:

Wrong: His courage or resolution were never in doubt.

Right: His courage or resolution was never in doubt.

Wrong: Neither his courage nor his resolution were ever in doubt.

Right: Neither his courage nor his resolution was ever in doubt.

5. When one of the subjects is plural, *or* and *nor* take a plural verb and are placed next to the plural subject, e.g.:

Wrong: Tom or his friends was responsible for this.

Right: Tom or his friends were responsible for this.

Wrong: Neither the Taj Mahal nor the Pyramids impresses him.

Right: Neither the Taj Mahal nor the Pyramids impress him.

6. When two alternative subjects of different number or person are joined by correlative conjunctions, e.g. *either . . . or, neither . . . nor*, the verb should agree with the nearer, e.g.:

Wrong: Either you or I are responsible.

Right: Either you or I am responsible.

If this is felt to be awkward, it is better to reconstruct the sentence thus: 'Either you are responsible or I am.' See also EITHER . . . OR; NOT ONLY . . . BUT ALSO.

7. Adjectives and pronouns such as *each, every, everybody, anybody, nobody, no one, none* are singular and when used in the subject ought to be followed by singular verbs, e.g.:

Wrong: None of these apples are really ripe.

Right: None of these apples is really ripe.

8. If singular, the pronoun is followed by *his, hers, its*, not *their*, e.g.:

Wrong: Nobody received more than their fair share.

Right: Nobody received more than his fair share.

or: Nobody received more than her fair share.

Strictly speaking, *none* means 'no one' and *nobody* 'no one body', but in practice they often carry the sense of 'no ones' or 'no bodies', and if we look upon these – and *everybody, everyone*, etc. – as singular only, we soon find ourselves in trouble, an added difficulty being that in English there is no singular pronoun to refer to either male or female. The above sentences are factually correct only if the sharing was done among (a) males or (b) females. If the sharing was done among a mixed assemblage both *his* and *her* are factually incorrect. We could, of course, write 'his or her fair share', but such grammatical accuracy can become pedantic. Consider these examples:

'We all entered for the singing contest, but none of us was good enough to distinguish himself or herself.'

'Nobody at the meeting, whatever his or her feelings might have been, seemed inclined to commit himself or herself by openly stating his or her views.'

When, therefore, *everybody*, *none*, *nobody* are used with a strong plural idea, a plural verb and plural adjectives are allowable, e.g.:

Wrong: As soon as it began to rain everybody rushed for his or her car.

Right: As soon as it began to rain everybody rushed for their cars.

Here we so clearly picture all the people rushing for a number of cars that usage demands a plural verb and a plural noun.

All this is not to suggest that *everybody*, *none*, etc. are not usually followed by the singular, e.g. (a) 'Everybody was very pleased about this.' (b) 'He complains a great deal, but nobody ever takes him seriously.' (c) 'Of all the dramatists of that period, none was greater than William Shakespeare.'

9. Care must be taken to ensure that a relative pronoun agrees with the correct ANTECEDENT, e.g.:

Wrong: It is one of the best plays that has ever been written.

Right: It is one of the best plays that have ever been written.

The pronoun 'that' relates back to 'plays', not 'one'.

10. Care must also be taken to ensure that a verb agrees with its subject. When a singular subject is separated from the verb by a plural ENLARGEMENT, or the verb is followed by a plural COMPLEMENT, the verb must be singular, e.g.:

Wrong: A bouquet of red roses were presented to the vicar's wife.

Right: A bouquet of red roses was presented to the vicar's wife.

Wrong: The period of greatest prosperity were the five years following World War II.

Right: The period of greatest prosperity was the five years following World War II.

The tendency of a plural noun or pronoun to draw into the plural a verb that should agree with a singular subject is known as ATTRACTION.

See also AGREEMENT; and for number in the sense of countable things, see AMOUNT, NUMBER.

numerals   figures or symbols used to represent numbers. Those in everyday use, 0, 1, 2, 3, 4, 5, 6, 7, 8, 9, are known as Arabic numerals. ROMAN NUMERALS are more cumbersome but not yet entirely obsolete.

This is not an arithmetic book or a manual on business procedure or accountancy, and the following notes are intended for the guidance of writers of English, who often have to choose between (for example) '21' and 'twenty-one'.

1. Use words in such examples as these:

    (a) William is twelve years of age and his brother Frank is nearly ten.

    (b) As the letter weighed less than two ounces, it cost three pence for the stamp.

    (c) The meeting was attended by twenty-six members.

    (d) 'If I have said it once,' shouted Mr Mitchell angrily, 'I have said it a hundred times.'

    (e) The pupils at this school now number nearly six hundred.

    (f) 'No!' she cried. 'A thousand times no!'

2. When numbers over a hundred are not in round figures (200, 300, etc.), they are not as a rule written out, e.g. *The pupils at this school now number 589*. However, figures at the beginning of a sentence, where they look awkward, should be avoided.

Wrong: 589 pupils now attend this school.

Right: There are now 589 pupils at this school.

3. Commas should be inserted as follows: 1,000, 10,000, 100,000, 1,000,000 (a million). The best way to ensure that the commas are correctly placed is to work backwards from the end, adding a comma after every three figures.

4. Years should be in figures and without commas, e.g. 1875, 1963. See also DATES.

5. In descriptive matter such as we are now discussing, fractions should be written out, thereby avoiding these:

    (a) He threw the book aside before he had read $\frac{1}{4}$ of it.

    (b) Well begun is $\frac{1}{2}$ done.

    (c) $\frac{3}{4}$ of the class are now suffering from influenza.

6. For decimals, figures should always be used: 2.25, 25.5 (but £25.50), etc. Note that it should be 0.25, not .25.

7. Sums of money should be written out whenever possible, e.g.:

    (a) Michael borrowed ten pounds from his uncle.

    (b) We tipped the waiter fifty pence.

When the amounts cannot be written out briefly, figures are prefer-

able, e.g. 'The lowest estimate for painting the house was £120.75.
See also CARDINAL NUMBERS; CENTURIES; DATES.

O

O, Oh The general rule is that the first is used when it is not
detached from the word in the vocative case that follows it, e.g. 'O
Chatterton! how very sad thy fate!' (Keats). 'O mighty Caesar!
dost thou lie so low?' (Shakespeare). It is also better than the second
in such ejaculations as 'O dear!' though usage tends towards 'Oh,
dear!' or 'Oh dear!' without a comma. When there is detachment
from the word that follows, the second is preferred, e.g. 'Oh, what a
beautiful morning!' 'Oh, is it?' As a cry of pain or distress 'Oh!' is
correct, not 'O!' Note also that when 'Oh' forms part of an exclamatory phrase, the exclamation mark is placed at the end of the
phrase, e.g. 'Oh, how greedy you are!' 'Oh, the little more, and
how much it is!' (Browning).
See also under CAPITAL LETTERS.

obelus the dagger (†) used to draw attention to a footnote. It
usually refers to the second footnote on a page, the first one being
marked with an ASTERISK.
See also FOOTNOTE.

object a noun or noun-equivalent used to name the person or
thing affected by the action of a transitive verb in the active voice.
The *direct* object is that affected primarily by the verb; the *indirect*
object is that affected secondarily by the verb. 'He gave his sister a
present.' The direct object is 'present', for that is what he gave; the
indirect object is 'sister', the recipient of the gift. The case of the
direct object is accusative; the case of the indirect object is dative.

objective dealing only with outward things; that is, without
colouring them with the writer's own thoughts and feelings; scientific rather than personal. 'The field is green' is an objective fact.
'The field is a lovely green' has become a subjective fact, since it
expresses a personal taste that may not necessarily be shared by
others. Thence the opposite of *objective* is *subjective*.

objective case   another name for ACCUSATIVE CASE.

oblivious   This means 'forgetful of' and is followed by 'of', not 'to', e.g. 'After a while he became oblivious of the noise around him.' Today, however, it is often used to mean simply 'unaware of', e.g. 'He was so absorbed in the conversation that he was oblivious of the approaching car.'

obscenity   See PORNOGRAPHY.

obscurantism (L. 'to cover') the prevention of the spread of knowledge; the placing of every obstacle in the way of intellectual progress. It is based on the theory that what matters is not what actually happens but what the mass of people can be made to believe.

obsequial, obsequious   The singular noun *obsequy* is seldom used. The plural *obsequies* means 'funeral rites or ceremonies', particularly those of a stately nature. The term 'funeral obsequies' is a PLEONASM, since it gives us 'funeral funeral rites'. The adjective is *obsequial*. Though similar in structure, *obsequious* means something quite different, i.e. 'servile; fawning; compliant in a cringing way'.

observance, observation   We shall not confuse these if we remember that *observance* means 'attending to a duty or custom', whilst *observation* means 'noticing or watching things'.

obsolete, obsolescent   Both derive from the Latin meaning 'to grow old', but there is a shade of difference between them. To be *obsolete* is to be out of date; out of use; no longer current, e.g. words such as *eke* (also), *esperite* (spirit), *sweb* (spoon), *crescence* (increase). To be *obsolescent* is to be on the way to becoming obsolete, but not yet completely so, e.g. *shew* (show), *especial* (special), *whilom* (former). Modern motor-cars are said to incorporate 'built-in obsolescence' since the manufacturer knows that a new design will, sooner rather than later, make them out of date.

   An obsolete word, spelling, phrase or construction is called an ARCHAISM.

obtain   Besides its usual meaning of 'to get' or 'to acquire', this verb is used in the sense of 'to be prevalent; to be customary or in use', e.g.: 'Democratic government does not obtain in Communist countries.' 'Different local regulations obtain in different areas.'

octameter (oktæmˡətə) (Gk. 'eight measures') in PROSODY a line of verse consisting of eight feet, e.g.:

> Nobly, / nobly / Cape St. / Vincent / to the / North-west /
>   died a / way

See METRE.

octave in PROSODY a division of eight lines, especially the first eight lines of a SONNET. The last six lines of a sonnet are called a *sestet*.

octavo (okteiˡvou) (abbreviated 8vo) an eighth of a sheet of printing paper. The sheet is folded three times to give eight leaves. Sheets vary in size, and the size of the leaves varies accordingly. The usual size for a novel, known as 'crown 8vo', is 5 in. wide by 7½ in. long. For slightly larger books, the usual size is 5⅝ in. wide by 8¾ in. long, which is known as 'demy (dimaiˡ) 8vo'. All these dimensions are slightly reduced when the leaves are cut and trimmed before the book is bound.

See also FOOLSCAP; QUARTO.

oculist, optician The first is one skilled in the treatment of diseases of the eye; the second is one who makes or sells spectacles and other optical instruments.

ode (Gk. 'a song') at one time a poem set to music and sung by a chorus. The traditional ode (known as the *Pindaric ode*, after Pindar, the greatest lyric poet of ancient Greece) was in three stanzas: the *strophe*, the *antistrophe* and the *epode*. These formed the accompaniment to a dance. The *strophe* ('turning') was chanted by the chorus as it moved across the ORCHESTRA away from the stage in the first figure of the dance. The *antistrophe* ('counter-turning') was chanted as the chorus retraced its steps in the second figure of the dance. The *epode* was chanted standing still. There is some element of doubt as to the exact procedure. For instance, it has been suggested that the strophe was chanted by one half of the chorus, the antistrophe by the other half, and the epode by the full chorus.

In English prosody the term *ode* has come to be used for a lyric of up to about two hundred lines, written in the form of an address or

in celebration of some special occasion. The Romantic Movement
(see ROMANTICISM) produced many great odes, e.g. *Ode to the West
Wind* by Shelley, *Ode to Autumn* and *Ode to a Nightingale*, both by
Keats, and *The Hound of Heaven* by Francis Thompson. Here is a
stanza from Wordsworth's *Ode on Intimations of Immortality*, in which
he looked back on his childhood:

> Our birth is but a sleep and a forgetting:
> The Soul that rises with us, our life's Star,
>   Hath had elsewhere its setting,
>   And cometh from afar:
>   Not in entire forgetfulness,
>   And not in utter nakedness,
> But trailing clouds of glory do we come
>   From God, who is our home:
> Heaven lies about us in our infancy!
> Shades of the prison-house begin to close
>   Upon the growing Boy,
> But he beholds the light, and whence it flows,
>   He sees it in his joy;
> The Youth, who daily farther from the east
>   Must travel, still is Nature's priest,
>   And by the vision splendid
>   Is on his way attended;
> At length the Man perceives it die away,
> And fade into the light of common day.

offbeat   In music the *offbeat* is that part of a measure other than
the accented one; it is similar to the unstressed part of a metrical
foot in PROSODY. In modern usage the term also means anything
'diverging from the main stream of current thought' (Webster).
Thus we have offbeat comedy, offbeat advertising, offbeat plays,
offbeat books.

Old (Anglo-Saxon) English   see DERIVATION.

older   see ELDER.

omnibus   a volume containing a number of stories, plays, etc.,
usually by the same author. Sometimes several books, already published singly, are published together in an omnibus edition. This

practice is not universally popular; the volumes are too heavy to
read with comfort in bed!

See also BUS.

one   Errors arising through the confusion of this indefinite pronoun
with *they, he, you,* etc. are treated under PRONOUN, *personal.*

one's   the only possessive with an apostrophe: *yours, hers, ours,
theirs, its,* but *one's.*

oneself   This is the usual spelling of this reflexive pronoun, but
one's self is not incorrect, especially when used with *own,* e.g. 'It is
better to be one's own self than to act a part.'

one time, one-time   The hyphen should be added when the use
is adjectival. It has the meaning of 'former', whilst 'at one time' has
the meaning of 'once' or 'formerly', e.g.:

(a) He was at one time a close friend of mine.
(b) My one-time friend has now been sent to prison.

only   Make sure that *only* comes at the right point in the sentence
to show your exact meaning, e.g.:

1. '*Only* Mac went in the coach as far as Glasgow.' The others
   went by train.
2. 'Mac *only went in the coach as far as Glasgow.*' That was all he did.
3. 'Mac went *only in the coach* as far as Glasgow.' He did not do part
   of the journey by train.
4. 'Mac went in *the only coach* as far as Glasgow.' There were no
   other coaches.
5. 'Mac went *in the coach only as far as Glasgow.*' This is ambiguous;
   it means either 3 or 6.
6. 'Mac went in the coach *as far only as Glasgow.*' He did the rest of
   the journey by train.
7. 'Mac went in the coach *as far as Glasgow only.*' He did not go as
   far as London or Plymouth.

onomatopoeia   (ɔnəmætoupiˡə) (Gk. 'word-making')   the technical name given to the formation of words in imitation of the sound
made. Thus the word *hiss* makes roughly the same sound as the
action named, as do *bang, buzz, crack, crash, cuckoo, flap, mumble, pop,*

quack, *splash*, *squelch*, *twitter*, *whiz*. These are mostly original creations. That is to say, they have no history, no etymology; they are root words created to represent a sound. This is probably how some of the first human sounds came into existence, and we are still bringing more into existence today. Some recent ones are *ping-pong* and, representing the sound of crashing aircraft, *prang*. STRIP CARTOONS produce onomatopoeic words almost daily, usually to indicate violence, e.g. 'wham!', 'boiing!' Whole sentences or even passages may be onomatopoeic, e.g. 'I heard the water lapping on the crag, And the long ripple washing through the reeds' (Tennyson).

onto, on to   These have different meanings, corresponding to those between INTO and IN TO. The first has the meaning of 'to a position on or upon'; the second expresses movement to another position. Thus:

(a) The baby fell from her cradle onto the floor.
(b) We walked on to the next village.

As with *into*, the use of *onto* to form an infinitive is clearly wrong, e.g. 'He went onto give his reasons.' Here 'onto' should be 'on to'.

opera (plural of OPUS)   DRAMA set to music. It takes several forms. In *grand opera* there is usually no spoken dialogue, everything being sung, and the theme is tragic. *Faust* by Gounod, *Lohengrin* by Wagner and *Aida* by Verdi are all grand operas. In *light opera* (or *operetta*) the singing is interspersed with spoken dialogue. Good examples of light opera are *Die Fledermaus* by Johann Strauss and *The Merry Widow* by Lehar. In *comic opera* there is usually much more dialogue than in a light opera. The best known of English comic operas are those by Gilbert and Sullivan – *The Mikado*, *Patience*, *H.M.S. Pinafore*, *The Pirates of Penzance* and others. In France comic opera is known as *opéra bouffe*. The acknowledged master was Offenbach, whose seventy *opéras bouffes* include *Orphée aux Enfers* (*Orpheus in the Underworld*) and *La Vie Parisienne*.

The *book* – that is, the words – of an opera is called the LIBRETTO.

operetta   originally a short opera, usually in one act. Later the word was used to describe any light opera. See OPERA above.

optician   see OCULIST.

opus (L. 'work')   used to refer to a musical composition (see under MUSICAL TERMS) and also to a literary or an artistic undertaking. Its most frequent use is in the term *magnum opus* ('great work'), meaning the chief production of a writer or artist. For example, Milton's *magnum opus* was *Paradise Lost*, and Michelangelo's *magnum opus* was the painting on the ceiling of the Sistine Chapel in Rome, which he completed, lying on his back, in four years.

oral   see VERBAL.

orchestra (Gk. 'a dance')   the space in front of the stage in the theatre of ancient Greece, where the chorus sang and danced. Nowadays it refers not only to the place where the musicians sit but also to the musicians themselves.
    See also ODE.

ordinal numbers   the numbers that show order or position, e.g. *first* (*1st*), *second* (*2nd*), *third* (*3rd*), *fourth* (*4th*), *fourteenth* (*14th*), *fortieth* (not *fourtieth*) (*40th*), *hundredth* (*100th*), *hundred and twenty-fifth* (*125th*).
    The abbreviated form is used chiefly in dates, e.g. 14th November 1963. It should be noted that, unless they end a sentence, *st, nd, rd* and *th* should never be followed by a full stop, e.g.:
    Wrong: With reference to your letter of 29th. September last and
                 to our telephone conversation on 1st. October . . .
    Right: With reference to your letter of 29th September last and
                 to our telephone conversation on 1st October . . .
    Apart from dates, lists, sporting results, etc., it is better to spell out the word than to use the abbreviated form, e.g.:

    (a) The first guest to arrive was Harry Johnson.
    (b) They always visit us on the second Sunday in the month.
    (c) Today is my nineteenth birthday.
    (d) My sister is now in her twenty-third year.

    See also CENTURIES; DATES; NUMERALS.

ordinance, ordnance   The first is a decree issued by a higher authority. *Self-denying ordinance*, now used as a general phrase meaning 'self-imposed discipline', dates back to the Civil War, when by an order passed in 1645, all Members of Parliament were requested to give up certain executive offices, particularly commands in the Army and Navy. *Ordnance* refers to mounted guns and, in a wider sense, artillery of all kinds. The Royal Army Ordnance Corps is responsible for the issue of munitions of war and numerous other supplies. The Ordnance Survey maps the whole of Britain and Ireland in great detail.

ordinand   the name given to one who is preparing to take holy orders. As does *ordinance* above, it derives from *ordain*, which means, among other things, 'to confer holy orders on'.

orthography   the art of spelling words correctly. See GRAMMAR; SPELLING.

overworked words   These can be divided into two classes:

1. Those that suddenly become popular, live for a while and then are heard no more. Among these are CATCHWORDS and the colloquialisms used by successive generations, e.g. *top-hole, topping, ripping, smashing, wizard*. A recent favourite was *fabulous*. It was soon replaced by the simple *great*, applied to anything from a wedding to an ice cream.

2. Those that have been with us for a long time and threaten to go on for ever. High up on the list are GOT and NICE. Others are: *awful, awfully, lovely, definitely, weird and wonderful, terrible, phenomenal, ghastly, terrific, nostalgia, nostalgic, shocking, fantastic, frightful, dreadful, hectic, chronic, beastly, deadly, simply, horrible, fearful, frantic, stupendous, livid, colossal, gorgeous, fiendish, literally, sweet*. Many of these (and scores of others) have been so treated that they have lost most, if not all, of their original meaning. Oliver Wendell Holmes called it *verbicide*, the 'violent treatment of a word with fatal results to its legitimate meaning, which is its life'. This sad state of affairs is touched on in *Through the Looking-Glass*.

'When *I* use a word', Humpty Dumpty said in rather a scornful tone, 'it means just what I choose it to mean – neither more nor less.'

'The question is,' said Alice, 'whether you *can* make words mean so many different things.'

'The question is,' said Humpty Dumpty, 'which is to be Master – that's all.'

Alice was much too puzzled to say anything, so after a minute Humpty Dumpty began again. 'They've a temper, some of them – particularly verbs, they're the proudest – adjectives you can do anything with, but not verbs – however, *I* can manage the whole lot of them . . .'

It is a fact that most overworked words are adjectives – or their adverbs.

A study of overworked words reveals the fact that they are never too busy to deputise for each other as INTENSIVES. For example, both a headache and the weather could be described as 'awful', 'terrible', 'ghastly', 'frightful', 'dreadful' – and so on.

One result of overworking words is that we run out of superlatives. Hollywood is much to blame for this: *greatest, mightiest, most stupendous* – and then what? There is a story, probably apocryphal, about Mr Sam Goldwyn.

'Well, Mr Goldwyn,' said a friend, 'how's business?'

'It's colossal,' he replied, 'but it's improving.'

To sum up, in serious writing or conversation it is worth a moment's extra thought to make our meaning clearer and add fresh-ness to our style.

See also VOCABULARY; VOGUE WORDS; and *vulgarisation* under VULGAR.

owing to   see DUE TO.

oxymoron (oksimoːrˡən)   a FIGURE OF SPEECH in which two words or phrases of opposite or contrasting meaning are placed together for effect, e.g. 'bitter sweet', 'cruel to be kind', 'agonising joy', 'cordial dislike', 'precious bane', 'dear enemy', 'busy doing nothing'. An oxymoron is thus a very concise PARADOX.

P

page proof   see PRINTERS' PROOFS.

pagination   see PRINTERS' PROOFS.

palindrome   a word or sentence that reads the same in either direction, e.g. (a) *Ada*; (b) *madam*; (c) *Able was I ere I saw Elba.*

pan- (Gk. 'all') a prefix meaning 'the whole of', e.g. *Pan-American*, relating to the whole of America, all the countries of North, Central and South America. A *panacea* is a cure-all.

pantomime an exotic and nonsensical Christmas entertainment on the stage, remotely based on fairy stories but padded out with popular songs of the moment, topical references, comic stage business and audience participation. It requires the hero (principal boy) to be played by a girl in tights and the comic 'dame' to be played by a man.

See also HARLEQUINADE.

parable a FIGURE OF SPEECH; a short story told to teach a moral lesson; an ALLEGORY in brief. It is the same as a FABLE except that usage has now confined its use to religion – 'an earthly story with a heavenly meaning', as it has been described. The best-known parables are those of Jesus, such as the Parable of the Good Samaritan.

paradox a FIGURE OF SPEECH; a seemingly absurd or contradictory statement that on closer examination is found to contain an important truth, e.g. (a) 'Hasten slowly' (from the Latin *Festina lente*). (b) 'The child is father of the man' (Wordsworth). (c) 'He who goes against the fashion is himself its slave' (Logan Pearsall Smith). (d) 'If a thing is worth doing it is worth doing badly' (G. K. Chesterton). See also OXYMORON.

paragraph A whole composition or story if not broken up into sections would be difficult to follow. There would be nowhere to pause and no guide to the development of the whole. We should have to work out the stage-by-stage development unaided by the author. It is to enable the reader to advance by easy stages and quickly appreciate the development of the whole that we divide it into paragraphs.

Just as here, the beginning of a new paragraph is indicated by indenting (that is, the leaving of a gap between the margin and the first word of the paragraph). The first line of a composition or story should not be indented, for the reader will know without guidance that it is the first line of the first paragraph.

In days gone by, paragraphs were marked by the symbol ¶.

paraphrase This came originally from two Greek words meaning 'telling alongside'. By the time it was taken over by Latin it had the meaning of 'equal phrasing'. Today in English its meaning is much the same, namely an alternative version in the same language. Usually it implies a simpler version, though a version of something simple rendered into a more difficult style could still be called a paraphrase. For example, if one wrote a piece of modern English in the way in which it would have been written by Defoe, the author of *Robinson Crusoe*, one would be making a paraphrase; and so would one be if one wrote a piece of slangy English in a manner acceptable to a conference of educated people.

Paraphrasing is therefore a kind of translation, yet we must do more than make a word-for-word translation: we must interpret it. Suppose we have to paraphrase these lines from Cowper's *The Task*:

> Some to the fascination of a name
> Surrender judgement hoodwink'd.

To interpret this adequately in simple modern English, our paraphrase will run something like this:

> 'Some people are so impressed by the name of a famous person that they accept his views and carry out his instructions without exercising any critical judgement at all.'

parenthesis (pæren׀θəsis) a word or group of words inserted in a sentence that is grammatically complete without it. This aside, so to speak, is indicated by being separated off by commas, brackets or dashes, e.g. (1) 'The duchess, very tall and stately, swept into the room.' (2) 'On the following day (a fine one for a change) we played cricket.' (3) 'The farmer was furious – and one cannot really blame him – when he caught the boys stealing apples.' A parenthesis does not necessarily come in the body of the sentence; it can come at the end, e.g. 'This unexpected legacy has not added to his happiness, I suspect.'

Parenthesis (or the plural *parentheses*) refers also to the curved lines ( ) known as 'round' BRACKETS. Words in brackets are described as being 'in parenthesis', or, more usually, 'in parentheses'. The style of the novelist Henry James is markedly parenthetical.

parody a deliberately exaggerated imitation of another piece of writing, usually aimed at making fun of the original writer by turn-

ing his work to ridicule. For example, here are a few lines from Longfellow's *The Song of Hiawatha*:

> He had mittens, Minjekahwun,
> Magic mittens made of deer-skin;
> When upon his hands he wore them,
> He could smite the rocks asunder,
> He could grind them into powder.

And here is *The Modern Hiawatha*, by an unknown author:

> He killed the noble Mudjokivis.
> Of the skin he made him mittens,
> Made them with the fur side inside,
> Made them with the skin side outside.
> He, to get the warm side inside,
> Put the inside skin side outside.
> He, to get the cold side outside,
> Put the warm side fur side inside.
> That's why he put the fur side inside,
> Why he put the skin side outside,
> Why he turned them inside outside.

Authors have been known to parody themselves. Here is Swinburne on Swinburne:

> It's as plain as a newspaper leader
>   That a rhymester who scribbles like me
> May feel perfectly sure that his reader
>   Is sick of the sea.

parse to divide a sentence into its grammatical parts, and to
describe a word, stating which part of speech it is, what form it takes,
and how it is used in the sentence. The noun is *parsing*. This was once
a school exercise much used by teachers and much disliked by
pupils. Not much time is spent on parsing today. If we had to parse
the verb *heard*, for example, in the sentence 'He heard a noise' we
should write:

> *heard*: verb, transitive, weak, active, indicative mood, past tense
>   simple, third person singular agreeing with subject 'he'.

partially, partly The first means 'to a limited degree'; the
second means 'with respect to a part of the whole', e.g. (a) 'He was

partially reassured when I told him that nobody could blame him for what had happened.' (b) 'Although he could not be held entirely responsible, there is no doubt that he was partly to blame for what happened.'

participles non-finite parts of the verb that either qualify nouns (or noun-equivalents) or help to form tenses, e.g. 'Now that I have *finished* my work I am *drawing* up plans for the *coming* year.' Of the two participles, the present participle always ends in -*ing* (*eating*, *biting*, *swimming*), and the past participle usually ends in -*ed*, -*d*, -*t*, -*en* or -*n* (*voted*, *heard*, *learnt*, *chosen*, *thrown*), though some are quite irregular (*begun*, *brought*, *dug*, *gone*, *struck*).

The following tenses are formed with the help of participles: present continuous active (*he is helping*); present continuous passive (*he is being helped*); present perfect active (*he has helped*); present perfect passive (*he has been helped*); future continuous active (*he will be helping*); future continuous passive (*he will be being helped*); future perfect active (*he will have helped*); future perfect passive (*he will have been helped*); past continuous active (*he was helping*); past continuous passive (*he was being helped*); past perfect active (*he had helped*); past perfect passive (*he had been helped*); past perfect continuous active (*he had been helping*). And similarly for the conditional tenses, e.g. *he would have helped*.

When used adjectivally, the participle may function as a simple adjective (the *rising* sun, a *broken* knife) or as part of a participial phrase qualifying a noun or its equivalent in the rest of the sentence, e.g. '*Entering the paddock*, we saw the damage. *Snapped in two by the gale*, the tree had fallen right across the fence.'

Care must be taken in the use of participles. 'Running across the field, he climbed over the gate.' This means that he climbed over the gate while he was running across the field. 'Cycling along the lane, a bull suddenly appeared in front of me.' This is an example of the *misrelated* participle. The participle functions as an adjective and qualifies a noun or pronoun. Here it appears to qualify 'bull', and so creates the ludicrous picture of a bull cycling. Sometimes the mis-related participle, along with its phrase, can be moved to a more sensible position; but more frequently, as here, the sentence must be recast: 'As I was cycling along the lane, a bull suddenly appeared in front of me.' Certain words like *judging* and *considering* are used in phrases that have almost lost their participial character, e.g. 'Considering your views, your action was odd, to say the least.' In such sentences it would be pedantic to insist on the strict rule of grammar.

Another trap is the *unrelated* or *hanging* participle. Instead of being related to the wrong noun or pronoun, it is related to nothing; it is left hanging in the air, e.g. (a) 'Having been disappointed twice, there is no reason to suppose the third time will be lucky.' (b) 'Eating his supper in the kitchen, there was a knock on the front door.' To avoid these hanging participles we must recast the sentences, thus: 'Since you have been disappointed twice, there is no reason to suppose that the third time will be lucky.' 'While he was eating his supper in the kitchen, there was a knock on the front door.'

Fused participles occur when the GERUND is confused with the present participle. 'Jill disliked you saying that.' Here 'saying' is treated as a participle, which functions as an adjective, and then made to qualify 'you'. But in fact it is a gerund, which functions as a noun, and therefore needs to be qualified by a possessive adjective. In other words, Jill did not dislike you in the act of saying that; she disliked the act itself. The distinction can be readily seen in these two sentences:

'I watched Brian swimming.'
'I watched Brian's swimming.'

The first is a participle, 'swimming' qualifying the noun 'Brian'. It was Brian whom I watched. The second is a gerund, 'swimming', functioning as a noun. It was not Brian but his swimming that I watched.

However, usage seems to be changing, so that few writers now make the distinction between the gerund and the present participle at all regularly. This is perhaps not unnatural, since the possessive leads to such ungainly sentences as: 'My mother disliked Jack's and his sister's being so late.' 'Owing to Ian's and Bob's falling ill, we had to cancel the party.' In speaking or writing these sentences, most educated people would omit the possessives, and they would have such grammarians as Professor Jespersen on their side.

Participial phrases are treated also under PHRASE. See also ABSOLUTE.

particles   a term used to cover the minor parts of speech, viz. articles, prepositions, adverbs and conjunctions, together with affixes.

See ADVERBIAL PARTICLE; PHRASAL VERBS.

parts of speech the eight classes into which words may be grouped according to their function in a sentence. In this book they are treated separately under NOUN; VERB; ADJECTIVE; ADVERB; PRONOUN; CONJUNCTION; PREPOSITION; INTERJECTION. The parts of speech are important to any understanding of the use and meaning of words, since a single word may be used as several different parts of speech, and its meaning will naturally vary accordingly, as may be seen from the use of *brown* in the following:

As a noun: Brown is a colour I dislike intensely.
As a verb: I always brown very quickly at the seaside.
As an adjective: Suddenly they came face to face with a brown bear.

A word that is normally one part of speech may take on a new use and meaning by being used as another part of speech. Thus *park* was first a noun meaning a grassland with a few trees. Then it meant an open space in which to put cars. From this latter meaning we have the verb *to park*, which is quite different from the original noun.

Sometimes an adjective comes to have the force of a noun by the omission of the noun. Thus *submarine* formerly was an adjective only. It was later so often used in the term 'a submarine vessel' that the noun was dropped and the adjective became a noun and produced a further noun *submariners*. The following also began as adjectives only and later became nouns too: *offensive* (the act of attacking), *panic* (fear), *principal* (a chief or head), *wireless* (telegraphy or telephony).

passage part of a speech or literary work taken for quotation, etc.

passed, past The first is used in a verbal sense; the second is an adjective or a preposition, e.g.:

(a) 'We passed a week in Paris.'
     'We have been in Paris for the past week.'
(b) 'Ten minutes passed and there was still no sign of him.'
     'It was ten past seven when he arrived.'

passive voice see VOICE.

pastiche a literary or other work of art done in the style of another, but not as PARODY. Thackeray's imitation of the *Spectator* essays in *Henry Esmund* is pastiche. The term is also used to denote a musical composition or picture made up from various sources.

pastoral any play, poem or romance mainly concerned with the life of shepherds or simply country folk portrayed in an idealised way. Originating in Greek literature, the pastoral was revived during the Renaissance. Spenser's *Shepheard's Calendar* is a pastoral, as is Shakespeare's *As You Like It*.

pathetic fallacy Here *pathetic* means 'capable of feeling'. The term was coined by Ruskin and refers to the ascribing of human emotions to inanimate nature, e.g. 'the cruel sea'; 'the mocking laughter of the wind'; 'the genial sun'; 'the pitiless desert'; 'the happy autumn fields'. See also PERSONIFICATION.

pathos (peiθˡos) that which awakens tender, sympathetic emotions. There is pathos in the death of Falstaff as described by his old friend Mistress Quickly in *Henry V*. Pathos carried too far can descend into BATHOS.

pedantic making an unnecessary display of learning. It is pedantic to refer to a taxi as a 'taximeter cabriolet'; to a flea as '*Pulex irritans*'; or to a conjuror as a 'prestidigitator'; and it is pedantic to say:

'We are in a position analogous to that of Julius Caesar when, in the year 49 B.C., he crossed the Rubicon, that little stream dividing his province of Cisalpine Gaul from ancient Italy, and advanced with his troops upon the army of Gnaeus Pompeius, better known as Pompey the Great. As Caesar remarked at the time, *Alea jacta est*, which may be translated, "The die is cast".'

Anyone other than a pedant would say, 'We've crossed the Rubicon'; or 'We can't go back now'; or 'We've reached the point of no return.'

peninsula, peninsular The first is a noun meaning 'a piece of land almost surrounded by water'; the second is an adjective meaning 'pertaining to or resembling a peninsula'. The Peninsular War (1808–14) was so called because it was fought by Great Britain against France in the Iberian peninsula – that is, Spain, Portugal and south-west France.

pen name another name for PSEUDONYM.

pentameter (pentæmˡətə) (Gk. 'five measures') in PROSODY a line of verse consisting of five feet. The most popular form of pentameter is the *iambic pentameter* – that is, five disyllabic feet with the stress on the second syllable of each foot. It is the measure of BLANK VERSE, the HEROIC COUPLET and the SONNET.

See also METRE.

per annum   by the year; annually, e.g. 'The subscription is two guineas per annum.' In the following sentence, either 'yearly' or 'per annum' is redundant: 'The yearly subscription is two guineas per annum.'

per cent (abbr. of L. *per centum*, 'by the hundred')   for, in, or to every hundred. The symbol is % but in literary usage *per cent* (without a full stop) is preferable. Percentage can range from 1 (or less) to 100 (or more), thus:

$$
\begin{array}{rll}
\tfrac{1}{2}\% & (\text{or} \quad \tfrac{1}{2} \text{ per cent}) = & \tfrac{1}{2} \text{ per } 100 \\
1\% & (\text{or} \quad 1 \text{ per cent}) = & 1 \text{ per } 100 \\
10\% & (\text{or} \quad 10 \text{ per cent}) = & 10 \text{ per } 100 \\
25\% & (\text{or} \quad 25 \text{ per cent}) = & 25 \text{ per } 100 \\
50\% & (\text{or} \quad 50 \text{ per cent}) = & 50 \text{ per } 100 \\
75\% & (\text{or} \quad 75 \text{ per cent}) = & 75 \text{ per } 100 \\
100\% & (\text{or } 100 \text{ per cent}) = & 100 \text{ per } 100 \\
110\% & (\text{or } 110 \text{ per cent}) = & 110 \text{ per } 100 \\
200\% & (\text{or } 200 \text{ per cent}) = & 200 \text{ per } 100 \\
\end{array}
$$

It has been argued that inasmuch as a percentage is part of the whole, and the whole is 100%, there can be no such thing as 200% or 300%, since a part cannot be greater than the whole. This is a fallacy. Let us assume that we have picked up a bargain for £10 and wish to sell it at a profit. Should we sell it for £15 the rate of profit on our original outlay is 50%; should we sell it for £20 we have doubled our money, and the rate of profit on our original outlay is 100%; and should we be fortunate enough (or unprincipled enough) to sell it for £30 we have trebled our money, and the rate of profit on our original outlay is 200% – that is, 200 per 100.

The word *percentage* does not mean 'a small part'. Consider this: 'Only a percentage of the members attended the meeting.' This means that the meeting was attended by a mere 1-100% of the members, which is nonsense. Unless the percentage is stated, e.g. 'Only ten per cent', 'Only twenty per cent', it is better to write: 'Only a few', 'Only fifteen', 'Only about half', etc.

See also VOGUE WORDS.

period another name for the FULL STOP.

periphrasis (pərif'rəsis) another name for CIRCUMLOCUTION. The adjective is *periphrastic* (perifræs'tik).

permissive tolerant; used especially, now, in the phrase *permissive society*, indicating a new climate of tolerance on the part of the community in the field of morals, particularly sexual morals. The *permissive society* has been praised, or abused, for encouraging the spread of FOUR-LETTER WORDS in 'polite' speech, in novels, and on the stage; for ceasing to frown on promiscuity; for allowing all conventions of speech, dress and behaviour to be challenged.

The phrase is frequently used loosely, usually by opponents as a CATCHWORD, as are *Welfare State* (beneficent government) and *Affluent Society* (more money for more people).

person the form of pronouns that indicates whether they refer to the person speaking (first person – *I, me, we, us*), the person spoken to (second person – *you*) or the person spoken about (third person – *he, she, it, him, her, they, them*). The use of *thou* and *thee* (second person singular), though once widespread, is now almost wholly confined to poetry and references to God.

See also PRONOUN, *personal*.

personal letters See CORRESPONDENCE.

personification a FIGURE OF SPEECH in which inanimate or abstract things are referred to as if they were human beings. It is thus a form of metaphor in which the inanimate thing is seen to have some similarity with humans, e.g. (a) 'Exploitation reared its ugly head.' (b) 'Love laughs at locksmiths.' (c) 'Justice is blind.' (d) 'Green-eyed jealousy.' (e) 'A tree whose hungry mouth is pressed Against the earth's sweet flowing breast' (*Trees* by Joyce Kilmer). (f) 'The moon stepped out of her mantle of cloud to smile momentarily upon us.'

Just as the moon is referred to as *she*, so is the sun referred to as *he* – the 'centre and sire of light' according to P. J. Bailey, and 'Father of rosy day' according to Thomas Hood. Night is a 'sober-suited matron, all in black' (Shakespeare), 'the mother of counsels' (George Herbert), the 'sable goddess' (Edward Young). Day would seem to be masculine, e.g. 'The joyous morning ran and kissed the grass And drew his fingers through her sleeping hair' (John Free-man).

A country is *she* and so is a ship; a train and an aircraft can be either *she* or *it*, more usually *it*. A motor-car is often *she*. Necessity is 'the mother of invention', and England 'the mother of parliaments', whilst philosophy, according to Cicero, is 'the mother of all the arts'. Father is not so often used in personification. Apart from being time itself and the parent of 'rosy day' he is associated with Old Father Thames, the Mississippi, which is the 'Ol' Man River' of *Showboat*, and the Nile, which is 'the Father of Rivers'. Sons are not con-spicuous in personification, but daughters are numerous, e.g. America is the 'gigantic daughter of the West' (Tennyson), Spring is 'Daughter of Heaven and Earth' (Emerson), Duty is 'Stern Daughter of the Voice of God' (Wordsworth), whilst Omar Khayyám wrote that he 'Divorced old barren Reason from my Bed, And took the Daughter of the Vine to Spouse'.

See also APOSTROPHE (2).

petitio principii (L. 'taking the beginning for granted')   see BEGGING THE QUESTION.

phenomenal (Gk. 'to appear')   the adjective of the noun *pheno-menon* (plural *phenomena*), which is anything that appears or is per-ceived by the senses. When we see a flash of lightning we are wit-nessing an electrical phenomenon. The adjective, therefore, does not have the meaning popularly ascribed to it, which is synonymous with 'extraordinary', 'marvellous', 'wonderful', 'unexpected', 'tremendous'. Literally, 'a phenomenal success' is one that we can see, hear, touch or smell.

philology   the study of languages, including their ETYMOLOGY and GRAMMAR; now more commonly called LINGUISTICS.

philosophy (Gk. 'the love of wisdom')   the study of the general principles of knowledge or existence; a searching into the reason and nature of things. A *philosopher* is a lover of wisdom and also one who should accept misfortune without complaint.

phoneme   a linguistic term to denote the basic units of sound. Phonemes come together to form SYLLABLES.

phonetics (Gk. 'the uttering of sounds')   the branch of PHONOLOGY
that deals with speech sounds and pronunciation. The main head-
ings under which it is treated in this work are PRONUNCIATION; and
GUIDE TO PRONUNCIATION on page 7. See also AFFRICATES; ALPHA-
BET; ASPIRATE; CONSONANTS; DIAERESIS; DIGRAPH; DIPHTHONG;
EUPHONY; FRICATIVES; GUTTURALS; HIATUS; INITIAL TEACHING ALPHA-
BET; LATERALS; NASALS; SIBILANTS; SYNAERESIS; VOWEL LIGATURES;
VOWELS.

phonology (Gk. 'description of sounds')   the science of vocal
sounds, one of the main divisions of GRAMMAR. A branch of phonology is PHONETICS, under which heading are grouped such matters
relating to speech sounds and pronunciation as are treated in this
work.

phrasal verbs   are those that consist of a main verb to which is
linked an ADVERBIAL PARTICLE. The two then function as one verbal
unit with an idiomatic meaning that is different from the sum of its
parts, e.g. to turn down, to come to, to get by, to give in, to put
across, to put up. A phrasal verb must be distinguished from a verb
that is followed by a preposition. In the sentence 'he ran up the
hill', *up* is a preposition introducing the phrase 'up the hill'; in the
sentence 'she ran up a dress', *up* is an adverbial particle belonging
to the phrasal verb 'ran up' meaning 'quickly made'.

phrase   a group of words containing no finite verb but making a
unit that functions as a noun, an adjective or an adverb within the
sentence. It is thus always dependent upon the rest of the sentence
and cannot stand on its own, e.g. '*Eating peas with a knife* requires a
gross kind of skill' (noun phrase). 'The girl *in the blue dress* is my
cousin' (adjectival phrase). 'The pony galloped *across the field*' (adverbial phrase).
  As a means of constructing compact sentences, and as an aid in
producing variety, the *participial* phrase justifies special mention. The
participle, whether past or present, always has the function of an
adjective as well as a verb. For this reason the participial phrase
always qualifies a noun or its equivalent in the rest of the sentence,
e.g. 'Entering the field, we saw the damage. Snapped in two by the
gale, the tree had fallen right across the fence.' In the first sentence
'entering' is the present participle; in the second sentence 'snapped'
is the past participle.

Often the participial phrase has also an adverbial function telling how, when or why something happens, as you can see from these examples:

(a) 'We saw the moon *reflected brilliantly in the glassy water*.'
(b) '*Having made her purchases*, Sheila retraced her steps.'
(c) '*Thinking he was early*, James did not hurry.'
(d) 'He did not worry unduly, *convinced that he could do better*.'

In(a) the phrase qualifies the noun 'moon' and is adjectival. In (b) it qualifies the noun 'Sheila' and is again adjectival, but it also modifies the verb 'retraced', telling us why or when she retraced her steps, and is therefore adverbial.

Another kind of participial phrase is the *absolute* phrase, so called because it is absolutely free from any agreement with another part of the sentence. In other words, the noun it qualifies is contained within its own phrase, e.g. '*The weather being fine*, we decided to go for a picnic.' The participle 'being (fine)' qualifies the noun 'weather'. In this sense it is absolutely free of the rest of the sentence; but in an adverbial sense it is not free, since it gives the reason for our going for a picnic.

In this connection see also ABSOLUTE; ADJECTIVAL PHRASE; AD-VERBIAL PHRASE; NOUN PHRASE; PARTICIPLES; VERB; VERBAL PHRASE (under VERB)

picaresque the type of fiction that relates the adventures of rogues. Fielding's *Tom Jones* is a picaresque novel. The term is used both as a noun and as an adjective.

Pindaric ode see ODE.

pitch the pitch with which a sound is spoken depends on the frequency of vibrations of the vocal cords; it is a matter of higher or lower notes.

See also INTONATION.

plagiarism (*g* soft) using another's words or thoughts as one's own. It derives from the Latin meaning 'to kidnap'. A plagiarist is a literary kidnapper. It has been said that to copy from one book is *plagiarism*, but to copy from four books is *research*! Voltaire had this to say about 'honest plagiarists':

All the makers of dictionaries, all compilers who do nothing else than repeat backwards and forwards the opinions, the errors, the impostures, and the truths already printed, we may term plagiarists; but honest plagiarists, who arrogate not the merit of invention.

platitude a trite or commonplace remark, especially one that is solemnly.delivered, as if to give originality and importance to a worn-out TRUISM. Let us assume that Mr Braithwaite has heard of the death of a rich acquaintance, and produces this string of platitudes as being observations suitable to the occasion: 'Well, that's the way it goes. It comes to us all in the end. What comes must come, and you can't take it with you. We're only born once and we've got to make the most of it. The sun's not always shining. Life goes on and time cures all.'

pleonasm (pli:ʹənæzm) (Gk. 'more than enough') a superfluous addition. It is a form of REDUNDANCY, but not quite the same as TAUTOLOGY, which is saying a thing twice in different ways. Pleonasm is the inclusion in a sentence of words that could be omitted without affecting its meaning, e.g.:

1. 'The two boys were both given five pence each.' Omit 'both'.
2. 'The man continued to go on working.' Omit 'to go on'.
3. 'The two twins were exactly identical.' Omit 'two' and 'exactly'.
4. 'He hurried in haste to the station.' Omit 'in haste'.
5. 'She said that, provided she received it in writing, that she would accept his apology.' Omit second 'that'.
6. 'The two books I read last week were equally as good.' Omit 'as'.
7. 'This one is more superior.' Omit 'more'. (See COMPARISON, DEGREES OF.)
8. 'We have now gone over to oil heating and hope this new innovation will prove a success.' Omit 'new'.
9. 'The brown hat belonged to Mr Jones and the grey hat to Mr Smith respectively.' Omit 'respectively'. (See RESPECTIVELY.)
10. 'Mary and Elizabeth had a mutual affection for each other.' Omit 'for each other'. (See MUTUAL.)
11. 'Any clever remarks he heard he remembered and, at a suitable opportunity, repeated them as his own.' Omit 'them'.

12. 'Every gallon of fuel oil used by this bus bears a tax of 2/9 per gallon!!' Omit 'per gallon' (and one of the exclamation marks). This notice was exhibited in buses run by the Aldershot & District Traction Co. Ltd.

13. 'The reason why he shouted was because we had made him angry with our taunts.' This is a more subtle form of pleonasm. The sense of 'why' is already contained in 'reason', and 'why' should therefore be omitted. 'Because' means 'for that reason' and is therefore repeating 'reason', so it also should be omitted and replaced by 'that', giving us: 'The reason he shouted was that we had made him angry with our taunts.'

Poets are sometimes guilty of pleonasm, probably for the sake of metre. Here is the first stanza of the Clown's song in the last act of Shakespeare's *Twelfth Night*:

When that I was and a little tiny boy,
   With hey, ho, the wind and the rain,
A foolish thing was but a toy,
   For the rain it raineth every day.

In the first line 'that', 'and' and 'little' are superfluous, as is 'it' in line four.

plosives   in PHONETICS the sounds made by air that escapes with a small explosion. See GUIDE TO PRONUNCIATION on page 7.

pluperfect tense   another name for the past perfect tense, which is treated under TENSE.

plural   the form of words indicating that more than one is referred to. In English only nouns, pronouns and verbs are inflected to indicate plural NUMBER. The general rule for making the plural of nouns is: add -s to the singular form. But in doing this we may influence the spelling of the word, so it is convenient to make eight sub-rules:

1. Nouns ending in the sibilants (hissing sounds), *s*, *sh*, *ch*, *z*, *x*, add -*es* to show the phonetic change, e.g. *gas – gases*, *mass – masses*, *brush – brushes*, *watch – watches*, *buzz – buzzes*, *box – boxes*. Surnames ending in -*s* or -*es* add -*es*, e.g. *Davis – the Davises*, *Jones – the Joneses*.

2. Nouns ending in a consonant plus -*y* change the *y* into *i* and add -*es*, e.g. *berry – berries*, *ruby – rubies*. But those ending in a vowel

plus *-y* follow the general rule, e.g. *donkey – donkeys, money – moneys, monkey – monkeys, valley – valleys, toy – toys.*

3. Some nouns ending in *-f* or *-fe* follow the general rule; some change the *f* into *v* and add *-es* (or *-s* in the case of *-fe* words). Here are the main ones:

bailiff – bailiffs	calf – calves
carafe – carafes	elf – elves
chief – chiefs	half – halves
cliff – cliffs	knife – knives
cuff – cuffs	leaf – leaves
dwarf – dwarfs	life – lives
giraffe – giraffes	loaf – loaves
hoof – hoofs	self – selves
plaintiff – plaintiffs	sheaf – sheaves
roof – roofs	shelf – shelves
scarf – scarfs	thief – thieves
turf – turfs	wife – wives
wharf – wharfs	wolf – wolves

The *-ves* list is complete, but there are many more *-fs* words, so the quickest way of dealing with the problem is to memorise those ending in *-ves*, though it must be pointed out that *hoofs, scarfs, turfs* and *wharfs* are increasingly spelt with *-ves*.

4. Most of the familiar nouns ending in *-o* add *-es* for the plural, e.g. *hero – heroes, negro – negroes, no – noes, potato – potatoes.* (The main exceptions are *dynamos, magnetos, photos, pianos, stylos*, which are contractions of longer words.) The less familiar words – longer words, rare words, foreign words, proper names – follow the general rule by adding *-s*, e.g. *archipelagos, bravados, cameos, folios, generalissimos, ghettos, infernos, manifestos, Romeos.*

5. There is a small collection of nouns that have only one form to indicate both singular and plural. They are *aircraft, cod, deer, forceps, grouse* (bird), *salmon, sheep, swine.*

6. Then there are those with no singular form, e.g. *alms, eaves, measles, news, riches, tidings* and all the many nouns ending in *-ics*, e.g. *athletics, mathematics, phonetics, politics.* These plural nouns often take a singular verb, e.g. (a) 'The news is most encouraging today.' (b) 'Mathematics is his favourite subject.' Others are plural nouns taking plural verbs but describing single things, e.g. *bellows, breeches, pants, pincers, pliers, scissors, shears, tongs, trousers.* With these we always imply 'a pair of', and 'pair' is singular.

7. Those nouns that depart entirely from -*s* for the plural are either: odd survivors of Old English, e.g. *man – men, woman – women, child – children, brother – brethren, penny – pence, ox – oxen, foot – feet, tooth – teeth, louse – lice, mouse – mice, goose – geese*; or words borrowed from other languages and retaining their foreign plurals, e.g. *terminus – termini, bureau – bureaux*. Generally speaking, when these become fully absorbed into our language they lose their foreign plural and take an ordinary English plural. Thus the plural of *index* was *indices*, but already we speak of *indexes*, except in mathematics. But if the English plural would be awkward, the foreign plural may continue to be used. Thus it is unlikely that the plural of *crisis* will ever be *crisises*, since *crises* is much easier to say. Below is a list of the more common foreign plurals:

addendum – addenda	medium – media
analysis – analyses	memorandum – memoranda
antenna – antennae	minimum – minima
appendix – appendices	nebula – nebulae
automaton – automata	nucleus – nuclei
axis – axes	oasis – oases
basis – bases	parenthesis – parentheses
criterion – criteria	phenomenon – phenomena
datum – data	plateau – plateaux
erratum – errata	radius – radii
focus – foci	sanatorium – sanatoria
formula – formulae	spectrum – spectra
fungus – fungi	stimulus – stimuli
hypothesis – hypotheses	stratum – strata
index – indices	synopsis – synopses
larva – larvae	tableau – tableaux
libretto – libretti	terminus – termini
maximum – maxima	thesis – theses

8. Most compound nouns consist of adjective plus noun. Such words form their plurals in the same way as the noun part alone forms it, e.g. *blackberry – blackberries, Frenchman – Frenchmen*. If the adjective, or adjective equivalent, comes after the noun part, the plural ending still has to be added to the noun part and therefore comes in the middle of the compound word, e.g. *courts-martial, fathers-in-law, knights-errant, lookers-on*. Where the single ending is -*ful*, the plural ending is not added to the noun part but to the suffix, e.g. *basketfuls, cupfuls, spoonfuls*. In a few instances, where the parts of the

compound are two nouns, both parts take the plural ending, e.g. *menservants*, *Lords Justices*.

plutocracy   see under DEMOCRACY.

poetic justice   In his *Dunciad* Pope wrote:

Poetic Justice, with her lifted scale,
Where, in nice balance, truth with gold she weighs,
And solid pudding against empty praise.

It is the justice meted out by poets to the good and to the bad; and in the punishment of the wrongdoer poetic justice has more than a touch of irony. As the Mikado sings in *The Mikado*:

My object all sublime
I shall achieve in time –
To let the punishment fit the crime –
The punishment fit the crime.

There is poetic justice in the fate of the scientist mentioned under ENJAMBMENT.

poetic licence   By the limitations imposed upon them by the medium in which they work, poets are sometimes forced to break grammatical rules. Consequently they are allowed a certain licence not permitted to prose writers. W. S. Gilbert touches on this in the last of the Gilbert and Sullivan operas, *The Grand Duke, or the Statutory Duel*:

But each a card shall draw,
And he who draws the lowest
    Shall (so 'twas said)
    Be thenceforth dead –
  In fact a legal 'ghoest'.
(When exigence of rhyme compels,
Orthography foregoes her spells,
    And 'ghost' is written 'ghoest'.)

That this is but a shadow of the real Gilbert need not concern us here.

poet laureate   a poet appointed by the king or queen of England to write verses in celebration of Court and national events. *Laureate* derives from the Latin meaning 'laurel-wreath'. Inasmuch as he was appointed by James I to the office of poet attached to the royal household, Ben Jonson can be regarded as the first official poet laureate. Some authorities date the laureateship back to Edmund Spenser, but this claim is based only on the fact that Queen Elizabeth I granted him a pension of £50 because of the flattering references to her in *The Faerie Queene*.

Since Ben Jonson there have been sixteen poets laureate. Below are listed the last seven of these:

William Wordsworth	1843–50
Lord Tennyson	1850–92
Alfred Austin	1896–1913
Robert Bridges	1913–30
John Masefield	1930–68
Cecil Day Lewis	1968–72
John Betjeman	1972–

poetry   any form of writing that is not in PROSE. Webster defines it as: 'the art or work of poets; the embodiment in appropriate language of beautiful or high thought, imagination, or emotion, the language being rhythmical, usually metrical, and characterised by harmonic and emotional qualities which appeal to and arouse the feelings and imagination; metrical composition; also the production or productions of a poet or poets; poetical writings; poems collectively; verse; rime . . .'

Cross-references to poetry in this work are listed under PROSODY.

polemic   As an adjective this (or *polemical*) means 'controversial'; 'disputatious'. As a noun it means 'a controversial discussion'. The plural *polemics* refers to the practice of theological controversy.

pomposity   speech or writing that crudely tries to seem magnificent. It is a DEROGATORY term. Pompous words are inflated ones with which a lazy writer tries to make good his deficiencies.

pop   abbreviation for *popular* which gained wide currency in the 1960s with specific reference to *pop music* and *pop art*. *Pop music* was an extension of *rock 'n' roll*, itself borrowed from the strong Negro rhythms in *jive* and *jazz* music. It was exemplified at its best by The Beatles, whose international popularity, beginning in 1963, led to the NEOLOGISM *Beatlemania* to describe the extraordinary enthusiasm they evoked in the liberated young. The name of the *group* (a term that completely displaced the older compound noun *dance-band*) was a PUN on *beat*, a musical term that acquired a more specific meaning in jazz and pop circles, and led to such adjectives as OFFBEAT and *downbeat*. Pop groups were sometimes followed on tour, usually a series of *one night stands*, by hysterical nymphets known as *groupies*. *Pop art* was the portrayal of instantaneously recognised objects supposed to be representative of *pop culture*, as with a large painting of a tin of Campbell's soup by the American *pop artist* Andy Warhol.

pornography (Gk. 'writing about whores') as an abstract noun, was widely used in the 1960s by traditionalists to describe the new PERMISSIVE literature which, if not devoted to whores, certainly dwelt in unloving detail on the facts of lust. Simultaneously there was an uprush of deliberate pornography, particularly in some magazines, to take advantage of the new tolerance. Defenders of liberty were sometimes embarrassed to have to put up a case for this *hard-core pornography*. At this period, too, charges of obscenity were frequently levelled. Everyone knew what *obscene* meant, but the courts of law were hard put to it to define *obscenity* in punishable terms.

portmanteau words These are made up by joining part of one word to part of another in order to convey the ideas behind both words. The term was invented by Lewis Carroll, who created the portmanteau word *galumph* from *gallop* and *triumph*. More recent examples are *electrocute* from *electric* and *execute*; *radiogram* from *radio* and *gramophone*; *Benelux* from *Belgium, Netherlands and Luxembourg*. Three of the many combinations invented to serve the needs of modern times are *docudrama* (documentary drama), *motel* (motorists' hotel) and *traddict* (traditional jazz addict).

See also NEOLOGISM and TELESCOPING.

poser, poseur A *poser* is a question difficult to answer. The word is also used for one who poses for a photograph or portrait. A *poseur* (from the French) also poses but with a different intention; he behaves in an affected manner in order to impress others.

possessive see under APOSTROPHE (1); GENITIVE (POSSESSIVE) CASE.

possessive adjectives and pronouns These should be clearly distinguished. Possessive adjectives are *my, your, his, her, one's, its, our, their*. They can never be used without the noun they qualify, e.g. 'my book', 'your car', 'their house'. Note that there is an apostrophe in *one's* but not in *its*, e.g. 'one's head', 'its head'. Possessive pronouns are *mine, yours, his, hers, its, theirs*. They are always used on their own instead of a noun plus the possessive adjective, e.g. (a) 'This book is mine (= 'my book')', (b) 'Which car is yours (= 'your car')?', (c) 'They have been to our house and we have been to theirs (= 'their house').' Note that there is no apostrophe in *yours, hers, its, ours* or *theirs*.

A word that is both a possessive adjective and a possessive pronoun is *whose*. It is a possessive adjective when it has a noun following it, e.g. 'I asked him whose house was on fire, but he could not tell me.' Here 'whose' is a possessive adjective qualifying 'house'. It is a possessive pronoun (i.e. the possessive form of the relative pronoun *who*) when it is used without a following noun, e.g. 'He told me a house was on fire, but he did not know whose.' Here 'whose' is in the same class as *mine, yours*, etc., e.g. 'He told me a house was on fire, but he did not know if it was mine.'

The purist argues that as *whose* is the possessive form of *who*, it should be used only for persons, and that when we refer to things we should use *of which*, the possessive form of the relative pronoun *which*. According to him we may say 'This is the man whose car has been stolen', but we may not say 'This is the car whose owner cannot be traced'. Grammar, however, was made for man, not man for grammar, and usage has ruled that *whose* is permissible, mainly because it is so much less ungainly than *of which*.

The need to distinguish between *whose* and *who's* is treated under WHOSE, WHO'S, and the use of *whose* as an interrogative pronoun ('Whose car is this?') is treated under PRONOUN.

postscript (L. 'written afterwards') something added to a letter already finished; an afterthought. It is abbreviated PS, and a further postscript is abbreviated PPS. Here are two postscripts added by Jack to a letter to his friend:

Yours sincerely,
Jack

PS I forgot to say I've bought a new bicycle.
PPS You owe me a letter!

practicable, practical   The first means 'able to be put into practice or to be accomplished', whilst the second means 'adapted to actual conditions, not merely theoretical'. It follows that a person can be practical, but he can never be practicable. An idea, however, can be both practical and practicable. It helps to remember that practical is the opposite of theoretical.

pragmatism (Gk. 'the practice of doing')   in PHILOSOPHY the doctrine that tests the value and truth of ideas by their practical bearing upon human affairs. To be *pragmatic* is to be businesslike, to be concerned with practical results. In a DEROGATORY sense, it means to be interfering, to be meddlesome in other people's affairs; or to be more concerned with practical results than with matters of principle.

precede, proceed   The first means 'to go before', either in rank, importance, sequence or time, e.g.:

(a) In the order formally observed on ceremonial occasions, the Archbishop of York precedes the Prime Minister.
(b) The task of building more houses precedes all others.
(c) In the alphabet the letter *c* is preceded by *a* and *b*.
(d) My fortnight's holiday in Bournemouth was preceded by a week in London.

The second (*proceed*) means 'to go forward from point to point', e.g. 'We proceeded from the public library to the museum, then from the museum to the aquarium.' Do not use *proceed* when there is no element of *procession* (going from point to point), e.g.:

Wrong: Acting on this information, the police proceeded to a house in Deptford.

Right: Acting on this information, the police went to a house in Deptford.

Right: Acting on this information, the police went to a house in Deptford, then proceeded to search other houses in the neighbourhood.

precedence, precedent   Both these nouns derive from *precede*, but they have different meanings. The first means 'priority' in the sense of superior rank or importance, e.g.:

(a) At the Universities of Oxford and Cambridge, the High Sheriff takes precedence of the Vice-Chancellor.

(b) Precedence was given to those who had most urgent need of medical attention.

A *precedent* is something that has happened in the past and can be used to justify a present action, or give guidance in dealing with any particular matter, e.g. 'Our precedent for holding the meeting on a Wednesday is that it was held on a Wednesday last year.'

Opinion as to the pronunciation of these two words is divided. Here recommended are presə|dens and presə|dent, but not with the z sound as in *president*.

precious   This means literally 'of great price; very costly'. Gold and silver are precious metals; a diamond is a precious stone. It is used also: (a) with the meaning of 'much loved', 'beloved', e.g. 'The little girl was in tears because the head had come off her precious doll.' (b) with the meaning of 'affected', 'over-refined', e.g. 'I do not much care for that precious young man, with his conceited manner and superior attitude.' (c) ironically, as a synonym of EGREGIOUS, e.g. 'That precious brother of hers made an ass of himself, as usual.' (d) as an INTENSIVE, e.g. 'We had precious few customers in the shop today.'

précis (prei|si)   an abstract or summary; a condensed version of an original passage of prose. Précis-writing provides very good practice in the art of discriminating between the relevant and the irrelevant, the essential and the inessential.

predicate   the part of the sentence that is predicated (asserted) about the subject. It consists of (a) the finite verb alone, e.g. 'The girls *sang*.' (b) the finite verb and the object, e.g. 'The girls *sang a hymn*.' (c) The finite verb and the complement, e.g. 'He *became an actor*.' Anything that adds to the information given by the verb and the object, or by the verb and the complement, is known as the **extension of the predicate**, e.g.:

verb + object + extension: 'The girls *sang a hymn by Charles Wesley at the evening service*.' We now know who wrote the hymn and when it was sung by the girls.

verb + complement + extension: 'He *became a professional actor in his eighteenth year*.' We now know that it was a professional actor he became and that this happened in his eighteenth year.

The predicate is not always to be found after the subject; it can come before it, e.g. '*Along the High Street came* the procession.'

See also COMPLEMENT; OBJECT; SENTENCE; SUBJECT; VERB.

preface the introduction to a book, usually written by the author himself. It may state his reasons for writing the book, the scope and aim of it, and may also contain other matters that should be explained to the reader before he starts on the book. Bernard Shaw was as famous for his prefaces to his plays as he was for the plays themselves. For example, his preface to *Major Barbara* is very nearly half as long as the play. But this is unusual. Most prefaces run to no more than a page or two.

See also FOREWORD.

prefix an affix placed before a root word to modify its meaning and so build a new word, e.g. *pre*paid, *un*cover, *im*port, *ex*port, *trans*port. See also SUFFIX; WORD-FORMATION.

prejudice This derives from the Latin meaning 'judging before'. Ambrose Bierce defined it in *The Devil's Dictionary* as 'a vagrant opinion without visible means of support'. It is a bias against or in favour of a person or thing without knowledge of the facts. We may say, for example, that we have never eaten olives because we do not like them. But how can we form an opinion until we have tasted one? After we have tasted one we may still say that we do not like olives, but we are no longer prejudiced against them.

Prejudice stands in the way of any objective approach in an argument. It is a form of FALLACY to persuade your hearers to prejudge an issue before all the facts have been laid before them. For example, the dismissal of the steward of your sports club is under discussion. You believe him to be dishonest, but if you have no facts to support this belief, you ought not to prejudice the minds of the committee by such remarks as: 'You can tell he's a crook by his shifty expression'; or 'I for one have never trusted the fellow.'

premise (or **premiss,** but the first spelling is recommended) an assumption made for the purpose of an ARGUMENT. See SYLLOGISM; DEDUCTION.

preposition a structural word (*at, by, for, in, of, on, to, out, with,* etc.) introducing a phrase made up of a preposition and a noun or its equivalent, along with any qualifications, e.g. '*in* a hurry', '*at* long last', '*alongside* the quay'. Some prepositions are compound, e.g. '*out of* this world', '*with regard to* your suggestion'. A few are verbal in character, e.g. '*considering* his age', '*notwithstanding* his resistance'.

Certain prepositions are used incorrectly as conjunctions. For instance, *like* is a preposition, not a conjunction. The corresponding conjunction is *as*, e.g.:

Right: That boy can swim like a fish.

Wrong: I wish I could swim like that boy can.

Right: I wish I could swim as that boy can.

The distinction is usually maintained in literary English, though in colloquial English it is customary to say, 'I wish I could swim like that boy (can).' This use of *like* is increasingly common in American usage: 'like the man said' is a popular expression, and phrases such as 'like the President has always maintained' are already creeping into the written language.

Like should not be used instead of *as if*, e.g.:

Wrong: I felt like I was being smothered.

Right: I felt as if I was being smothered.

In the same way, the prepositions *without* and *except* should not be used in place of the conjunction *unless*.

Wrong: I shan't go without you come with me.

Wrong: I shan't go except you come with me.

Right: I shan't go unless you come with me.

There is nothing wrong about using a preposition to end a sentence with. Each case must be judged on its own merits. If the sentence sounds well and looks sensible it must be all right. It is, however, obviously awkward to end the sentence with more than one preposition ('What,' the small boy asked his mother, 'did you want to bring the book I didn't want to be read to out of up for?'), and we must also watch sentences where the preposition is separated too far from the noun it goes with. Sometimes, especially with compound verbs, the end position is much more natural, as we can see from these two sentences: (a) 'Is that the room you sleep in?' (b) 'Is that the room in which you sleep?'

prepositional idiom   the idiomatic use of prepositions. It is important to use the correct preposition, especially after certain words, to introduce the phrase following, e.g. to agree *to* a thing, but to agree *with* a person; to converse *with* a person *on* a subject or *about* something; to substitute something *for* something else, but to replace something *by* something else; to be answerable *to* a person for something one has done, but to be answerable *for* having done it. Here are a few more prepositional idioms:

to be averse *to*	to be endowed *with*
to connive *at*	to gloat *over*
to culminate *in*	to be impervious *to*
to be deterred *from*	to be intent *upon*
to be devoid *of*	to be marred *by*
to dissent *from*	to be sensitive *to*

Press Use the capital letter when the reference is to newspapers in general, e.g. 'He wrote innumerable letters to the Press, but very few of them were published.'

See also METONYMY.

presumptive, presumptuous The first means 'presumed' or 'probable', e.g. 'The heir presumptive to the throne in 1950 was Princess Elizabeth.' One also speaks of 'the heir apparent'. The second is a DEROGATORY adjective meaning the opposite of 'modest', e.g. 'His presumptuous behaviour in occupying the seat intended for the guest of honour earned him a sharp rebuke from the chairman.'

pretentious laying claim to greater importance than is justified; showing off. A pretentious style of writing uses words and constructions that are more difficult and important-looking than the matter to be expressed justifies.

prevent The literal meaning of this is 'to come before' rather than 'to stop or hinder'.

(a) 'His election to the presidency of the association was prevented by the sudden death of his wife.'
(b) 'The commissionaire barred their way and prevented them from entering the building.'

In the second example, 'stopped' would be better than 'prevented' if we wished to allow for the origin of the word, but few do, and usage has now accepted *prevent* as a synonym for *stop* or *hinder*.

preventive, preventative Use the first if you are referring to something that prevents; the second is used artificially to refer to a contraceptive device, though this is being superseded by 'protective'.

principal, principle   We shall avoid confusing these if we remember that the former means 'chief' and may be an adjective or a noun. Thus the principal member of a business and its principal are one and the same person. *Principle* means 'a rule of conduct', and is often used in the plural, e.g. 'It was against his principles to mock the aged.'

printers' proofs   After the type of a book has been set by the compositor, it must be read for corrections before it is printed. A trial impression from the composed type is therefore taken. This is called a *proof*. There are two stages of correction: one before the matter is paginated (made up into pages) and the other after pagination.

The first trial impression is called the *galley proof*, so called because *galley* is the name of the oblong tray on which the matter is placed as it is set up by the compositor. The galley proof is usually about eighteen inches long. Collectively these proofs are referred to as 'galleys'. In preparation for the second stage, they are read for 'literals', which are errors made by the compositor. These are some of the marks used in the correction of proofs:

ℐ	delete
⋀	insert
#	insert space (*and is* for *andis*)
trs.	transpose letters (e.g. *the* for *teh*)
×	change damaged letter
⌒	close up (e.g. *the* for *t he*)
cap.	change to capital letter(s)
l.c.	(lower case) change from capital letter(s) to lower-case letter(s), i.e. small letter(s) (e.g. *doctor* for *Doctor*; *prime minister* for *Prime Minister*)
n.p.	begin a new paragraph
ital.	change to italics
↻	turn letter (e.g. *the* for *thǝ*)
stet	'let it (the original word) stand'; ignore the correction

When the type has been reset in accordance with the corrections made in the galleys, the matter is paginated and a second trial impression (*page proof*) is taken from the type. After the page proofs have been read and corrected (there's many a slip 'twixt the galley and the page!), the book is 'ready for press' – that is, ready to be printed off.

The advantage of galley proofs is that corrections can be made more easily and more cheaply at that stage than at the page-proof stage. A word, a line or even a whole paragraph can be added to or deleted from the galleys without much difficulty, but the page proofs are another matter. Uniformity requires that, apart from the first and last pages of chapters, all the pages in a book must have the same number of lines, say 38. It is obvious, therefore, that when the page-proof stage has been reached, we cannot add a line to a page, or strike one out, without disturbing the pagination of that and successive pages. Even the addition of a single word to a line can cause an 'overrun' from one page to the next – and so on until a space on the last page of a chapter allows us to add an extra line and so not have to carry the repagination farther.

In the normal course of things, there is no need for any extensive emendation of the proofs unless the author has second thoughts and wishes to revise his text. Unless instructed not to, printers always submit galley proofs to the publishers, but the publishers do not always forward them to the author, for he is more than likely to treat them as he might a draft typescript, peppering them with alterations and sending the printers mad. Instead the publishers clip the author's wings by withholding the galleys and sending him a copy of the page proofs, usually with the warning, courteous yet stern, that alterations must be kept to an absolute minimum.

The author will do well to remember that the majority of printers make a charge for all alterations other than the correction of literals, and that the publishers may require him to bear a part of the cost of these. In consequence, should he decide that some emendation is essential, he must avoid the necessity for repagination by altering the text in such a way that there are no more and no fewer than the standard number of lines on that page. This can be done by (a) making room for an addition by striking out something less important and of equal length; or (b) substituting for a deletion a word or phrase of equal length; which is not always as easy as it sounds.

The obvious remedy is for the author to satisfy himself that his typescript, technically known as COPY, is correct and complete before he submits it to the publishers. It is a foolish mistake to say, 'I don't want to spoil the look of my typescript, so I'll put that right in the proofs.' Though neatness and clarity are desirable, neither

publishers nor printers will attach any importance at all to the un-
blemished beauty of the typescript.

printing terms   See COPY; FOOLSCAP; FORMAT; FOUNT; GALLEY
PROOF (under PRINTERS' PROOFS); INDENTATION; LEADING ARTICLE;
LITERAL MISTAKES; LOWER CASE; OCTAVO; PAGE PROOF (under
PRINTERS' PROOFS); PAGINATION (under PRINTERS' PROOFS); QUARTO.

prise, prize   'John tried to prise open the chest with a crowbar.'
Though *prise* is acceptable, the usual spelling is *prize*.

prolepsis (proulep¹sis) (Gk. 'taken beforehand') in RHETORIC a
device by which objections are *forestalled* by being answered in
advance, e.g. (a) 'My advice to you gentlemen is that, *although our
resources are at present inadequate*, we go ahead with this project.' (b) '*I
am the first to acknowledge that it was unwise for a public servant to accept this
gift*, but I submit that his motives were not dishonourable.'
    Prolepsis is also a FIGURE OF SPEECH in which an adjective is used
to denote in advance the result of the action of the verb, e.g. (a) 'The
winning horse was last away at the start of the race.' (b) 'The man
killed by the blast was standing in the boiler-house when the explosion
occurred.' In (a) we are told in advance that the horse won the race;
in (b) we are told in advance that the man was killed by the explosion.

prologue (Gk. 'to speak before')   an introduction to a play, poem,
etc. either in prose or verse. Sometimes it is sung, as in the famous
prologue to *I Pagliacci*, the opera by Leoncavallo. Shakespeare used
prologues, as in the speech introducing *Henry V*, the opening lines of
which are:

> O for a Muse of fire, that would ascend
> The brightest heaven of invention,
> A kingdom for a stage, princes to act
> And monarchs to behold the swelling scene!

See also EPILOGUE.

pronoun   a word used instead of a noun, usually to avoid repeating
the noun, e.g. 'Give John the books and then *he* will give *them* to the
manager.' Pronouns may be classified as:

1. *Personal pronouns* (*I, me, you, he, him, she, her, one, it, we, us, they, them*) stand for those speaking, those spoken to, or those spoken of, e.g. '*I* was waiting outside the cinema with *her* when *you* went past with *him*.'

The neuter pronoun *it* corresponds to *he* and *she* in the third person and has the same plural (*they, them, their, theirs*). It is used (a) as a substitute for any neuter noun, e.g. 'He gave me a penny and told me to spend *it* wisely.' (b) as the subject of an impersonal verb, e.g. 'When *it* thunders I am frightened.' 'Does *it* frighten you?' (c) in such impersonal expressions as: '*It* is four o'clock'; 'I did not think *it* was so late'; '*It* is one hundred and ten miles from London to Birmingham.' See also ANTICIPATORY SUBJECT; IDIOM.

Errors arise through the confusion of person – through the mixing of *they, he, you*, etc., with the indefinite pronoun *one*, e.g.:

Wrong: One is bound to succeed as long as you persevere.

Right: One is bound to succeed as long as one perseveres.

Wrong: What can one do when he finds himself in such a position?

Right: What can one do when one finds oneself in such a position?

2. *Demonstrative pronouns* (*this, these, that, those, such, the other, the same*) indicate the person or thing referred to, e.g. '*That* is the hat I am going to wear instead of *this*.'

3. *Relative pronouns* (*who, whom, those, which, that*) express a relationship to an antecedent and introduce a subordinate adjectival clause, e.g. 'I know *nobody* in the firm *who* has the right qualifications.' The relative pronoun *who* relates back to the antecedent *nobody* and introduces the adjectival clause *who has the right qualifications*. Agreement between a relative pronoun and its antecedent is shown only in the verb, e.g.: 'I know only two men in the firm who *have* the right qualifications.'

When a relative pronoun introduces a subordinate adjectival clause, it must agree with the noun or pronoun in the main clause, e.g.:

Wrong: This is the boy which won the race.

Right: This is the boy who won the race.

Wrong: They that believed him supported him.

Right: They who believed him supported him.

See also ACCUSATIVE (OBJECTIVE) CASE, section (d).

The use of *which* instead of *that* is all too common and gives rise to AMBIGUITY, e.g.:

Wrong: Toys which are dangerous should not be given to young children.

Right: Toys that are dangerous should not be given to young children.

The first sentence suggests that all toys are dangerous. The second conveys the writer's true meaning, which is that dangerous toys should not be given to young children. Alternatively, if the warning is of a particular rather than a general nature, *which* should be used instead of *that*, and the subordinate clause marked off by commas, e.g. 'Fireworks, which are dangerous in the wrong hands, should not be given to young children.'

A safe rule is: never use *which* in place of *that* when *that* makes your meaning clearer; and always omit the comma (or commas) when *which* can be used instead of *that* without risk of ambiguity, e.g.:

Wrong: The thing, which really angers me, is his stubbornness.

Right: The thing which really angers me is his stubbornness.

or: The thing that really angers me is his stubbornness.

4. *Interrogative pronouns* (*who? which? what? whom? whose?*) ask a question, e.g. (a) '*What* are you doing this afternoon?' (b) '*Whose* gloves are these?'

5. *Possessive pronouns* (*mine, yours, his, hers, its, ours, theirs, whose*) denote possession or appurtenance – the possessor or the thing possessed, e.g. 'The gloves are *mine* and the umbrella is *hers*.' See also POSSESSIVE ADJECTIVES AND PRONOUNS.

6. *Reflexive pronouns* (*myself, yourself, himself, herself, oneself, itself, ourselves, yourselves, themselves*) serve as the object of a reflexive verb (see REFLEXIVE), e.g. 'The children enjoyed *themselves* at the seaside.' The verb *enjoyed* has as its object *themselves*, which turns back upon the subject *children*. (Note that *hisself* and *theirselves*, although used in dialect, are not good English.) An archaic use of reflexive pronouns is seen in such sentences as: (a) 'I sat *me* down awhile.' (b) 'He hied *him* to London.' In (a) *me* has the same meaning as *myself*. In (b) *him* has the same meaning as *himself*. The old-fashioned verb *to hie* means *to hasten*.

7. *Emphatic pronouns* are reflexive pronouns used for emphasis, e.g. 'He *himself* was to blame.'

8. Indefinite pronouns (*any, one, anyone, anybody, nobody, nothing, something*) refer in general terms to an unspecified number of persons or things, e.g. (a) '*One* cannot expect *anybody* to endure such treatment.' (b) '*Something* attempted, *something* done, has earned a night's repose.' (Longfellow.)

9. *Distributive pronouns* (*each, every, either, neither*) refer to persons or things individually, e.g. '*Each* tried hard, but *neither* succeeded.'

See also AMBIGUITY; APOSTROPHE (1); CASE; NOUN-EQUIVALENTS; NUMBER.

pronunciation Most of the difficulties of English spelling arise from the fact that it is etymological rather than phonetic, words being spelt according to their historical form rather than their present sound. Thus the word *enough* is spelt thus because in Old English it was pronounced with a guttural sound represented by *gh*, though today it is pronounced as if it were spelt *enuff*.

In earlier times spelling was much more phonetic than it is today. Chaucer, Shakespeare and Milton, for example, were all sensible enough to let the spelling as far as possible represent the sound. But during the eighteenth century the pedants came along and fixed the spelling according to what they considered to be sound etymology.

Since spellings were finally 'decided', pronunciation has changed considerably; so that today our spellings are so remote from their pronunciation that if English is to become a real international language, some reform of its spelling will be essential. In the meantime the compilers of dictionaries must adopt some system whereby the pronunciation of words can be shown.

In its simplest form this is the replacement of letters by those nearer to the sound of the word, e.g. *rough* (*ruff*), *cough* (*coff*), *trough* (*troff*), *through* (*throo*), *thought* (*thawt*). But this will not do for certain other words in this class, e.g. *bough* and *dough*. The entry *bough* (*bow*) would be ambiguous, for *bow* rhymes with either *cow* or *go*, whilst the entry *dough* (*do*) might well suggest that *dough* is pronounced like the verb *do*. This difficulty is overcome by making the entries read *bough* (*bou*) and *dough* (*dō*); but those who refer to the dictionary must have further guidance, so at the beginning of the dictionary is printed a 'Key to Pronunciation', which tells them that the *ou* sound in *bou* is pronounced like the *ou* sound in *doubt*, and that the sign over the *o* in *do*, known as the MACRON, indicates that the vowel has the long sound of the *o* in *go*, not the *u* sound of the *o* in *do*.

In order to pronounce a word correctly, we must know not only the sounds that go to make it, but also where the stress or accent falls. The stress will fall on a particular syllable; so we must be able to break the word into syllables. There is no problem with single-syllable words; but words of more than one syllable fall into the following main patterns:

(a) Words of two syllables with the stress on the first: *sis¹-ter*, *pain¹-ter*, *doc¹-tor*, *a¹-gile*, *for¹feit*, *her¹-o*.

(b) Words of two syllables with the stress on the second: *be-hind*ˡ, *ob-scure*ˡ, *a-dore*ˡ, *be-gin*ˡ, *con-sist*ˡ, *mo-rose*ˡ.

(c) Words of two syllables with both stressed: *thir*ˡ-*teen*ˡ, *Chi*ˡ*nese*ˡ, *arm*ˡ-*chair*ˡ, *back*ˡ-*fire*ˡ, *half*ˡ-*term*ˡ, *White*ˡ-*hall*ˡ.

(d) Words of three syllables with the stress on the first: *com*ˡ-*i-cal*, *su*ˡ-*i-cide*, *pos*ˡ-*i-tive*, *per*ˡ-*i-od*, *el*ˡ-*e-gant*.

(e) Words of three syllables with the stress on the second: *co-loss*ˡ-*al*, *de-lic*ˡ-*ious*, *con-ges*ˡ-*ted*, *ig-no*ˡ-*ble*.

(f) Words of three syllables with the stress on the third, though sometimes there is a slight stress also on the first: *in-di-rect*ˡ, *dis-re-gard*ˡ, *rep-ar-tee*ˡ, *in-ter-fere*ˡ.

(g) Words of four or more syllables usually stress the third from last: *pho-tog*ˡ-*raph-er*, *de-moc*ˡ-*ra-cy*, *i-den*ˡ-*tic-al*, *pa-ren*ˡ-*the-sis*, *har-mon*ˡ-*i-ous*, *ge-o-met*ˡ-*ri-cal*, *val-e-tu-din-ar*ˡ-*i-an*, *un-i-den-ti-fi*ˡ-*a-ble*.

MEANING CHANGED BY SHIFT OF STRESS

The position of the stress is so important that some words change their meaning or function completely with a shift of stress, as can be seen from this list:

1. *ab*ˡ*stract* (adj.), considered apart from any application to a particular object; not concrete
   *abstract*ˡ (verb), to draw away; to separate
2. *alter*ˡ*nate* (adj.), done or happening by turns
   *al*ˡ*ternate* (verb), to make or come in turn
3. *at*ˡ*tribute* (noun), a quality or property
   *attrib*ˡ*ute* (verb), to ascribe as belonging or appropriate to
4. *com*ˡ*pact* (noun), an agreement between parties
   *compact*ˡ (adj.), well-arranged; closely pressed
5. *con*ˡ*tent* (noun), what is contained in a book, vessel, etc.
   *content*ˡ (adj.), satisfied with what one has
6. *con*ˡ*vert* (noun), one who adopts a new opinion
   *convert*ˡ (verb), to change into another form or state
7. *con*ˡ*vict* (noun), a person held in prison
   *convict*ˡ (verb), to prove guilty
8. *des*ˡ*ert* (noun), a sandy waste
   *desert*ˡ (verb), to forsake; to run away
9. *es*ˡ*cort* (noun), a guard for protection or honour
   *escort*ˡ (verb), to go as a guard

10. *fre*ˈ*quent* (adj.), often occurring; numerous
    *frequent*ˈ (verb), to go often or habitually to a place

11. *in*ˈ*valid* (noun), a sick person
    *inval*ˈ*id* (adj.), not valid; without legal force

12. *min*ˈ*ute* (noun), one-sixtieth of an hour
    *minute*ˈ (adj.), very small

13. *ob*ˈ*ject* (noun), a thing presented to the senses or the mind
    *object*ˈ (verb), to oppose; to give a reason against

14. *per*ˈ*vert* (noun), a person turned from right to wrong
    *pervert*ˈ (verb), to turn a person or a thing from right to wrong;
    to misapply

15. *ref*ˈ*use* (noun), garbage
    *refuse*ˈ (verb), to decline

GUIDES TO PRONUNCIATION AND STRESS

In the above examples stress is indicated by means of a vertical stroke. In some dictionaries it is indicated by means of what is called a turned period, thus: *ref·use*. Guides to pronunciation also vary from dictionary to dictionary. For example, picking three words at random:

	water	*plumage*	*expostulate*
Concise Oxford	wawter	plōō·mĭj	expŏ·stulate
Webster	wôˈtĕr	plōōmˈāj	ĕks-pŏsˈtū-lāt
Thorndike	wôˈtər	plümˈij	eks posˈ chù lāt
New Elizabethan	wawˈtėr	plooˈmȧj	ek sposˈtū lāt

Whatever the system, the pronunciation key is for the guidance of English-speaking people; it is of little help to those to whom English is a foreign language. This has led to the introduction of a system by which the forty-four sounds that make up the English language have been given international phonetic symbols, which, once mastered, will enable the overseas student to find his way through the labyrinth of English pronunciation.

As this system of international phonetic symbols is becoming more and more widely used, it has been adopted for the present work. On pages 7 and 8 there are complete lists of the twenty vowel sounds and the twenty-four consonant sounds.

See also ACCENT; ALPHABET; CONSONANTS; DERIVATION; GUTTURALS; INITIAL TEACHING ALPHABET; SIBILANTS; SPELLING; VOWELS; STANDARD ENGLISH; RECEIVED PRONUNCIATION.

proofs   see PRINTERS' PROOFS.

proper adjectives   These are the adjectives corresponding to proper nouns, and like their nouns they begin with a capital letter. There is no one way in which these adjectives are formed; they make use of most of the adjectival endings available to English, and a few are oddities, e.g. Switzerland – Swiss; Isle of Man – Manx; Holland – Dutch. The following list will give some idea of the variety of proper adjectives:

Alps – Alpine
Britain – British
China – Chinese
Cornwall – Cornish
Denmark – Danish
Edward – Edwardian
Egypt – Egyptian
Europe – European
Finland – Finnish
Flanders – Flemish
George – Georgian
Ghana – Ghanaian
Glasgow – Glaswegian
Greece – Greek
Hitler – Hitlerite
Holland – Dutch
Iceland – Icelandic
Iraq – Iraqi
Ireland – Irish
Isle of Man – Manx
Israel – Israeli
James – Jacobean

Jew – Jewish
Malta – Maltese
Manchester – Mancunian
Naples – Neapolitan
Napoleon – Napoleonic
Netherlands (Holland) – Dutch
Norway – Norwegian
Pakistan – Pakistani
Paris – Parisian
Poland – Polish
Rome – Roman
Scotland – Scottish
Shakespeare – Shakespearian
Sicily – Sicilian
Shaw (Bernard) – Shavian
Slav – Slavonic
Sweden – Swedish
Switzerland – Swiss
Venice – Venetian
Victoria – Victorian
Wales – Welsh

It is worth noting that few adjectives have been formed from the names of towns, and those few are rarely used. The noun itself is made to do service as an adjective. We may speak, for example, of a Glaswegian characteristic, i.e. a characteristic of a native or resident of Glasgow, but we do not speak of the Glaswegian streets, but of the Glasgow streets or of the streets of Glasgow. The same applies to Manchester and Mancunian. It is also to be noted that Edwardian, Georgian and Jacobean relate to the reigns of English kings. Edwardian means anything characteristic of the reign of King

Edward VII, e.g. Edwardian clothes; Georgian means (a) anything characteristic of the reigns of George I, George II, George III, George IV, e.g. Georgian architecture; (b) some things characteristic of the reign of George V, e.g. the Georgian poets; and Jacobean means anything characteristic of the reign of James I, e.g. Jacobean furniture.

proper nouns see NOUN; CAPITAL LETTERS.

prophecy, prophesy The noun is spelt with a *c*, the verb with an *s*.

proportion This has a more precise meaning than *portion* or *part*. It is the comparative relation of one thing to another (or one part to another) with respect to size, number or degree, e.g.:

(a) Our success will be in proportion to our industry.
(b) If wages are increased, the cost of living will rise in proportion.
(c) The proportion of young men entering university is greater than it was before World War II.
(d) The room was well-proportioned and beautifully furnished.

In sentences such as the following, *proportion* should not be used instead of *portion* or *part*:

(e) Only a small portion of the Abbey still stands.
(f) Even on his summer holidays he spent a part of his time studying.

pros and cons This derives from the Latin *pro*, meaning 'for' and *contra*, meaning 'against'. When we 'consider the pros and cons', we look at both sides of the matter, weighing the advantages against the disadvantages before deciding what to do.

prose (L. 'straightforward') any form of writing that is not in verse. In his *Le Bourgeois Gentilhomme* ('The Citizen Turned Gentleman') Molière makes his character say: 'For more than forty years I have been talking prose without knowing it.'

prosody (prosˈədi) (Gk. 'to a song') the science treating of the quantity of syllables (stressed or unstressed) and the rules of verse. It is divided into METRE and RHYME, which are dealt with under those headings. For convenience of reference there are listed below, in three sections, the headings under which matters relating to prosody are separately treated in this work.

PROSODY

ANTISTROPHE; BALLAD; BALLADE; BLANK VERSE; CANTO; CLERIHEW; COUPLET; DOGGEREL; ELEGY; EMOTIVE LANGUAGE; END-STOPPED LINE; ENJAMBMENT; ENVOY; EPIC; EPIGRAM; EPILOGUE; EPITAPH; FEMININE ENDING; FREE VERSE; HAIKU; HEROIC COUPLET; IDYLL; IMAGERY; INVERSION; JINGLE; LAMPOON; LEONINE VERSE; LIMERICK; LYRIC; NARRATIVE; NONSENSE VERSE; OCTAVE; ODE; PARODY; PINDARIC ODE; POETIC LICENCE; POETRY; QUATRAIN; ROMANTICISM; RONDEAU; SATIRE; SESTET; SONNET; STANZA; STROPHE; THRENODY; TRIOLET; TRIPLET; VERS LIBRE; VERSE.

METRE

ACATALECTIC; ACCENT; ALEXANDRINE; AMPHIBRACH; ANAPAEST; BREVE; CAESURA; CATALECTIC; DACTYL; DECASYLLABIC; DIMETER; DISYLLABIC; ELISION; FEMININE ENDING; FOOT; HEPTAMETER; HEXA-METER; IAMBUS; MACRON; MONOMETER; MONOSYLLABIC; OCTAMETER; PENTAMETER; PLEONASM; POETRY; QUANTITY; RHYTHM; SCANNING; SPONDEE; SPRUNG RHYTHM; STRESS; TETRAMETER; TRIMETER; TRI-SYLLABIC; TROCHEE.

RHYME

ASSONANCE; EYE RHYME; FEMININE RHYME; INTERNAL RHYME; LEON-INE VERSE; MASCULINE RHYME; POETIC LICENCE; POETRY; RHYMING SLANG.

protagonist A *protagonist* is not the opposite of an *antagonist*. He is not one who fights for you instead of against you, but one who takes the leading part in a contest or champions a cause. You cannot have more than one protagonist at a time.

See also VOGUE WORDS.

protogram a modern word borrowed from the Greek meaning 'first letter'. A protogram is a word formed by combining the initial letters of other words.

Another term for words of this kind is *acronym*, from the Greek meaning 'beginning name'.

See ABBREVIATIONS (4).

proverb a short pithy saying. Many proverbs still in general use are centuries old; they are based on human nature, which does not change. 'Far from eye, far from heart' (thirteenth century); 'Opportunity makes the thief' (thirteenth); 'A wonder lasts but nine days' (fourteenth); 'Silence gives consent' (fourteenth); 'Enough is as good as a feast' (fifteenth); 'There's no rose without a thorn' (fifteenth); 'One good turn deserves another' (fifteenth); 'Birds of a feather flock together' (sixteenth); 'Revenge is sweet' (sixteenth); 'Do as you would be done by' (sixteenth); 'The pot calls the kettle black' (seventeenth); 'There is honour among thieves' (eighteenth); 'Nothing succeeds like success' (nineteenth).

A large number of our proverbs have been borrowed from other languages. 'A man without a smiling face must not open a shop' (Chinese); 'An iron hand in a velvet glove' (French); 'Better be envied than pitied' (Greek); 'No man is wise at all times' (Latin); 'See Naples and (then) die' (Italian); 'The morning hour has gold in its mouth' (German); 'There are no fans in hell' (Arabic); 'They who live longest will see most' (Spanish); 'If you would make an enemy, lend a man money, and ask it of him again' (Portuguese).

Some proverbs contradict each other, proving the contrariness of human nature, e.g.:

(a) More haste less speed.
    He who hesitates is lost.
(b) Many hands make light work.
    Too many cooks spoil the broth.

Some popular quotations have become proverbs, e.g. 'Discretion is the better part of valour' (Shakespeare, though he put it round the other way: 'The better part of valour is discretion'); 'Be sure your sin will find you out' (Old Testament); 'Kind hearts are more than coronets' (Tennyson); 'The child is father of the man' (Wordsworth).

pseud, pseudo DEROGATORY terms for POSEURS, persons who air pretensions. The satirical magazine *Private Eye* instituted a column entitled '*Pseuds' Corner*', composed entirely of extracts from contemporary writers caught in a pretentious posture.

pseudonym, alias, incognito   All these apply to a person who does not use his own name, but they are not interchangeable. A *pseudonym* (sjudˈənim) is a pen-name adopted by a writer, e.g. Mark Twain (Samuel Langhorne Clemens), Lewis Carroll (Charles Lutwidge Dodgson). An *alias* (eiˈliæs) is a name assumed by a person to conceal his identity. 'While in hiding from the police he lived under an alias, calling himself plain John Smith.' *Incognito* (in-cogˈnitou), used more often as an adverb than as a noun or an adjective, refers to an important person who does not wish to attract attention to his high station in life. 'It was the custom of the king to travel incognito in order to mix with his subjects and hear their true opinions.'

psychological moment   That this means 'in the nick of time' is a popular fallacy. The excellent Mr Fowler writes in *Modern English Usage*: 'The original German phrase, misinterpreted by the French and imported together with its false sense into English, meant the psychic factor, the mental effect, the influence exerted by a state of mind, and not a point of time at all, *das Moment* in German corresponding to our *momentum*, not our *moment*. Mistake and all, however, it did for a time express a useful notion, that of the moment at which a person is in a favourable state of mind (such as a skilled psychologist could choose) for one's dealings with him to produce the effect one desires. But, like other popularised technicalities, it has lost its special sense and been widened till it means nothing more definite than *the nick of time*, to which as an expression of the same notion it is plainly inferior.'

pun   It is because it has so many homonyms and homophones that the English language lends itself to puns more than do most languages. A pun is a FIGURE OF SPEECH that may be defined as a (usually humorous) play on words having a similar sound but different meanings. 'Is life worth living? It depends upon the liver.' Here the play is upon the homonyms 'liver', meaning one who lives, and 'liver', meaning a glandular organ. 'At the drunkard's funeral four of his friends carried the bier.' This time it is a play on the homophones 'bier' and 'beer'. The humour falls flat in print. A pun based upon homophones is better heard, not seen. Charles Lamb wrote in his *Essays of Elia*: 'An Oxford scholar, meeting a porter who was carrying a hare through the streets, accosts him with this extraordinary question, "Prithee, friend, is that thy own hare, or a wig?"'

Perhaps the most deplorable pun in English literature was put by Shakespeare into the mouth of Lady Macbeth, who, after her husband has murdered Duncan, king of Scotland, suggests that the blame can be placed on Duncan's two attendants, now lying in a drunken sleep. 'If he do bleed,' she says, 'I'll gild the faces of the grooms withal, for it must seem their guilt.'

In everyday conversation most of our puns are based on neither homonyms nor homophones, but on words that have to be stretched to be made to sound similar. This is a poor type of pun that passes muster only in quick exchanges. Such a pun might be made if someone lost his car and his friend quickly said: 'That is very car(e)less of you.'

punctuation signs used to make reading matter more readily intelligible. The full stop may be regarded as essential to break the matter into sentences; but the other marks are purely for convenience in reading. See AMBIGUITY; APOSTROPHE (I); BRACKETS; COLON; COMMA; DASH; DIALOGUE; EXCLAMATION MARK; FULL STOP; HYPHEN; INVERTED COMMAS; LACUNA; QUESTION MARK; REPORTED SPEECH; SEMI-COLON.

pupil see SCHOLAR.

purist a stickler for purity in language; one who condemns all words and expressions that are not traditionally correct, thus suspecting all slang and colloquialisms. The purist insists on DIFFERENT FROM and retains WHOM whenever it is accusative, even in 'I did not know the artist whom he was praising.'

pygmy, pigmy The first spelling is recommended here. It comes from the Latin *pygmaeus*, which derives from the Greek word meaning 'three spans large' – that is, three times the distance from the end of the thumb to the end of the little finger when fully extended.

Q

qualify in grammar, to describe more fully. It is used in the definition of an adjective, which qualifies a noun or pronoun, e.g. (a) 'The *black* cat.' (b) '*Lucky* you!' When describing the functions of an adverb grammarians usually use MODIFY.

Qualification means also any modification or limitation of a statement. If a statement is made without any qualification it is meant to be absolute – true without any limitation. If it is hedged round with qualification, it will be true only in certain circumstances or on certain conditions; it will be expressed with many *ifs, buts, thoughs* and *provided thats*.

quantity in classical verse, the relative length or shortness of sounds in a metrical foot, determined by the time required to pronounce the sounds or syllables. In modern PROSODY it refers to the degree of emphasis of the sounds – that is, whether they are stressed or unstressed.

See ACCENT; METRE; SCANNING.

quarto (abbreviated qto or 4to) a quarter of a sheet of printing paper. The sheet is folded twice to give four leaves. Sheets vary in size, and the size of the leaves varies accordingly, the average size for printing being 9 in. wide by 12 in. long. Quarto typing paper is usually 8 in. wide by 10 in. long, 3 in. shorter than FOOLSCAP.

See also OCTAVO.

quasi- (kweizˈai) a hyphenated prefix, especially to a noun or an adjective, to indicate 'apparent(ly)', 'almost', 'half-', etc., e.g. 'We can do no more than describe Mr Williams's new book as a quasi-historical romance.'

quatrain (kwotˈrein) (F. 'four') in PROSODY four successive lines of verse, usually expressing a complete thought. Here is a quatrain by Walter Savage Landor:

> I strove with none, for none was worth my strife;
>   Nature I loved; and next to Nature, Art;
> I warm'd both hands before the fire of life;
>   It sinks, and I am ready to depart.

The quatrain is a popular form in the composition of the rhymed EPIGRAM. See also LAMPOON.

question   see BEGGING THE QUESTION; LEADING QUESTION; RHETORICAL QUESTION; NEGATIVE QUESTIONS; QUESTION TAGS. Indirect questions are treated under REPORTED SPEECH.

question mark   the punctuation mark (?) used to indicate that a question has been asked, e.g. *Have you forgotten it?* As does the EXCLAMATION MARK, it takes the place of a full stop at the end of a sentence. When used in dialogue it is placed before the closing quotation mark, e.g. '*Have you forgotten it?*' *asked Sheila*. When other writers are quoted it comes within the quotation marks if it forms part of the quotation, e.g. '*Where are the songs of Spring? Ay, where are they?*' (Keats). If it does not form part of the quotation it is placed outside the quotation marks, e.g. *How many of us will agree that* (to quote Voltaire) '*all is for the best in the best of possible worlds*'?

Another use of the question mark is to indicate an element of doubt, as in this encyclopaedia reference: *Chaucer, Geoffrey* (?1340–1400). This means that, although the year of his death is not in doubt, the year of his birth is uncertain. The abbreviation *c.* (*circa*, about) is sometimes used instead of the question mark, e.g. *Chaucer, Geoffrey* (*c.* 1340–1400).

For the use of question marks in indirect speech see REPORTED SPEECH.

question tags   or tail questions are sentences consisting of a NEGATIVE statement followed by a positive question, e.g. 'They aren't going to take him to hospital, are they?' or a positive statement followed by a NEGATIVE QUESTION, e.g. 'They are going to take him to hospital, aren't they?'. The tag, whether positive or negative, contains an ANOMALOUS FINITE. The questions beginning with a negative statement normally expect the answer *No*; those beginning with a positive statement normally expect the answer *Yes*.

quite   completely; wholly; entirely; to the fullest extent. This adverb can be used to modify an adjective, a verb, a phrase or another adverb, e.g. (a) 'You are quite wrong.' (b) 'I have not quite finished.' (c) 'Make yourself quite at home.' (d) 'He was annoyed – and quite rightly so.' But in good writing it should not be used to qualify a noun, e.g. (a) 'There was quite an argument.' (b) 'I don't

think it's quite the thing to talk about him behind his back.' Colloquially this usage is permissible (as is the use of the affirmative
'quite' instead of the more correct 'quite so'), but there is little to be
said in favour of 'quite a few' when the speaker means 'more than
a few'.

quotation marks　another name for INVERTED COMMAS.

R

rationalising　Literally this means 'making rational'. By extension it means 'finding a reason for'. We rationalise when we manufacture arguments to justify our line of conduct. For example, we
rationalise our laziness by saying that the longer we stay in bed, the
harder we work when we get up. Rationalising is a form of WISHFUL
THINKING and also FALLACY.

See also OBSCURANTISM.

re (L. 'thing; affair')　in the matter of; with reference to. In law
and business it is used in headings, e.g.:

> Dear Sir,
> 　　　　　　　　re Lansdowne Trust
> 　We are in receipt of your letter of 29th November
> and now take pleasure in informing you that . . .

Except in business correspondence, memoranda and informal
notes ('Thanks for p.c. re Birmingham trip'), it is not recommended
as a synonym for 'about' or 'concerning', e.g.:
Wrong:　The doctor invited the opinion of a specialist re the con-
　　　　　dition of his patient.
Right:　The doctor invited the opinion of a specialist concerning
　　　　　the condition of his patient.

realism　representing things as they really are and not as we would
like them to be; the opposite of ROMANTICISM. In literature realism

applies to the method used by writers of fiction who describe life in factual terms without glamorising it.

For realism on the stage see ALIENATION; METHOD.

reasoning   see ARGUMENT; LOGIC.

received pronunciation   the pronunciation that is adopted by the majority of educated people in Britain and generally accepted as standard. It is, however, biased towards Southern England and the Public Schools.

recount, re-count   The first means 'to narrate; to tell in detail'; the second means 'to count again', e.g. 'The shepherd counted his sheep, padlocked the gate leading into the field and went home. An hour later old Mr Gummidge called at the cottage and recounted at great length how he had just seen a covered truck being driven away from the field. The shepherd hurried to the scene, re-counted the sheep and found that ten were missing.'

redbrick   The *Shorter Oxford Dictionary* (1959) defines this new compound adjective as being 'applied attributively to denote a university of modern foundation the official buildings of which are conceived as being built of red brick (in contrast to the stone of the ancient universities); also collectively such universities in general'. When we speak, therefore, of a 'redbrick university' we mean one of the newer universities, whether it is built of red brick, yellow brick or ferro-concrete.

redress, re-dress   The first means 'reparation for wrong'; the second means 'to dress again', e.g. 'When the bather had re-dressed, he demanded redress for the theft of his watch from the cubicle.'

redundancy (L. 'an overflowing')   the use of more words than we need to express our meaning. It takes various forms, which are treated under CIRCUMLOCUTION (PERIPHRASIS), which is talking round the subject; PLEONASM, which is a superfluous addition; and TAUTOLOGY, which is saying the same thing twice in different ways.

refrain   a recurring phrase or line, especially at the end of STANZAS. The refrain of a song in which the audience joins may run to several lines and is called the chorus.

reflexive   a term used to describe a verb of which the object names the same thing or person as the subject, or the pronoun that serves as the object of such a reflexive verb, e.g. (a) 'He cursed himself for a fool.' (b) 'On leaving the village behind I found myself walking between the hedges of a narrow winding lane.' (c) 'We congratulated ourselves on our good fortune.'

See also PRONOUN, *reflexive*.

reform, re-form   The first means 'to improve; to lead a better life'; the second means 'to form again', e.g. 'After all the players had promised to reform, the football club was re-formed.'

regalia   see INSIGNIA.

region, neighbourhood   These should not be used in the sense of 'about' or 'approximately', e.g.:
Wrong: He earns something in the region of ten pounds a week.
Right: He earns about ten pounds a week.
Wrong: The total weight will be in the neighbourhood of ten tons.
Right: The total weight will be approximately ten tons.

register   a term used in modern linguistics to indicate the variations in structure, vocabulary and sound which can occur in different language situations. The language used by a teacher in a classroom of infants will clearly differ from that used by a university lecturer. Language has to adapt itself to a wide variety of purposes. It may have to be informative, factual, emotive, or formal, technical, ceremonial, casual, intimate, social, commercial, political. Every language situation has its appropriate type of language or register.

See COLLOQUIALISM; JARGON; SLANG.

relation, relative   When referring to a member of the same family, it is better to use the second, though the first is used with effect in the (satiric?) couplet:

'God bless the squire and his relations
And keep us in our proper stations.'

relative clause   another name for ADJECTIVE CLAUSE because usually introduced by a RELATIVE PRONOUN.

relative pronoun   See PRONOUN.

Renaissance Deriving from the French meaning 'rebirth', this word, usually spelt with a capital letter, is the name given to the revival of learning and the arts in Europe during the fourteenth, fifteenth and sixteenth centuries. This rediscovery of the classics of Latin and Greek had a profound effect on the English language. See DERIVATION.

repartee the making of witty retorts. Repartee consists of quick, clever replies to remarks so that, instead of damaging the person addressed, they are turned back on their maker. Someone once made a very uncomplimentary remark about George Bernard Shaw at a meeting. G.B.S. immediately retorted: 'Yes, I am inclined to agree with you, sir, but who are we among so many?' This was repartee, since it turned the laugh against the critic.

repel, repulse The difference is shown in these two examples:

(a) I was repelled by his manner.
(b) I was repulsed by his manner.

In the first I was sickened or disgusted by his manner, which I found repulsive; whilst in the second I was deterred or rebuffed by his manner, which repelled me. As Fowler points out in *Modern English Usage*: 'That is repellent that keeps one at arm's length; that is repulsive from which one recoils.'

repertory company A *repertoire* is a stock of pieces – songs, recitations, plays, etc. – that a performer or theatrical company is ready to perform, e.g. 'Mr Bartlett sang a number of songs from his extensive repertoire.' Originally a repertory company relied upon a repertoire of plays, with which it toured the country. Nowadays *repertory* has taken on a different meaning. A repertory company no longer draws on a repertoire, but presents a fresh play every week (or every second week), the hard-working performers spending their time acting in this week's play, rehearsing next week's play and learning their parts for the week after.

replace, substitute Be careful to use the correct preposition. We replace something *by* something else; we substitute something *for* something else, e.g.:

Wrong: A new book was replaced for the one that had been lost.
Right: A new book was substituted for the one that had been lost.

Wrong: The book that had been lost was substituted by a new one.
Right: The book that had been lost was replaced by a new one.
See also PREPOSITIONAL IDIOM.

reported speech   When we write down the exact words used by a speaker, we are using what is known in grammar as *direct speech*, e.g.:

(a) 'I am a Scotsman,' explained Mr Macgregor on his arrival at London Airport, 'and I have flown down here this morning from my home in Glasgow.'

When we give a report of what he said, but do not write down his exact words, we are using *indirect* or *reported speech*, e.g.:

(b) Mr Macgregor explained on his arrival at London Airport that he was a Scotsman, and that he had flown down there that morning from his home in Glasgow.

Let us briefly notice what happens when we make a reported rendering.

1. First of all, we have to make it clear who is being reported, so our report opens with an introductory main clause containing the VERB OF SAYING: *Mr Macgregor explained* . . . The person who spoke usually becomes a third person in the reported speech: *I* becomes *he* and *my* becomes *his*.

In the case where the reporter was himself engaged in the conversation that he is reporting, the *I* or *me* that refers to the reporter will remain, and the *you* that refers to him will become *I* or *me*.

(c) 'You will live to regret your decision,' Alan told me.
(d) Alan told me that I should live to regret my decision.

2. Because the report is made after the words were spoken, the words become more remote. Each tense takes one step back into the past. Thus the present *I am* in (a) becomes the past *he was* in (b); and the future *you will live* in (c) becomes the future in the past *I should live* in (d). In the same way, the past becomes the pluperfect, e.g.:

(e) 'You were misinformed,' Mr Brown said to me.
(f) Mr Brown told me that I had been misinformed.

There can, of course, be no change in the pluperfect because there is no tense to take us farther into the past. Nor is there any change in the participles or the infinitives. We can illustrate these changes with the verb *to eat*, thus:

DIRECT	REPORTED
'I eat,' he said.	He said that he ate.
'I am eating,' he said.	He said that he was eating.
'I have eaten,' he said.	He said that he had eaten.
'I shall eat,' he said.	He said that he would eat.
'I shall have eaten,' he said.	He said that he would have eaten.
'I may eat,' he said.	He said that he might eat.
'I ate,' he said.	He said that he had eaten.
'I was eating,' he said.	He said that he had been eating.
'I can eat,' he said.	He said that he could eat.

3. Certain adjectives, pronouns and adverbs referring to things or times close at hand are changed into corresponding ones referring to things or times more remote, thus:

now	then	today	on that day
here	there	yesterday	on the previous day *or* on the day before
this	that		
these	those	tomorrow	on the next day *or* on the following day
hence	thence		
hither	thither	last week	in (*or* during) the previous week

4. In reported speech, a question usually becomes a statement that someone asked something. It thus begins with an introductory main clause containing the verb of saying, and the question mark disappears.

(g) 'Can you help me, Brian?' asked his mother.
(h) Brian's mother asked him if he could help her.

Sometimes, however, the question form may be retained, e.g. *Could Brian, his mother asked, help her?* But this question form is not recommended unless the statement form is awkward.

5. A command is usually rendered by a verb of saying followed by the infinitive. The exclamation mark, if there is one, always disappears.

(i) 'Be quiet and sit down!' said the teacher.
(j) The teacher told him to be quiet and to sit down.

A suitable verb of saying should, of course, be chosen to express the exact firmness of the command. It might range from *the teacher asked him* to *the teacher commanded him*. Sometimes an adverb may also be necessary to express the exact shade of meaning, e.g. *The teacher politely asked him* or *the teacher angrily ordered him*.

Notice that after certain verbs of saying we have to use a noun clause rather than the infinitive.

(k) 'Be quiet,' he suggested, 'and then you will hear it.'
(l) He suggested that they should be quiet and then they would hear it.

Similarly we say: *He insisted that . . . He demanded that . . . He shouted that . . . He cried out that . . .*

6. Words of address like 'old chap', 'Ladies and gentlemen', 'Mum' cannot be reproduced in reported speech. We avoid them by making it clear to whom the words were spoken.

(m) 'How are you feeling, old chap?' asked Charles.
(n) Charles asked Frank how he was feeling.

'Ladies and gentlemen' might be rendered as *those present* or *the audience*; and 'Mum' as *his mother*.

7. As our report must be as exact as possible, we should be conservative in changing words. If the speaker used the word 'started' there is nothing to be gained by changing it to 'began'. There is therefore no justification for toning down or BOWDLERISING the original, however formal the report may be, as is done in the following reported speech:

(o) 'Good-o!' cried Ian. 'That's a wizard idea.'
(p) Ian thought it was an excellent idea.

Since reported speech should convey the atmosphere of the direct speech, a better version would be:

(q) Ian cheerfully approved by saying he thought it was a wizard idea.

8. In direct speech the convention is to make a new paragraph every time the speaker changes. In reported speech this is unnecessary.

DIRECT	INDIRECT
'Are you going to Italy again for your holidays, Tom?' asked Jack.	Jack asked Tom whether he was going to Italy again for his holidays. Tom replied that he hoped to go to Spain that year.
'This year I hope to go to Spain,' was the reply.	

9. Finally we should remember that from the point of view of style we can set our characters before our readers much more vividly with direct speech, for reported speech inevitably irons out the MAN-NERISMS of speech. Reported speech has its place in composition, especially for covering the ground, but for actuality we need direct speech.

repulse For the difference between this and *repel* see REPEL.

respectively This adverb is used to indicate that the persons or things secondly mentioned apply in the same order to those first mentioned, e.g. 'Tom, Dick and Harry received respectively a cricket bat, a football and an English dictionary.' The word is un-necessary when there is no element of apportionment. This is wrong: 'The potatoes were planted by Tom, Dick and Harry respectively.' It is a PLEONASM.

Restoration Spelt with a capital letter, this refers to the re-establishment of the monarchy in 1660, when Charles II was pro-claimed king after the death of Oliver Cromwell. In English litera-ture and arts, the Restoration period can be dated from 1660 to 1702, when Queen Anne acceded to the throne. The period was marked in literature and the drama by a sharp reaction from the strict code of morals imposed by the Puritans.

reverend, reverent The first means 'deserving reverence'; the second means 'feeling or showing reverence'. A reverend gentleman is a clergyman; a reverent gentleman is one who venerates and treats someone or something with deep respect.

As a title given to clergymen, the first (abbreviated *Rev.*) is used thus: *The Reverend Charles Jones* or *The Rev. Charles Jones*; the abbre-viation is not used in conversation. An initial or initials can, of course, take the place of the Christian name, e.g. *The Rev. C. R. Jones*, but he must never be referred to as *Reverend Jones* or *Rev. Jones*. If we do not know his Christian name or initials, we address him in writing as *The Reverend Mr Jones* or *The Rev. Mr Jones*.

Very Reverend is a title reserved for a dean, *Right Reverend* for a bishop, and *Most Reverend* for an archbishop.

In conversation it is usual to refer to a Protestant priest as *Mr* (*Jones*) and to a Catholic priest as *Father* (*O'Hara*).

review, revue   A review is a survey; a re-examination; a periodical publication; an inspection of troops. A revue is a stage entertainment with songs, dances, etc., the emphasis being on the parodying of events and fashions of the day. In the 1960s the satirical revue *Beyond the Fringe* was notably successful.

rhetoric   the art of speaking eloquently and persuasively, but not always sincerely and from the heart. Disraeli once described Gladstone as 'a sophistical rhetorician, inebriated with the exuberance of his own verbosity'.

rhetorical question   a FIGURE OF SPEECH; a question designed to vividly suggest rather than demand an answer, e.g. 'Where in the world would you find another country like Australia?' The speaker is not wanting an answer; he is trying to suggest as vividly as possible that Australia is unique. It is a device much favoured by orators, who are apt to indulge in rhetoric; hence its name.

In ARGUMENT the rhetorical question is a form of BEGGING THE QUESTION, e.g. 'Is there anyone who would dare deny the supremacy of our team?' The speaker does not require an answer. He is prejudging the matter, assuming that their team is supreme before it has been proved so.

See FALLACY.

rhyme   one of the two main divisions of PROSODY. The etymological spelling of *rhyme* should be *rime*, as in *The Rime of the Ancient Mariner* by Coleridge. By its association with *rhythm* it has assimilated the *hy*. Rhyme is the identity of sounds between words, considered from the last accented vowel to the end of the word. Identity of spelling does not necessarily constitute a rhyme, e.g. *flănge* does not rhyme with *chănge* (but see EYE RHYME). A single or masculine rhyme is when the final syllable of one line rhymes with the final syllable of the other, e.g.:

Row, brothers, row, the stream runs fast,
The Rapids are near and the daylight's past.

                            (Moore)

A double or feminine rhyme is when the penultimate (last but one) syllable of one line rhymes with the penultimate syllable of the other, e.g.:

> Trip no further, pretty sweeting;
> Journeys end in lovers meeting.
> > (Shakespeare)

A triple rhyme is when the antepenultimate (last but two) syllable of one line rhymes with the antepenultimate syllable of the other, e.g.:

> I'd rather have a tricycle
> Than I would have a bicycle,
> For skidding on an icicle
> Is safer on a tricycle.
> > (Anon)

It is essential that the sounds preceding the last accented vowel should be different, e.g. *incision* does not rhyme with *decision*. It is equally essential that the sounds following the last accented vowel should be identical, e.g. *exclaim* does not rhyme with *complain* because the first ends with an *m* and the second with an *n*. It should be added that not all poets agree with this rule; some gain their effects by means of ASSONANCE, which is the agreement of vowel sounds in two syllables without the agreement of consonant sounds, e.g. *roam – bone, leap – neat.*

A third rule is that the rhyming syllables must be similarly stressed, e.g. *irate* does not rhyme with *pirate*, and *ally* does not rhyme with *pally* (but see POETIC LICENCE).

A point to be borne in mind when reading the poetry of long ago is that pronunciation has changed with the years – and so accordingly has rhyme. For example, we find in *The Rape of the Lock* by Pope this couplet:

> Here thou, great Anna! whom three realms obey,
> Dost sometimes counsel take – and sometimes tea.

This was a perfect rhyme when Pope wrote it in 1713, for *tea* was pronounced 'tay' (as in the French *thé*) until about the middle of the eighteenth century. In passing, 'great Anna' was Queen Anne, who was renowned for her homely virtues.

A convention observed in the writing of poetry is that rhyming lines are indented equal distances from the left-hand margin. Here is a stanza by the seventeenth-century poet, James Shirley:

> The glories of our blood and state
> > Are shadows, not substantial things;
> There is no armour against fate;
> > Death lays his icy hand on kings:

Sceptre and crown
Must tumble down
And in the dust be equal made
With the poor crooked scythe and spade.

For convenience of reference all headings under which matters relating to prosody, metre, and rhyme are separately treated in this work are listed under PROSODY.

rhyming slang   the cockney and, now, Australian use of slang words disguised by rhyme. Thus *sky rocket* means *pocket*; *apples and pears* means *stairs*; *trouble and strife* means *wife*; *butcher's hook* means *look*. The point of rhyming slang is to conceal the subject of conversation from eavesdroppers, particularly police ears. So having established the rhyme, you then dispense with it, so that 'I put it in my sky' means 'I put it in my pocket', and 'let's have a butcher's' means 'let's have a look'. As a simple exercise in the art, what does this mean: 'He ran round the Johnny Horner with the tom he had half-inched'? It means: 'He ran round the corner with the jewellery (*tomfoolery = tom*) he had stolen (*half-inched = pinched*).' Some of the words from rhyming slang have passed into everyday use without the users being aware of their seamy origin. Thus 'raspberry', an audible sound of disapproval, is *raspberry tart* = 'fart', and 'berk', colloquially a moron, is frequently heard on TV even though in origin it is an abbreviation of 'Berkeley Hunt'.

rhythm   in PROSODY another name for METRE.

rhythmic prose   see SPRUNG RHYTHM.

riddle   from the Old English meaning 'to read'. It has a wider sense than CONUNDRUM and refers to anything puzzling or obscure, though the traditional child's riddle takes the form of: 'What goes up when the rain comes down?' Answer: an umbrella.

rime   see RHYME.

roman numerals   These are represented by a series of symbols, the basic ones being:

I	1
V	5
X	10
L	50
C	100
D	500
M	1,000

If one symbol is *preceded* by another of less value, the lesser one is subtracted from the greater one to give the total, e.g. IV = 4 (5 minus 1). If a symbol is *followed* by another of less or equal value, the whole is equal to their sum, e.g. XI = 11 (10 plus 1) and XX = 20 (10 plus 10). Both capital letters and small letters (iv, cccx) are used.

I	1	XVII	17	LXXXV	85
II	2	XVIII	18	XC	90
III	3	XIX	19	XCV	95
IV*	4	XX	20	C	100
V	5	XXV	25	CC	200
VI	6	XXX	30	CCC	300
VII	7	XXXV	35	CD	400
VIII	8	XL	40	D	500
IX	9	XLV	45	DC	600
X	10	L	50	DCC	700
XI	11	LV	55	DCCC	800
XII	12	LX	60	CM	900
XIII	13	LXV	65	M	1,000
XIV	14	LXX	70	MD	1,500
XV	15	LXXV	75	MCM	1,900
XVI	16	LXXX	80	MM	2,000

* IIII on clocks.

1958	MCMLVIII	1963	MCMLXIII
1959	MCMLIX	1964	MCMLXIV
1960	MCMLX	1965	MCMLXV
1961	MCMLXI	1970	MCMLXX
1962	MCMLXII	1976	MCMLXXVI

Although not so general as they once were, Roman numerals have not yet been entirely superseded by Arabic numerals (see NUMERALS). They are still used for some clocks, dates (particularly on tombstones, public monuments, statues, etc.) and the names of kings and queens, e.g. *Elizabeth I, George II, Richard III, Henry IV.* Unless the numerals end a sentence they should not be followed by a full stop, e.g. *George IV was formerly the Prince Regent*. Do not write *Elizabeth Ist, George IInd, Richard IIIrd*, etc. If you wish to use the full title write *Elizabeth the First, George the Second*, and so on.

romanticism   a never-satisfied desire for the unknown or un-attainable. The romantic attitude tends to see more in things than the bare objective facts, and hence often refuses to call a spade a spade. Romanticism is inclined to glamorise life, to flinch away from REALISM. The *Romantic Movement* in English literature began towards the end of the eighteenth century. It was a revolt against classicism (see CLASSIC), the restrained style of writing that had persisted for over a century – a revolt that produced the romances of Scott and the poems of Wordsworth, Byron, Coleridge, Keats and Shelley.

Romanticism is in this literary sense to be contrasted with REALISM and CLASSICISM. The term is also popularly used for an outlook that would glamorise life. A romantic young lady is one who tries to believe that everyday life is much more glamorous than it really is.

rondeau   In the terminology of music a *rondo* is a work or move-ment having a main theme that is returned to after each subordinate theme. Similarly, in PROSODY a *rondeau* (the French word from which the Italian word *rondo* is derived) has a recurring refrain. It is a poem in three parts, with the opening words of the first part repeated at the end of the second and third parts. There are five lines in the first part and (without the refrain) three in the second and five in the third. The metre is iambic, the stress being on the second syllable of each disyllabic foot, and there are only two rhymes throughout. The following shows the construction of a rondeau. No claim is made for any poetic merit!

You fled from me the other day.
I know not why you went away.
   No parting note you left behind,
   No single clue that I could find;
Of hope, no tiny fickle ray.

Why did you, darling, not delay
The moment for this harsh display?
   Was it with cruelty designed
          You fled from me?

Alas, the price that I must pay,
The lonely part that I must play!
  And yet . . . the thought creeps into mind
  It is not you who are unkind;
It is not *I* but *you* should say,
            'You fled from me.'

root   a word or element of language from which other words are derived or built. It is therefore the ultimate or unanalysable element of language. Thus *rupt* (from *ruptus*, the past participle of *rumpere*, 'to break') is the common root of the following words: *abrupt, bankruptcy, corrupt, eruption, rupture.* See also AFFIXES; PREFIX; STEM; SUFFIX; WORD-FORMATION.

ruminant (L. 'throat')   adjective or noun referring to animals that chew their cud. Cows, sheep and camels are ruminants. The verb *to ruminate* means not only to chew the cud but also, figuratively, 'to meditate', e.g. 'Robinson Crusoe ruminated on his unhappy fate.'

running title (or **running headline**)   In book production, a running title over the text on a left-hand page repeats the title of the book; on the right-hand page, it usually repeats the title of the chapter.
  See SIGNATURE.

S

saga   This derives from the Old Norse meaning 'a story'. It has the same root as SAW. The *Concise Oxford Dictionary* defines it as: 'A medieval Icelandic or Norwegian prose narrative, especially one embodying history of Icelandic family or Norwegian king.' Nowadays it has come to be applied to the story of a family through succeeding generations. John Galsworthy wrote a number of books and short stories all about a London family, beginning in 1886 and covering a period of over forty years. These stories were televised as *The Forsyte Saga.*

same   Do not use *same* or *the same* as a substitute for a pronoun, e.g.:
  Wrong: The goods have now arrived and we thank you for same.
  Right: The goods have now arrived and we thank you for them.
  Wrong: He bought himself a new suit and paid fifteen guineas for
      the same.
  Right: He bought himself a new suit and paid fifteen guineas
      for it.

same, similar   The first denotes identity – an absolute sameness.
The second denotes resemblance.

'The same again, sir?' asked the barmaid.
'That is impossible,' replied the professor of English, 'for I have
already drunk it, but I will have something similar.'

sanction   Our tendency to use this word in the sense of 'permission' or 'consent' (or verbally, 'to permit' or 'to allow') has
obscured its original wider sense. The word derives from the Latin
meaning 'to make sacred or inviolable'. A sanction is a law or decree,
and it is also a punishment or reward in accordance with that law or
decree, so that 'a sanction' is not only 'a permit' but also 'a prohibition'. A government may sanction the export of arms – that is,
consent to their being exported; but should the actions of one nation
be thought by other nations to be a breach of international law, they
may impose sanctions by such measures as the withholding of loans,
the limiting of trade relations, or by blockade or the use of military
force.

sang, sung   At one time these were interchangeable for the past
tense of the verb *to sing*, but nowadays *sang* is preferred, *sung* being
used only as the past participle, e.g.:
  Wrong: She sung four songs at the concert.
  Right: She sang four songs at the concert.
  Right: She has sung four songs this evening.

sank, sunk, sunken   As with *sang* and *sung*, the first two were at
one time interchangeable for the past tense of the verb *to sink*. The
past participle was either *sunk* or *sunken*. Nowadays *sank* is preferred
for the past tense, and *sunk* or *sunken* for the past participle. Used
adjectivally *sunk* and *sunken* are not interchangeable in every case.
For example, a ha-ha is a *sunk* (not *sunken*) fence, and we speak of
sunken (not *sunk*) cheeks or eyes.

sarcasm (Gk. 'to tear flesh like dogs') a remark that is bitter and, though indirect, clearly intended to wound. It is thus ironically worded, taking the form of such remarks as: 'That's right – smash every plate in the house!' 'I suppose you'll get this job finished by Christmas?' 'Why be just difficult when, with a little more effort, you could be impossible?' The difference between sarcasm and IRONY is mainly one of intention. Whereas sarcasm uses words ironically to wound, irony is merely a witty use of words, not necessarily meant to wound at all.

satire the use of ridicule, irony, sarcasm, etc. in speech or writing for the ostensible purpose of exposing and discouraging vice or folly. Satirical writing is therefore DIDACTIC; it sets out to teach the reader to have better ideas. For example, in *Gulliver's Travels* Swift satirises various ideas and practices of his time that he considered to be bad. Alexander Pope was a satirist in rhyme. Here are two of his couplets:

> The hungry judges soon the sentence sign,
> And wretches hang that jurymen may dine.

> Damn with faint praise, assent with civil leer,
> And, without sneering, teach the rest to sneer.

In the 1960s the term *satire* was applied to such TV shows as *That Was the Week that Was* or Rowan and Martin's *Laugh In*, which are really LAMPOONS.

saw This derives from the same root as SAGA and means a proverb or maxim, e.g. 'Full of wise saws and modern instances.' It is no longer in current use.

scanning (or **scansion**) In PROSODY to *scan* is to mark off lines of verse into feet (see FOOT), i.e. the parts into which the line is divided by stresses rather than by syllables, e.g.:

> Two souls / with but / a sin / gle thought,
> Two hearts / that beat / as one.

Here the accent sign indicates the stressed syllables of the four feet in the first line and of the three feet in the second line. In prosody the accent sign is not used, a stressed syllable being indicated by the MACRON (–), and an unstressed one by the BREVE (∪), which marks a short vowel sound, thus:

Two souls / with but / a sin / gle thought,

   Two hearts / that beat / as one.

'To scan' also means 'to be metrically correct'.

There was a young bard of Japan,
Whose limericks never did scan.
   When told this was so,
   He replied, 'Yes, I know,
But I always like to get as many words in
       the last line as I possibly can.'

Scanning is dealt with more fully under METRE.

scarcely   see HARDLY.

scholar, pupil   These are not interchangeable. A pupil is a child who goes to school to learn. A scholar is a learned person who devotes himself to original thought, and as there is no other word to describe him, *scholar* is best reserved for that purpose. A *student* is one who is receiving higher or technical training at a university or college. The use of *scholar* for a pupil is, fortunately, dying out, but the use of *student* for a pupil in a secondary school is gaining ground.

semantics   is the branch of linguistics concerned with the meanings of words. It is a very wide subject, since the meaning of a word depends upon the context or semantic field in which it is used. This involves a consideration of both the STRUCTURE and the subject matter. The word *rose*, for example, has one meaning if we are talking about flowers, and another if we are talking about colours. Semantics also involves WORD BUILDING and the change of meaning in the past.

semi-colon   the punctuation mark (;) indicating a break stronger than that represented by a comma, but weaker than that represented by a full stop. It is mainly used:

  1. To separate two related clauses of a sentence that are not actually joined by a conjunction, e.g. 'Never speak about what you are ignorant of; speak briefly of what you know; and whether you speak or keep silent, do so tactfully.'

  2. Similarly to separate antithetical clauses, e.g. 'The distance is long; our time is short.'

3. Before a clause beginning with a SENTENCE ADVERB such as *so, therefore, however, thereupon, in this way, for instance*, e.g. 'The roads have become slippery; therefore take care.'

4. To separate items in a list when commas are insufficient because they have already been used within the individual items, e.g. 'Take the following with you: a clean shirt; a pair of shorts, not too short; two towels, more if you have them; a thick sweater; a spare pair of shoes and several pairs of socks, as hard-wearing as possible.'

5. To act as a kind of rest, especially in long sentences before the last clause when it tends to sum up the preceding clauses, e.g. 'When I am bored or have nothing much to occupy myself with, I begin to nibble whatever comes my way, whether it is sweets, chocolate, fruit, or even oddments lying around in the larder; and this I believe to be the downfall of many a top-heavy heavyweight.'

sentence Otto Jespersen defines this as: 'A relatively complete and independent unit of communication – the completeness and independence being shown by its standing alone or its capability of standing alone, i.e. of being uttered by itself.' Grammatically the sentence may be defined as the unit of language containing a subject and a predicate expressed or understood (SEE SUBJECT; PREDICATE).

Sentences may be classified according to their purpose, thus:

1. *Statements*, which make statements or assertions, e.g. 'It is going to be a fine day.'

2. *Questions*, which ask for an answer, e.g. 'Is it going to be a fine day?'

3. *Commands*, which give orders or requests, e.g. 'Let us go, now it has stopped raining.'

4. *Exclamations*, which express various cries of the heart, e.g. 'If only the sun would come out!'

5. *Greetings* and other amorphous sentences, i.e. having no definite form, e.g. (a) 'Surely not.' (b) 'Good morning.' (c) 'Not on your life.' (d) 'Many happy returns.' See also EXCLAMATION; EJACULATION.

Sentences may also be classified according to their clause structure, thus:

1. The *simple sentence* consists of one clause only, i.e. one subject and predicate, e.g. 'The dog barked furiously.'

2. The *complex sentence* consists of one main clause and one or more subordinate clauses, e.g. 'The dog barked furiously when we ap-

proached the house, though we called it all the pet names that we could think of.'

3. The *compound sentence* consists of two or more main clauses, e.g. 'The dog barked furiously and the parrot screeched beyond endurance, but no one took the slightest notice.'

4. The *compound-complex sentence* is a combination of the last two kinds, i.e. two or more main clauses, combined with one or more subordinate clauses, e.g. 'The dog barked more furiously than we had supposed possible, and the parrot screeched beyond endurance, but no one took the slightest notice when we protested, though our protest was perfectly reasonable and polite.'

Clauses are treated also under ADJECTIVAL CLAUSE; ADVERBIAL CLAUSE; CLAUSE; NOUN CLAUSE.

Sentences can also be classified according to their construction – that is, where the main point comes. If we begin with the main point and then tack on subordinate details we construct a *loose sentence*, e.g.:

'The search party began their climb up a steep winding path leading into the mountains, undaunted by the hazards that darkness might bring.'

This is the commonest and most natural way of writing because it is the main point that usually occurs to us first; but it is a loose way of writing and becomes slovenly if overdone. We construct a tighter and more disciplined sentence if we keep the reader waiting by means of a *periodic sentence*, so called because the main point comes last and is ended by the period (full stop), e.g.:

'Up a steep winding path leading into the mountains, undaunted by the hazards that darkness might bring, the search party began their climb.'

If we wish, we can compromise by placing the main point somewhere in the middle, e.g.:

'Up a steep winding path leading into the mountains, the search party began their climb, undaunted by the hazards that darkness might bring.'

Being a mixture of the loose and the periodic, this is called a *mixed sentence*.

Another type is the *balanced sentence*, in which two or more main points are balanced against each other, e.g. 'The weather was warm, the sea calm, the captain and crew in the best of spirits.' When two contrasted ideas are so balanced we get the *antithetical sentence*, e.g. 'He praised their courage, but condemned their recklessness.' See also ANTITHESIS; ELLIPSIS.

sentence adverbs adverbs of interpolation. Unlike ordinary adverbs, they do not tell us about a verb but about the whole sentence. They are, so to speak, inserted in the whole sentence and, to show that they are inserted, they are marked off from the rest of the sentence by commas, e.g.:

(a) The sun, *however*, continued to shine.
(b) You may, *for example*, have some old clothes you wish to dispose of.
(c) He was, *perhaps*, the greatest actor of his day.
(d) Children are human, *after all*.

Other sentence adverbs are *nevertheless, in the meantime, as a matter of fact, even so, well, please, thank you, yes, no, indeed*.

See also SEMI-COLON, section 3.

sententious tersely full of meaning. It is now often a DEROGATORY word used to describe a person so given to wise sayings that he becomes a tedious moraliser.

sentiment, sentimentality The first is a feeling towards something, especially a sympathetic one, unaffected by reason. Thus one can have or express a sentiment of reverence, pity, admiration, love, patriotism, respect, etc. The second is an excessive display of sentiment; emotion out of proportion to the situation. This is a DEROGATORY term, implying that the person accused of sentimentality should bring his emotions more under the control of reason.

See also EMOTIONS.

sequence of tenses see under TENSE.

serial a story divided into sections and published by instalments (one section at a time) in a newspaper or magazine. Some serials are adapted from novels; others are written with a view to serialisation – that is, all the instalments are of about the same length, and each instalment ends in such a way that the reader is left eager to know what is going to happen next. Dickens wrote *The Pickwick Papers* by monthly instalments, often under such pressure that he scribbled away while the printers' boy waited on the doorstep for the 'copy'.

sestet   in PROSODY a division of six lines, especially the last six lines of a SONNET. The first eight lines of a sonnet are called an *octave*.

shaggy-dog story   a long-drawn-out story intended to be funny, rich with circumstantial detail and leading up to an absurd or irrelevant punch line which frequently takes the form of an excruciating PUN. One such involves a knight in armour, who at the climax of the story is obliged to leave a castle on a stormy night mounted on a large and presumably shaggy dog, complaining that 'no one should turn out a knight on a dog like this'.

shall, will   The full distinction between them is summed up in this rule: for the simple future use *shall* in the first person and *will* in the second and third ('I shall, 'we shall', 'you will', 'he will', 'they will'); to express determination use *will* in the first person and *shall* in the second and third ('I will, 'we will', 'you shall', 'he shall', 'they shall'). 'I shall not go' means that it is not my intention to go. 'I will not go' means that I am determined not to go. In Shakespeare's *Julius Caesar*, one of the conspirators, named Decius Brutus, comes to fetch Caesar to the senate house. Caesar replies:

> And you are come in very happy time,
> To bring my greetings to the senators
> And tell them that I will not come to-day:
> Cannot, is false, and that I dare not, falser:
> I will not come to-day: tell them so, Decius.

This distinction in the first person is fast disappearing because neither Scotsmen nor Americans take any notice of it. The distinction is more important in the second and third persons. 'You will not do it' shows that you believe it is not his intention to do it. 'You shall not do it' is a threat of your determination to prevent him. Which is the stronger of the following? 'They will not pass.' 'They shall not pass.'

See also CORRECT ENGLISH.

should, would   These are the past tense of SHALL and WILL and their use is similar. There is, however, a further use of *should* in the sense of 'ought to', e.g. 'I warned him that he should be more careful and he promised that he would try to be.'

show, shew   Use the first spelling; the second is now obsolete, although still used in legal documents.

sibilants letters sounded with a hiss, e.g. the *s* in *sing*, the *sh* in *shame*, the *ch* in *choose*, the *j* in *just*, the *z* in *quiz* and the *x* in *fix*. The ʒ sound in such words as *leisure* and *measure* is also a sibilant. The letters *c* and *g* are sibilants when they are soft, e.g. *receive, cellar, decent; George, gentle, region*. The hard *c* and *g* are GUTTURALS.

See also GUIDE TO PRONUNCIATION on pages 7–9.

sic (L. 'so; thus; in this manner') When there is a word or expression in a quoted passage that might be taken as a misquotation we use *sic* in brackets to indicate that the fault does not lie with the quoter but with the original writer. We are as much as saying: 'This is as it was written.' For example, (a) 'On the following day we had a visiter [*sic*] in the person of the Bishop of London.' (b) 'The poet and playwright, Ben Johnson [*sic*], was a familiar figure at the convivial gatherings in the Mermaid Tavern, Cheapside.' We do not correct the original writers' work by altering 'visiter' to 'visitor', and 'Johnson' to 'Jonson'; we leave these as they are, but we show that we know they are wrong by adding [*sic*].

See also MISQUOTATION.

sick humour a heartlessly cynical form of humour. We also have *sick jokes* and *sick comedians*. Here is an example of the first:

'Dad,' said Tommy to his father, 'why don't you ever let me go out and play with the other boys?'

'Shut up,' replied his father, 'or I'll put you in a smaller cage.'

There is a sadistic element in sick humour which may match the environment (most originated in New York) but is a revelation of its creators' attitudes.

signature In book production, a *signature* is a code appearing at the foot of a page to indicate to the binder the start of a 16- or 32-page collation. For example, on page 289 the small letters at the foot FOE–K indicate the title of the book *Facts of English* and the 10th series of 32-page sections (the letter K is the 10th in the alphabet, omitting J, which is not used). The word is also used to refer to the 16- or 32-page section itself. Signatures to letters are treated under CORRESPONDENCE.

signs and symbols These are used as a form of shorthand in various specialist fields, such as astronomy, botany, chemistry, finance, mathematics, medicine, meteorology, music, and science. Below are given those likely to be encountered by the student of English. Strictly speaking, some of them are not signs or symbols but abbreviations. A number of other abbreviations are treated under that heading.

WRITING AND PRINTING

.   FULL STOP

:   COLON

;   SEMI-COLON

,   COMMA

?   QUESTION MARK

!   EXCLAMATION MARK

'   APOSTROPHE

'   TURNED COMMA

' '   Single quotation marks. See INVERTED COMMAS

" "   Double quotation marks. See INVERTED COMMAS

-   HYPHEN

–   DASH

( )   BRACKETS

[ ]   Square brackets or crochets. See BRACKETS

}   Brace, used to join words, lines, etc., e.g.:

$$\left.\begin{array}{l}\text{gorse}\\ \text{furze}\end{array}\right\} \textit{Ulex europaeus}$$

/   Virgule or Oblique, used in abbreviations, e.g. c/o (care of), 2/- (two shillings in pre-decimal coinage), a/c (account), and in such useful compounds as and/or

*   ASTERISK. See also under FOOTNOTE

†   Dagger or obelus. See under FOOTNOTE

&   AMPERSAND

∧   CARET

‾   MACRON

˘   BREVE

¶   PARAGRAPH

··   DIAERESIS

'   Acute accent, used in French to indicate the closed 'e' sound, e.g. *école* (school). See also ELISION

`   Grave accent, used in French to indicate the open 'e'

sound, e.g. *manière* (manner). Grave is pronounced gra:v, as in the French

^ Circumflex accent, used in French to indicate that the sound of a vowel followed by a consonant is long, e.g. *même* (same)

¸ CEDILLA

~ Tilde, a Spanish variant of *titulo*, meaning 'title'. It is put over the Spanish *n* to show that it is followed by a *y* sound, e.g. *señor, señora*. The equivalent sound in English is as in *canyon* and the surname *Denyer*

MONEY AND COMMERCE

£ Pound(s) sterling. It derives from the Latin *libra*, meaning 'a pound' (in weight)

s Shilling(s). It derives from the Latin *solidus* (plural *solidi*), which was in fact worth about a guinea, i.e. twenty-one shillings; now replaced by decimal coinage

d Penny or pence. It derives from the Latin *denarius* (plural *denarii*); now replaced by decimal coinage

p Symbol for penny under decimal coinage

$ Dollar

% PER CENT

@ *at*, used when referring to the cost of articles, e.g. '4 shirts @ £1·25 each'

MATHEMATICS

= Equals

+ Plus, the sign of addition, e.g. $8 + 5 = 13$ (eight plus five equals thirteen)

— Minus, the sign of subtraction, e.g. $8 - 5 = 3$ (eight minus five equals three)

× Multiplied by, e.g. $4 \times 2 = 8$ (four multiplied by two equals eight)

÷ Divided by, e.g. $4 \div 2 = 2$ (four divided by two equals two)

nth (pronounced *enth*). In mathematics *n* is the symbol for an indefinite number. To raise to the nth degree is to raise to an indefinite degree. Colloquially we use it to imply a large number without being precise, e.g. 'He's just finished writing his nth book.' The SLANG equivalent is umpteenth.

∴　Therefore
∵　Because or since

MEASUREMENT

′　Minute(s) or foot (feet), e.g. 16′ (sixteen minutes or sixteen feet)

″　Second(s) or inch(es), e.g. 11″ (eleven seconds or eleven inches)

°　Degree. Used in indicating temperatures, e.g. 32° is freezing point on the Fahrenheit scale and 0° on the centigrade scale. It is also used in geometry, e.g. 'A circle contains 360°, so half a circle is 180°, and a quarter of a circle (a right angle) is 90°.'

4to　QUARTO
8vo　OCTAVO

similar　see SAME.

simile, metaphor　A simile is a FIGURE OF SPEECH in which two things or actions are likened on the strength of some common quality though they are in all other respects unlike, in order to increase the imaginative perception of what is being asserted. It is therefore from the start an imaginatively perceived likeness, so that factual information about a likeness does not constitute a simile, e.g. 'Miss Amelia Jones is like her sister Dorothy' is not a simile, it is a literal comparison; but 'Miss Amelia Jones is like a fussy old hen' is a simile.

A metaphor is like a simile condensed. In a simile the comparison is explicitly stated with the help of some such word as *like* or *as*, whilst in a metaphor the comparison is implied by an identification of the two things compared. Thus the above simile would become a metaphor if we said, 'Miss Amelia Jones is a fussy old hen.'

There are scores of similes in current use, e.g. *as cool as a cucumber, as dead as mutton, as deaf as a post, as fit as a fiddle, as good as gold, as happy as a sandboy, as mad as a hatter, as red as a beetroot, as thick as thieves, like a bull in a china shop, like a fish out of water, like hot cakes, like wildfire.*

The language is full, too, of metaphorical usage, e.g. *the sands of time, too many irons in the fire, nipped in the bud, a bed of roses, in the pink, crocodile tears, coming down to brass tacks, the countess sailed across the room.* Many apparently literal words began as metaphorical applications and may now not be recognised as metaphors, e.g. 'She *poisoned* her sister's mind.' 'The camel is the *ship* of the desert.' In this sense the metaphor is the life-blood of our language, for without it no new idea could be expressed, no new thing named, without the invention of a completely fresh word (see NEOLOGISM). Some words are now much more often used in their metaphorical sense than in their original literal sense. For example, we more often hear of someone being petrified with fear than of something petrifying in the literal sense of 'turning into stone'.

Many figures of speech were good and convincing when first used, but they have been so often repeated that we no longer take any notice of them. They obviously serve a not very useful purpose if they pass unnoticed. This applies to all overworked figures that have become CLICHÉS We should therefore be wary of using clichés such as 'leaving no stone unturned' or being 'as hard as nails'. If we cannot find a fresh and stimulating figure it is often better to stick to literal language.

In addition to making a figure good in itself, we must take care that it is apt. The metaphor of saddling oneself with something unwanted is a useful one, but it would be inept to talk of saddling oneself with a lame horse. A special case of ineptness is the MIXED META-PHOR. For instance, it would be a bad mixture to talk about the conflagration of war drowning all hope of prosperity, or to say that Mr Robinson caused a storm in a teacup by barking up the wrong tree.

simply This means 'plainly; unaffectedly; naturally; clearly'. It is not synonymous with *merely* or *only*, e.g.:

Wrong: We are simply wasting our time.

Right: We are merely wasting our time.

  Or: We are only wasting our time.

Here is the correct use of simply: 'The suggestion I have to make is simply this: that we work to rule.'

Colloquially *simply* is much in use, e.g. (a) 'The weather was simply glorious.' (b) 'As an actress she's simply marvellous.' (c) 'Her cooking is simply awful.' In good writing it should be used only as the adverb of *simple*, e.g. (a) 'She was simply dressed in a neat tailor-made suit.' (b) 'He spoke simply but with great conviction.'

simulate, stimulate The first means 'to feign; to put on the appearance without the reality'; the second means 'to spur on; to rouse to action'.

(a) The stick insect avoids detection by simulating a twig.
(b) The pirate captain stimulated his crew by promising them rich plunder.

singular   grammatically the form of the noun, pronoun or verb that indicates one person or thing only. See also NUMBER; PLURAL.

skit   a light and usually short SATIRE, often in the form of PARODY.

slander, libel   At one time the distinction was easy; to *slander* someone was to speak a false report about them, and to do so maliciously would AGGRAVATE the offence; to *libel* someone was to perform a similar act in print. Broadcasting brought difficulties; was a radio defamation a *slander* (spoken) or a *libel* (published)?   And what of television? Could a picture be defamatory? English law is slowly adapting itself to these new MEDIA. Generally, it is not a defence against a suit for libel or slander to plead ignorance; it *is* a defence, often difficult to sustain, to plead justification.

slang   highly colloquial expressions. Slang is more removed from literary English than are merely colloquial expressions. It is thus frowned upon in polite conversation as well as in written communications. Its only place in formal writing is in DIALOGUE where the use of slang is necessary to be true to the character who is speaking, e.g. 'Keep your 'air on, mate,' said the old road-sweeper. 'There's no need to fly off the 'andle.'

   In the course of time many slang words have become respectable and entered the language proper. The word *slang* was not used till about 1756; before that it was called *cant* and meant the secret language of the underworld of thieves and rogues. Here are some examples of the words that were cant in 1725 and have since become good English: *bet, cheat, filch, flog, fun, jilt, prig, shabby, trip* (voyage). When he compiled his Dictionary, which was published in 1755, Dr Johnson dismissed the following as slang, or 'low words', as he called them: *coax, dodge, fuss, simpleton.* Today they are all quite unobjectionable. In 1912 *bogus, rollicking, rowdy* were still slang.

   Where do slang words come from? In many instances from the JARGON of colourful groups, as with RHYMING SLANG. *Jazz* was originally Negro slang as used in the southern states of America – and so was its successor *jive. To blow your top* (get angry) is a trumpet player's phrase. From the Negro sub-culture of the United States also comes the phrase *and all that jazz* (meaning *and so on*); the DEROGATORY noun *fuzz* for policemen; a number of ephemeral words for weapons of violence that may well puzzle future American etymologists; and a participial adjective brought to England by the comedian Lenny Bruce and used in his act at the Establishment Club, that is the longest OBSCENITY, a 13-letter word, in the language. The concept of *Black Power* has released the adjective *black* from its taboo in relation to skin colour, and rendered obsolescent a number of offensive slang words – *nig, wog, fuzzy-wuzzy, sambo* – about Negroes and a number of EUPHEMISMS (*coloured, dark-skinned, Ethiopian*) which genteel manners had produced when black people themselves disliked the straightforward adjective.

Slang starts off as *in-group* language, and spreads to wider groupings if the original group holds a sort of illicit fascination for the respectable. The criminal underworld in England, apart from producing RHYMING SLANG and exporting it to Australia, gave us slang nouns for policemen (*coppers, rozzers, bluebottles, the law*); for magistrates (*beaks*); for prison (*stir, time, bird*) in general and in particular (*the Moor, the Ville, the Scrubs*, meaning Dartmoor, Pentonville and Wormwood Scrubs); and for dubious activities (*cracking a crib, casing a joint, putting the boot in, bending*, i.e. bribing a *copper*).

From the Turf and the fraternity of bookmaking have come e.g. *pipped at the post, welshing, nobbled* i.e. of a horse doped to lose, *ten to one* (in the sentence e.g. *I'll lay you ten to one he won't marry her.*), and a variety of expressions using the betting term *odds*, at least one of which, *against heavy odds*, has moved into formal writing. In general, 'respectable' sport produces COLLOQUIALISMS (all those cricketing metaphors) rather than slang.

From the stage or *show-business* (*showbiz* in stage slang) come e.g. *putting on an act, to upstage* i.e. obscure someone, *hog the limelight* (*to steal the limelight* is now a respectable metaphor) or, more simply, *hogging it, adlib* (see AD LIBITUM), *spot on* i.e. accurate (from *spotlight*).

See also COLLOQUIALISM; DERIVATION; JARGON; RHYMING SLANG.

sobriquet (sou'brikei) The dictionary tells us briefly that a sobriquet is a nickname. Its meaning, however, can be much more precisely defined. It is a second name given to some well-known person or thing, with whom or with which it is so closely identified in our minds that recognition is immediate. Few need to be told that 'the Bard of Avon' refers to Shakespeare; 'the Iron Duke' to Wellington; 'the Old Lady of Threadneedle Street' to the Bank of

England; 'the Merry Monarch' to Charles II; 'the Grand Old Man' (or 'G.O.M.') to Gladstone; the 'Big Smoke' (or the 'Great Wen') to London; 'the staff of life' to bread; 'Reynard' to the fox; 'Chanticleer' to the barnyard cock; 'Bruin' to the bear; 'the sport of kings' to hunting; 'the herring pond' to the Atlantic Ocean; 'the willow' to the cricket bat; 'the leather' to the cricket ball. There are hundreds of others, many of them less obvious than those just mentioned. To whom, for instance, do the following refer? (1) 'the wicked wasp of Twickenham'; (2) 'the Father of Learning'; (3) 'the Great Commoner'; (4) 'Ursa Major' ('the Great Bear'); (5) 'the Knight of the Rueful Countenance'; (6) 'the Widow of Windsor'; (7) 'the Swedish Nightingale'; (8) 'Farmer George'; (9) 'the Ariosto of the North'; (10) 'the English Virgil'; (11) 'the Seagreen Incorruptible'; (12) 'the Man of Destiny'; (13) 'the Lady with the Lamp'. They refer to: (1) Alexander Pope; (2) Aristotle; (3) William Pitt, first Earl of Chatham; (4) Samuel Johnson; (5) Don Quixote; (6) Queen Victoria; (7) Jenny Lind; (8) King George III; (9) Sir Walter Scott; (10) Edmund Spenser, author of *The Faerie Queene*; (11) Maximilien Robespierre, a leading figure in the French Revolution; (12) Napoleon; (13) Florence Nightingale. Too free use of sobriquets is not to be recommended; there is much to be said for calling a spade a spade.

solecism (sol'əsizm)   any offence against the accepted, educated, grammatical usage, idiom or pronunciation. Thus, to use the double negative 'I don't want no cake' instead of 'I don't want any cake' would be a solecism; and so would be the pronunciation of *pronunciation* as if it were spelt *pronounciation*.

Below are a number of common 'wrongs' and 'rights':
Wrong: I don't deny I wasn't frightened.
Right: I don't deny I was frightened.
Wrong: I didn't use to like tomatoes.
Right: I used not to like tomatoes.
Wrong: I've drank it.
Right: I've drunk it.
Wrong: Don't lay on the wet grass.
Right: Don't lie on the wet grass.
Wrong: I can't hardly believe it!
Right: I can hardly believe it!
Wrong: He came through the war without hardly a scratch.
Right: He came through the war with hardly a scratch.

Wrong: My aunt sent me an Xmas present.
Right: My aunt sent me a Christmas present.
Wrong: Those sort of hats don't suit her.
Right: That sort of hat doesn't suit her.
Wrong: I hate the sight of them people.
Right: I hate the sight of those people.
Wrong: She jumped off of the bus.
Right: She jumped off the bus.
Wrong: Tom is about your heighth.
Right: Tom is about your height.
Wrong: Tom is taller than what I am.
Right: Tom is taller than I am.
Wrong: Dad has took your book back to the library.
Right: Dad has taken your book back to the library.
Wrong: I did just like what you told me.
Right: I did just as you told me.
Wrong: I don't say as I enjoyed it.
Right: I don't say that I enjoyed it.
Wrong: This here book is the one I want.
Right: This book here is the one I want.
Or: This book is the one I want.
Wrong: That there clock isn't right.
Right: That clock there isn't right.
Or: That clock isn't right.
Wrong: Elsie hasn't never seen the sea.
Right: Elsie has never seen the sea.
Wrong: You never cleaned your teeth this morning!
Right: You didn't clean your teeth this morning!
Wrong: Mr Templeton sung three songs at the concert.
Right: Mr Templeton sang three songs at the concert.
Wrong: She was that tired she went straight to bed.
Right: She was so tired she went straight to bed.
Wrong: The next party I saw was an old woman with a basket.
Right: The next person I saw was an old woman with a basket.
Wrong: My sister plays the piano real good.
Right: My sister plays the piano really well.
Wrong: Mary enjoyed herself and John enjoyed hisself too.
Right: Mary enjoyed herself and John enjoyed himself too.
Wrong: They were all thoroughly enjoying theirselves.
Right: They were all thoroughly enjoying themselves.
Wrong: The man as said that was a liar.

Right: The man who said that was a liar.
Wrong: I might of gone if it hadn't rained.
Right: I might have gone if it hadn't rained.
Wrong: Between you and I, she's only after his money.
Right: Between you and me, she's only after his money.
Wrong: Me and you are the same age.
Right: You and I are the same age.
Wrong: What would you do if you was him?
Right: What would you do if you were he?
Wrong: I won't go without you come with me.
Right: I won't go unless you come with me.
Wrong: It learnt me a lesson I shall never forget.
Right: It taught me a lesson I shall never forget.
Wrong: It depends what you said to her.
Right: It depends on what you said to her.
Wrong: Will you please loan me five pence?
Right: Will you please lend me five pence?
Wrong: Tommy asked for the lend of a pencil.
Right: Tommy asked for the loan of a pencil.
Wrong: I don't doubt but what you aren't right.
Right: I don't doubt that you are right.
Wrong: It was her what done it.
Right: It was she who did it.

See also VULGAR; CORRECT ENGLISH.

soliloquy (solil'əkwi)   When the author of a play wishes the audience to know a character's thoughts, he makes the actor talk to himself, usually when alone on the stage. This is called a *soliloquy*. The most famous of all soliloquies is Hamlet's speech beginning: 'To be, or not to be: that is the question.' (*Hamlet*, Act III, Sc. i.) A one-sided telephone conversation can be the modern dramatist's equivalent of a soliloquy, a device brilliantly used in *Inadmissible Evidence* by John Osborne.

sometimes, sometime, some time   The following examples may help to show the different shades of meaning:

(a) I meet him sometimes in London.
    Sometimes I'm happy, sometimes I'm sad.
(b) I must attend to it sometime.
    I am nearly always at home, so please call in and see me sometime.

(c) This book will take me some time to finish.

There are some times when play is harder than work.

The word *sometime* has the additional meaning of 'former' or 'formerly', e.g. 'Mr William Harrison, sometime chairman of Wessex County Council, has died at the age of eighty-two.'

sonnet (O.F. 'a little song')   in PROSODY a poem of fourteen lines in iambic metre, each line containing five feet. The early or Petrarchan sonnet consisted of an octave rhymed *abba abba*, and a sestet rhymed *cde cde*. The variation that Shakespeare used came to be known as the Shakespearean or English sonnet. It was rhymed *abab cdcd efef gg*, and was in effect three quatrains and a final couplet. Later on many more variations were introduced – even blank verse – till today all we can say with any certainty is that it must have fourteen lines and is normally decasyllabic, but how the lines are arranged is a problem that each poet solves for himself.

Here is a sonnet by Milton, who used the Petrarchan form:

When I consider how my light is spent
Ere half my days, in this dark world and wide,
And that one talent which is death to hide
Lodged with me useless, though my soul more bent

To serve therewith my Maker, and present
My true account, lest He returning chide, –
Doth God exact day-labour, light denied?
I fondly ask: – But Patience to prevent

That murmur, soon replies; God doth not need
Either man's work, or His own gifts: who best
Bear His mild yoke, they serve Him best: His state

Is kingly; thousands at His bidding speed
And post o'er land and ocean without rest: –
They also serve who only stand and wait.

sophistry (sof'istri)   specious reasoning; clever argument intended to deceive. Such an argument is called a *sophism*. Bacon wrote in *The Advancement of Learning*: 'The great sophism of all sophisms being equivocation or ambiguity of words and phrase.' Sophistry is a form of FALLACY.

special, especial   Although synonymous to the extent that they
are both the opposite of 'general' or 'ordinary', the second, used in
the sense of 'extra special', is obsolescent. We no longer refer to our
'especial friend', using instead 'special', 'best' or 'particular'. It is
in its adverbial form that the second has its separate function in our
vocabulary, e.g. 'The hall was specially decorated for the occasion
and we were delighted to entertain so many old friends, especially
those who had travelled long distances to be with us on that happy
day.'

speciosity   plausibility. The adjective is *specious*, meaning 'apparently fair or right; giving a surface impression of genuineness'. A
specious excuse is one that sounds reasonable enough, but does not
bear close inspection. For example, Mr Brown spent his summer
holidays at home last year. Early on he received a letter, which he
neglected to answer for over a fortnight. He then wrote: 'I am sorry
to keep you waiting, but I have been on holiday'. This was a specious
excuse because it gave his correspondent the impression that he had
been away from home.
   A specious argument is a verbal FALLACY.

spelling   English is not, unfortunately, a phonetic language. Most
of its spelling difficulties arise from the fact that words are spelt
according to their historical form rather than their present pronunciation. Thus the word *rough* is spelt as it is because in Old
English it was pronounced with a guttural sound represented by *gh*,
though today it is pronounced as if it were spelt *ruff*.
   In past centuries, spelling was much more phonetic than it is now,
and writers more or less allowed the spelling to change with the pronunciation. Then in the eighteenth century the spelling was fixed
once and for all according to what was considered sound ETY-
MOLOGY. Even so, mistakes were made which have been perpetuated.
Dr Johnson, for example, in his Dictionary spelt the Old English
verb *ake* with a ch (*ache*) as if it came from Greek. This has given us
an odd spelling that hasn't even the justification of etymology for its
oddness. Since spellings were finally fixed, pronunciation has gone
on changing, leaving many spellings very remote from their present-
day pronunciation.
   However, there are certain rules and patterns that spelling still
follows. By being taught these, schoolchildren can learn some 80%
of the words they need; the rest they have to learn individually. The

commonest patterns consist of letter combinations, such as *oo, ow, ee, air, ish,* representing a consistent sound even though there may be other combinations representing the same sound. Thus, all the *ea* words (seat, cheat, beat, etc.) may be learnt as an associated series, kept quite separate from the *ee* words (meet, feet, greet, etc.), which are learnt at a different time as another associated series.

Modern spelling courses such as *Word Perfect* (Ginn) are based on the belief that this pattern arrangement together with a few simplified rules brings an insight into the composition of words that makes it still worth while teaching spelling in school despite the many irregularities. The main rules are:

1. *i* comes before *e* except after *c* when the sound is i: e.g. field, pier, siege, belief; *but* ceiling, deceive, receipt, conceit
   Exceptions: seize, weird, counterfeit

2. When you add a suffix to a word ending in *y,* you change the *y* into *i* only when a consonant comes before the *y,* e.g. tidy – tidies – tidied – tidier – tidiest; *but* stray – strays – strayed – strayer lady – ladies, story – stories; *but* valley – valleys, essay – essays
   Exceptions: You keep the *y* when adding -*ing* to avoid a double *i,* e.g. tidy – tidying, fly – flying

3. Words ending in a single *e* drop the *e* when a suffix beginning with a vowel is added, e.g. care – caring – cared; *but* careless – careful; measure – measuring – measured – measurable; *but* measurement – measureless
   Exceptions: If a soft *c* or *g* comes before the *e,* the *e* must be retained to keep the *c* or *g* soft, e.g. courage – courageous, replace – replaceable. A few other exceptions are true – truly, due – duly, awe – awful

4. When you add a suffix beginning with a vowel to a word of one syllable ending in a single consonant with a single vowel letter before it, you double the consonant letter, e.g. fit – fitting – fitted – fitter – fittest; *but* fitness – fitful
   star – starry – starred – starring; *but* starless – starlet
   Exceptions: bus – buses, gas – gases

5. In words of more than one syllable ending in a single consonant letter with a single vowel letter before it, you double the consonant letter only if the last syllable is stressed, e.g. omit – omitting – omitted; *but* rivet – riveting – riveted – riveter prefer – preferring – preferred; *but* preference – preferable

6. When you add *-ly* to words ending in *-le*, you drop the *-le*, e.g. gentle – gently, capable – capably

7. Words ending in *c* add a *k* when adding *-ed*, *-ing*, *-y*, *-er*, in order to keep the *c* hard, e.g. picnic – picnicker, panic – panicky, mimic – mimicked, bivouac – bivouacking

8. A few words ending in double *l*, such as *full, till, will, all*, lose an *l* when used to form compound words, e.g. full – careful, till – until, well – welcome, all – already

See also PLURAL; PRONUNCIATION.

split infinitive   when an adverb or phrase comes between the *to* and the verb or the first part of the verb, e.g. *to readily agree, to utterly deny, to badly need, to at least attempt*. Often a split infinitive is ungainly and should be avoided, e.g.:

Wrong: He asked us to slowly and distinctly say our lines.
Right: He asked us to say our lines slowly and distinctly.

Sometimes a split infinitive can be avoided by placing the adverb before the *to*, e.g. 'I was bitterly to regret this decision.' But consider the result when the same method is applied to the above, thus: 'He asked us slowly and distinctly to say our lines.' (He asked us slowly and distinctly?) Here is another example: 'In an angry tone the speaker asked the hecklers kindly to refrain from interrupting him.' (He asked them kindly in an angry tone?) Yet if we place the adverb after the infinitive, the sentence becomes ungainly: '. . . to refrain kindly from interrupting him'. If we must retain *kindly*, there is no alternative but to split the infinitive: '. . . the speaker asked the hecklers to kindly refrain from interrupting him'.

If by splitting an infinitive we can avoid awkwardness or ambiguity, we are perfectly justified in doing so, as in these examples: (a) 'To half finish a task is almost as bad as not attempting it.' (b) 'Why don't we join together to flatly forbid this shameful practice?' (c) 'To but meet him in the street was to know that here was no ordinary man.'

It is a mistake to imagine that an infinitive has been split in such sentences as: 'Mr Brown is to be particularly remembered for the help he gave to refugee children.' The infinitive here is *to be* and it is not split, so it is unnecessary to write: 'Mr Brown is particularly to be remembered . . .'

spondee   in PROSODY a disyllabic foot with equal stress on both syllables, e.g. *bōat-hōok*. See METRE.

spoonerism   the result of the accidental interchanging of two sounds, usually syllables in neighbouring words. It derives its name from Dr William Archibald Spooner, who was Warden of New College, Oxford, from 1903 to 1924, and was doubtless responsible for very few of the spoonerisms that have gained currency over the years. A genuine example is said to be: 'Kinquering congs their tatles tike' for 'Conquering kings their titles take.' Others, less authentic, are: (a) 'Excuse me, but you are occupewing my pie.' 'No, I was sewn into this sheet.' (b) 'Who has never felt within his breast a half-warmed fish?' (c) 'It is pleasant to travel on a well-boiled icicle.'

See also METATHESIS.

sprung rhythm   is the measure made famous by Gerard Manley Hopkins. Instead of adhering to the traditional foot of two or three syllables, he used a foot of any number of syllables, the stress always falling on the first syllable. In this way one stress could immediately follow another or be separated from the next by a number of so-called slack syllables. In sprung rhythm, as Robert Bridges has pointed out, 'the feet are assumed to be equally long or strong and their seeming inequality is made up by pause or stressing'.

To differentiate the two kinds of rhythm, the traditional kind is usually referred to as *running rhythm*. Sprung rhythm is clearly much more flexible than running rhythm. Its very naturalness has made it popular in modern poetry, since it is more like the rhythm of common speech and is the rhythm of all but the most monotonously regular music.

Here are some scanned lines from the opening of Hopkins's *Pied Beauty*:

$$\text{Glory be to / God for / dappled / things –}$$
$$\text{For / skies of / couple- / colour as a / brindled cow;}$$
$$\text{For / rose-moles all in / stipple upon / trout that / swim;}$$

Notice that the scanning of each line continues from the one before. In fact it goes on without a break from the beginning of a stanza to the end. This still further increases the flexibility of the lines till the division into lines appears to be almost unnecessary. Some critics have therefore referred to this type of verse as *rhythmic prose*.

Rhythm is discussed under METRE.

stage   the acting profession in general (see METONYMY). Dramatists are said to 'write for the stage'; and being 'on the stage' means being employed as an actor or actress. The verb 'to stage' means to put a play on the stage. *Stage fright* is nervous apprehension when appearing before an audience, especially for the first time. A *stage whisper* is a whisper loud enough for an audience to hear; as a figurative phrase, it refers to a whisper intended to be heard by others than the person addressed.

See also DRAMA; THEATRE.

standard English   a term used to denote the sort of English that is supposedly accepted by a consensus of opinion among educated people. It is sometimes referred to as BBC English, and is spoken with RECEIVED PRONUNCIATION.

stanza   in PROSODY a group of two or more lines forming the unit which, repeated, makes up a poem. Nowadays it is often called a VERSE, though *verse* originally meant a single line of poetry. The stanza may be compared to a paragraph in prose. In conventional poetry all stanzas follow the same pattern. For example, if there is a line shorter than the rest in one stanza, a similar short line occupies the same position in succeeding stanzas.

See METRE.

stationary, stationery   The first is an adjective meaning 'standing still'; the second is a noun meaning 'writing materials'. They both derive from the Latin meaning 'having a fixed station'. In medieval times a bookseller who was not an itinerant vendor but had his own shop was called a 'stationer'; hence 'stationery'.

stem   often regarded as being synonymous with ROOT. Technically, however, it is not quite the same; it is the root with any slight alteration or addition of letters to facilitate the addition of a prefix or a suffix. For example, *emerge* and *immerse* have the same root (*mergo, mersum*, 'I plunge'), but each is a separate stem: *emerge – emergence – emerges*; *immerse – immersing – immersion*.

See also WORD-FORMATION.

stet (L. 'let it stand')   used in the correction of printer's proofs and other written matter, and indicating that a former correction is to be disregarded; that, for example, a word, phrase, sentence, etc. marked for deletion is not now to be deleted but allowed to remain.

stilted   referring to expression that strives to be superior in an artificial way. Sometimes a person's conversation is stilted because he does not feel at ease in his surroundings; in trying to correct his speech he pronounces his words in too precise a fashion. He is, as it were, endeavouring to increase his height by walking awkwardly on stilts.

stimulus, stimulant   The first, together with its plural *stimuli*, is borrowed direct from the Latin, which means 'a goad'. A stimulus is something that rouses to action, and the adjective *stimulant* (or the alternative *stimulating*) means 'causing increased action; acting as a spur'. The noun *stimulant* applies specifically to anything that causes a temporary increase in activity, as *an alcoholic stimulant*. We can say that words of encouragement are a stimulus, and that brandy is a stimulant.

See also SIMULATE, STIMULATE.

storey, story   Though some authorities are not in agreement, it is better to use the first spelling when referring to the floor of a building. Strictly speaking, the ground floor is not a storey, for the word comes from the Latin *instaurare*, which means 'to build up'. See also 'first floor' under AMERICAN ENGLISH.

strait   This is sometimes confused with *straight*. The adjective *strait* means 'narrow; limited; confining'. We read in the Bible: 'Enter ye in at the strait gate: for wide is the gate, and broad is the way, that leadeth to destruction . . .' A *strait-jacket* or *strait-waistcoat* is a garment used to restrain maniacs. The figurative expression *strait-laced* means 'prudish; strictly moral; narrow in opinion'. The noun *strait* means a narrow channel connecting two larger bodies of water. It is used in the plural, e.g. *the Straits of Dover*. To be *in dire straits* is to be in a desperate position, and a person badly in need of money is *in straitened circumstances*.

stress   the same as ACCENT, which can be defined as the stronger tone of voice given to a particular syllable of a word. It is dealt with more fully under ACCENT, METRE, PRONUNCIATION and SCANNING.

stringed, strung   The first derives from the noun *string* and means 'having strings'; the second is the past tense and past participle of the verb *to string*. Thus violins and harps are *stringed* instruments, and the washing is *strung* on the clothes line.

strip cartoons   a form of story-telling in drawings and words that began as a method of illustrating children's comic papers and quickly spread to newspapers and magazines all over the world. Quintessentially, a strip cartoon is an illustrated account of one person's adventures, usually against heavy odds (Dick Tracy is a policeman; Rip Kirby is a 'private eye'; Garth and Superman are, respectively, British and American super-heroes who act out school-boy fantasies of ubiquity and superhuman strength for a supposedly adult audience); or a girl in search of romance (Jane was a famous forerunner in the *Daily Mirror* with the piquancy that she was per-petually being revealed in a state of undress – the strip cartoon in which she was finally seen naked pushed the art form over some sort of threshold and was hailed as a breakthrough by the bulk of the British Army in World War II, avid followers of Jane); or a group of characters easily identifiable (Peanuts, featuring Charlie Brown and a gang of American children, has a world-wide following; Andy Capp is a satire on the English working man which is immensely popular with the English working man and, indeed, all over North America and Europe in translation).

Traditionally, the strip cartoon is designed to go across four or five columns of a newspaper, and consists of three or four 'frames' to each strip. Equally traditionally, story-line and dialogue are conveyed in hand-drawn capital letters – the description continuity ('RIP FACES THE HOODED MENACE') in 'boxes' and the dialogue in 'balloons' conventionally thought to be issuing from the charac-ters' mouths ('TAKE THAT, YOU FILTHY SPY!!!'). American strips were first on the scene and appear as syndicated material all over the world.

At first 'quality' newspapers sneered at strips as being suitable only for 'tabloid' newspapers. This attitude is changing fast. *The Observer Colour Magazine* prints a syndicated weekly cartoon of Peanuts in colour; and it was this newspaper that pioneered a series of cookery hints written and drawn by the author Len Deighton: the 'factual' strip – golfing instruction, great moments of history, true stories of animals – is the sole important development from the originals.

It should be noted that strip cartoons are not 'read', as is a SERIAL: they are 'followed' by their devotees, who number millions.

strong verbs   See VERB; WEAK VERBS.

strophe (strou'fi)   the first stanza of a Pindaric ode. See ODE.

structural linguistics a recent development in the study of languages, less rigidly grammatical and taking far more account of actual usage, which in practice leads to a study of the standard patterns of the language. Leading exponents of this new approach to the teaching of English as a foreign language are Professor C. C. Fries and Noam Chomsky of America. In Britain this modern approach to linguistics in general has been championed by Professors R. Quirk and P. Strevens, among many others.

structure the manner in which a thing is constructed. In SYNTAX it refers to the arrangement of the component parts of a SENTENCE, whose generous variety of forms enables us to express every shade of meaning. In popular modern linguistics, the term 'structure' is used to denote a regular pattern of language – a sentence pattern. It is also used for any word group that has a characteristic structural function. 'Structural words' as opposed to LEXICAL WORDS are those that perform a structural function rather than providing content. They include the ARTICLES, CONJUNCTIONS, PREPOSITIONS, ADVERBIAL PARTICLES, AUXILIARY VERBS, INTENSIFIERS.

student see under SCHOLAR.

subject the word or group of words denoting the person or thing about which the verb makes an assertion. The subject is always a noun or noun-equivalent. In practice there are two distinct uses of the word. The first, sometimes called the *simple subject*, means the noun or noun-equivalent, stripped of all qualifications, that names whatever is doing, suffering or being, e.g. 'The *car* swerved violently.' Here *car* is the simple subject of the verb *swerved*. The other use is where it means all that part of the sentence which is not the predicate – that is to say, the simple subject plus what is known as the **enlargement of the subject**, which includes even an adjectival clause, e.g. '*The big red sports car that suddenly appeared over the brow of the hill* swerved violently and missed the cyclist by inches.' Here the simple subject is *car*, and the rest of the italicised words are the enlargement of the subject.

For the agreement of subject and verb see NUMBER. See also ANTICIPATORY SUBJECT; IDIOM; INFINITIVE; OBJECT; PREDICATE; SENTENCE; VERB.

subjective not OBJECTIVE, but expressing the thoughts or opinions of the speaker, writer or artist; belonging to the person thinking rather than to the thing he is thinking about. An objective account of a bull-fight tells the hearer or reader just what happened and no more; a subjective account describes the bull-fight from the narrator's point of view, bringing into prominence his opinion of bull-fighting in general and this bull-fight in particular.

subjunctive   see under MOOD; TENSE.

subordinate clause   a clause dependent upon another. It is treated under CLAUSE.

substantive   another name for a NOUN. The adjective is *substantival*.

substitute   The distinction between this and *replace* is considered under REPLACE.

sub-title   an additional title subordinate to the main title of a book, play or opera, often prefaced by 'or'. Thus: *The Mikado, or The Town of Titipu* (Gilbert and Sullivan), *Twelfth Night, or What You Will* (Shakespeare). The practice has gone out in recent years, but one famous example lingers – and is never referred to by its main title alone; it is *Eric, or Little by Little*, written by Dean Farrar in 1858.

suffer   In grammar the verb *to suffer* means 'to be affected by'. Thus in 'Jack hits George', George doubtless undergoes physical suffering, whilst in 'Jack praises George', George is occasioned no pain or distress; but he still suffers in a grammatical sense the action of the verb.

suffix   an affix placed at the end of a word or root to form a new word. Suffixes are either grammatical INFLEXIONS (boy's, walked, walking) or endings indicating various parts of speech, e.g. -*ly* indicates an adverb; -*ness* an abstract noun; and -*able* an adjective.
  The following list contains all the main suffixes in use in the English language, apart from suffixes used in the formation of plurals, case endings, declensions and non-finite parts of verbs:

-*able*	used to form adjectives from verbs, giving the meaning of *able* or *liable*, or *worthy to be—ed*, e.g.: marriageable, distinguishable, insupportable, valuable.
-*al*	forms nouns and adjectives, e.g.: nouns: removal, acquittal; adjectives: musical, fatal, official.

-*age*   forms nouns: breakage, carriage, usage.

-*an (ean)*   forms adjectives meaning *pertaining* or *belonging to*, e.g.: suburban, Shakespearean, Euclidean.

-*ance*   forms nouns from verbs with the meaning of *the state or quality of*, e.g.: perseverance, endurance, ignorance, deliverance.

-*ant*   forms nouns with meaning of *agent* or *doer*, e.g.: assistant, accountant.

-*ate*   forms verbs from nouns or adjectives, e.g.: estimate, hyphenate, formulate, liquidate, validate.

-*ation*   forms nouns from verbs, with the meaning of *the act* or *state of*, e.g.: emendation, consideration, exclamation, damnation, temptation.

-*dom*   forms nouns from nouns, with the meaning of *rank*, *domain* or *condition*, e.g.: Kingdom, serfdom, martyrdom, earldom.

-*en*   forms verbs from adjectives with the meaning of *to make*, e.g.: soften, lighten, thicken.
Also forms adjectives expressing material, e.g.: golden, wooden, woollen.

-*ence*   indicating a state, e.g.: permanence, corpulence, concurrence, precedence, transference.

-*er*   forms nouns from nouns, adjectives or verbs, to give the meaning of *one who performs the action*, *person belonging to a place* or *instrument* or *object that does something*, e.g.: follower, gardener, Londoner, foreigner, paper-cutter, decanter.

-*ess*   feminine formation as in goddess, lioness, countess, giantess, governess, adventuress.

-*ful*   forms adjectives with the meaning of *full of* or *having the quality of*, e.g.: beautiful, masterful, tasteful, wasteful.

-*fy*   forms verbs with the sense of *to make*, *to make into*, *to produce*, e.g.: amplify, classify, purify, stupefy.

-*hood*   forms nouns of condition or quality, e.g.: motherhood, fatherhood, manhood, statehood.

-*ible*   forms adjectives with the meaning *that can be—ed*, e.g.: contemptible, digestible, divisible, legible.

-*ion*   forms nouns of condition, action, e.g.: abstraction, constitution, delegation, speculation, suggestion.

-*ish*   forms adjectives meaning *belonging to*, *in the nature of*, or sometimes with the meaning of *somewhat*, e.g.: boyish, girlish, foppish, bookish, greenish, reddish.

-ism   forms nouns from adjectives, suggesting a disposition to be what the adjective describes, e.g.: barbarism, socialism, idealism, modernism, spiritualism.

-ist   forms nouns meaning an *agent, believer* or *one who follows* and *practises*, e.g.: violinist, atheist, fatalist, cyclist, organist, specialist.

-ise   is the suffix ending of a small group of words of which the most common are: advertise, chastise, compromise, despise, disguise, enterprise, exercise, supervise, surprise.

-ity (*ty*) forms nouns meaning the *quality of being what the adjective describes*, e.g.: liberality, formality, humility, reality, universality.

-ive   forms adjectives from verbs meaning *to have the nature of, tending to*, e.g.: impressive, active, coercive.

-ize   forms verbs from nouns and adjectives, e.g.: civilize, patronize, equalize, realize, sympathize. (But '-ise' is becoming more common in these cases. See -ISE, -IZE.)

-less   forms adjectives meaning *without, devoid, free from*, e.g.: witless, useless, guileless, countless, fearless.

-ly   (a) an adverbial suffix, e.g.: cruelly, beautifully, quickly, slowly, etc.
            (b) an adjectival suffix, e.g.: kingly, scholarly, soldierly, lovely.

-ment   forms nouns with the meaning of *the act of* or *the means of*, e.g.: atonement, amendment, requirement, payment.

-ness   forms nouns expressing a state or quality, e.g.: sweetness, bitterness, tiredness, laziness, etc.

-or   forms nouns with the meaning of *agent* or *instrument*, e.g.: editor, surveyor, donor.

-ory   forms adjectives meaning *the state* or *quality of*, e.g.: compulsory, perfunctory, illusory.

-ship   forms abstract nouns with the meaning of *the quality of* or other nouns meaning *the status* or *office of*, e.g.: hardship, salesmanship, scholarship, lordship.

-some   forms adjectives with the meaning *productive of* or *apt to be*, e.g.: quarrelsome, lonesome, wholesome, awesome.

-th   forms nouns from verbs and adjectives: growth, health, stealth, truth, width.

-ure   forms nouns from verbs: closure, seizure, departure, mixture.

-*y*   (a) forms adjectives meaning *having the character* or, *composed of*, e.g.: milky, thorny, slangy, bluey, misty.
(b) forms nouns from verbs: delivery, flattery, discovery.

See also PREFIX; WORD-FORMATION.

suggestio falsi (L. 'the suggestion of an untruth')   a verbal FALLACY, of which we are guilty when we make a statement that is not in itself untrue but implies something that is. For example, our friend Tom may ask us: 'The Joneses are living as husband and wife, but are they really married?' To this we reply: 'Thank heaven we're all more tolerant these days than we used to be.' We thus leave Tom under the false impression that we know the Joneses not to be married.

superlative   the form of the adjective or adverb indicating the highest degree of comparison. It is treated under COMPARISON, DEGREES OF.

surprise   The University professor slipped his arm round the waist of the housemaid just as his wife entered the room. 'Really, George,' she exclaimed, 'I'm surprised at you!' 'To the contrary, my dear,' he replied, 'it is we who are surprised. You are astonished.' He was right. Literally, to surprise is to take unawares; to come upon or attack suddenly.

surrealism   a movement in the arts in the 1920s, defined by one of its founders (André Breton) as, 'Pure psychic automatism, by which it is intended to express verbally, in writing or by other means, the real process of thought, in the absence of all control exercised by reason and outside all aesthetic or moral preoccupations'.

syllable (Gk. 'take together')   the unit of pronunciation, i.e. part of a word that can be sounded by itself. Thus *man* has one syllable (monosyllabic), *man-ly* has two syllables (disyllabic), and *man-li-ness* has three syllables (trisyllabic). By adding a prefix we get *wo-man-li-ness*, which has four syllables (quadrisyllabic).

For the division of words into syllables see PRONUNCIATION.

syllepsis (silep'sis) (Gk. 'a taking together')   a TURN OF EXPRESSION in which a word that has both a literal meaning and a figurative meaning is applied in both these senses to two nouns, e.g.:

(a) The officer spurred on his horse and troops to still greater efforts.

(b) Tom threw a glance and the Latin dictionary at me.

(c) The hairdresser's scissors were not so sharp as the customer's tongue.

(d) The landlord came into the room wearing an angry frown and a bowler hat.

Strictly speaking, syllepsis is not the same as ZEUGMA, but it is common usage to make zeugma the name for both.

syllogism (sil'oudʒizm) (Gk. 'to reckon together') in LOGIC an argument based on deductive reasoning (see DEDUCTION), e.g.:

All poisons are harmful things.
Arsenic is a poison.
Therefore arsenic is a harmful thing.

Any assumption made for the purpose of an argument is called a *premise*. The first premise is an assumption in the form of a generalisation. We call this the *major premise*, in this case: *that all poisons are harmful things*. The second premise is not general but particular. We call this the *minor premise*, in this case: *that arsenic is a poison*. By applying the minor premise to the major premise we can draw or deduce the *conclusion*: *that arsenic is a harmful thing*.

Looked at in another way, a syllogism contains three items or *terms*. The *major term* in the above syllogism is 'harmful things', the *minor term* is 'arsenic', and the *middle term*, which connects the major and minor terms but is absent from the conclusions, is 'poisons'.

A syllogism can be represented diagrammatically by three discs, one within the other. To be logically sound, the major term (A) must include all of the middle term (B), and the middle term must include all of the minor term (C). The terms are said to be *distributed* – that is, used to their fullest extent.

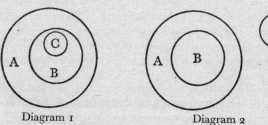

Diagram 1   Diagram 2

In a negative syllogism, the middle term does not include the minor term. Therefore the major term does not include it either. This can be seen from the second diagram, which represents this style of syllogism:

All poisons (B) are harmful (A).
Lemonade (C) is not harmful.
Therefore lemonade is not poisonous.

FALLACIES

Sometimes arguments are false because there is a flaw in the construction of the syllogism. Logical flaws are called *fallacies*. There are two main types of fallacies resulting from wrong construction: the fallacy of the *undistributed middle*, and the fallacy of the *missing middle*. The first is illustrated by the following:

All squirrels (B) are arboreal (A).
This small animal (C) is arboreal.
Therefore it is a squirrel.

The conclusion may be true, but on the other hand it is quite likely that the small animal may be some other kind of arboreal creature. The arguer has wrongly assumed that squirrels constitute the whole of the arboreal class, whereas they constitute only a part of it. If we refer to the second diagram, we can see that C could be within B, but it could also be within any other part of A. The middle term is not distributed all over A because squirrels are not the only creatures that are arboreal. In other words, the major premise is made to apply to the whole class – everything living in trees – when in fact it applies to only part of it – squirrels.

This fallacy of the undistributed middle is important because it is often used to draw correct conclusions and so escapes notice by the unwary, e.g.:

All birds can fly.
Kingfishers can fly.
Therefore kingfishers are birds.

The conclusion is correct, but the argument is fallacious, as can be seen by using the same argument to produce another conclusion known to be false, e.g.:

All birds can fly.
Helicopters can fly.
Therefore helicopters are birds.

The fallacy of the undistributed middle is also common in negative syllogisms, e.g.:

All cows have cloven hoofs.
This animal is not a cow.
Therefore it has not cloven hoofs.

Cows do not cover the whole of the cloven-hoof class; there are plenty of other cloven-hoof animals, and this may be one of them.

A sound syllogism must have a middle term that occurs in both premises. The absence of this middle term is the other type of fallacy, e.g.:

All poisons are harmful things.
Frost-bite is a harmful thing.
Therefore frost-bite is a poison.

Here again the major term is 'harmful things', but now the minor term is 'frost-bite'; and there is no middle term – no term occurring in both the major and the minor premises – to connect 'frostbite' with 'poisons'. Here is another example:

All monkeys have tails.
This lion has a tail.
Therefore it is a monkey.

There is no middle term connecting the major premise and the minor, so it is not possible to make any deduction. In effect, in order to prove his conclusion, the arguer wrongly assumes that the particular case, 'this lion', is included in the generalisation, 'all monkeys'.

Other fallacies in syllogistic reasoning derive from the material or content of the syllogism. The construction of the syllogism may be sound, but the conclusion is unsound because it is drawn from a false premise. The major premise may be false, e.g.:

All cats are bipeds.
This is a cat.
Therefore it must have two legs.

The major premise here is obviously wrong; but sometimes it is so subtly wrong that it may pass unnoticed, e.g.:

Fungi are poisonous.
This is a fungus.
Therefore it is poisonous.

The major premise here is based on a rash generalisation. It needs qualification: only some fungi are poisonous; some are perfectly edible. Hence this particular one may or may not be poisonous. In any case the conclusion is logically unsound, since the major premise is false.

Sometimes it is the minor premise that is false, e.g.:

Vitamins protect our health.
Potatoes are full of vitamins.
Therefore potatoes should be eaten for good health.

The argument here breaks down because it is not true that potatoes are full of vitamins, and you cannot draw a sound conclusion from such a false premise.

Still another type of fallacy is based upon ambiguity, e.g.:

All sovereigns are made of gold.
A king is a sovereign.
Therefore a king is made of gold.

Both the construction and the premises appear to be sound, and yet the conclusion is patently absurd. The word 'sovereign' does not mean the same thing in the major premise as it does in the minor; it is used ambiguously. Consequently we have in reality four terms, and a syllogism may have only three.

In its less obvious form this fallacy is often used by unscrupulous propagandists. It is important to see that the terms used do not change their meaning or application during the course of an argument, e.g.:

Without liberty we are but slaves.
We do not have the liberty of smoking in church.
Therefore we are nothing more than slaves.

The argument seems sound, until we realise that 'liberty' in the major premise means freedom in a broad sense, whilst in the minor premise its meaning is restricted to a very trivial aspect of freedom.

It may be thought that syllogisms are rather remote from the actualities of everyday argument, for we seldom state our arguments in syllogistic form. It is true that few arguments are put in syllogistic form, but only by reducing them to their syllogistic form can we be quite sure of testing their validity. So many arguments are based on fallacies, and often we can prove these arguments to be false by means of a syllogism.

symbol   a sign or mark representing something else. See SYM-BOLISM below and also SIGNS AND SYMBOLS. International phonetic symbols are listed under GUIDE TO PRONUNCIATION on page 7.

symbolism   the use of symbols to represent ideas, persons or things in such a way that the symbols have an emotional significance. Thus the crucifix reminds us of Jesus Christ and the Christian Church; the national flag reminds us of our country; the hammer and sickle reminds us of Russia and Communism; the dove reminds us of peace.

symposium (Gk. 'drinking together')   a pleasant recreation accompanied by music and conversation. Its modern meaning is a collection of the views of various writers on a given topic, e.g. 'The next issue of this periodical will contain a symposium on fox-hunting, the opinions of a number of eminent persons on this controversial matter being frankly expressed.'

synaeresis (sineər'əsis) (Gk. 'a taking or drawing together')   the opposite of DIAERESIS. When two successive vowels are pronounced as one sound, that is synaeresis. Examples are *extraordinary*, in which *a* and *o* form a single vowel sound, and *aeroplane*, which is pronounced as if spelt *airoplane*. By comparison *aerated* has a diaeresis, the first *a* and *e* being pronounced separately.

syncope (sink'əpi)   the shortening of a word by dropping a letter or syllable from the middle of it, e.g. *e'er* for *ever*, *ne'er* for *never*, *shepherd* for *sheepherd*, *pacifist* for *pacificist*. This shortening is often for the sake of EUPHONY.
  See also CONTRACTION.

synecdoche (sinek'dəki)   a FIGURE OF SPEECH in which a part is made to stand for the whole, or the whole for a part, e.g. 'The brains of New Zealand' for the brainy people of New Zealand, and 'Australia' for the Australian test team.

synonyms (sin¹ənimz) words having approximately the same meaning and use. The English language is specially rich in synonyms because it is derived from so many languages that it has tended to borrow the same word from several different sources. Thus we have:

to wed (Old English) and *to marry* (Norman French)
kingly (Old English), *royal* (Norman French) and *regal* (Latin)
meal (Old English) and *repast* (Norman French)
child (Old English) and *infant* (Norman French)
friendly (Old English) and *amicable* (Latin)
fatherly (Old English) and *paternal* (Latin)
manly (Old English) and *virile* (Latin)
holiday (Old English) and *vacation* (Latin)

It will be noted that the Old English word is usually more homely and direct and usually to be preferred, though the longer word of more recent introduction has its place on formal occasions. Thus *conflagration* might sound right in a history book, but we should call it 'a great fire' in conversation; and we should certainly cry 'Fire! Fire!' if one broke out, rather than 'Conflagration! Conflagration!'

Not many English synonyms have exactly the same meaning and use. For example, to say that a husband pursued his wife along the passage when all he did was to follow her is to create an entirely wrong impression. It is therefore important to be able to choose the right synonym for the particular context.

See also DERIVATION; VOCABULARY.

Words of opposite meaning are called ANTONYMS.

synopsis (sinop¹sis) a summary; a tabulation or setting out of details; a short statement giving a general impression of a play, book, etc. The difference between a synopsis and a PRÉCIS is that the first is in note form and the second is in continuous prose. Some books have at the head of each chapter a synopsis of the events described in the chapter. Here is the synopsis of Chapter XXV of *The Pickwick Papers* by Charles Dickens:

SHOWING, AMONG A VARIETY OF PLEASANT MATTERS, HOW MAJESTIC AND IMPARTIAL MR. NUPKINS WAS; AND HOW MR. WELLER RE-TURNED MR. JOB TROTTER'S SHUTTLECOCK AS HEAVILY AS IT CAME. WITH ANOTHER MATTER, WHICH WILL BE FOUND IN ITS PLACE.

syntax (Gk. 'to put in order') the branch of GRAMMAR dealing with (a) the arrangement of words in a sentence, and the rules governing this arrangement; (b) the classification of sentences according to their clause structure; (c) the correct use of the PARTS OF SPEECH, the eight classes into which words can be grouped according to their function in a sentence.

In English, which is largely uninflected, much depends upon the order of words to express meaning. The same words may have a very different meaning when placed in a different order, as may be seen from these two sentences, made up of the same words: 'John hit the ball.' 'The ball hit John.' Syntax is therefore particularly important, as is fully recognised in STRUCTURAL LINGUISTICS, a recent development in teaching English as a foreign language.

For a selection of cross-references see under GRAMMAR.

T

table a list setting out facts or figures in compact form; a SYNOPSIS. A *contents table* gives a summary of the subject-matter of a book; a *multiplication table* shows the products of quantities taken in pairs $(2 \times 1 = 2, 2 \times 2 = 4, 2 \times 3 = 6,$ etc.); a *time-table* shows the times of departure and arrival of trains, buses, etc.

For the use of the word *table* in another sense see METONYMY.

tag a trite quotation, especially a familiar Latin expression, e.g. *in vino veritas* ('There is truth in wine'), *veni, vidi, vici* ('I came, I saw, I conquered', said by Julius Caesar), *facilis descensus Averno* ('It is easy to descend into hell'). A number of others are to be found under LATIN WORDS AND PHRASES. *Cherchez la femme* is a French tag. It means 'Look for the woman', the implication being that a woman is usually the cause of the trouble. When we murmur lazily, '*Dolce far niente*', we are using an Italian tag meaning 'sweet idleness'.

tail questions another name for QUESTION TAGS.

tautology (tɔːˈtɒlədʒi) (Gk. 'saying the same thing') the useless or ineffective repetition of the same idea in different words, e.g. (a)

'The concert hall was a large one and of considerable extent.' (b) 'The early explorers courageously dared the perils of the sea.' (c) 'Without shoes or socks the boy ran bare-footed across the field.' (d) 'Henry II was a medieval king who ruled during the Middle Ages.' In (a) the tautology is obvious; in (b) 'dared' means that they had the courage to make the attempt, so 'courageously' is tautological; in (c) we are told that the boy was not wearing his shoes and socks, so we need not be told that he was bare-footed when he ran across the field; in (d) 'medieval' is an adjective meaning 'of the Middle Ages', so here it is tautological and should be omitted.

Many tautological terms have become so much a part of our everyday speech that they cannot be condemned on the score of useless repetition. Indeed, they have value as INTENSIVE phrases, which is what they were when first coined. Here are a few of them, those printed in small capitals being treated under their own headings: *to all intents and purposes*; *by hook or by crook*; *cool and collected*; *first and foremost*; *for ever and aye*; *free, gratis and for nothing*; HUE AND CRY; *jot or tittle*; *kith and kin*; NULL AND VOID; *over and above*; *part and parcel*; *rack and ruin*; *rules and regulations*; *ways and means*; WEIRD AND WONDERFUL; WITHOUT LET OR HINDRANCE.

See also ARCHAISM.

Tautology is a form of REDUNDANCY because it is saying the same thing twice in different ways. It is not quite the same as PLEONASM, which is the use of unnecessary words.

teach see LEARN.

telescoping the bringing of two words together to form one word, e.g. *alone* (all one), *atone* (at one, i.e. set at one, reconcile), *doff* (do off), *don* (do on), *pinafore* (pin afore, i.e. in front).

See also PORTMANTEAU WORDS.

tense (L. 'time') the form of the verb that indicates the time of the action. There are three main tenses: 1. *past* ('I took'); 2. *present* ('I take'); 3. *future* ('I shall take'). There are also (4) the future tense of reported speech, called the *future in the past* ('I should take', e.g. 'I told them that I should take my young brother with me'), and (5) the *conditional* tense ('I would take'), which expresses a condition, e.g. 'I said I would take my young brother with me if he promised to behave himself.'

Each of these tenses may be sub-divided into *simple, continuous* (or *imperfect*) and *perfect*, thus:

	Simple	Continuous	Perfect
Past	I took	I was taking	I had taken
Present	I take	I am taking	I have taken
Future	I shall take	I shall be taking	I shall have taken
Future in past	I should take	I should be taking	I should have taken
Conditional	I would take	I would be taking	I would have taken

When the action is viewed for its effect on events now, we use the present perfect rather than the simple past, e.g.: 'I took the tablets' (simple past); 'I have taken the tablets' (present perfect). We can therefore usually add *now* after its use, e.g. 'I have taken the tablets now that I have the doctor's permission.' In the same way, the past perfect (sometimes called the *pluperfect*) views the action for its effect on events at a certain time in the past, e.g. ('I had taken the tablets.' We can therefore usually add 'already . . . when' or 'before', e.g. 'I had already taken the tablets when the doctor advised me against them'; or 'I had taken the tablets before getting the doctor's permission.'

All the above tenses are in the indicative mood, active voice. They are slightly different in the subjunctive mood, now obsolescent, and quite different in the passive voice, e.g.:

	Simple	Continuous	Perfect
Subjunctive	(If) I were taken	(If) I were being taken	(If) I had been taken
Past passive	I was taken	I was being taken	I had been taken

SEQUENCE OF TENSES

When writing sentences with more than one finite verb we must be careful to see that the tenses correspond.

Wrong: Nobody would say such a thing unless he believes it.

Right: Nobody would say such a thing unless he believed it.

In the first sentence 'would say' is conditional, which is a past tense, whilst 'believes' is in the present tense. The saying and the believing must therefore have happened at different times. But this is clearly nonsense; they must have both happened either in the past or in the present.

This rule does not always apply. For example, the future tense may be followed by any other tense, e.g.:

(a) 'I shall see what you wrote' (future followed by simple past).
(b) 'I shall see what you are writing' (future followed by present continuous).
(c) 'Tomorrow I shall see what you had written by teatime yesterday' (future followed by past perfect).

Again, the past tense may be followed by the present tense when the present tense expresses a universal truth, or fact, that is valid regardless of time, e.g. 'The physics master showed us how acid turns blue litmus red.' (It happened not only on that occasion, but happens also on every other occasion.) Again, following a main clause in the past tense by a subordinate clause in the same tense may produce a statement that is not in accordance with the facts, e.g. 'I heard this afternoon that Mr Jones was a Roman Catholic.' This might well mean that Mr Jones is no longer a Roman Catholic. Any doubt is dispelled by the use of the present tense for the subordinate clause, thus: 'I heard this afternoon that Mr Jones is a Roman Catholic.'

See also HISTORIC PRESENT; INFINITIVE.

terminology basically the science of the correct use of terms. More generally it refers to the terms used in any branch of learning or activity. For example, medical terminology is the system of terms used in the medical profession. Similarly there are the terminology of art, the terminology of engineering, the terminology of the theatre, the terminology of music and the terminology of printing; the last two are treated under MUSICAL TERMS and PRINTING TERMS.

tetrameter (tetræmˈətə) (Gk. 'four measures') in PROSODY a line of verse consisting of four feet, e.g.:

Courage, / brother! / do not / stumble,
    Though thy / path be / dark as / night;
There's a / star to / guide the / humble:
    'Trust in / God and / do the / right.'
                                        (Macleod)

Here the metre is trochaic – that is, with the stress falling on the first syllable of each disyllabic foot ('Cóurage, / bróther! / dó not / stúmble'). Each line, then, is a *trochaic tetrameter*. Because the last feet of lines 2 and 4 are not complete trochees, having one syllable instead of two, these lines are called CATALECTIC.

The *iambic tetrameter* (a line of four disyllabic feet with the stress on the second syllable of each foot) is often to be found in lyric poetry. Here are two examples, the first from a poem by Tennyson (*In Memoriam*), the second from a poem by Christopher Marlowe (*The Passionate Shepherd to his Love*):

(a)   I hold / it true, / whate'er / befall;
      I feel / it, when / I sor / row most;
      'Tis bet / ter to / have loved / and lost
  Than nev / er to / have loved / at all.

(b)   Come live / with me / and be / my Love,
  And we / will all / the pleas / ures prove
  That hills / and val / leys, dales / and fields,
  Or woods, / or steep / y mount / ain yields.

See METRE.

than   SEE ACCUSATIVE CASE; AS, THAN; DIFFERENT FROM, TO, THAN.

that, which   see PRONOUN, *relative*.

the   the definite article, indicating the one or more persons or things under discussion; usually pronounced ðə. Only when it is used emphatically is it pronounced ði:.

theatre   from the Greek meaning 'to look on'. The American spelling is *theater*. Besides referring to a playhouse, a building in which dramatic performances are given, the word is used as a METONYMY to describe dramatic art, literature, etc. as a whole, e.g. 'The French theatre suffered both a financial and an artistic crisis during 1962.' (*Britannica Book of the Year 1963*) An *operating theatre* is a place in which medical students watch surgeons operating upon patients. A place of action is also called a theatre. For example, Burma became a *theatre of war* when the Japanese invaded it in 1941.
See also DRAMA; STAGE.

theatre of the absurd   a type of drama developed in the 1950s by Beckett, Ionesco, Genet, Pinter, Orton and others, in which the absurdity stems from man's predicament in the universe, which is seen as a belief in living coupled with the contradictory belief in the purposelessness of living. The result is a blend of wild comedy and outrageous tragedy, exemplified in *Waiting for Godot* by Samuel Beckett or *Loot* by Joe Orton.

See also KITCHEN-SINK DRAMA; METHOD; THREE UNITIES, THE.

thence see HENCE.

therefor, therefore The first means 'for this; for that; for it'; the second means 'for that reason', e.g.:

- (a) The millionaire was anxious to buy the property and offered ten thousand pounds therefor.
- (b) The millionaire was anxious to buy the property and therefore offered ten thousand pounds for it.

thesaurus (θiːsɔːrˈləs or θiːsɔːrˈləs) (Gk. 'treasure') a treasurehouse of words. The term would have gone out of use years ago had it not been for *Roget's Thesaurus*, the famous dictionary of English synonyms and antonyms by Peter Mark Roget.

thesis (Gk. 'thing laid down') a proposition advanced or maintained; an argument that substantiates a theory or contention. A thesis is also an essay based on original research in some specific subject and written or delivered by a candidate for university honours. Thus Mr Jones gained his degree with his thesis 'Concerning the longevity of fish under varying temperatures of water'. The plural is *theses*.

though, although The second is synonymous with the first when the meaning is 'notwithstanding that'. (a) and (b) below are both correct; which to use is a matter of personal choice.

- (a) Although he was over seventy he still walked ten miles a day.
- (b) Though he was over seventy he still walked ten miles a day.

But *although* is not synonymous with *though* when the meaning is (c) 'as if', (d) 'even if', (e) 'however'.

- (c) It looks as though we shall lose this match.
- (d) It is bound to be an enjoyable match, even though we lose.
- (e) I hoped I was going to enjoy the match; I didn't, though.

An abbreviated form of *though* sometimes encountered is *tho'*.

thrash, thresh   Both come from the Anglo-Saxon word meaning 'to beat', but nowadays the first refers to corporal punishment and the second to the process of beating out grain.

Three Unities, the   the three principles of the canon of dramatic composition as laid down by Aristotle. They are the unities of *place*, of *time*, and of *action*, requiring that a play should be represented as occurring in one place, on the same day, and with nothing irrelevant in the plot, which must be a continuous sequence of events. With the return to the classics during the Renaissance, certain Italian and French writers adopted the Aristotelian canon, but there was no general acceptance, Shakespeare being among those who attached more importance to the unity of action than to the unities of place and time. Since his time the Unities have, quite properly, been more and more discarded as an irrelevant formalism.

See KITCHEN-SINK DRAMA; METHOD; THEATRE OF THE ABSURD.

threnody (θren¹ədi) (Gk. 'a dirge song')   a song of lamentation; an ODE on a person's death.

thriller   an exciting crime story depending more on action than does a novel of detection, which is a battle of wits between the author and the reader. The novels of Ian Fleming and Alistair MacLean fall into this class.

till, until   These are to a large extent interchangeable, *until* being the more formal of the two. It tends also to be used instead of *till* when it begins a sentence, e.g. 'Until my employers sent me to Ghana in 1960, I had never been out of England.' Note the double *l* in *till* and the single *l* in *until*.

tragedy   a literary work, usually a play, that is preoccupied with the serious or unhappy aspects of life. It is sombre in tone and ends in misfortune, yet produces CATHARSIS in the audience from its sense of rightness. Shakespeare's *Macbeth* and Ibsen's *Ghosts* are typical tragedies. The great periods of tragedy were Classical Greece and Elizabethan England.

tragi-comedy   is used to denote either a play that is a mixture of tragic and comic elements, such as Chekov's *The Cherry Orchard*, or a play that is sombre in tone and theme but has a happy ending, such as Shakespeare's *The Winter's Tale*.

transferred epithet when an adjective or adverb is transferred from the word with which it normally goes to another with which it is associated, e.g.:

(a) He stopped shivering when he had drunk a cup of hot coffee.
He stopped shivering when he had drunk a hot cup of coffee.
(b) The old gentleman was angrily brandishing an umbrella.
The old gentleman was brandishing an angry umbrella.

In (a) the epithet 'hot' is transferred from the coffee to the cup; in (b) the anger is transferred from the old gentleman to his umbrella.

transitive verbs see under VERB.

transpire The literal meaning of this is 'to breathe through; to pass off as a vapour'. Figuratively it means 'to leak out; to become known gradually'. It should not therefore be used in the sense of 'happen' or 'occur'.

Wrong: Rushton Wanderers played consistently well throughout the season, so when it transpired that they won the Football Cup nobody was surprised.

Right: Mrs Bailey told the neighbours that her husband had gone to America on business and would be away for six months, but it later transpired that he had left her for good.

trendy a VOGUE WORD to describe those eager to show themselves abreast of current fashions in clothes, culture and life-style generally. *Trendy* people use vogue words readily and sometimes create them.

trilogy (trilˈədʒi) three plays or pieces of writing complete in themselves but with a common theme. Shakespeare's *Henry VI* is a trilogy, being in three distinct parts. In more modern times, Arnold Wesker constructed a trilogy of plays around a Jewish family – *Chicken Soup with Barley*, *Roots* and *I'm Talking About Jerusalem*.

trimeter (trimˈətə) (Gk. 'three measures') In PROSODY a line of verse consisting of three feet. The following lines from *The Mikado* are in *iambic trimeters* – that is, three disyllabic feet with the stress on the second syllable of each foot:

My ŏb / jéct áll / sŭblíme
Ĭ shall / ăchíeve / ĭn tíme

See METRE.

triolet (traiᴵoulet or triːᴵoulet)   in PROSODY a poem of eight lines, with the first line repeated in the fourth and seventh lines, and the second line repeated in the last. Although the following is of no literary merit it shows the rhyme and metre.

> I have to write a triolet
>   And so my Muse must not desert me.
> It is to win a shilling bet
> I have to write a triolet
> And though I've not succeeded yet,
>   To lose the bet will really hurt me.
> I *have* to write a triolet
>   And so my Muse must *not* desert me!

triplet   in PROSODY three lines rhyming together, e.g.:

> Theirs not to make reply,
> Theirs not to reason why,
> Theirs but to do and die.
>   (Tennyson)

trisyllabic (traisilæbᴵik)   having three syllables, e.g. *telephone, elephant, bungalow.*
    See METRE.

trite   hackneyed; worn out; commonplace. Thus the Bellman in Lewis Carroll's *The Hunting of the Snark*:

> 'For England expects – I forbear to proceed:
> 'Tis a maxim tremendous, but trite.'

trochee (troukᴵi)   in PROSODY a disyllabic foot with the stress on the first syllable, e.g. ´*sunset.*
    See METRE.

truism   a self-evident truth; a PLATITUDE. 'You can only die once' is a truism.

try to, try and   'I decided to try and get another bicycle.' This implies a twofold decision, not only to try but also to get, even though the speaker means no more than he will try to get another bicycle, with no certainty of success. Take another example: 'You try and do it!' The speaker knows the difficulties or has himself attempted it and failed. If that is the meaning, he should say 'you try to do it!' But if the words are intended not as a challenge but by way of encouragement, there is some justification for 'you try and do it' in the sense of 'just try and you'll find that you can do it'. Apart from such rare exceptions as this, *to* is better than *and*.

turned comma   one of the pair of punctuation marks known as INVERTED COMMAS. It is the mark (') used to begin the quotation; the mark (') used to end the quotation is the APOSTROPHE. The turned comma is also to be found in certain surnames, e.g. M'Dowell, M'Kay, M'Kenzie, M'Mahon.

U

uncountable noun   unlike a COUNTABLE NOUN, it represents something that cannot be counted and therefore has no separate plural form. *Rice, water, furniture, wisdom, biology* are all uncountable nouns.

Underground newspapers   self-inflicted description of a group of 'rebel' newspapers produced mainly in London, New York and the American West Coast in the 1960s and 1970s, and united only by their dissident approach to conventional society. The English pioneer was *Private Eye*, a magazine whose purpose, stoutly maintained, was to LAMPOON society. Later arrivals on the scene were *International Times* (abbreviated to *I.T.*), *Rolling Stone* and *Oz* (prosecuted for alleged obscenity at the Old Bailey in 1971). FOUR-LETTER WORDS were used with what frequently looked like schoolboy defiance. Some were openly in favour of drug-taking, and some accepted small advertisements advertising homosexual and other deviations. As a source of SLANG, they are invaluable to the literary historian, at least.

understatement   see MEIOSIS.

uninterested   see DISINTERESTED.

unique   an adjective that can have no comparative or superlative. It means 'of which only one exists'. A thing is therefore unique or not unique. It cannot be more unique or most unique. The purist would apply the same argument to *perfect*, *correct*, *round*. The difficulty can be overcome by saying that something is 'more nearly unique, perfect', etc.

upper case a printing term for capital letters. Though *lower case* (*l.c.*) is invariably used for small letters, the term *caps.* is more common for capital letters.

urban, urbane The first applies to a town (from L. *urbs*), as in Urban District Council, and the same idea is seen in *conurbation*, a string of towns connected by ribbon-development. The second means civilised, polite, as opposed to the supposedly rude manners of country people. The noun from *urbane* is 'urbanity'.

V

valet a man who looks after his master's clothes. The verb (*valet*, *valeted*) means to carry out these duties. They derive from the French, but should be pronounced væˈlet, not væˈlei, except in *valet de chambre*. The cleaning and pressing of clothes is called *valeting*, often found in trade names, e.g. *The Premier Valeting Service.*

venal, venial The first means 'that may be bought', referring to a person who is ready to accept a bribe. It includes also the conduct of that person. The second means something entirely different. It means 'that may be pardoned'. A *venial offence* is one of a trifling kind, e.g.:

(a) A venal footballer is a disgrace to British sportsmanship, for he has been bribed to lose the game.
(b) A footballer commits a venial offence when he inadvertently breaks some minor rule of the game.

verb the part of speech that expresses action (*hit*), the suffering of action (*is hit*), or existence (*is*). It also expresses TENSE, MOOD and

VOICE, e.g. 'I am fond of cabbage, but dislike it when it has been boiled for more than a few minutes.' In this sentence 'am' is in the indicative mood, 'dislike' is in the present tense, and 'has been boiled' is in the passive voice.

Verbs are either *transitive* or *intransitive*, both words deriving from the Latin meaning 'going across'. A transitive verb requires an object to complete it, the action of the verb going over to the object, e.g. 'The car hit the fence.' An intransitive verb does not require an object to complete it, e.g. 'The fence collapsed.' An intransitive verb that cannot make a complete statement without the addition of a COMPLEMENT is known as a *verb of incomplete predication*, e.g. 'The weather grew worse.' Here 'The weather grew' cannot stand by itself; it requires 'worse' to make a complete statement. Some verbs may be both transitive and intransitive, e.g. (a) 'He sang a new song' (transitive). 'He sang well' (intransitive).

A *weak* (or *regular*) *verb* is one that (a) forms its past tense by adding a *d* or a *t* to its present tense, e.g. *move – moved*; *deal – dealt*; (b) forms its past tense by shortening its present tense, e.g. *meet – met*; or (c) takes the same form for the past as for the present, e.g. *cast – cast*.

A *strong* (or *irregular*) *verb* is one that forms its past tense by a variation in the root vowel, e.g. *drive – drove*, and the past participle by adding *n* or *en*, e.g. *draw – drawn*; *drive – driven*.

A *compound verb* is a verb phrase made up of a verb and one or more prepositions and functioning as a single verb, e.g. *to come in, to stand up, to watch out for, to do away with*. This should not be confused with the verb that is a compound word, e.g. *to browbeat* (noun plus verb), *to whitewash* (adjective plus verb).

Other names for a compound verb are *phrasal verb* and *verbal phrase*, which may also be used to describe verbs formed with the aid of one or more auxiliary verbs, e.g. *had gone, would have gone, had been eaten*.

See also AGREEMENT; AUXILIARY VERBS; COMPLEMENT; FINITE VERBS; GERUND; HISTORIC PRESENT; INFINITIVE; MOOD; NUMBER; PARTICIPLES; PERSON; PREDICATE; REFLEXIVE; REPORTED SPEECH; TENSE; VERB OF SAYING; VOICE.

verbal, oral   As an adjective descriptive of something given by word of mouth, *oral* is the better word. Technically, *a verbal answer* is an answer given in words, either spoken or written, whilst *an oral answer* is one given in spoken words. Another meaning of *verbal* is 'of, pertaining to, or derived from a verb'.

verbal phrase see under VERB.

verb of saying a verb used in direct speech to show who is speaking, e.g. 'I said', 'Tom said', 'said Tom'. Besides the simple 'said', there are many others that show not only who is speaking but also the manner in which the words are said, e.g.:

'How I hate the winter!' complained Mr Wilson.
'Never mind, dear,' smiled his wife. 'Spring will soon be here.'
'How soon?' demanded young Tommy.
'In about a month,' explained Mrs Wilson.
'About a month,' repeated Tommy, then asked: 'How long is that?'
'You ask too many questions,' grumbled his father.
'That's the only way he can learn,' pointed out Mrs Wilson.

See also INVERTED COMMAS; REPORTED SPEECH.

verbose using more words than are needed; words for words' sake. Here, in full spate, is Serjeant Buzfuz, counsel for the plaintiff in the breach-of-promise action brought by Mrs Bardell, a widow, against Mr Pickwick:

I entreat the attention of the jury to the wording of the document placed by Mrs Bardell in her front parlour-window, 'Apartments furnished for a single gentleman'! Mrs Bardell's opinions of the opposite sex, gentlemen, were derived from a long contemplation of the inestimable qualities of her lost husband. She had no fear, she had no distrust, she had no suspicion, all was confidence and reliance. 'Mr Bardell,' said the widow; 'Mr Bardell was a man of honour, Mr Bardell was a man of his word, Mr Bardell was no deceiver, Mr Bardell was once a single gentleman himself; *to* single gentlemen I look for protection, for assistance, for comfort, and for consolation; *in* single gentlemen I shall perpetually see something to remind me of what Mr Bardell was, when he first won my young and untried affections; to a single gentleman, then, shall my lodgings be let.' Actuated by this beautiful and touching impulse (among the best impulses of our imperfect nature, gentlemen), the lonely and desolate widow dried her tears, furnished her first floor, caught her innocent little boy to her maternal bosom, and put the bill up in her parlour-window. Did it remain there long? No. The serpent was on the watch, the train was laid, the mine was preparing, the sapper and miner was at work. Before the bill had been in the parlour-window three days – three days, gentlemen – a Being, erect upon two legs, and bearing all the outward semblance of a man, and not of a monster, knocked at the door of Mrs Bardell's house. He inquired within; he took the lodgings; and on the very next day he entered into possession of them. This man was Pickwick – Pickwick, the defendant.

No wonder that Serjeant Buzfuz paused here for breath, his face, the author tells us, 'perfectly crimson'.

vernacular the language of one's native country; also used as an adjective, e.g. 'The medium of instruction in secondary schools in Enugu (Nigeria) is English, but the vernacular language of the pupils is Ibo.' The term is also used to denote the home language of a person as opposed to the 'posh' language of school or polite society.

verse strictly speaking, a metrical line containing a definite number of feet. It derives from the Latin *verto* (I turn) because, after writing one line, the poet turns back to write the next. Loosely, verse is synonymous with STANZA, and with POETRY in a general sense. The divisions of chapters in the Bible are known as verses. Each one is numbered, so that Genesis xlii, 3 refers us to the third verse of the forty-second chapter of Genesis: 'And Joseph's ten brethren went down to buy corn in Egypt.' We speak too of the verses, not the stanzas, of a hymn or a song.

See also METRE.

vers libre the name comes from a turn-of-the-century revolt against the extreme restraints of classical French PROSODY. Rhythm was said to be more important than SCANSION, feeling more important than RHYME. Rimbaud, Lafargue, Baudelaire and Mallarmé showed the way; the SURREALISTS followed; soon, all over Europe 'free verse' was the mark of the *avant garde*. In the English language, two American expatriates, T. S. Eliot and Ezra Pound, blazed a trail eagerly followed for the next half-century by poets mature and fledgeling.

This is the way the world ends;
Not with a bang but a whimper,

wrote Eliot in a famous 'free verse' couplet that could have been taken as a threnody for rhyming, scanning verse.

vicious circle two or more undesirable things, each of which keeps causing the other. To put it another way, there is a vicious circle when a cause produces an effect that produces the original cause. For example, war breeds hate, and hate in turn breeds war, which breeds more hate – and so on. The problem of a vicious circle is how to break it, how to stop it going round and round. In this particular case it might be possible to prevent effect following cause so disastrously if we tried to remove by means of education the hate left behind by war.

See also ARGUING IN A CIRCLE.

virtual, virtuous The first means 'being such in effect but not in name'; the second means 'pure in thought and deed'.

'Although the firm still traded under the name of old Mr Jones, the virtual head of the business was his nephew, who was not quite so virtuous and honest as his uncle believed!'

The adverb *virtually* has come to have the meaning of 'to all intents and purposes', e.g. 'Nearly twenty villages were virtually destroyed by the hurricane.'

virtuosity skill in the performance of some fine art, especially music. A person who is a lover of the fine arts, or a brilliant player on some instrument, or a collector of works of art – paintings, antique furniture, etc. – is called a *virtuoso*.

viz. abbreviation of *videlicet*, the Latin for 'one may see'. It is used to introduce an enlargement upon a previous statement, e.g. 'These facilities are not available during certain months of the year, viz. February, June, September and November.' The use of *viz.* is not recommended; it is better to write *namely*: and even if it appears as *viz.* on the printed page, it should be read aloud as 'namely'.

vocabulary Without a large vocabulary all our attempts to express ourselves must needs be crude, for the subtle shades of meaning will be beyond us. Clear thinking and arguing are then impossible; and where words fail, blows often ensue. Words with their different meanings are like so many bricks of varying shapes, colours and textures with which to build sentences to express thoughts for every occasion. Without this raw material of words we must remain inarticulate. We cannot write effectively without having the right word in the right place.

There are 500,000 words listed in the huge *Oxford English Dictionary*. Although the dictionaries to which most of us have access are not nearly so comprehensive, we can still find the right word to fit our meaning if we make the effort. A dictionary of SYNONYMS will help us to do this, but we must use it with care and intelligence, for synonyms are rarely of exactly the same meaning and use. Even such obvious synonyms as *big* and *large* are not always interchangeable. A small child could say that his big brother would soon be leaving school. But if he said that his large brother would soon be leaving school he would convey quite a different meaning. Again, consider these synonyms of *hard*:

The opposite of *soft*: *solid, dense, firm, rigid, unyielding, compact*

The opposite of *tender*: *unfeeling, unkind, hard-hearted, harsh, cruel, exacting, callous, obdurate, stony*

The opposite of *easy*: *difficult, arduous, complex, perplexing, puzzling, wearying, laborious, intricate*

The opposite of *pleasant*: *unpleasant, painful, distressing, grievous, disagreeable, calamitous*

As an adverb it is synonymous with *laboriously, industriously, earnestly, diligently, energetically*; and, in the sense of *hard by*: *near, close*.

Even with the great choice of words at our disposal, we still tend to overwork certain words because we are too slack, neglectful, indolent, idle, supine, inert, torpid, dronish, careless, negligent, apathetic, uninterested, indifferent, lazy to find better ones. Thus we use OVERWORKED WORDS.

We say here, as we say elsewhere, that in serious writing or conversation, it is worth a moment's extra thought to make our meaning clearer and add freshness to our style; and style begins with the better word.

vocative case the case of a word indicating that the person or thing being named is being addressed, e.g. (a) 'Yes, *sir*, that is what happened.' (b) 'Tell me, young *fellow*, what is your name?'

See also under CASE.

vogue words We cannot do better than borrow from *Modern English Usage*: 'Every now and then a word emerges from obscurity, or even from nothingness or a merely potential and not actual existence, into sudden popularity. It is often, but not necessarily, one that by no means explains itself to the average man, who has to find out its meaning as best he can; his wrestlings with it have usually some effect upon it; it does not mean quite what it ought to, but in compensation it means some things that it ought not to, before he has done with it . . .'

Among the examples Fowler went on to quote were: FEASIBLE; HECTIC; INDIVIDUAL; PERCENTAGE; PROTAGONIST; PSYCHOLOGICAL MOMENT. To these we add ALLERGIC; CHRONIC; COMMUTER; contemporary; EXPERTISE; LIQUIDATE; LITERALLY; nostalgic; PHENOMENAL; SUMMIT. See also OVERWORKED WORDS.

voice a form of the verb that shows whether the thing named by the subject is performing the action (active voice) or suffering the action (passive voice). 'Jack hit the ball.' The subject is 'Jack'. He is performing the action of hitting the ball, so the form of the verb is active. 'The ball was hit by Jack.' Here the subject is 'ball', which suffers the action of being hit, so the form of the verb is passive.

vowel ligatures two vowel letters joined together to form one sound, e.g. æ, œ. At one time scholars used them in words derived from the Latin and Greek, e.g. *Cæsar, Phœnicia, encyclopædia*, but nowadays vowel ligatures are confined to Old English and French words, e.g. *Cædmon* (O.E.) and *manœuvre* (F.). See also DIGRAPH.

vowels in PHONETICS the sounds produced when the breath passes through the mouth without obstruction. The letters representing such sounds are also referred to as vowels. They are *a, e, i, o* and *u*, the rest of the alphabet being made up of CONSONANTS.

The letters *w* and *y* are known as *semi-vowels* because in some words the sound of them is very like that of a consonant, whilst in others it is the same as that of a vowel. *W* is a consonant before vowels, e.g. *we, women, onward*, and a vowel in diphthong sounds, when it comes after a vowel, e.g. *howl, sewing, coward. Y* is a consonant when it begins a word or syllable, e.g. *yes, young, beyond*. When it comes at the end, it is a vowel with the sound of a short *i*, e.g. *ugly, pony, merry*, or a vowel with the sound of a long *i*, e.g. *try, fly, my*. When not at the beginning or the end, it has either the sound of the short *i*, as in *physic, typical, system, mystery*, or the sound of the long *i*, as in *type, scythe, python, lyre*.

Vowel sounds and consonant sounds are treated under GUIDE TO PRONUNCIATION on page 7.

vulgar (L. 'the common people') an adjective that has come to mean 'coarse; low'. A *vulgarian* is a person, usually rich, who is lacking in good manners and taste. The literal meaning of the adjective is 'ordinary; general; vernacular'. The *vulgar tongue* refers to the common speech of the people, whether it be English, French or Spanish, not to the low conversation associated with the fish-porters of Billingsgate Market. The *Vulgate* refers to the translation of the Bible from Hebrew into Latin made by Jerome in the fifth century. The verb *to vulgarise* means 'to make common'. As applied to the English language it means 'to debase by making popular'. Fowler has this to say: 'Vulgarization of words that should not be in common use robs some of their aroma, others of their substance, others again of their precision; but nobody likes to be told that the best service he can do to a favourite word is to leave it alone, and perhaps the less said here on this matter the better.'

Vulgarisation is treated under OVERWORKED WORDS. Vulgarism, which is violation of the rules of grammar and syntax, is treated under SOLECISM.

W

was, were For the use of the subjunctive *if I were, if he were*, etc. see under MOOD.

way, weigh When a ship is in motion, is she *under way* or *under weigh*? The question is often asked. The answer is that she is *under way*. The confusion doubtless arises because the anchor is *weighed*, i.e. lifted out of the water, before the ship puts to sea. *To weigh anchor* means to start a voyage, and thereafter the ship is on the way to her destination; she is under way.

weak verbs those regular verbs that form their past participles and past tenses by adding *-ed*, or *-t* to the INFINITIVE form, e.g. listen – listened, hope – hoped, burn – burnt, as opposed to the STRONG or IRREGULAR VERBS that change the vowel sound to form the past participle and past tense, e.g. find – found, begin – begun – began, speak – spoken – spoke.

were   For the use of the subjunctive *if I were, if he were*, etc. see under MOOD.

whence, whither   Though considered rather old-fashioned today, *whence* is still not ousted by *from where, where from, from which, from what place*. The following are all in good, plain English:

(a) He lived for ten years in Bournemouth, whence he moved in 1962 to Hastings.
(b) Whence comes it that we now face a crisis that could have been avoided?
(c) I take that remark whence it comes. (i.e. I know the character of the man who said it, so I am not going to let it hurt my feelings.)

In a similar position stands *whither*, still better in some contexts than *where, to which place, to what place*.

(d) This strange man stayed in the village for a week, then left as quietly as he had arrived. Whence he had come and whither he went, none of us ever knew.

Compare this with: 'Where he had come from and where he went to . . .' or the even clumsier: 'From which place he had come and to which place he went . . .'

Note that *whence* is not preceded by the redundant *from*; or *whither* by the redundant *to*. 'From whence he came and to whither he went . . .' is wrong.

See also HENCE.

which, that   see PRONOUN, *relative*.

while, whilst   These are not entirely synonymous. The second cannot be used in sentences such as the following: 'It was a long while before I saw my friend again.' In the sense of 'during the time that', *while* is correct, e.g. 'My brother waited outside the shop while I went in and bought a camera'; but when the sense is that of comparison, *whilst* is correct, e.g. 'My brother bought his camera from a friend, whilst I bought mine from a shop.' Here there is no question of 'during the time that', so the use of *while* would be not only incorrect but also ambiguous, for it might convey the meaning that the two purchases were made simultaneously.

whisky, whiskey   Scotch *whisky*, Irish *whiskey*.

whither see WHENCE, WHITHER.

who, whom see under ACCUSATIVE (OBJECTIVE) CASE.

whole When used as an adjective this means 'complete; un-divided; unbroken; uninjured; entire', e.g.:

(a) Within an hour the whole village was in flames.
(b) He devoted his whole life to the relief of suffering.
(c) I'll give you ten pounds for the whole lot.

As will be seen from these examples, *whole* can be used when refer-ring to a unit or a group, but it should not be used when referring to the individual items comprising a group; that is to say, it should not be used in the sense of *all*, e.g.:

Wrong: My mother found that the whole twelve eggs were bad.
Right: My mother found that all twelve eggs were bad.
  Or: My mother found that the whole dozen eggs were bad.
Wrong: At the court-martial the whole twenty mutineers were found guilty.
Right: At the court-martial all twenty mutineers were found guilty.

whose, of which The first is the possessive form of the relative pronoun *who*, e.g. 'Mr Jones, whose tree it was, was not consulted before it was cut down.' The second is the possessive form of the relative pronoun *which*, e.g. 'The tree, the owner of which was Mr Jones, was cut down before he was consulted.' The use of *whose* in-stead of *of which* ('The tree, whose owner was Mr Jones . . .') is treated under POSSESSIVE ADJECTIVES AND PRONOUNS.

whose, who's The first is defined above; the second is an abbre-viation of *who is* or *who has*, e.g.:

(a) Whose pencil is this?
(b) Who's the owner of this pencil?
(c) Who's stolen my pencil?

will see SHALL, WILL.

wishful thinking believing a thing to be so because we wish it to be so, in order to avoid facing unpleasant facts. In World War II there were many wishful thinkers, deluding themselves into the conviction that victory was in sight, when in fact it was a very long way off. 'It'll all be over by Christmas,' said they.

Wishful thinking is a form of RATIONALISING.

wit   the ability to see and express unexpected associations with a view to amusing. It therefore satisfies a more intellectual sense of humour than mere funniness does. When used to refer to a quality in a piece of writing or speech, wit might be defined as verbal sword play which, though intended to amuse, has a sting in it.

without   The misuse of this preposition as a conjunction is treated under PREPOSITION.

without let or hindrance   a tautological term. Here 'let' is used in its old sense, which was synonymous with 'hinder'. As Hamlet says when his friends try to stop him from following the ghost of his father: 'Unhand me, gentlemen; by heaven, I'll make a ghost of him that lets me.'

See also ARCHAISM.

Women's Lib   an accepted abbreviation, without full stop, for *Women's Liberation Front*, an Anglo-American re-creation of a SUFFRAGETTE movement for even fuller women's emancipation. The movement, fiercely articulate, produced a number of books in the early 1970s, notably *The Female Eunuch* by Germaine Greer, and was responsible for a new compound, *male chauvinism*, to indicate men's self-centred reaction to their demands.

word-formation   the branch of GRAMMAR dealing with the formation of words, either by DERIVATION, or by joining two or more words together (see COMPOUND), or by adding a PREFIX and/or a SUFFIX to a ROOT or a STEM.

Understanding how words are built up from their component parts is one of the most helpful guides to correct meaning. The central brick, which tells us what family the word belongs to, is the root. The brick that goes before it is the prefix, and the one that comes after it is the suffix. Words may be built up in the following patterns: (a) the root alone; (b) prefix + root; (c) root + suffix; (d) prefix + root + suffix. Thus:

(a)	do	man	port	stamp
(b)	over-do	un-man	trans-port	re-stamp
(c)	do-ing	man-ly	port-able	stamp-ed
(d)	over-do-ing	un-man-ly	trans-port-able	re-stamp-ed

The root may not, of course, be a recognisable word, but a French, Latin or Greek root. Thus the root in *conscious* is the Latin root *sci* that appears in *scio* (I know). The word is therefore built up like this: *con-sci-ous*.

Sometimes the pattern is complicated by there being more than one prefix or suffix. The word *unconsciously*, for example, has two prefixes and two suffixes, and is built up like this: *un-con-sci-ous-ly*.

Knowing how a word is built up is a vital guide to meaning. For instance, if we know that *describe*, *inscribe* and *subscribe* are made up of the Latin root *scribo* (I write) plus the prefixes *de-*, *in-* and *sub-* respectively, we automatically know that *describe* means 'to write about', *inscribe* 'to write in' and *subscribe* 'to write under' and so show agreement.

Other ways in which many of our words are formed are treated under BACK-FORMATION; NOUN; ONOMATOPOEIA; PORTMANTEAU WORDS; PROPER ADJECTIVES; PROTOGRAM; TELESCOPING.

worth while, worth-while   The HYPHEN should be added only when the use is adjectival, e.g.:

(a) Let's stay at home and look at the television. It's not worth while going out to the cinema on a night like this.

(b) It was a worth-while visit to the cinema; much better than staying at home looking at the television.

would   see SHOULD, WOULD.

X

-xion, -ction   The majority of nouns ending in either of these take the second. Those with the *-xion* ending are *complexion*, *crucifixion*, *deflexion*, *effluxion*, *flexion*, *fluxion*, *transfixion*. Modern usage favours *connection*, *deflection*, but *inflexion* (of which the adjective is *inflective*).

Reflection is more general than *reflexion*, which has a scientific application. The adjective *reflexive* is used in grammar, denoting an action directed back upon the agent or subject, e.g. 'He killed himself'. For general use the adjective is *reflective*.

Xmas   see CHRISTMAS, XMAS.

Y

Y   This semi-vowel is treated under VOWELS and also under GUIDE TO PRONUNCIATION on page 9.

Z

Z   the last letter of the English alphabet. Americans pronounce it *zee*, not *zed*.

zeugma (zuːgˡmə) (Gk. 'to yoke; to join')   a TURN OF EXPRESSION in which a verb or adjective (usually a verb) is applied to two or more nouns or noun-equivalents and either (a) is grammatically incorrect in its application to the more distant noun; or (b) does not make sense in its application to that noun. Here is an example of (a): 'I was in the front of the train and my bags in the guard's van at the rear.' The verb 'was' cannot be applied to 'bags'. It should read: 'and my bags were in the guard's van . . .' The most famous example of (b) is from Pope: 'See Pan with flocks, with fruits Pomona crowned.' For Pomona, the Roman goddess of fruits, crowning with these makes sense, but Pan would not be crowned with flocks of goats. Under (b) falls also the adjective performing a double duty, e.g. 'He was a man of deep learning and ideals.' This should read: 'and high ideals.'

   By common usage, zeugma includes SYLLEPSIS, although grammarians distinguish between them.

BIOGRAPHICAL PARTICULARS CONCERNING WRITERS AND OTHERS MENTIONED IN THIS BOOK

ADDISON, Joseph (1672–1719), English poet and essayist.

ARISTOPHANES (448?–370? B.C.), Greek writer of comedies, including *The Frogs* and *The Wasps*.

ARISTOTLE (384–322 B.C.), Greek philosopher, 'the Father of Learning'.

BACH, Johann Sebastian (1685–1750), German composer and musician.

BACON, Francis, Baron Verulam, Viscount St. Albans (1561–1626), English philosopher and statesman.

BAILEY, Philip James (1816–1902), English poet.

BECKETT, Samuel (b. 1906), Anglo-Irish dramatist, author of *Waiting for Godot*.

BELLOC, Joseph Hilaire Pierre (1870–1953), British author, son of French father and English mother.

BENTLEY, Edmund Clerihew (1875–1956), English author and the inventor of the short form of verse known as the CLERIHEW.

BESANT, Annie (1847–1933), English freethinker and theosophist.

BIERCE, Ambrose (1842–1914?), American satirist, poet and writer of short stories. His death in Mexico was reported in 1916, but it is not known when and how he died.

BIRDSEYE, George (1844–1919), American writer of verse.

BOSWELL, James (1740–95), Scottish biographer of Samuel Johnson.

BOWDLER, Thomas (1754–1825), English editor from whose name derives the verb *to bowdlerise*.

BROWNING, Robert (1812–89), English poet.

BUNYAN, John (1628–88), English preacher, author of *The Pilgrim's Progress*.

BURGESS, Frank Gelett (1866–1951), American humorist, novelist and illustrator.

BURNS, Robert (1759–96), Scottish poet, author of *Auld Lang Syne*.

BYRON, George Gordon Noel sixth Lord (1788–1824), English poet.

CAESAR, Gaius Julius (100–44 B.C.), Roman general, statesman and writer.

CAMPBELL, Thomas (1777–1844), Scottish poet.

CARROLL, Lewis (real name Charles Lutwidge Dodgson) (1832–98), mathematician and author of *Alice in Wonderland, Through the Looking-Glass*, etc.

CERVANTES SAAVEDRA, Miguel de (1547–1616), Spanish author of *Don Quixote*.

CHAUCER, Geoffrey (1340?–1400), the father of English poetry, author of *The Canterbury Tales*.

CHESTERTON, Gilbert Keith (1874–1936), English essayist, novelist, poet and critic.

CHOPIN, Frédéric François (1809–49), French-Polish pianist and composer.

CHURCHILL, Charles (1731–64), English clergyman, poet and satirist.

CHURCHILL, Sir Winston Leonard Spencer (1874–1965), English statesman and author.

CICERO, Marcus Tullius (106–43 B.C.), Roman orator.

CLOUGH, Arthur Hugh (1819–61), English poet, best known for his *Say not the Struggle naught availeth*.

COLERIDGE, Samuel Taylor (1772–1834), English metaphysician and poet, author of *Kubla Khan* (which he left unfinished) and *The Rime of the Ancient Mariner*.

COWPER, William (1731–1800), English poet, author of many poems, including *John Gilpin* and *Verses Supposed to be Written by Alexander Selkirk*, beginning with the line, 'I am monarch of all I survey'.

CRUDEN, Alexander (1701–70), Scottish compiler of Bible Concordance.

DANTE Alighieri (1265–1321), Italian poet, author of *La Divina Commedia* ('The Divine Comedy').

DARWIN, Charles Robert (1809–82), English naturalist, author of *The Origin of Species*.

DAY LEWIS, Cecil (1904–72), Poet Laureate from 1968 to 1972.

DEFOE, Daniel (1659?–1731), English author of *Robinson Crusoe* and much else. He was born Daniel Foe, later changing Foe to Defoe.

DE MORGAN, Augustus (1806–71), English mathematician.

DICKENS, CHARLES (1812–70), English novelist, author of *The Pickwick Papers, David Copperfield, Oliver Twist*, etc.

DISRAELI, Benjamin, first Earl of Beaconsfield (1804–81), statesman and author.

DRYDEN, John (1631–1700), English poet, dramatist and satirist. He was Poet Laureate from 1670 to 1689.

EDISON, Thomas Alva (1847–1931), American electrician and inventor.

ELGAR, Sir Edward William (1857–1934), English composer.

EMERSON, Ralph Waldo (1803–82), American essayist, poet and philosopher.

EPICURUS (342?–270 B.C.), Greek philosopher.

EUCLID (c. 300 B.C.), Greek mathematician, author of *The Elements of Geometry*.

EURIPIDES (484?–406 B.C.), Greek dramatist.

FARRAR, Dean Frederick William (1831–1903), English clergyman and author of *Eric, or Little by Little*.

FREEMAN, John (1880–1929), English poet.

GALSWORTHY, John (1867–1933), English novelist and dramatist.

GAY, John (1685–1732), English poet and dramatist.

GILBERT, Sir William Schwenck (1836–1911), English dramatist, writer of the librettos of the Gilbert and Sullivan comic operas, *The Mikado*, *H.M.S. Pinafore*, *The Pirates of Penzance*, *Iolanthe*, etc.

GLADSTONE, William Ewart (1809–98), English statesman.

GOLDSMITH, Oliver (1728–74), Irish poet, novelist and dramatist, author of the long poem, *The Deserted Village*, the novel, *The Vicar of Wakefield* and the play, *She Stoops to Conquer*.

GOLDWYN, Samuel (b. 1882), Polish-born American film producer.

GOUNOD, Charles François (1818–93), French composer.

GRAY, Thomas (1716–71), English poet, author of *Elegy written in a Country Churchyard* and *Ode on a Distant Prospect of Eton College* ('Alas, regardless of their doom, The little victims play! No sense have they of ills to come, Nor care beyond to-day.').

HAMMERSTEIN II, Oscar (1895–1960), American lyricist, song-writer and theatrical producer.

HANDEL, George Frederic (1685–1759), German composer, becoming a naturalised British subject in 1726.

HERBERT, George (1593–1633), English poet and divine.

HOLMES, Oliver Wendell (1809–94), American poet and essayist.

HOMER, epic poet of Greece in about the ninth century B.C. Nothing is known of him except that he wrote those two great epic poems, the *Iliad* and the *Odyssey*.

HOOD, Thomas (1799–1845), English poet of Scottish descent. He wrote *The Song of the Shirt*, some lines from which are quoted under EMOTIVE LANGUAGE.

HOPKINS, Gerard Manley (1844–89), English poet and Jesuit.

HORACE (Quintus Horatius Flaccus) (65–8 B.C.), Roman poet.

JOHNSON, Rossiter (1840–1931), American author and essayist.

JOHNSON, Dr Samuel (1709–84), English writer and lexicographer. His *Dictionary of the English Language*, which took seven years to complete, was published in 1755.

JONSON, Ben (1573?–1637), English poet, first official Poet Laureate. He is remembered best for his *To Celia*, which begins: 'Drink to me only with thine eyes, And I will pledge with mine . . .'

KEATS, John (1795–1821), English poet. His best-known poems are *Endymion, Ode to a Nightingale, Ode on a Grecian Urn* and *To Autumn*.

KILMER, Joyce (1886–1918), American poet. He was killed in action in France a few days before the Armistice. His famous poem *Trees* was set to music by Oscar Rasbach.

KINGSLEY, Charles (1819–75), cleric, poet and author.

KIPLING, Rudyard (1865–1936), English author of verse and fiction.

KNOX, J. Mason, American humorist in the early part of this century.

LAMB, Charles (1775–1834), English essayist, writing under the name of Elia.

LANDOR, Walter Savage (1775–1864), English author and poet.

LEAR, Edward (1812–88), English author and landscape artist. He is remembered for his nonsense verse, and did much to popularise the limerick.

LEHAR, Franz (1870–1948), Hungarian composer. His best-known work was the light opera *The Merry Widow*.

LEONCAVALLO, Ruggiero (1858–1919), Italian composer of the opera *I Pagliacci*.

LISZT, Franz (1811–86), Hungarian pianist and composer.

LONGFELLOW, Henry Wadsworth (1807–82), American poet, author of *Hiawatha*.

MACINTOSH, Charles (1766–1843), Scottish chemist and inventor.

MACLEOD, Norman (1812–72), Scottish minister.

MARLOWE, Christopher (Kit) (1564–93), English dramatist, poet and friend of Shakespeare's. He wrote *Tamburlaine, The Tragical History of Dr Faustus* and *The Jew of Malta*. He was murdered in a brawl.

MASEFIELD, John Edward (1878–1967), English poet, novelist and dramatist. He was Poet Laureate from 1930 to 1967, and was awarded the Order of Merit in 1935. His longer poems include *The Everlasting Mercy*, *Dauber* and *Reynard the Fox*.

MENDELSSOHN-BARTHOLDY, Felix (1809–47), German composer.

MERCATOR, Gerardus (1512–94), Flemish geographer.

MICHELANGELO (1475–1564), Italian artist and sculptor.

MILTON, John (1608–74), English poet and writer, author of *Paradise Lost*.

MOLIÈRE (real name John Baptiste Poquelin) (1622–73), French dramatist.

MONTAIGNE, Michel D'Eyquem, Sieur de (1533–92), French essayist.

MOORE, Thomas (1779–1852), Irish poet.

MORE, Sir Thomas (1478–1535), English statesman, author and philosopher, author of *Utopia*. He was beheaded for high treason because he would not acknowledge Henry VIII as supreme head of the Church of England.

MOZART, Wolfgang Amadeus (1756–91), Austrian composer.

NAPOLEON BONAPARTE (1769–1821), Emperor of France.

OFFENBACH, Jacques (1819–80), naturalised French composer of comic operas, born in Cologne of Jewish parents.

OWEN, Wilfred (1893–1918), English poet, killed in the First World War.

PALGRAVE, Francis Turner (1824–97), English poet, critic and editor of anthologies, including *The Golden Treasury*.

PENN, William (1644–1718), English Quaker, founder of Pennsylvania.

PEPYS, Samuel (1633–1703), English diarist, and secretary to the Admiralty. His famous diary was written in cypher or shorthand and was not translated into longhand until 1825.

PINDAR (*c.* 522–443 B.C.), greatest lyric poet of ancient Greece.

PINTER, Harold (b. 1930), English dramatist, author of *The Caretaker*, *The Birthday Party* and *A Slight Ache*.

PITT, William, first Earl of Chatham (1708–78), English statesman and Prime Minister.

POPE, Alexander (1688–1744), English poet and satirist, described by Lady Mary Wortley Montagu as 'the wicked wasp of Twickenham'.

QUILLER-COUCH, Sir Arthur Thomas (1863–1944), English writer and Professor of English.

ROCHESTER, John Wilmot, second Earl of (1647–1680), courtier and poet, dissolute associate of Charles II.

ROGET, Peter Mark (1779–1869), Anglo-Swiss scientist, his chief claim to fame being his *Thesaurus of English Words and Phrases*, published in 1852. New editions were published in 1879 and 1936, and a completely revised and modernised edition appeared in 1962.

ROMBERG, Sigmund (1887–1951), Hungarian-born American composer of operetta and musical comedy, including *The Student Prince*, *The Desert Song* and *New Moon*.

RUSKIN, John (1819–1900), English author, art critic and social reformer. Son of a Scottish wine merchant.

SCOTT, Sir Walter (1771–1832), Scottish novelist and poet. Among his novels were *Old Mortality*, *Rob Roy*, *The Heart of Midlothian*, *Ivanhoe* and *Redgauntlet*; among his poems were *The Lay of the Last Minstrel* and *Marmion*.

SEWELL, Anna (1820–78), English author of *Black Beauty*, the autobiography of a horse.

SHAKESPEARE, William (1564–1616), English poet and dramatist. His plays fall under three headings: Histories, Tragedies, Comedies. Among the first were: *Henry IV* (in two parts), *Henry V*, and *Richard III*; among the second were: *Romeo and Juliet*, *Julius Caesar*, *Macbeth*, *Hamlet*, *King Lear* and *Othello*; among the third were *The Tempest*, *Much Ado About Nothing*, *A Midsummer Night's Dream*, *The Merchant of Venice*, *As You Like It* and *Twelfth Night*.

SHAW, George Bernard (1856–1950), Irish dramatist and critic. He made a fortune out of the English by abusing them.

SHELLEY, Mary Wollstonecraft (1797–1851), second wife of the poet, her fame resting on her novel, *Frankenstein*.

SHELLEY, Percy Bysshe (1792–1822), English poet. Among his poems were *The Revolt of Islam*, *Ode to the West Wind*, *To a Skylark*, *Prometheus Unbound*, and his lament for the death of John Keats, *Adonais*.

SHERIDAN, Richard Brinsley Butler (1751–1816), Irish dramatist and politician. His two great comedies were *The Rivals*, and *The School for Scandal*. His powers as a Parliamentary orator were considerable.

SHIRLEY, James (1596–1666), English dramatic poet.

SOCRATES (*c.* 470–399 B.C.), Greek philosopher.

SPENCER, Herbert (1820–1903), English philosopher. In his *Principles of Biology* he coined the phrase, 'survival of the fittest'.

SPENSER, Edmund (1552?–1599), English poet, author of *The Faerie Queene*. See also under POET LAUREATE.

SPOONER, Dr William Archibald (1844–1930), English scholar, Warden of New College, Oxford. From his name derives SPOONER-ISM.

STANISLAVSKY, Constantin (1863–1938), Russian theatrical director, founder of the Moscow Art Theatre.

STEELE, Sir Richard (1672–1729), essayist and dramatist of mixed Irish and English parentage.

STEVENSON, Robert Lewis Balfour (1850–94), Scottish author and poet, he dropped his third Christian name and altered the second to 'Louis'. His best-known book was *Treasure Island* originally called *The Sea Cook*. Others were *Kidnapped, Dr Jekyll and Mr Hyde* and *Catriona*.

SULLIVAN, Sir Arthur Seymour (1842–1900), English composer. Although he aspired to the composition of more serious music, he is remembered best for his collaboration with W. S. Gilbert (see above) in the comic operas known collectively as 'Gilbert and Sullivan'.

SWIFT, Jonathan (1667–1745), author of *Gulliver's Travels*. Of English descent, he was born in Dublin and became Dean of St. Patrick's in that city.

SWINBURNE, Algernon Charles (1837–1909), English poet and dramatist.

TCHAIKOVSKY, Piotr Ilich (1840–93), Russian composer. Among his works are *The Swan Lake* ballet, the piano concerto in B flat minor, the *Casse-Noisette* suite and *The Sleeping Beauty* ballet.

TENNYSON, Alfred Tennyson, first Baron (1809–92), English poet, and Poet Laureate from 1850. His poems include *In Memoriam, Idylls of the King, The Charge of the Light Brigade* and *The Revenge* ('Sink me the ship, Master Gunner – sink her, split her in twain! Fall into the hands of God, not into the hands of Spain!').

THOMPSON, Francis (1859–1907), English poet, author of *The Hound of Heaven*.

VERDI, Giuseppe (1813–1901), Italian composer. Among his operas are *Rigoletto, Il Trovatore* and *La Traviata*.

VIRGIL (70–19 B.C.), Roman poet. His full name was Publius Vergilius Maro, so it can be argued that we should spell it *Vergil*. Usage, however, has decided upon *Virgil*. He is remembered for his epic poem, the *Aeneid*. Though the Romans adopted him as their own, he was born near Mantua, in Cisalpine Gaul.

VOLTAIRE (real name François Marie Arouet) (1694–1778), French philosopher and author. His best-known work is *Candide*, in which comes the famous observation by Dr Pangloss, 'Tout est pour le mieux dans le meilleur des mondes possibles.' ('All is for the best in the best of possible worlds.')

WAGNER, (Wilhelm) Richard (1813–83), German composer. His operas include *The Flying Dutchman*, *Tannhäuser* and *Lohengrin*.

WALLACE, Alfred Russel (1823–1913), English naturalist and scientist. Independently he arrived at the same conclusion as Darwin as to the origin of species.

WESKER, Arnold (b. 1932), English dramatist, author of *The Kitchen* and *Chips With Everything*.

WESLEY, Charles (1707–88), English hymn writer, brother of John Wesley. He wrote over six thousand hymns, including *Jesu, Lover of my Soul*.

WILDE, Oscar Fingall O'Flahertie Wills (1856–1900), Irish poet, playwright and wit, who, in his own words, 'died beyond his means'. His stage comedies include *Lady Windermere's Fan* and *The Importance of Being Earnest*.

WORDSWORTH, William (1770–1850), English poet, and Poet Laureate from 1843. His acceptance of the laureateship and a pension was considered by some to be a defection from the Liberal cause, which impelled Browning to write *The Lost Leader*, which begins: 'Just for a handful of silver he left us, Just for a riband to stick in his coat.' Wordsworth wrote a large number of poems, many of them didactic. Among the greatest of them were his *Ode on Intimations of Immortality* (see page 222), and his sonnets on liberty.

YOUNG, Edward (1685–1765), English poet. He wrote a great deal of verse, only one line of which is known to most of us: 'Procrastination is the thief of time.'

BIBLIOGRAPHY

A Dictionary of Modern English Usage, by H. W. Fowler (O.U.P.)

The Shorter Oxford English Dictionary (O.U.P.)

The Concise Oxford Dictionary of Current English (O.U.P.)

Webster's New International Dictionary of the English Language (G. Bell & Sons, Ltd.)

The Encyclopædia Britannica

The New Elizabethan Reference Dictionary (George Newnes Ltd.)

Thorndike English Dictionary (English Universities Press Ltd.)

New College Standard Dictionary (Funk & Wagnalls Company, New York)

A Dictionary of Modern American Usage, by H. W. Horwill (O.U.P.)

Roget's Thesaurus of English Words and Phrases (Longmans, Green & Co. Ltd.)

Usage and Abusage, by Eric Partridge (Hamish Hamilton)

A Dictionary of Slang and Unconventional English, by Eric Partridge (Routledge & Kegan Paul Ltd.)

Brewer's Dictionary of Phrase and Fable (Cassell & Co. Ltd.)

A Dictionary of Abbreviations, by Cecily C. Matthews (George Routledge & Sons, Ltd.)

Essentials of English Grammar, by Oscar Jespersen (George Allen & Unwin, Ltd.)

The Use of English, by Randolph Quirk (Longmans, Green & Co. Ltd.)

The Structure of English, by C. C. Fries (Longmans, Green & Co. Ltd.)

Everyman's Roget's Thesaurus £1.25
Edited by D. C. Browning

Roget's Thesaurus is one of the English-speaking world's most valuable and celebrated works of reference. It is a treasury of synonyms, antonyms, parallel and related words, designed to help you find the right word or phrase to express your ideas with force and clarity.

This edition preserves the original plan of classification and categories (including the vast and ingenious index) and has been completely revised to bring all words and phrases into accordance with current usage. Over ten thousand more of these have been added, including many technical terms, everyday neologisms, Americanisms and slang.

Chambers Essential English Dictionary 60p
Edited by A. M. MacDonald

A dictionary of the words essential to daily life, with clear, precise and informative definitions; giving interesting derivations, illustrative examples of usage, and idiomatic expressions.

This is outstanding among small dictionaries for legibility and ease of reference. And although the background of our language makes up the body of the book, it fully reflects modern developments in words, meanings and outlook.

A Dictionary of Famous Quotations 60p

This collection took over five years to compile. Its exceptionally clear and attractive presentation makes it a delight to read, and the lively selection of quotations encourages the browser as well as the seeker of specific references. The comprehensive index, with over 25,000 entries, enables one to trace a partly-remembered quotation with maximum speed.

The Best English 60p
G. H. Vallins

Dealing with the techniques of composition in poetry, drama and prose, the author shows that words properly used communicate not only with our minds but also with our hearts and our emotions.

The many examples of the uses of language taken from sources as varied as Shakespeare and P. G. Wodehouse, Pepys and George Bernard Shaw, Chaucer and Dylan Thomas, all add enormously to the reader's knowledge and appreciation of the treasures of literature.

'Valuable not only for the sensible criticisms that he makes, not only for the delightful quotations that he introduces, but also for his common sense' OBSERVER

The Story of Language 75p
C. L. Barber

In the first half of this book, general topics such as the nature of language, its origins, the causes of linguistic changes, and language families, are examined; the second half is, in effect, a history of the English language.